THE BIBLE AS HISTORY, now thoroughly updated with the latest scientific and archaeological breakthroughs in biblical investigation.

Including:

- Revolutionary new evidence that confirms some of the most monumental and controversial events in the Bible—including the destruction of Sodom and Gomorrah

- Recently deciphered texts from the ancient world that offer an intriguing look back at the origin of the Ten Commandments

- An entirely new chapter revealing the extraordinary techniques that may soon prove the authenticity of the Shroud of Turin

THE BIBLE AS HISTORY will take you on a breathtaking journey to the heart of Holy Scripture as it pieces together one of the most stunning spiritual puzzles in the history of mankind.

THE BIBLE AS HISTORY

2nd Revised Edition

WERNER KELLER
Translated from the German by
William Neil

Revised and with a postscript by
Joachim Rehork

New material translated from the German by
B. H. Rasmussen

BANTAM BOOKS
TORONTO · NEW YORK · LONDON · SYDNEY

*This low-priced Bantam Book
has been completely reset in a type face
designed for easy reading, and was printed
from new plates. It contains the complete
text of the original hard-cover edition.*
NOT ONE WORD HAS BEEN OMITTED.

RL 9, IL AGE 12 AND UP

THE BIBLE AS HISTORY

*A Bantam Book/ published by arrangement with
William Morrow and Company, Inc.*

PRINTING HISTORY

*Morrow edition published February 1981
3 printings through May 1981*

*A Selection of Preferred Choice, December 1980; Catholic Digest,
February 1981 and History Book Clubs, March 1981*

*New revised edition originally published in Great Britain in 1980
by Hodder and Stoughton Ltd.*

First Bantam edition / June 1974

Bantam revised edition / February 1982

*Bantam Books are published by Bantam Books, Inc. Its trade-
mark, consisting of the words "Bantam Books" and the portrayal of a rooster, is Registered in U.S. Patent and Trademark
Office and in other countries. Marca Registrada. Bantam
Books, Inc., 666 Fifth Avenue, New York, New York 10103.*

To my parents
and
my friend Th. Ruth

CONTENTS

over the ''chariots of iron''—Israelite crockery at
Megiddo—Marauders from the desert—Traces of
Abimelech's destruction of Shechem—Gideon's successful tactics—First battle in history against a
camel-corps—A new breed of long-distance carriers.

Krethi and Plethi—Invasion by the ''Sea Peoples''—
The great trek from the Aegean—Triumphal progress with ox-waggons and ships—The Hittite empire disappears—Seaports in flames on the coast of
Canaan—General mobilisation on the Nile—Pharaoh
Ramesses III saves Egypt—The great land and sea
engagement—Interrogation in P.O.W. camps—Life
size portraits of the Philistines.

Philistines on the coast—Swan pattern pottery—
Beer mugs with filters—Carefully guarded iron
monopoly—Philistines occupy the highlands—Traces
of the burning of Shiloh—Choosing a king from dire
necessity—Allenby successfully uses Saul's tactics—
Surprising the Turks—Albright finds Saul's castle—
Two temples in Beth-Shan—The end of Saul.

V When Israel Was an Empire
—from David to Solomon

A man of genius—From armour-bearer to monarch—Unintentional military aid for Assyria—From
the Orontes to Ezion-Geber—Revenge at Beth-
Shan—New buildings with casemated walls—Finding
of the Pool of Gibeon—Jerusalem fell by a
stratagem—Warren discovers a shaft leading to the
city—The Sopher kept the ''Imperial Annals''—
Was David called David?—Ink as a novelty—
Palestine's climate is unpropitious for keeping records.

DIGGING UP THE NEW TESTAMENT

I *Jesus of Nazareth*

INTRODUCTION TO THE NEW REVISED EDITION

My book *The Bible as History* was first published in 1955. It was translated into 24 languages and used for religious instruction in schools, for Bible Seminars in Universities as well as by Bible Study Groups both Christian and Jewish. More than ten million copies have been printed throughout the world.

Since that time Biblical archaeology has brought to light hitherto undiscovered facts by the use of new techniques and the most up-to-date methods of investigation. It has been possible to confirm and reinforce a number of theories, while other accepted opinions, previously considered to be scientifically established, have had to be called into question and the conclusions even of well-known scholars revised. In order to preserve the scholarly reliability of my book, it has become necessary to include the most recent research results. One cannot and should not shut oneself off from new discoveries even if they are inconvenient.

I would have liked to bring my book into line with the most recent research myself, but a serious illness of some years' duration has unfortunately prevented me from undertaking this costly and responsible task. I have consequently been obliged, much against my will, to entrust this project to another. I am happy, however, to have obtained the collaboration of Dr. Joachim Rehork. In his appendix he has explained the principles according to which we agreed that the revision should be carried out.

To him I tender my sincere thanks.

Ascona 1978   WERNER KELLER

INTRODUCTION

"The greatest happiness of the thinking man is to have fathomed what can be fathomed, and quietly to reverence what is unfathomable."

GOETHE

When a non-theologian writes a book about the Bible it is a rare enough occurrence to entitle the reader to ask for some explanation of how the writer managed to make himself master of his subject.

As a journalist I have been for many years exclusively concerned with the results of modern science and research. In 1950 in the course of my ordinary routine work I came across the reports of the French archaeologists Professors Parrot and Schaeffer on their excavations at Mari and Ugarit. Cuneiform tablets discovered at Mari on the Euphrates were found to contain Biblical names. As a result, narratives of the patriarchs which had been for a long time regarded as merely pious tales were unexpectedly transferred into the realm of history. At Ugarit on the Mediterranean, evidence of the Canaanite worship of Baal had for the first time come to light. By a coincidence, a scroll of Isaiah discovered in a cave by the Dead Sea was in the same year dated as pre-Christian. These sensational reports—and indeed in view of the significance of these finds it is not too much to use the word "sensational"—awakened in me the desire to come to closer grips with Biblical archaeology, the most recent and, generally speaking, least known province in the field of investigation into the ancient world. I therefore ransacked German and foreign literature for a comprehensive and intelligible summary of the results of previous research. I found none for there was none to find. So I went to the sources myself in the libraries of many lands—aided in this bit of real detective work by my wife's enthusiasm—and collected all the hitherto scientifically established results of investigations which were to be found in the learned works of Biblical archaeologists. The deeper I went into the matter the more exciting it became.

The door into the historical world of the Old Testament had been already thrown open by a Frenchman, Paul-Emile Botta, in 1843. In the course of excavations at Khorsabad in Mesopotamia he suddenly found himself confronted by reliefs of King Sargon II of Assyria, who ravaged Israel and led its people off into captivity. Accounts of this conqueror's campaigns deal with the conquest of Samaria, which is also described in the Bible.

For a century now, American, English, French and German scholars have been digging in the Middle East, in Mesopotamia, Palestine and Egypt. All the great nations have founded institutes and schools specifically for this type of research. The Palestine Exploration Fund began in 1869, the German Palestine Association in 1877, the Dominican Ecole Biblique de St. Etienne in 1892. The German Oriental Society followed in 1898: then in 1900 the American Schools of Oriental Research and in 1901 the German Protestant Institute of Archaeology.

In Palestine, places and towns which are frequently mentioned in the Bible are being brought back once more into the light of day. They look exactly as the Bible describes them and lie exactly where the Bible locates them. On ancient inscriptions and monuments scholars encounter more and more characters from the Old and New Testaments. Contemporary reliefs depict people whom we have hitherto only known by name. Their features, their clothes, their armour take shape before our eyes. Colossal figures and sculptures show us the Hittites with their big noses; the slim tall Philistines; the elegant Canaanite chiefs with their "chariots of iron" which struck terror into the hearts of the Israelites; the kings of Mari, contemporary with Abraham, with their gentle smiles. During the thousands of years that divide us from them the Assyrian kings have lost nothing of their fierce and forbidding appearance: Tiglath-Pileser III, well known as the Old Testament "Pul"; Sennacherib who destroyed Lachish and laid siege to Jerusalem; Esarhaddon who put King Manasseh in chains, and Ashurbanipal the "great and noble Asnapper" of the book of Ezra.

As they have done to Nineveh and Nimrud—old-time Calah—or to Ashur and Thebes, which the prophets called No-Amon, the scholars have also awakened from its ancient slumber the notorious Babel of Biblical story with its legendary tower. In the Nile Delta archaeologists have found the cities of Pithom and Raamses, where the resentful Hebrews toiled as slaves. They have laid bare strata which tell of the flames and destruction which accompanied the children of Israel on their conquering march into Canaan. In Gibeah they found Saul's mountain stronghold, whose walls once echoed to the strains of David's harp. At Megiddo they came upon the vast stables of King Solomon, who had "12,000 horsemen".

From the world of the New Testament reappeared the palatial edifices of King Herod. In the heart of Old Jerusalem The Pavement was discovered, where Jesus stood before Pilate, as is mentioned in St. John's gospel. Assyriologists deciphered on the astronomical tables of the Babylonians the exact dates on which the Star of Bethlehem was observed.

These breathtaking discoveries, whose significance it is impossible to grasp all at once, make it necessary for us to revise our views about the Bible. Many events which previously passed for "pious tales" must now be judged to be historical. Often the results of investigation correspond in detail with the Biblical narratives. They do not only confirm them, but also illumine the historical situations out of which the Old Testament and the Gospels grew. At the same time the chances and changes of the people of Israel are woven into a lively colourful tapestry of daily life in the age in which they lived, as well as being caught up into the political, cultural and economic disputes of the nations and empires which struggled for power in Mesopotamia and on the Nile, from which the inhabitants of the tiny buffer state of Palestine were never able completely to detach themselves for over 2,000 years.

The opinion has been, and still is widely held, that the Bible is nothing but the story of man's salvation, a guarantee of the validity of their faith for Christians everywhere. It is however at the same time a book about things that actually happened. Admittedly in this sense it has limitations, in that the Jewish people wrote their history in the light of their relationship to

Yahweh, which meant writing it from the point of view of their own guilt and expiation. Nevertheless the events themselves are historical facts and have been recorded with an accuracy that is nothing less than startling.

Thanks to the findings of the archaeologists many of the Biblical narratives can be better understood now than ever before. There are, of course, theological insights which can only be dealt with in terms of the Word of God. But as Professor André Parrot, the world-famous French archaeologist, has said: "How can we understand the Word, unless we see it in its proper chronological, historical and geographical setting?"

Until now, knowledge of these extraordinary discoveries was confined to a small circle of experts. Only fifty years ago Professor Friedrich Delitzsch of Berlin was asking "Why all this effort in these distant barren and dangerous lands? Why all this costly rummaging among the rubble of past ages when we know there is neither gold nor silver to be found there? Why this mad competition among different countries to get control of these dreary looking mounds for the sole purpose of digging them up?" The German scholar Gustav Dalman gave him the right answer from Jerusalem itself when he expressed the hope that one day all that the archaeologists had "experienced and seen in their scientific labours would be turned to good account and would help to solve the practical problems of school and church". This latter hope has so far however remained unfulfilled.

No book in the whole history of mankind has had such a revolutionary influence, has so decisively affected the development of the western world, or had such a world-wide effect as the "Book of Books", the Bible. Today it is translated into 1,120 languages and dialects (1,660 in 1979), and after 2,000 years gives no sign of having exhausted its triumphal progress.

In gathering together and working over the material for this book, which I in no way claim to be complete, it seemed to me that the time had come to share with those who read their Bibles and those who do not, with churchmen and agnostics alike, the exciting discoveries which have resulted from a careful examination of the combined results of scientific investigation along many different lines. In view of the overwhelming mass of authentic and well-attested evidence now available, as I thought of the sceptical criticism which from the eighteenth century onwards would fain have demolished the Bible altogether, there kept hammering on my brain this one sentence: "The Bible is right after all!"

WERNER KELLER

Hamburg,
September 1955

THE BIBLE AS
HISTORY

DIGGING UP THE OLD TESTAMENT

I

The Coming of the Patriarchs from Abraham to Jacob

Chapter 1
IN THE "FERTILE CRESCENT"

Four thousand years ago—Continents asleep—The great cradle of our civili-sation—Culture in the Ancient East—Staged towers and pyramids had been built long before—Giant plantations on the banks of canals—Arab tribes attack from the desert.

If we draw a line from Egypt through the Mediterranean lands of Palestine and Syria, then following the Tigris and Euphrates, through Mesopotamia to the Persian Gulf, the result is an unmistakable crescent.

Four thousand years ago this mighty semi-circle around the Arabian Desert, which is called the "Fertile Crescent", embraced a multiplicity of civilisations lying side by side like a lustrous string of pearls. Rays of light streamed out from them into the surrounding darkness of mankind. Here lay the centre of civilisation from the Stone Age right up to the Golden Age of Graeco-Roman culture.

About 2000 B.C., the further we look beyond the "Fertile Crescent", the deeper grows the darkness and signs of civilisation and culture decrease. It is as if the people of the other continents were like children awaiting their awakening. Over the Eastern Mediterranean already a light is shining—it is the heyday of the Minoan kings of Crete, founders of the first sea-power known to history. For 1,000 years the fortress of Mycenae had protected its citizens, and a second Troy had long been standing upon the ruins of the first. In the nearby Balkans, however, the Early Bronze Age had just begun. In Sardinia and Western France the dead were being buried in vast stone tombs. These megalithic graves are the last great manifestation of the Stone Age.

In Britain they were building the most famous sanctuary of the Megalithic Age—the Temple of the Sun at Stonehenge—that giant circle of stones near Salisbury which is still one of the sights of England about which many tales are told. In Germany they were tilling the soil with wooden ploughs.

At the foot of the Himalayas the flickering lamp of an isolated outpost of civilisation in the Indus valley was fast going out. Over China, over the vast steppes of Russia, over Africa, darkness reigned supreme. And beyond the waters of the Atlantic lay the Americas in twilight gloom.

But in the "Fertile Crescent" and in Egypt, on the other hand, cultured and highly developed civilisations jostled each other in colourful and bewildering array. For 1,000 years the Pharaohs had sat upon the throne. About 2000 B.C. it was occupied by the founder of the XII Dynasty, Amenemhet I. His sphere of influence ranged from Nubia, south of the second cataract of the Nile, beyond the Sinai peninsula to Canaan and Syria, a stretch of territory as big as Norway. Along the Mediterranean coast lay the wealthy seaports of the Phoenicians. In Asia Minor, in the heart of present day Turkey, the powerful kingdom of the ancient Hittites stood on the threshold of its history. In Mesopotamia, between Tigris and Euphrates, reigned the kings of Sumer and Akkad, who held in tribute all the smaller kingdoms from the Persian Gulf to the sources of the Euphrates.

Egypt's mighty pyramids and Mesopotamia's massive temples had for centuries watched the busy life around them. For 2,000 years farms and plantations, as big as any large modern concern, had been exporting corn, vegetables and choice fruits from the artificially irrigated valleys of the Nile, the Euphrates and the Tigris. Everywhere throughout the "Fertile Crescent" and in the empire of the Pharaohs the art of cuneiform and hieroglyphic writing was commonly known. Poets, court officials and civil servants practised it. For commerce it had long been a necessity.

The endless traffic in commodities of all sorts which the great import and export firms of Mesopotamia and Egypt despatched by caravan routes or by sea from the Persian Gulf to Syria and Asia Minor, from the Nile to Cyprus and Crete and as far as the Black Sea, is reflected in their business correspondence, which they conducted on clay tablets or papyrus. Out of all the rich variety of costly wares the most keenly sought after were copper from the Egyptian mines in the mountains of Sinai, silver from the Taurus mines in Asia Minor, gold and ivory from Somaliland

FIG. 1.—The "Fertile Crescent" and Egypt—the great centres of civilisation about 2000 B.C.

in East Africa and from Nubia on the Nile, purple dyes from the Phoenician cities on the coast of Canaan, incense and rare spices from South Arabia, the magnificent linens which came from the Egyptian looms and the wonderful vases from the island of Crete.

Literature and learning were flourishing. In Egypt the first novels and secular poetry were making their appearance. Mesopotamia was experiencing a Renaissance. Philologists in Akkad, the great kingdom on the lower Euphrates, were compiling the first grammar and the first bilingual dictionary. The story of Gilgamesh, and the old Sumerian legends of Creation and Flood, were being woven into epics of dramatic power in the Akkadian tongue which was the language of the world. Egyptian doctors were producing their medicines in accordance with text-book methods from herbal compounds which had proved their worth. Their surgeons were no strangers to anatomical science. The mathematicians of the Nile by empirical means reached the conclusion about the sides of a triangle which 1,500 years later Pythagoras in Greece embodied in the theorem which bears his name. Mesopotamian engineers were solving the problem of square measurement by trial and error. Astronomers, admittedly with an eye solely on astrological prediction, were making their calculations based on accurate observations of the course of the planets.

Peace and prosperity must have reigned in this world of Nile, Euphrates and Tigris, for we have never yet discovered an inscription dating from this period which records any large-scale warlike activities.

Then suddenly from the heart of this great "Fertile Crescent", from the sandy sterile wastes of the Arabian desert whose shores are lashed by the waters of the Indian Ocean, there burst in violent assaults on the north, on the north-west, on Mesopotamia, Syria and Palestine a horde of nomadic tribes of Semitic stock. In endless waves these Amorites, "Westerners" as their name implies, surged against the kingdoms of the "Fertile Crescent".

The empire of the kings of Sumer and Akkad collapsed in 1960 B.C. under their irresistible attack. The Amorites founded a number of states and dynasties. One of them was eventually to become supreme: the first dynasty of Babylon, which was the great centre of power from 1830 to 1530 B.C. Its sixth king was the famous Hammurabi.

Meantime one of these tribes of Semitic nomads was destined to be of fateful significance for millions upon millions throughout the world up to the present day. It was a little group, perhaps only a family, as unknown and unimportant as a tiny grain of sand in a desert storm: the family of Abraham, forefather of the patriarchs.

Chapter 2
UR OF THE CHALDEES

Station on the Bagdad railway—A staged tower of bricks—Ruins with Biblical names—Archaeologists in search of scriptural sites—A consul with a pick—The archaeologist on the throne of Babylon—Expedition to Tell al-Muqayyar—History books from rubble—Tax receipts on clay—Was Abraham a city dweller?

"And Terah took Abram his son, and Lot the son of Haran, his son's son, and Sarai, his daughter in law, his son Abram's wife; and they went forth with them from Ur of the Chaldees" (Gen. 11^{31}).

...and they went forth with them from Ur of the Chaldees—Christians have been hearing these words for almost 2,000 years. Ur, a name as mysterious and legendary as the bewildering variety of names of kings and conquerors, powerful empires, temples and golden palaces, with which the Bible regales us. Nobody knew where Ur lay. Chaldea certainly pointed to Mesopotamia. Sixty years ago no one could have guessed that the quest for the Ur which is mentioned in the Bible would lead to the discovery of a civilisation which would take us farther into the twilight of prehistoric times than even the oldest traces of man which had been found in Egypt.

Today Ur is a railway station about 120 miles north of Basra, near the Persian Gulf, and one of the many stops on the famous Bagdad railway. Punctually the train makes a halt there in the grey light of early morning. When the noise of the wheels on their northward journey has died away, the traveller who has alighted here is surrounded by the silence of the desert.

7

His glance roams over the monotonous yellowish-brown of the endless stretch of sand. He seems to be standing in the middle of an enormous flat dish which is only intersected by the railway line. Only at one point is the shimmering expanse of desolation broken. As the rays of the rising sun grow stronger they pick out a massive dull red stump. It looks as if some Titan had hewn great notches in it.

To the Bedouins this solitary mound is an old friend. High up in its crevices the owls make their nests. From time immemorial the Arabs have known it and have given it the name Tell al-Muqayyar, "Mound of Pitch". Their forefathers pitched their tents at its base. Still as from time immemorial it offers welcome protection from the danger of sandstorms. Still today they feed their flocks at its base when the rains suddenly charm blades of grass out of the ground.

Once upon a time—4,000 years ago—broad fields of corn and barley swayed here. Market gardens, groves of date-palms and fig trees stretched as far as the eye could see. These spacious estates could cheerfully bear comparison with Canadian wheat farms or the market gardens and fruit farms of California. The lush green fields and beds were interlaced by a system of dead straight canals and ditches, a masterpiece of irrigation. Away back in the Stone Age experts among the natives had utilised the water of the great rivers. Skilfully and methodically they diverted the precious moisture at the river banks and thereby converted desert wastes into rich and fruitful farmland.

Almost hidden by forests of shady palms the Euphrates flowed in those days past this spot. This great life-giving river carried a heavy traffic between Ur and the sea. At that time the Persian Gulf cut much deeper into the estuary of the Euphrates and the Tigris. Even before the first pyramid was built on the Nile Tell al-Muqayyar was towering into the blue skies. Four mighty cubes, built one upon the other in diminishing size, rose up into a 75 feet tower of gaily coloured brick. Above the black of the square foundation block, its sides 120 feet long, shone the red and blue of the upper stages, each studded with trees. The uppermost stage provided a small plateau, on which was enthroned a Holy Place shaded by a golden roof.

Silence reigned over this sanctuary, where priests performed their offices at the shrine of Nannar, the moon-god. The stir and noise of wealthy metropolitan Ur, one of the oldest cities of the world, hardly penetrated into it.

In the year 1854 a caravan of camels and donkeys, laden with an unusual cargo of spades, picks and surveyor's instruments, approached the lonely red mound, under the leadership of the British consul in Basra. Mr. J. E. Taylor was inspired neither by a lust for adventure nor indeed by any motive of his own. He had undertaken the journey at the instigation of the Foreign Office, which in its turn was complying with the request from the British Museum that a search should be made for ancient monuments in Southern Mesopotamia, where the Euphrates and the Tigris came closest together just before entering the Persian Gulf. Taylor had often heard in Basra about the strange great heap of stones that his expedition was now approaching. It seemed to him a suitable site to investigate.

About the middle of the 19th century all over Egypt, Mesopotamia and Palestine investigations and excavations had started in response to a suddenly awakened desire to get a scientifically reliable picture of man's history in this part of the world. The goal of a long succession of expeditions was the Middle East.

Up till then the Bible had been the only historical source for our knowledge of that part of Asia before about 550 B.C. Only the Bible had anything to say about a period of history which stretched back into the dim twilight of the past. Peoples and names cropped up in the Bible about which even the Greeks and the Romans no longer knew anything.

Scholars swarmed impetuously into these lands of the Ancient East about the middle of last century. Nobody then knew names that were soon to be in everyone's mouth. With astonishment the age of progress and enlightenment heard of their finds and

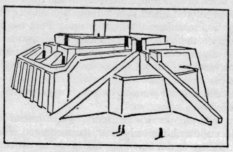

FIG. 2.—The great staged tower at Ur (Reconst.).

discoveries. What these men with infinite pains extracted from the desert sand by the great rivers of Mesopotamia and Egypt deserved indeed the attention of mankind. Here for the first time science had forced open the door into the mysterious world of the Bible.

The French vice-consul in Mosul, Paul-Emile Botta, was an enthusiastic archaeologist. In 1843 he began to dig at Khorsabad on the Tigris and from the ruins of a 4,000 year old capital proudly brought to light the first witness to the Bible: Sargon, the fabulous ruler of Assyria. "In the year that Tartan came unto Ashdod, when Sargon the king of Assyria sent him . . ." says Isaiah 20[1].

Two years later a young English diplomat and excavator, A. H. Layard, uncovered Nimrud (Kalchu), the city which the Bible calls Calah (Gen. 10[11]) and which now bears the name of the Nimrod of the Bible, "a mighty hunter before the Lord. And the beginning of his kingdom was Babel and Erech, and Accad and Calneh in the land of Shinar. Out of that land he went forth into Assyria and builded Nineveh and Rehoboth-Ir and Calah. . . ." (Gen. 10[10-11]).

Shortly after that, excavations under the direction of an English major, Henry Creswicke Rawlinson, one of the foremost Assyriologists, unearthed Nineveh, the Assyrian capital with the famous library of King Ashurbanipal. This is the Nineveh whose wickedness the Biblical prophets constantly denounced (Jonah 1[2]).

In Palestine the American scholar Edward Robinson devoted himself in 1838 and 1852 to the reconstruction of the topography of the ancient world.

From Germany, Richard Lepsius, later director of the Egyptian Museum in Berlin, recorded the monuments of the Nile area during an expedition which lasted from 1842–46.

Just as the Frenchman Champollion had the good fortune to decipher Egyptian hieroglyphics, so Rawlinson, the discoverer of Nineveh, was, among others, successful in solving the riddle of cuneiform writing. The ancient documents were beginning to talk!

Let us return to the caravan which is approaching Tell al-Muqayyar.

Taylor pitches his tents at the foot of the red mound. He had neither scientific ambitions nor previous knowledge. Where is he to begin? Where is the best spot to deploy his native diggers?

The great brick mound, architectural masterpiece of a shadowy past though it might be, conveys nothing to him. Perhaps in the heart of it lies something which might eventually be exhibited in the museum and might interest the London experts. He thinks vaguely of old statues, armour, ornaments or even perhaps buried treasure. He takes a closer look at the curious mound. Step by step he taps at its surface. No indication of a hollow cavity within. The great edifice appears to be completely solid. Thirty feet above him the wall of the lowest block rises straight and sheer out of the sand. Two broad stone ramps lead to the next and smaller cone above, then above them rise the third and fourth stages.

Taylor clambers up and down, crawls along the ledges on hands and knees in the broiling sun, finding only broken tiles. One day, bathed in sweat, he reaches the topmost platform and a few owls fly startled from the dilapidated walls. Nothing more. However he is not discouraged. In his efforts to get to the heart of the secrets of the mound he makes a decision which today we can only deeply regret. He takes his labour gangs away from the base of the mound and sets them to work at the top.

What had survived for centuries, what had withstood sand-storm and blazing sun alike, became now the victim of tireless pickaxes. Taylor gives orders to pull down the top story. The work of destruction begins at the four corners simultaneously. Day after day masses of bricks crash dully down the sides to the ground. After many weeks the chattering voices on the top of the mound are suddenly hushed, the clanging and banging of the pickaxes stop abruptly. Falling over each other in their haste a few men rush down the side of the mound and up to Taylor's tent. In their hands they hold little bars, cylinders made of baked clay. Taylor is disappointed. He had expected more. As he carefully cleans his finds he recognises that the clay rolls are covered over and over with inscriptions—cuneiform writing! He understands none of it but he is highly delighted. The cylinders, carefully packed, are despatched to London. The scholars on Thames-side are however not impressed—and small wonder. These were the years when the experts were looking to North Mesopotamia, where, under their fascinated gaze, the emergence from the hills of Nineveh and Khorsabad on the upper Tigris of the palaces and colossal reliefs of the Assyrians, as well as thousands of clay tablets and statues, was enough to put everything else in the shade. What significance compared with them had the little clay cylinders from Tell al-Muqayyar? For two years more Taylor hopefully continued his search. But there were no further results from Tell al-Muqayyar and the expedition was abandoned.

It was seventy-five years later before the world learned what priceless treasures were still lying under that ancient mound.

As far as the experts were concerned Tell al-Muqayyar was once more forgotten. But it was by no means neglected. No sooner had Taylor left than hordes of other visitors arrived. The broken walls and above all the top tier of the mound, which Taylor's gangs had shattered, provided a welcome and inexhaustible supply of inexpensive building material for the Arabs who over the years came from far and near and departed with as many bricks as their pack-mules could carry. These bricks, fashioned by men's hands thousands of years before, still bore plainly the names of Ur-Nammu, the first great builder, and of Nabonidus, the Babylonian conqueror who restored the staged tower which they called the Ziggurat. Sandstorms, rain, wind and the heat of the sun have all added their quota to the process of destruction.

During the First World War when British troops on the march to Bagdad in 1915 camped near this ancient structure they found that its former appearance had been completely altered. It had become so flat due to dilapidation and theft in the intervening years since 1854 that one of the soldiers was able to indulge in a piece of daredevilry. The step-formation of the tower which had previously been so clearly marked had disappeared so completely that he was able to ride his mule right to the summit of the mound.

By a lucky chance there was an expert among the officers of the party, R. Campbell Thompson, of the Intelligence Staff of the army in Mesopotamia. In peace time he had been an assistant in the British Museum. Thompson rummaged with an expert eye through the huge heap of bricks and was shocked at the deterioration of the material. Examination of the terrain led him to suppose that there were further areas worth investigating in the neighbourhood of the Tell, ruins of settlements which lay buried under the sand. Thompson recorded all this with great care and sent an urgent message to London. This prompted them to blow the dust off the insignificant looking little clay cylinders which had almost been forgotten and to look at them again with greater attention. The inscriptions on them were then found to contain some extremely important information as well as a curious story.

Almost 2,500 years before Taylor someone else had been searching and rummaging on the same spot with the same concern—Nabonidus, king of Babylon in the 6th century B.C., venerator of the past, man of renown, ruler of a mighty kingdom and archaeologist rolled into one. In his day he established that "the Ziggurat was now old". But his tactics were different from Taylor's. "I restored this Ziggurat to its former state with mortar and baked bricks." When the weakened structure of the staged tower had been restored he had caused the name of the first builder, which he had discovered, to be cut out on these little clay cylinders. His name, as the Babylonian had been able to decipher from a damaged inscription, had been King Ur-Nammu. Ur-Nammu? Was the builder of the great staged tower king of the Ur that the Bible mentions? Was he the ruler of Ur of the Chaldees?

It seemed highly probable. The same Biblical name had cropped up several times since then. Ancient records which had been recovered from other sites in Mesopotamia also mentioned Ur. It appeared from these cuneiform writings that it was the capital city of the great Sumerian people. At once the battered remnants of Tell al-Muqayyar aroused eager interest. Scholars from the Museum of Pennsylvania University joined the archaeologists from the British Museum in fresh investigations. The staged tower on the lower Euphrates might hold the secret of this unknown Sumerian people—and of the Ur of the Bible. But it was not until 1923 that a joint American and British team of archaeologists could set out. They were spared the tiresome journey on the backs of swaying camels. They went by the Bagdad railway. Their equipment likewise went by train: trucks, rails, picks, spades, baskets.

The archaeologists had enough funds at their disposal to turn up the whole countryside. They begin their carefully planned excavation on a large scale. Since considerable finds might be expected, they reckon on taking several years. In charge of the expedition is Sir Charles Leonard Woolley. The forty-three year old Englishman had already won his spurs on expeditions and digs in Egypt, Nubia and Carchemish on the upper Euphrates. Now this talented and successful man makes Tell al-Muqayyar

his life's work. Unlike the zealous but unsuspecting Taylor
several decades before, his chief aim is not directed to the staged
tower at all. He is possessed with a desire above all to investigate
these flat mounds which rise all around him out of the vast sandy
plain.

Woolley's trained eye had not failed to note their striking
configuration. They look like little Table Mountains. Flat on top,
they slope downwards in an almost uniform pattern. Similar
mounds exist in great numbers, large and small, in the Middle
East, on the banks of the great rivers, in the midst of fertile
plains, by the wayside on the routes followed by caravans from
time immemorial. No one has yet been able to count them. We
find them from the delta of the Euphrates and Tigris on the
Persian Gulf to the highlands of Asia Minor where the river
Halys tumbles into the Black Sea, on the eastern shores of the
Mediterranean, in the valleys of the Lebanon, on the Orontes in
Syria and in Palestine by the Jordan.

These little eminences are the great quarries for archaeological
finds, eagerly sought and often inexhaustible. They are not
formed by the hand of Nature, but are artificially created, piled
high with the legacy of countless generations before us; vast
masses of rubble and rubbish from a bygone age which have
accumulated from the remains of huts and houses, town walls,
temples or palaces. Each one of these hills took shape gradually
in the same way through a period of centuries or even millennia.
At some point after men had first settled there the place was
destroyed by war or was burned down or was deserted by its
inhabitants. Then came the conquerors or new settlers and built
upon the selfsame spot. Generation after generation built their
settlements and cities, one on top of the other, on the identical
site. In the course of time the ruins and rubble of countless
dwellings grew, layer by layer, foot by foot, into a sizeable hill.
The Arabs of today call such an artificial mound a Tell. The
same word was used even in ancient Babylon. Tell means
"mound". We come across the word in the Bible in Josh. 11[13].
During the conquest of Canaan, where cities "that stood on their
mounds" are spoken of, it is these Tulul, which is the plural of
Tell, which are meant. The Arabs make a clear distinction
between a Tell and a natural eminence, which they call a Jebel.

Every Tell is at the same time a silent history book. Its strata
are for the archaeologist like the leaves of a calendar. Page by

page he can make the past come to life again. Every layer, if we read it aright, tells of its own times, its life and customs, the craftsmanship and manners of its people. This skill on the part of excavators in deciphering the message of the strata has reached astonishing heights of achievement.

Stones, hewn or rough, bricks or traces of clay betray the nature of the building. Even decayed and weathered stones or the remains of brick dust can indicate exactly the ground plan of a building. Dark shadows show where once a fireplace radiated its warming glow.

Broken pottery, armour, household utensils and tools which are to be found everywhere among the ruins, afford further help in this detective work on the past. How grateful are the scholars of today that the ancient world knew nothing of municipal cleansing departments! Anything that had become unusable or superfluous was simply thrown out and left to the tender mercies of time and the weather.

Today the different shapes, colours and patterns of pots and vases can be so clearly distinguished that pottery has become archaeology's Number One measurement of time. Single potsherds, sometimes only fragments, make it possible to give a precise dating. As far back as the second millennium B.C. the greatest margin of error in establishing a date in this way is at the outside about fifty years.

Priceless information was lost in the course of the first great excavations of last century because no one paid any attention to these apparently worthless bits of broken pottery. They were thrown aside. The only important things seemed to be great monuments, reliefs, statues or jewels. Much that was of value was thus lost for ever. The activities of Heinrich Schliemann, the antiquary, are an example of this sort of thing. Fired with ambition he had only one end in view: to find Homer's Troy. He set his gangs of labourers on to digging straight down. Strata, which might have been of great value in establishing dates, were thrown aside as useless rubbish. At length Schliemann unearthed a valuable treasure amid general acclamation. But it was not, as he thought, the treasure of Priam. His find belonged to a period several centuries earlier. Schliemann had missed the reward of his labours, that would have meant so much to him, by digging past it and going far too deep. Being a business man Schliemann was an amateur, a layman. But the professionals were, to begin with, no better. It is only during this century that the archaeologists have been working in accordance with approved methods. Beginning at the top and working down through the Tell they examine every square inch of the ground. Every tiny object, every piece of pottery is scrutinised. First they dig a trench deep into the mound. The different coloured strata lie open like a cut cake and the trained eye of the expert is able at a rough glance to place in their historical perspective whatever ancient human habitations lie embedded there. It was in accordance with this tried method that the Anglo-American expedition started work at Tell al-Muqayyar in 1923.

In early December there arose a cloud of dust over the rubble heap which lay east of the Ziggurat and only a few steps from the broad ramp up which ancient priests in solemn procession had approached the shrine of Nannar the moon-god. Fanned by a light wind it spread across the site until it seemed as if the whole area around the old staged tower was shrouded in fine mist. Powdery sand whirling up from hundreds of spades indicated that the great dig had started.

From the moment when the first spade struck the ground an atmosphere of excitement hovered over every shovelful. Each spadeful was like a journey into an unknown land where no-one knew beforehand what surprises lay ahead. Excitement gripped even Woolley and his companions. Would some important find richly reward them for their toil and sweat upon the hill? Would Ur give up its secrets to them? None of these men could guess that for six long winter seasons, till the spring of 1929, they would be kept in suspense. This large-scale excavation deep in Southern Mesopotamia was to reveal bit by bit those far off days when a new land arose out of the delta of the two great rivers and the first human settlers made their home there. Out of their painstaking research, carrying them back to a time 7,000 years before, events and names recorded in the Bible were more than once to take solid shape.

The first thing they brought to light was a sacred precinct with the remains of five temples, which had once surrounded King Ur-Nammu's Ziggurat in a semi-circle. They were like fortresses, so thick were their walls. The biggest one, which was 100 x 60 yards square, was dedicated to the moon-god. Another temple was in honour of Nin-Gal, goddess of the moon and wife of Nannar. Every temple had an inner court surrounded by a series of rooms. The old fountains were still standing, with long water troughs coated with bitumen. Deep grooves made with knives on the great brick tables showed where the sacrificial animals had been dissected. They were cooked as a common sacrificial meal on the hearths of the temple kitchens. Even the ovens for baking bread were there. "After 3,800 years," noted Woolley in his diary, "we were able to light the fire again and put into commission once more the oldest kitchen in the world."

Nowadays churches, law courts, tax offices and factories are quite separate establishments. It was otherwise in Ur. The sacred area, the Temple precinct, was not reserved exclusively for the worship of the gods. The priests had many other things to do besides their holy office. As well as receiving the sacrifices they collected the tithes and the taxes. That did not take place however without written confirmation. Every payment was noted on a little clay tablet—probably the first tax receipts ever issued. The amounts received were entered by scribes in weekly, monthly and yearly totals.

Minted currency was as yet unknown. Taxes were paid in kind: every inhabitant of Ur paid in his own coin. Oil, cereals, fruit, wool and cattle made their way into vast warehouses, perishable articles went to the temple shops. Many goods were manufactured in factories owned by the temple, for example in the spinning-mills which the priests managed. One workshop produced twelve different kinds of fashionable clothing. Tablets found in this place gave the names of the mill-girls and their quota of rations. Even the weight of the wool given to each worker and the number of garments made from it were meticulously recorded. In one of the legal buildings they found copies of the sentences carefully stacked exactly as they are in the administrative offices of modern law courts.

For three winter seasons the Anglo-American expedition worked on at the site of ancient Ur, and still this extraordinary museum of man's early history had not yielded up all its secrets. Outside the temple area the excavators had a further unprecedented surprise.

South of the staged tower, as they were clearing away a series of mounds, there suddenly emerged from the rubble solid structures: row upon row of walls and façades one after the other. As the sand was cleared away it revealed a complete checkerboard of dwelling-houses whose ruins were in places still 10 feet high.

Between them ran little alleyways. Here and there open squares broke the line of the streets.

Several weeks of hard work were necessary and endless loads of rubble had to be removed before the diggers were faced with an unforgettable sight.

Under the red slopes of Tell al-Muqayyar lay a whole city, bathed in the bright sunshine, awakened from its long sleep after many thousand years by the patient burrowing of the archaeologists. Woolley and his companions were beside themselves with joy. For before them lay Ur, the "Ur of the Chaldees" to which the Bible refers.

And how well its citizens lived, and in what spacious homes! No other Mesopotamian city has revealed such handsome and comfortable houses.

Compared with them the dwelling-houses which have been preserved in Babylon are modest, in fact miserable. Professor Koldewey, during German excavations there at the beginning of this century, found nothing but simple mud brick erections, one story high with three or four rooms surrounding an open courtyard. That was how people lived about 600 B.C. in the much admired and extolled metropolis of Nebuchadnezzar the Great of Babylon. But 1,500 years before that the citizens of Ur were living in large two-storied villas with thirteen or fourteen rooms. The lower floor was solidly built of burnt brick, the upper floor of mud brick. The walls were neatly coated with plaster and whitewashed.

A visitor would pass through the door into a small entrance hall where there was a basin to wash the dust off hands and feet. He then continued into the inner court, which was laid out in attractive paving. Round it were grouped the reception room, the kitchen, living rooms and private rooms and the domestic chapel. Up a stone staircase, which concealed a lavatory, he would reach a gallery from which branched off the rooms belonging to members of the family and the guest rooms.

From beneath the debris of brick and plaster there emerged into the light of day all the things that these patrician houses had contained in the way of domestic appliances for ordinary use. Countless sherds of pots, jugs, vases and small clay tablets covered with writing combined to form a mosaic from which piece by piece a picture of everyday life in Ur could be reconstructed. Ur of the Chaldees was a powerful, prosperous, colourful and busy capital city at the beginning of the second millennium B.C.

One idea was very much in Woolley's mind. Abraham is said to have come from Ur of the Chaldees—he must therefore have been born in one of these two-storied patrician houses and must have grown up there. Woolley wandered through these alleyways, past the walls of the great temple, and as he looked up he glimpsed this huge staged tower with its black, red and blue blocks and its fringe of trees. "We must radically alter", he writes enthusiastically, "our view of the Hebrew patriarch when we see that his earlier years were passed in such sophisticated surroundings. He was the citizen of a great city and inherited the traditions of an old and highly organised civilisation. The houses themselves reveal comfort and even luxury. We found copies of the hymns which were used in the services of the temples and together with them mathematical tables. On these tables were anything from plain addition sums to formulae for the extraction of square and cube roots. In other texts the writers had copied out the old building inscriptions to be found in the city and had compiled in this way a short history of the temples."

Abraham—no simple nomad, this Abraham, but son of a great city of the second millennium B.C.

That was a sensational discovery and one difficult to grasp. Newspapers and magazines carried photographs of the crumbling old staged tower and the ruins of the metropolis. They caused a tremendous sensation. People looked with astonishment at a drawing which bore the title: "A House of the time of Abraham". Woolley had had this done by an artist. It is a genuine reconstruction in accordance with the finds. It shows the inner court of a villa-type house; two tall jars stand on a tiled pavement; a wooden balustrade running round the upper story shuts off the rooms from the courtyard. Was the old familiar picture of the patriarch Abraham, as it had been held for generations, which saw him surrounded by his family and his cattle, suddenly to be called in question?

Woolley's idea did not remain unchallenged. Very soon theologians and even archaeologists registered their dissent.

In favour of Woolley's idea were the words of Gen. 11[31]: "And Terah took Abram his son and Lot . . . and they went forth . . . from Ur of the Chaldees." But there are other references in the Bible which point to somewhere else. When Abraham sends his old

servant from Canaan to the city of Nahor, to fetch a wife for his
son Isaac, he calls this place Nahor his "country" (Gen. 24[4]), his
"father's house" and "the land of my kindred" (Gen. 24[7]).
Nahor lay in the north of Mesopotamia. After the conquest of the
Promised Land Joshua addressed the people in these words:
"Your fathers dwelt on the other side of the flood in old time,
even Terah the father of Abraham and the father of Nahor"
(Josh. 24[2]). In this case the "flood" means as in other places in
the Bible, the Euphrates. The city of Ur was excavated on the
right bank of the Euphrates: looked at from Canaan it lay on this
side, not on the other side of the "flood". Had Woolley been too
hasty in his conclusions? What reliable evidence had the expedition produced? What proof was there that Terah and his son
Abraham lived actually in the city of Ur?

"The earlier journey from Ur of the Chaldees to Haran has,
apart from the discovery of the city itself, no archaeological
foundation," declares Professor W. F. Albright of Johns Hopkins
University. This scholar, who has himself conducted successful
excavations and is the foremost authority on the archaeology of
Palestine and the Middle East, goes further. "The remarkable
fact that the Greek translations [of the Bible] nowhere mention
Ur but read instead the more natural 'Land [of the Chaldees]'
might mean that the removal of Abraham's native place to Ur is
possibly secondary and was not generally known in the third
century B.C."

Ur emerged from the shadowy past as the capital city of the
Sumerians, one of the oldest civilisations in Mesopotamia. As
we know, the Sumerians were not Semites like the Hebrews.
When the great invasion of Semitic nomads streamed out of the
Arabian desert about 2000 B.C. its first encounter in the south
was with the extensive plantations of Ur, its houses and its
canals. It is possible that some recollection of that great journey
through the lands of the "Fertile Crescent", in which Ur was
involved, has resulted in its being mentioned in the Bible.
Painstaking research, particularly excavations in the last two
decades, make it almost certain that Abraham cannot ever have
been a citizen of the Sumerian metropolis. It would conflict with
all the descriptions which the Old Testament gives of the kind of
life lived by the patriarch: Abraham is a tent dweller, he moves
with his flocks from pasture to pasture and from well to well. He
does not live like a citizen of a great city—he lives the life of a
typical nomad.

As we shall see, it was much farther to the north of the "Fertile Crescent" that the stories of the Biblical patriarchs emerged out of their mystical obscurity on to the plane of history.

Chapter 3
DIGGING UP THE FLOOD

The graves of the Sumerian kings—A puzzling layer of clay—Traces of the Flood under desert sands—a catastrophic flood about 4000 B.C.

"And the Lord said unto Noah, Come thou and all thy house into the ark. For yet seven days and I will cause it to rain upon the earth, forty days and forty nights: and every living substance that I have made will I destroy from off the face of the earth.

"And it came to pass after seven days that the waters of the flood were upon the earth" (Gen. 7$^{1, 4, 10}$).

When we hear the word Flood, almost immediately we think of the Bible and the story of Noah's Ark. This wonderful Old Testament story has travelled round the world with Christianity. But although this is the best known tradition of the Flood it is by no means the only one. Among people of all races there is a variety of traditions of a gigantic and catastrophic Flood. The Greeks told the Flood story and connected it with Deucalion: long before Columbus many stories told among the natives of the continent of America kept the memory of a great Flood alive: in Australia, India, Polynesia, Tibet, Kashmir and Lithuania tales of a Flood have been handed down from generation to generation up to the present day. Are they all fairy tales and legends, are they all inventions?

It is highly probable that they all reflect the same world-wide catastrophe. This frightful occurrence must, however, have taken place at a time when there were human beings on earth who could experience it, survive it, and then pass on an account of it.

Geologists thought that they could solve this ancient mystery by pointing to the warm periods in the earth's history, between the Ice Ages. They suggested that when the huge ice-caps covering the continents, some of them many thousand feet high, gradually began to melt, the level of the sea rose to four times its normal height all over the world. This great additional volume of water altered land contours, flooded low lying coastal areas and plains, and annihilated their population, their animals, and their vegetation. But all these attempts at explanation ended in speculation and theory. Possible hypotheses satisfy the historian least of all. He constantly demands unambiguous factual evidence. But there was none: no scientist, whatever his line, could produce any. Actually it was by a coincidence—during research into something quite different—that unmistakable evidence of the Flood appeared, as it were, of its own accord. And that happened at a place we have already got to know: at the excavations at Ur.

For six years American and British archaeologists had been examining the ground at Tel al-Muqayyar, which by that time looked like one vast building site. When the Bagdad train stopped there for a moment, travellers looked with amazement at the soaring sandhills which had resulted from the diggings. Waggon loads of soil were removed, carefully searched, and put through the riddle. Rubbish thousands of years old was treated like precious cargo. Perseverance, conscientiousness, and painstaking effort had in six years yielded a handsome dividend. The Sumerian temples with their warehouses, workshops and law courts and the villa-type dwelling houses were followed, between 1926 and 1928, by discoveries of such magnificence and splendour that everything else so far paled into insignificance.

"The graves of the kings of Ur"—so Woolley, in the exuberance of his delight at discovering them, had dubbed the tombs of Sumerian nobles whose truly regal splendour had been exposed when the spades of the archaeologists attacked a 50 foot mound south of the temple and found a long row of superimposed graves. The stone vaults were veritable treasure chests, for they were filled with all the costly things that Ur in its heyday possessed. Golden drinking cups and goblets, wonderfully shaped jugs and vases, bronze tableware, mother of pearl mosaics, lapis lazuli and silver surrounded these bodies which had mouldered into dust. Harps and lyres rested against the walls. A young man, "Hero of the land of God" as an inscription described him, wore a golden helmet. A golden comb decorated with blossom in lapis lazuli adorned the hair of the beautiful Sumerian "Lady Puabi". Even the famous tombs of Nofretete and Tutankhamun contained no more beautiful objects. "The graves of the kings of Ur" are moreover 1,000 years older at least.

The graves of the kings had as well as these precious contents another more grisly and depressing experience in store for us, enough to send a slight shiver down the spine. In the vaults were found teams of oxen with the skeletons still in harness and each of the great waggons was laden with artistic household furniture. The whole retinue had clearly accompanied the noblemen in death, as could be gathered from the richly clad and ornamented skeletons with which they were surrounded. The tomb of the beautiful Puabi had twenty such skeletons, other vaults had as many as seventy.

What can have happened here so long ago? There was not the slightest indication that they were victims of a violent death. In solemn procession, it would seem, the attendants with the ox-drawn treasure-waggons accompanied the body to the tomb. And while the grave was being sealed outside they composed their dead master for his last rest within. Then they took some drug, gathered round him for the last time and died of their own free will—in order to be able to serve him in his future existence.

For two centuries the citizens of Ur had buried their eminent men in these tombs. When they came to open the lowest and last tomb the archaeologists of the 20th century A.D. found themselves transported into the world of 2800 B.C.

As the summer of 1929 approached the sixth season of digging at Tell al-Muqayyar was drawing to a close. Woolley had put his native diggers once more on to the hill of "the graves of the kings". It left him no peace. He wanted to be certain whether the ground under the deepest royal grave had fresh discoveries in store for the next season's excavation.

After the foundations of the tomb had been removed, a few hundred thrusts of the spade made it quite plain that further layers of rubble lay below. How far into the past could these silent chronometers take them?

When had the very first human settlement arisen on virgin soil under this mound? Woolley had to know. To make certain he very slowly and carefully sank shafts and stood over them to examine the soil which came up from the underlying strata. "Almost at once," he wrote later in his diary, "discoveries were made which confirmed our suspicions. Directly under the floor of one of the tombs of the kings we found in a layer of charred wood ash numerous clay tablets, which were covered with characters of a much older type than the inscriptions on the graves. Judging by the nature of the writing the tablets could be assigned to about 3000 B.C. They were therefore two or three centuries earlier than the tombs."

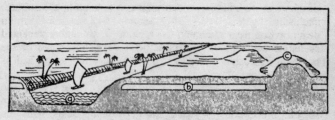

FIG. 3.—Traces of flood-clay about 4000 B.C.

(a) River bed (Euphrates).
(b) Layer of flood-clay.
(c) Hills which projected above the flood.

The shafts went deeper and deeper. New strata with fragments of jars, pots and bowls kept coming up. The experts noticed that the pottery remained surprisingly enough unchanged. It looked exactly like what had been found in the graves of the kings. Therefore it seemed as if for centuries Sumerian civilisation had undergone no radical change. They must, according to this conclusion, have reached a high level of development astonishingly early.

When after several days some of Woolley's workmen called out to him "We are on ground level" he let himself down onto the floor of the shaft to satisfy himself. Traces of any kind of settlement did in fact abruptly break off in the shaft. The last fragments of household utensils lay on the smooth flat surface of the base of the pit. Here and there were charred remains. Woolley's first thought was: "This is it at last." He carefully prodded the ground on the floor of the shaft and stopped short: it was clay, pure clay of a kind that could only have been deposited by water! Clay in a place like that? Woolley tried to find an explanation: it must be the accumulated silt of the Euphrates in bygone days. This stratum must have come into existence when

the great river thrust its delta far out into the Persian Gulf, just as
it still does, creating new land out of the sea at the river mouth at
the rate of 75 feet a year. When Ur was in its heyday, the
Euphrates flowed so close to it that the great staged tower was
reflected in its waters and the Gulf was visible from the temple
on its summit. The first buildings must therefore have sprung up
on the mud flats of the delta.

Measurements of the adjacent area and more careful calculations brought Woolley eventually however to quite a different
conclusion.

"I saw that we were much too high up. It was most unlikely
that the island on which the first settlement was built stood up so
far out of the marsh."

FIG. 4.—Pit showing flood-stratum at Ur.

1. Graves of the kings.   3. Band of clay (10 feet).
2. Sherds and vessels.   4. Antediluvian vessels.

The foot of the shaft, where the layer of clay began, was
several yards above the river level. It could not therefore be river
deposit. What was the meaning then of this remarkable stratum?
Where did it come from? None of his associates could give him a
satisfactory answer. They decided to dig on and make the shaft
deeper. Woolley gazed intently as once more basket after basket
came out of the trench and their contents were examined. Deeper
and deeper went the spades into the ground, 3 feet, 6 feet—still
pure clay. Suddenly at nearly 10 feet the layer of clay stopped as
abruptly as it had started. What would come now?

The next baskets that came to the surface gave an answer that none of the expedition would have dreamt of. They could hardly believe their eyes. They had expected pure virgin soil. But what now emerged into the glaring sunshine was rubble and more rubble, ancient rubbish and countless potsherds. Under this clay deposit almost 10 feet thick they had struck fresh evidence of human habitation. The appearance and quality of the pottery had noticeably altered. Above the clay-stratum were jars and bowls which had obviously been turned on the potter's wheel, here on the contrary they were hand-made. No matter how carefully they sifted the contents of the baskets, amid increasing excitement, metal remains were nowhere to be found, the primitive implement that did emerge was made of hewn flint. It must belong to the Stone Age!

That day a telegram from Mesopotamia flashed what was perhaps the most extraordinary message that had ever stirred men's imaginations, "We have found the Flood". The incredible discovery at Ur made headline news in the United States and in Britain.

The Flood—that was the only possible explanation of this great clay deposit beneath the hill at Ur, which quite clearly separated two epochs of settlement. The sea had left its unmistakable traces in the shape of remains of little marine organisms embedded in the clay. Woolley had to confirm his conclusions without delay: a chance coincidence—although the odds were against it—might conceivably have been making fools of them. Three hundred yards from the first shaft he sank a second one.

The spades produced the same result: sherds—clay—fragments of hand-made pottery.

Finally to remove all doubt, Woolley made them dig a shaft through the rubble where the old settlement lay on a natural hill, that is to say, on a considerably higher level than the stratum of clay.

Just at about the same level as in the two other shafts the sherds of wheel-turned vessels stopped suddenly. Immediately beneath them came hand-made clay pots. It was exactly as Woolley had supposed and expected. Naturally the intermediate layer of clay was missing. "About sixteen feet below a brick pavement," noted Woolley, "which we could with reasonable certainty date about 2700 B.C. we were among the ruins of that Ur which had existed before the Flood."

How far did the layer of clay extend? What area was affected by the disaster? A proper hunt now started for traces of the Flood in other parts of Mesopotamia. Other archaeologists discovered a further important check-point near Kish, south-east of Babylon, where the Euphrates and the Tigris flow in a great bend towards each other. There they found a similar band of clay, but only 18 inches thick. Gradually by a variety of tests the limits of the Flood waters could be established. According to Woolley the disaster engulfed an area north-west of the Persian Gulf amounting to 400 miles long and 100 miles wide, looking at the map we should call it today "a local occurrence"—for the inhabitants of the river plains it was however in those days their whole world.

FIG. 5.—The extent of the Flood in Mesopotamia.

After endless enquiry and attempts at some explanation, without achieving any concrete results, any hope of solving the great riddle of the Flood had long since been given up. It seemed to lie in a dark and distant region of time which we could never hope to penetrate. Now Woolley and his associates had through their tireless and patient efforts made a discovery which shattered even the experts: a vast catastrophic inundation, resembling the Biblical Flood which had regularly been described by sceptics as either a fairy tale or a legend, had not only taken place but was moreover an event within the compass of history.

At the foot of the old staged tower of the Sumerians, at Ur on the lower Euphrates, anyone could climb down a ladder into a narrow shaft and see and touch the remains of a gigantic and catastrophic Flood which had deposited a layer of clay almost 10 feet thick. Reckoning by the age of the strata containing traces of human habitation, and in this respect they are as reliable as a calendar, it could also be ascertained when the great Flood took place. It happened about 4000 B.C.

Clearly people in Woolley's day tended to give dramatic interpretations to the results of excavations more readily than they do nowadays, for shortly after Woolley, another excavator, Stephen Langdon, claimed, "with strong support from the press", that he in turn had found in Kish, that is to say, in Babylon, "material traces of the Flood". It was Langdon's, but also Woolley's bad luck that the datings of these two flood catastrophes did not agree. Which flood was the right one, the genuine, Biblical Flood? Woolley protested vigorously against Langdon's claim to have discovered it and a vehement argument followed which, however, did not in the least disturb a number of writers, among them, for example, Sir Charles Marston, who asserted that both Woolley and Langdon had discovered "simultaneously the deposits left by the Flood".

Since then the excitement has somewhat subsided and given place to more sober consideration. The following four main points emerge from the pronouncements of the experts:

Of Woolley's five shafts only two revealed any deposits at all from an inundation.

The inundation in Ur did not lead to the abandonment of the settlement. In fact, it did not even lead to an interruption in the occupation.

Traces of inundation were indeed discovered in other places in Mesopotamia, in Kish, as well as in Fara (Shuruppak), Nineveh and Uruk (Erech) but on the other hand, they are not found where they ought to be present if the whole of Mesopotamia was flooded.

The traces left by the inundations at the various excavation sites also vary, in some cases quite appreciably, in their chronological sequence. They belong to quite different periods; centuries separate them.

In other words, Woolley's "Flood" was obviously not of sufficient magnitude for the Biblical "Flood", unless we assume that one of the flood catastrophes shown by archaeology to have occurred in Mesopotamia had nevertheless had such a lasting effect on the inhabitants of those days that—with a considerable amount of exaggeration—the tradition of a catastrophe to humanity could arise from it. Naturally, however, this is mere supposition and the Biblical Flood, at any rate a flood of the unimaginable extent described in the Bible, still remains "archaeologically not demonstrated''. The question consequently remains: do all the various "flood" reports, which occur in practically all parts of the world, describe merely mankind's earliest experience of the phenomenon "flood catastrophe" and were all the traditional, relevant accounts of floods simply compressed or exaggerated to form a number of stories of the "great flood of all floods" or are they the vestiges of much older traditions going back hundreds of years *before* Woolley's flood at Ur, to the time of the melting of the gigantic glaciers of the Ice Age when the ocean rose some two hundred metres and the limits of today's land and sea were formed? That event had world-wide consequences which could explain why the traditions of a flood have persisted among so many peoples. The following pages will discuss one of the flood traditions, parallel to that in the Bible, although it derives to a large extent also from "Biblical lands".

Chapter 4
A FLOOD-STORY FROM OLD BABYLONIA

The Epic of Gilgamesh and the Bible—Twelve clay tablets from Nineveh—An ancient epic from the Library of Ashurbanipal—Utnapishtim, a Sumerian Noah?—The secret of Mt. Ararat—A gigantic ship in a museum of ice—Expeditions in quest of the Ark.

"And God said unto Noah...Make thee an ark of gopherwood: rooms shalt thou make in the ark and shalt pitch it within and without with pitch" (Gen. 6[13-14]).

About the turn of the century, long before Woolley discovered Ur, another find had aroused great interest and given rise to lively discussions about the nature of Holy Scripture.

From the dim recesses of the Ancient East an old mysterious story came to light: a heroic epic, of 300 quatrains, inscribed on twelve large clay tablets, which told of the wonderful experiences of the legendary king Gilgamesh.

The text was astonishing: Gilgamesh told a tale exactly like the Bible—of a man who was said to have lived before and after a mighty and disastrous Flood.

Where did this splendid and remarkable epic come from?

During excavations in the fifties of last century British archaeologists had found these twelve clay tablets, together with about 20,000 others, all in a good state of preservation, among the ruins of the library at Nineveh, which was reckoned to be the most famous in the ancient world. King Ashurbanipal had it built in the 7th century B.C. high above the banks of the Tigris in old

31

Nineveh. Today on the other side of the river the oil-derricks of Mosul tower into the sky.

A priceless treasure in packing cases started out on its long journey from Nineveh to the British Museum.

But it was not for several decades that the true value of these texts was revealed when they could finally be deciphered. At the time there was no one in the world who could read them. Despite every effort the tablets held their peace. Shortly before 1900 in the modest laboratories of the British Museum the old texts began, after an interval of twenty-five centuries, to unfold anew one of the finest narratives of the Ancient East. Assyriologists heard for the first time the Epic of Gilgamesh. It is written in Akkadian, the language of the court and of diplomacy in the time of King Ashurbanipal. Its form, however, dates not from the time when it was placed in the library at Nineveh but from 1,000 years earlier. It goes back as far as Hammurabi, the great king of Babylon, for soon a second copy was discovered in his capital on the Euphrates. Further finds confirmed the view that the Gilgamesh Epic belonged to the rich heritage of all the great nations of the Ancient East. Hittites and Egyptians translated it into their own tongues, and cuneiform tablets discovered by the Nile still show clearly the marks in red ink opposite those parts which the Egyptian scribes found difficulty in translating.

At last a little clay fragment gave the clue to the origin of the Epic of Gilgamesh. The world owes its original composition to the Sumerians, the people whose capital stood on the site of Ur.

Gilgamesh, as the cuneiform writing on the eleventh tablet from the library at Nineveh tells us, decided to ensure his immortality and set out on a long adventurous journey to find his ancestor Utnapishtim, from whom he hoped to learn the secret of everlasting life which the gods had bestowed upon him. When he reached the island on which Utnapishtim lived, Gilgamesh asked of him the "Secret of Life". Utnapishtim related that he had once lived in Shuruppak and had been a true worshipper of the god Ea. When the gods decided to destroy mankind by a Flood Ea warned his devotee Utnapishtim and issued this command: "O man of Shuruppak, son of Ubar-Tutu, tear down thy house, build a ship; abandon wealth, seek after life; scorn possessions, save thy life. Bring up the seed of all kinds of living things into the ship: the ship which thou shalt build. Let its dimensions be well measured."

We all know the wonderful story which follows. For what the

Sumerian Utnapishtim is said to have experienced, the Bible tells us about Noah.

> "And God said unto Noah... Make thee an ark of gopherwood.... And of every living thing of all flesh, two of every sort shalt thou bring into the ark, to keep them alive with thee; they shall be male and female" (Gen. 6¹³ff).

To make the comparison easier let us set side by side what Utnapishtim says of his great experience and what the Bible tells us of Noah and the Flood.

In accordance with the command of the god Ea, Utnapishtim builds the ship and says:

On the fifth day I decided upon its plan.	The length of the ark shall be 300 cubits the breadth of it 50 cubits and the height of it thirty cubits (Gen. 6¹⁵).
The floor was 200 ft. square.	
The walls were 200 ft. high.	
I gave it six stories and divided the breadth seven times.	With lower, second, and third stories shalt thou make it (Gen. 6¹⁶).
Its interior I divided into nine.	...Rooms shalt thou make in the ark (Gen. 6¹⁴),
6 sar of bitumen I poured into the kiln.	...and shalt pitch it within and without with pitch (Gen. 6¹⁴).

When Utnapishtim had finished building his ship he arranged a sumptuous banquet. He provided venison and mutton for those who had helped with the work of building and dispensed "cider, beer, oil and wine to the people as if it were running water". Then he continues:

All that I had I loaded, of the seed of all living things.	And Noah went in, and his sons, and his wife, and his sons' wives, into the ark because of the waters of the flood.
	Of clean beasts, and of beasts that are not clean, and of fowls,

	and of everything that creepeth upon the earth,
I brought into the ship my whole family and kinsfolk.	There went in two and two unto Noah into the ark, the male and the female, as God had commanded Noah (Gen. 7⁷⁻⁹).
The cattle of the field, the beasts of the field, all craftsmen—I made them go up into it.	
I went into the ship and closed my door.	And the Lord shut him in (Gen. 7¹⁶).
As soon as a gleam of dawn shone in the sky, came a black cloud from the foundation of heaven. Inside it Adad thundered.	And it came to pass, after seven days, that the waters of the flood were upon the earth. ... the same day were all the fountains of the great deep broken up, and the windows of heaven were opened (Gen. 7¹⁰⁻¹¹).
Adad's rage reached to the heavens: turning all light to darkness.	

The gods of Mesopotamia are terrified by the Flood and flee to the upper reaches of heaven where the god Anu has his abode. Before they enter "they crouch and cower like dogs". They are grieved and shattered by what is happening and tearfully and in utter dejection lodge their complaint.

A description worthy of Homer!

But the Flood rages on unceasing, as Gilgamesh learns:

| Six days and nights | And the flood was forty days upon the earth and the waters increased. And the waters prevailed exceedingly upon the earth, and all the high hills, that were under the whole heaven, were covered (Gen. 7¹⁷⁻¹⁹). |
| Raged the wind, the flood, the cyclone devastated the land. | |

When the seventh day came, the cyclone, the flood, the battle was over,	And God remembered Noah ...and God made a wind to pass over the earth and the waters assuaged (Gen. 8^1).
Which had battled like an army. The sea became calm, the cyclone died away, the flood ceased.	The fountains of the deep and the windows of heaven were stopped; and the rain from heaven was restrained. And the waters returned from off the earth continually, and after the end of the hundred and fifty days the waters were abated (Gen. 8^{2,3}).
And all mankind had turned to clay. The ground was flat like a roof.	And all flesh died that moved upon the earth...and every man (Gen. 7^{21}).

"And all mankind had turned to clay." Utnapishtim, the Sumerian Noah, is recording what he himself claimed to have lived through. Babylonians, Assyrians, Hittites and Egyptians who translated or read aloud or narrated these words had no more notion that they were describing something that actually happened, than did the modern Assyriologists who painfully deciphered them from the cuneiform tablets.

Today we know that line 134 on the eleventh tablet of the Epic of Gilgamesh must depend on an eye-witness account. Only someone who had himself seen the desolation caused by the catastrophe could have described it with such striking force.

The great layer of mud, which covered every living thing like a shroud and levelled the ground until it was as "flat as a roof", must have been seen with his own eyes by someone who had had a marvellous escape. The exact description of the great storm argues for this assumption. Utnapishtim expressly mentions a southern gale, which corresponds closely with the geographical situation. The Persian Gulf, whose waters were flung over the flat country by the gale, lies south of the estuary of the Tigris and Euphrates. To the last detail the weather conditions which he describes are characteristic of an unusual atmospheric disturbance. The appearance of black clouds and a roaring noise—sudden darkness in broad daylight—the howling of the southern gale as it drives the water in front of it. Any meteorologist recognises at once that this is a description of a cyclone. Modern weather experts recognise that, in tropical regions, coastal areas, islands, but above all alluvial river flats are subject to a spiral type of tidal wave which leaves devastation and destruction in its wake, and which is often caused by cyclones, accompanied by earthquakes and torrential rain.

All along the coast of Florida, in the Gulf of Mexico, and on the Pacific there is today an up-to-date alarm system with all the latest equipment. But for southern Mesopotamia in 4000 B.C. even a modern alarm system would not have been of much use. Sometimes cyclones produce an effect which takes the shape of the Flood. There is an example in recent times.

In 1876 a cyclone of this nature, accompanied by tremendous thunderstorms, swept across the Bay of Bengal and headed for the coast at the mouth of the Ganges. Up to 200 miles from its centre ships at sea had their masts splintered. It was ebb-tide along the coast. The receding water was seized by the broad high sweep of the cyclone and a gigantic tidal wave reared itself up. It burst into the Ganges area and sea water 50 feet high swept inland—141 square miles were buried and 215,100 people died.

Utnapishtim tells a horrified Gilgamesh what happened when the disaster was over:

I opened the window and the light fell on my face.	And it came to pass at the end of forty days, that Noah opened the window of the ark which he had made (Gen. 8⁶).
The ship lay upon Mt. Nisir.	And the ark rested in the seventh month, on the seventeenth day of the month, upon the mountains of Ararat (Gen. 8⁴).
Mount Nisir held the ship and allowed it not to move.	

Old Babylonian cuneiform texts describe with care where Mt. Nisir is to be found. It lies between the Tigris and the lower reaches of the river Zab, where the wild and rugged mountain ranges of Kurdistan rise sharply from the flat country bordering the Tigris. The alleged resting place corresponds perfectly with the last lap of the great catastrophe which burst inland from the south. We are told that Utnapishtim's home was in Shuruppak. It lay near the present day Fara in the middle of the flat fenland where Tigris and Euphrates part company. A tidal wave from the Persian Gulf must have carried a ship from here right to the Kurdistan mountains.

Despite the precise descriptions in the Epic of Gilgamesh, Mt. Nisir has never tempted the curious to search for the remains of this giant ship. Instead, Mt. Ararat, which belongs to the Biblical tradition, has been the goal chosen by a series of expeditions.

FIG. 6.—Mt. Ararat—where three countries meet: Turkey, Iran and U.S.S.R.

Mt. Ararat lies in Eastern Turkey, near the borders of Russia and Iran. Its snow capped summit is over 16,000 feet high.

Last century, many years before any archaeologist turned a spadeful of Mesopotamian soil, the first expeditions were making their way to Mt. Ararat. A shepherd's story had started them off.

At the foot of Ararat lies the little Armenian village of Bayzit, whose inhabitants have for generations recounted the remarkable experience of a mountain shepherd who was said to have seen one day on Ararat a great wooden ship. A report from a Turkish expedition in 1833 seemed to confirm the shepherd's story since it mentioned a wooden prow of a ship which in the summer season stuck out of the south glacier.

The next person to claim to have seen it was Dr. Nouri, Archdeacon of Jerusalem and Babylon. This agile ecclesiastical dignitary undertook a journey in 1892 to discover the sources of the Euphrates. On his return he told of the wreckage of a ship in the eternal ice: "The interior was full of snow: the outer wall was of a dark red colour." In the First World War a Russian flying officer, by name Roskowitzki, announced that he had spotted from his plane "the remains of wreckage of a fair-sized ship" on the south flank of Ararat. Although it was the middle of the war, Czar Nicholas II despatched a search party without delay. It is supposed not only to have seen the ship but even to have photographed it. All proof of this however perished, presumably in the Revolution.

From the Second World War there are likewise several cases of aerial observation. They come from a Russian pilot and four American fliers.

These latter reports brought into the field the American historian and missionary Dr. Aaron Smith of Greensborough, an expert on the Flood. As a result of years of labour he has collected a complete history of the literature on Noah's Ark. There are 80,000 works in seventy-two languages about the Flood, of which 70,000 mention the legendary wreckage of the Ark.

In 1951 Dr. Smith spent twelve days with forty companions to no purpose on the ice-cap of Ararat. "Although we found no trace of Noah's Ark," he declared later, "my confidence in the Biblical description of the Flood is no whit the less. We shall go back."

Encouraged by Dr. Smith the young French Greenland explorer Jean de Riquer climbed the volcanic peak in 1952. He too came back without accomplishing anything. Despite this, fresh expeditions are always getting ready for a further attempt on Mt. Ararat.

In 1955, in the early morning of July 6th, Fernand Navarra from France, searching for the most famous ship in history, succeeded to his great surprise in salvaging three fragments of a wooden beam embedded in solid ice on top of the mountain. The timber was at least 5,000 years old, although whether this was actually a relic of Noah's Ark it is of course impossible to say.

No tradition of the early days of Mesopotamia is in such close agreement with the Bible as the Flood story in the Epic of Gilgamesh. In some places we find almost verbal correspondence. Yet there is a significant and essential difference. The familiar story in Genesis knows of one God only. The oddly amusing and primitive conception has disappeared of a heaven overcrowded with gods, many of whom bear all too human characteristics.

In all the flood traditions which have been mentioned, problems arise from mankind's unfortunate tendency to believe what it wants to believe. This is shown especially in the search for the ark on the 5,165 metre-high Ağri Daği which lies on the frontier between Turkey and the Soviet Union. According to the account in the Bible (Gen. 8⁴), that is where Noah's Ark is supposed to have landed. When considered closely, however, the matter is by no means so unambiguous, for the Bible refers only to the "mountains of Ararat". Ararat is simply the name given to the old land of Urartu, which corresponds, roughly speaking, to present day Armenia. The Gilgamesh epic adds the "mountain Nisir" as the place where the ark came to rest, while Berossus, a Babylonian priest who lived in Hellenic times and who in his work *Babylonian Antiquities* also relates the Babylonian flood story, introduces a "Kordye mountain range" into the debate. Another claim for the honour of being regarded as the landing place of the ark is made for a mountain in Phrygia in Asia Minor, not far from the town of Kelainai, the centre of many legends in olden days, while the Mahometans prefer to situate the ark's landing place a good distance south of Ağri Daği on the mountain of Judi, which offers a view far across the Mesopotamian plain. One way and another there are in any case too many mountains figuring as landing places for the ark.

What has been done and is still being done on the mountain where according to Christian tradition the ark came to rest is, however, not yet sufficiently documented. André Parrot is of the opinion that silence is the only appropriate attitude to be adopted by scientific journals towards the periodically recurring attempts, usually accompanied by lively activity in the daily press, to discover remains of the Biblical ark high up amid the snow and ice. In fact, not a single specialist in archaeology has so far taken part in any of the attempts to recover the ark. The consequence is that we have no reliable account of methods used in the searches or of the circumstances in which finds have been made, not to mention photographic evidence providing proof of claims that have been put forward. This is not because professional archaeologists consider themselves too grand to undertake the strenuous exertions involved in climbing up Mount Ararat (or rather Ağri Daği), but because systematic archaeological investigations, particularly in such difficult terrain, involve enormous expenditure.

The necessary finance is granted, however, only when discoveries of great scientific and general interest are to be expected. Such finds are improbable on Mount Ararat, and so we are provisionally obliged to say that ever since the 5,165 metre peak has been in existence and men have inhabited the earth, no scientifically recorded inundation in the world has risen high enough to carry up to such an altitude any kind of floating construction of the nature of the ark. The terrain around Mount Ararat during this period has not undergone such spectacular changes that the ark could have been deposited there at a time when perhaps the summit was lower than it is today. From the outset, the search for the ark on Ağri Daği must be considered a failure and as André Parrot has so well expressed it, expeditions with Mount Ararat as their goal have more to do with mountain-climbing than with archaeology.

But does there not exist wood from Ararat "at least five thousand years old"? Certainly wood has been produced for examination which, it is claimed, has come from Ararat, but again there is a difficulty about the dating, which we are told is based on "estimates by a forestry institute in Madrid", while "a laboratory" in Paris is reported to have arrived at 4,484 years as the age of the wood. On the other hand, a "Research Institute in Pre-History" in Bordeaux is said to have been content with vague general statements about the "great age" of the material. Even if these institutes were shown on closer examination to be reputable, however, and their reports proved to be unassailable, we must take into account that the samples extracted by non-specialists and brought long distances to the above mentioned places must have been exposed to a considerable degree to the effects of dirt. This obscures the measurements obtained, so that there can scarcely be any question of the determination of that wood's age which is not open to objection. A subsequent Ararat expedition did not even locate the original spot where the wood had been found. On the other hand, it claimed to have discovered wood elsewhere on Ağri Daği, but its age has been assessed at only something between 1,300 and 1,700 years. This result coincides very nicely with the conjecture by a number of scholars that as a possible consequence of being traditionally linked with the account of the Flood, Ağri Daği was regarded as "holy" and so already in the early Christian era a few huts for pilgrims or hermits' dwellings may have been built there.

Chapter 5
ABRAHAM LIVED IN THE KINGDOM OF MARI

A stone corpse—Lieut. Cabane reports a find—A Syrian Tell has important visitors—King Lamgi-Mari introduces himself—Professor Parrot discovers an unknown empire—A royal palace with 260 apartments and courtyards— 23,600 clay tablets have survived for 4,000 years—Desert police report the "Benjamites"—Rebecca's home—A flourishing city—And Nuzi . . . ?

"Now the Lord had said unto Abram, Get thee out of thy country, and from thy kindred, and from thy father's house, unto a land that I will show thee" (Gen. 12¹).

The country of which the Bible is speaking in this case is Haran. Terah, his son Abram, his daughter-in-law Sarai, and his grand-son Lot lived there (Gen. 11³¹).

What was actually meant by Haran was until recently quite unknown. We knew nothing of its early history. All the old Babylonian documents are silent about the middle reaches of the Euphrates—Mesopotamia, the land between the rivers—where Haran once stood.

A chance find led to excavations in 1933, which here also gave rise to a great and exciting discovery and added considerably to our knowledge. They brought the Haran of the Bible and the kind of life lived by the patriarchs quite unexpectedly into a historical context.

On the line between Damascus and Mosul, where it cuts the Euphrates, lies the small obscure town of Abu Kemal. Since, as a result of the First World War, Syria was placed under a French mandate, there was a French garrison in the place.

41

Over the broad Euphrates plain in midsummer 1933 lay a brooding, paralysing heat. Lieut. Cabane, the station-commander, expected, when he was called into the orderly room, that it was merely another of these quarrels among the Arabs that he was supposed to settle. He had had more than enough of that already. But this time the excitement in the office seemed to be about something different. Eventually he managed to extract through the interpreter the following story: These people had been burying one of their relatives. They were digging the grave on a remote hillside, by name Tell Hariri, when out popped a stone corpse!

Perhaps, thought Lieut. Cabane, this might be something that would interest the museum at Aleppo. At any rate it was a pleasant change from the endless monotony of this God-forsaken post.

In the cool of the evening he drove out to Tell Hariri, which lay about 7 miles to the north of Abu Kemal near the Euphrates. The Arabs led him up the slope to the broken statue in a flat earthen trough which had so upset them the day before. Cabane was no expert, but he knew at once that the stone figure must be very old. Next day it was taken by French soldiers to Abu Kemal. The lights were on till long after midnight in the little command-post. Cabane was writing a detailed report on the find to the competent authorities, to Henry Seyrig, Director of Antiquities in Beirut, and to the Museum at Aleppo.

Months went past and nothing happened. The whole thing seemed to be either unimportant or forgotten. Then at the end of November came a telegram from Paris, from the Louvre. Cabane could hardly believe his eyes and read the message again and again. In a few days important visitors from Paris would be arriving: Professor Parrot, the well known archaeologist, accompanied by scientists, architects, assistants and draughtsmen.

On the 14th of December Tell Hariri was buzzing like a bee-hive. The archaeologists had begun their detective-work. First of all the whole mound was carefully measured and photographed in detail. Soundings were taken for echoes, specimens of soil were removed and submitted to expert opinion. December went by and the first weeks of the New Year. The 23rd of January 1934 was the decisive day.

As they were digging carefully through the outer crust of the Tell there appeared out of the rubble a neat little figure which had some writing pricked out on the right shoulder. Everyone bent over it, fascinated. "I am Lamgi-Mari . . . king . . . of Mari . . . the great . . . Issakkv . . . who worships his statue . . . of Ishtar."

Slowly, word by word, this sentence rings in the ears of the silent circle as Professor Parrot translates it from the cuneiform. This is an unforgettable moment for him and his companions. An almost uncanny scene and probably unique in the history of archaeology with its surprises and adventures!

The monarch had solemnly welcomed the strangers from distant Paris and introduced himself to them. It was as if he wanted politely to show them the road into his kingdom of long ago which lay in a deep sleep beneath him, and of whose pomp and power the Parisian scholars had as yet no conception.

Carved in stone, a marvellous piece of sculpture King Lamgi-Mari stood before Parrot: a commanding broad-shouldered figure upon its base. But the face lacks that incredible arrogance which is so typical of the portraits of other conquerors from the ancient East, the Assyrians, who without exception look fierce and bad-tempered. The king of Mari is smiling. He carries no weapons, his hands are folded in an attitude of worship. His robe, which leaves one shoulder bare, like a toga, is richly decorated with fringes.

Hardly ever has an excavation been so crowned with success from the word "go", and the first groping efforts. Mari, the royal city, must be lying slumbering under this mound.

Scholars had for a long time been familiar with the royal city of Mari which features in many old inscriptions from Babylonia and Assyria. One text maintained that Mari was the tenth city to be founded after the Flood. The great spade-offensive against Tell Hariri began.

With considerable intervals the digging went on from 1933 to 1939. For the greater part of the year the tropical heat made any activity impossible. Only in the cooler months of the rainy season, from the middle of December to the end of March, could anything be done.

The excavations at Tell Hariri brought a wealth of new discoveries to a chapter of the history of the Ancient East which is still unwritten.

No one knew as yet how close a connection the finds at Mari would prove to have with quite familiar passages in the Bible.

Year by year reports of the expedition provided fresh surprises. In the winter of 1933–34 a temple of Ishtar the goddess of fertility was exposed. Three of Ishtar's royal devotees have immortalised themselves as statues in the shrine which is inlaid with a mosaic of gleaming shells: Lamgi-Mari, Ebin-il, and Idi-Narum.

In the second season of digging the spades came upon the houses of a city. Mari had been found! However great was the satisfaction with their success, far more interest, indeed astonishment was aroused by the walls of a palace which must have been unusually large. Parrot reported: "We have unearthed 69 rooms and courts, and there are still more to come." One thousand six hundred cuneiform tablets, carefully stacked in one of the rooms, contained details of household management.

The record of the third campaign in 1935–36 noted that so far 138 rooms and courtyards had been found but that they had not yet reached the outer walls of the palace. Thirteen thousand clay tablets awaited deciphering. In the fourth winter a temple of the god Dagon was dug up and also a Ziggurat, the typical Mesopotamian staged tower. Two hundred and twenty rooms and courtyards were now visible in the palace and another 8,000 clay tablets had been added to the existing collection.

At last in the fifth season, when a further forty rooms had been cleared of rubble, the palace of the kings of Mari lay in all its vast extent before Parrot and his assistants. This mammoth building of the third millennium B.C. covered almost ten acres. Never before during any excavations had such an enormous building with such vast ramifications come to light.

Columns of lorries had to be commissioned to remove the cuneiform tablets from the palace archives alone. There were almost 24,000 documents. The great find of the tablets at Nineveh was put in the shade, since the famous library of the Assyrian king, Ashurbanipal, amounted to a "mere" 22,000 clay texts.

To get a proper picture of Mari palace aerial photographs were taken. These pictures taken from a low altitude over Tell Hariri gave rise to almost incredulous amazement when they were published in France. This palace at Mari was, around 2000 B.C., one of the greatest sights of the world, the architectural gem of the Ancient East. Travellers came from far and near to see it. "I have seen Mari," wrote an enthusiastic merchant from the Phoenician seaport of Ugarit.

The last king to live there was Zimri-Lim. The armies of the famous Hammurabi of Babylon subjugated the kingdom of Mari on the central reaches of the Euphrates and destroyed its mighty capital about 1700 B.C.

Under the wreckage of roofs and walls were found the fire-pans of the Babylonian warriors, the incendiary squad who set fire to the palace.

But they were not able to destroy it completely. The walls were left standing to a height of 15 feet. "The installations in the palace kitchens and bathrooms," wrote Professor Parrot, "could still be put into commission without the need of any repair, four thousand years after its destruction." In the bathrooms they found the tubs, cake-moulds in the kitchens, even charcoal in the ovens.

The sight of these majestic ruins is an overwhelming experience. A single gate on the north side ensured easier control and better defence. Passing through a medley of courts and passages one reaches the great inner courtyard and broad daylight. This was the centre both of official life and the administration of the kingdom. The monarch received his officials as well as couriers and ambassadors in the neighbouring audience-chamber, large enough to hold hundreds of people. Broad corridors led to the king's private apartments.

One wing of the palace was used exclusively for religious ceremonies. It contained also a throne-room, approached by a marvellous staircase. A long processional way passed through several rooms to the palace chapel in which stood the image of the mother-goddess of fertility. From a vessel in her hands flowed perpetually "the water of everlasting life".

The entire court lived under the king's roof. Ministers, administrators, secretaries and scribes had their own roomy quarters.

There was a Foreign Office and a Board of Trade in the great administrative palace of the kingdom of Mari. More than 100 officials were involved in dealing with the incoming and outgoing mail, which amounted to thousands of tablets alone.

Wonderful great frescoes added a decorative effect to the palace. Even to this day the colours have hardly lost any of their brilliance. They seem to have been laid on only yesterday but in fact they are the oldest paintings in Mesopotamia—1,000 years older than the renowned coloured frescoes in the splendid edifices of the Assyrian rulers at Khorsabad, Nineveh and Nimrud.

The size and grandeur of this unique palace corresponded to the land that was governed from it. Through these many thousands of years the palace archives have preserved the record.

Notices, public papers, decrees, accounts, scratched out on clay by the busy styli of well-paid scribes 4,000 years ago, had to be brought to life again with tireless industry. In Paris, Professor George Dossin, of the University of Liège, and a host of Assyriologists wrestled with the problem of deciphering and translating them. It would be years before all the 23,600 documents were translated and published.

Each of them contains a little piece of the mosaic which makes up the true facts about the kingdom of Mari.

Numerous orders for the construction of canals, locks, dams, and embankments make it plain that the prosperity of the country largely depended on the widespread system of irrigation, which was constantly under the supervision of government engineers, who saw to its care and maintenance.

Two tablets contain a list of 2,000 craftsmen, giving their full names and the names of their guilds.

FIG. 7.—This picture from Room 106 in the palace of Mari shows the investiture of Zimri-Lim by the goddess Ishtar.

The news service in Mari functioned so quickly and successfully that it would bear comparison with modern telegraphy. Important messages were sent by means of fire signals from the frontier of Babylon right up to present day Turkey in a matter of a few hours, a distance of more than 300 miles.

Mari lay at the intersection of the great caravan route from

West to East and North to South. It is not surprising therefore
that the traffic in goods, which extended from Cyprus and Crete
to Asia Minor and Mesopotamia, necessitated a lively correspondence on clay concerning imports and exports. But the
tablets do not merely record everyday matters. They also give an
impressive account of religious life, of New Year Festivals in
honour of Ishtar, auguries with the entrails of animals, and
interpretation of dreams. Twenty-five gods made up the Mari
pantheon. A list of sacrificial lambs, which Zimri-Lim presented,
refers to these occupants of heaven by name.

From countless individual bits of evidence on these tablets we
can form a picture of this masterpiece of organisation and
administration which the kingdom of Mari constituted in the 18th
century B.C. What is astonishing is that neither in their sculptures
nor in their paintings is there any indication of warlike activity.

The inhabitants of Mari were Amorites who had been settled
there for a long time, and who preferred peace. Their interests
lay in religion and ceremonial, in trade and commerce. Conquest, heroism, and the clash of battle meant little to them. As
we can still see from statues and pictures, their faces radiate a
cheerful serenity.

That did not mean, however, that they were absolved from the
necessity of defending and safeguarding their territory by force
of arms. On their frontiers lived tribes of Semitic nomads, who
found the lush pastures, market gardens and cornfields of Mari a
constant temptation. They were always crossing the border,
grazing their cattle over wide stretches of the countryside, and
disturbing the population. They had to be watched. Frontier
posts were therefore established as a check on this danger, and
any incident was immediately reported to Mari.

In Paris the Assyriologists were deciphering a clay tablet from
the archives of Mari. They read with astonishment a report from
Bannum, an officer of the desert police:

"Say to my lord: This from Bannum, thy servant. Yesterday I
left Mari and spent the night at Zuruban. All the Benjamites
were sending fire-signals. From Samanum to Ilum-Muluk, from
Ilum-Muluk to Mishlan, all the Benjamite villages in the Terqa
district replied with fire-signals. I am not yet certain what these
signals meant. I am trying to find out. I shall write to my lord
whether or not I succeed. The city guards should be strengthened
and my lord should not leave the gate."

In this police report from the central reaches of the Euphrates in the 19th century B.C. there appears the name of one of the tribes known to us from the Bible. It literally calls them Benjamites.

There is frequent mention of these Benjamites. They seem to have given the ruler of Mari so many headaches and caused so much trouble that periods of a king's reign were even called after them.

In the Mari dynasties the years of each reign were not numbered but were identified with some notable event, for example the building and consecration of new temples, the erection of great dams to improve irrigation, the strengthening of the banks of the Euphrates or a national census. Three times the chronological tables mention the Benjamites:

"The year in which Iahdulim went to Hen and laid hands upon the territory of the Benjamites" is referred to in the reign of King Iahdulim of Mari and

"The year that Zimri-Lim killed the dâvidum of the Benjamites"

"The year after Zimri-Lim killed the dâvidum of the Benjamites . . ." in the reign of the last monarch of Mari, Zimri-Lim.

An elaborate correspondence between governors, district commissioners, and administrators takes place over the single question: Dare we take a census of the Benjamites?

In the kingdom of Mari a census of the people was not uncommon. It provided a basis for taxation and for enlistment for military service. The population was summoned by districts and a nominal roll was made of every man liable for call-up.

The proceedings lasted several days, during which free beer and bread were distributed by government officials. The administration in the palace of Mari would fain have included the Benjamites in this but the district officers had their doubts. They advised against it since they understood only too well the temper of these roaming and rebellious tribes.

"Reference the proposal to take a census of the Benjamites, about which you have written me," begins a letter from Samsi-Addu to Iasmah-Addu in Mari. "The Benjamites are not well-disposed to the idea of a census. If you carry it out, their kinsmen the Ra-ab-ay-yi, who live on the other bank of the river, will hear of it. They will be annoyed with them and will not return to their country. On no account should this census be taken!"

Thus the Benjamites lost their free beer and bread and also escaped paying taxes and military service.

Later the children of Israel were to experience a census of this sort many times, conducted exactly on the Mari-pattern. The first time was on the command of Yahweh after Moses had led them out of Egypt. All men over twenty who were fit to fight were registered according to their families (Num. 1–4). A generation later, after their sojourn in the desert, Moses took a second census with a view to dividing up the land of Canaan (Num. 26). During the monarchy David ordered a national census. What he had in mind on that occasion was the building up of an army and his commander in chief, Joab, was entrusted with the arrangements (2 Sam. 24). As the Bible depicts the incident, Yahweh had put the idea into the king's mind in order to punish the people. The Israelites loved their freedom above all else. Registration and the prospect of being called up were equally hateful to them. Even in the year A.D. 6 the census carried out by Governor Cyrenius almost led to open revolt.

It is worth noting that it is to peace-loving Mari that the world owes the original pattern of all recruiting campaigns. It was later followed by Babylonians and Assyrians, by Greeks and Romans, in exactly the same way, as indeed in later days by the nations of modern times. Thus Mari has given the lead to the whole world in this matter of taking a census for purposes of taxation and conscription for military service.

In Paris the mention of Benjamites gave rise to conjecture and anticipation along a particular line. Not without reason.

On other clay tablets the Assyriologists dealing with these reports of governors and district commissioners of the Mari empire came across one after another a whole series of familiar sounding names from Biblical history—names like Peleg, and Serug, Nahor and Terah and—Haran.

"These are the generations of Shem," says Gen. 11. ". . . Peleg lived 30 years and begat Reu: And Reu lived two and thirty years and begat Serug: And Serug lived thirty years and begat Nahor: And Nahor lived nine and twenty years and begat Terah: And Terah lived seventy years and begat Abram, Nahor, and Haran."

Names of Abraham's forefathers emerge from these dark ages as names of cities in north-west Mesopotamia. They lie in Padan-Aram, the plain of Aram. In the centre of it lies Haran, which, according to its description, must have been a flourishing city in the 19th and 18th centuries B.C. Haran, the home of Abraham, father of the patriarchs, the birthplace of the Hebrew people, is here for the first time historically attested, for contemporary texts refer to it. Further up the same Balikh valley lay the city with an equally well-known Biblical name, Nahor, the home of Rebecca, wife of Isaac.

> "And Abraham was old and well stricken in age, and the Lord had blessed Abraham in all things. And Abraham said unto his eldest servant of his house, that ruled over all that he had: Put, I pray thee, thy hand under my thigh; And I will make thee swear by the Lord, the God of heaven, and the God of the earth, that thou shalt not take a wife unto my son of the daughters of the Canaanites, among whom I dwell; But thou shalt go unto my country, and to my kindred and take a wife unto my son Isaac. . . . And the servant took . . . of all the goods of his master . . . and he arose and went to Mesopotamia, unto the city of Nahor" (Gen. 24[1-4,10]).

The Biblical city of Nahor is unexpectedly drawn into a recognisable historical setting. Abraham's servant set out for the land of the kings of Mari. The instructions of his master, according to the Biblical tradition, clearly indicate that Abraham must have known Northern Mesopotamia, including Nahor, extremely well. How else could he have spoken of the city of Nahor?

If we follow the dates given in the Bible we find that Abraham left his native place, Haran, 645 years before the exodus of the people of Israel from Egypt. They wandered through the desert towards the Promised Land under the leadership of Moses in the 13th century B.C. This date is, as we shall see, assured by archaeology. Abraham must therefore have lived about 1900 B.C. The finds at Mari confirm the accuracy of the Biblical account. About 1900 B.C., according to the evidence of the palace archives, Haran and Nahor were both flourishing cities.

The documents from the kingdom of Mari produce startling proof that the stories of the patriarchs in the Bible are not "pious legends"—as is often too readily assumed—but things that are described as happening in a historical period which can be precisely dated.

The fact that the Bible contains genuine early Western Semitic names found surprising confirmation in written sources from the

Ancient East. Not only did personal names from the Biblical story of the patriarchs occur as place-names, but they also proved to be the names of individual persons and it is not at all rare or unusual for clay tablets to be found bearing the name of the patriarch Abraham. Yet has Abraham actually been brought nearer to us? The excavation of written sources at "Fennel Cape", Ras Shamra (ancient Ugarit), has revealed that there were even an Egyptian and a Cypriot among those bearing this name. The distinguished Bible archaeologist Father Roland de Vaux considered this "unusual and disturbing". Quite understandably so, for this being the case, Abraham, instead of drawing closer to us, is in danger of disappearing in the crowd of his numerous namesakes who appear during the various epochs of the history of the Near and Middle East.

Unfortunately the "Benjamites" of Mari have also disappeared. The conviction has established itself that the name in the texts from Mari which was interpreted as "Benjamites" really means simply "sons of the right (sc. hand)", that is to say, "sons of the south". It appears to have been a purely geographical designation rather than the name of a tribe, for in the Mari documents *banu rabbājā* and *banu śam'al* are contrasted with the "sons of the south". Moreover, the name of the territory Yemen in Southern Arabia has preserved the old Mari word across the millennia, for Yemen merely means south!

But Bible scholars have also learnt other things. A phrase such as "the year in which Zimri-Lim killed the *dâvidum* of the Benjamites" is now translated as "the year in which Zimri-Lim inflicted an annihilating defeat on the 'sons of the south'", for dâvidum does not mean "commander", as was previously thought, but "defeat".

Of course, the beginnings of Mari around 1800 B.C. agree extremely well with the traditional dating of the Biblical patriarchs, somewhere around or shortly after 2000 B.C. Paradoxically it was the astonishing confirmation of statements in the Bible connecting the time of the patriarchs with a period of the history of the Ancient East some 500 years later which thus raised doubts concerning the customary dating. This confirmation comes from the archives of Nuzi in Yorgan Tepe, fifteen kilometres south west of Kirkuk. The written documents from this Horite city of the kingdom of Mitanni (*c.* 1500 B.C.) cast a light not only on the ancient laws of the Horites, but also on the legal

practices of the Biblical patriarchs which agree to an amazing
degree with the Biblical texts. Three examples will suffice as
illustrations:

1) Abraham laments the fact that he will die without a son
   and that a certain Eliezer will inherit from him (Gen.
   15^2). From the Nuzi tablets we know that it was customary for a childless couple to adopt a "son" who
   looked after his foster-parents and in return inherited
   from them. This arrangement could be reversed to a
   certain degree if an heir was subsequently born.

2) If a marriage remained childless, the wife had to provide
   a "substitute wife". This is what Sarah did when she
   presented Hagar to Abraham (1. Gen. 16^2) and in the
   same way Rachel at a later time gave her husband Jacob
   her maid Bilhah (1. Gen. 30^3). The custom was precisely
   the same in Nuzi.

3) Jacob's wife Rachel stole the "images" of her father
   Laban (1. Gen. 31^{3ff}) and Laban moved heaven and
   earth to get these "images" back. The Nuzi tablets tell
   us why. The person who was in possession of these
   domestic images (*teraphim*) also had the rights to the
   inheritance.

Taken together there is a striking conformity between the
Bible and the Nuzi texts. Yet there is a bitter conclusion to be
drawn, for if the patriarchs followed the legal customs of the
Horites of the 15th century before the birth of Christ, how
could they have lived in the 18th, 19th or even the 20th century
before Christ? In other words, did Abraham really live in the
"kingdom of Mari"? Or ought we to look for him centuries later
in the kingdom of Mitanni? In fact, we shall see that certain
concepts of the "patriarchal period", in the religious sphere this
time, are matched by ideas contained in texts from the coastal
town of Ugarit (Ras Shamra) whose "classical" period came
still later, in the 15th to 14th centuries before Christ. Do we
have, in consequence, to put Israel's Biblical ancestors even
later? The questions still facing us today are innumerable!

If it seems that science is abandoning us to ourselves with a
large number of new problems and if it seems that it is consequently so much more difficult for us to connect the above

mentioned names and facts with definite and familiar individuals, this very same science has amazingly confirmed other Biblical statements as will become apparent later. And as our knowledge is continually advancing, it is by no means impossible that Biblical archaeology will one day provide us with further sensational discoveries.

Chapter 6
THE LONG JOURNEY TO CANAAN

Six hundred miles by the caravan route—Nowadays four visas are required— The land of purple—Punitive expeditions against "Sanddwellers"—Proud seaports with a troublesome hinterland—An Egyptian best-seller about Canaan—Sinuhe praises the Good Land—Jerusalem on magic vases—Strongholds—Sellin finds Shechem—Abraham chooses the high road.

"And Abram took Sarai his wife, and Lot his brother's son, and all their substance that they had gathered, and the souls that they had gotten in Haran: and they went forth to go into the land of Canaan" (Gen. 12⁵).

The road from Haran, the home of the patriarchs, to the land of Canaan runs south for more than 600 miles. It follows the river Balikh as far as the Euphrates, thence by a caravan route thousands of years old via the oasis of Palmyra, the Tadmor of the Bible, to Damascus, and from there in a south-westerly direction to the Lake of Galilee. It is one of the great trade routes that have always led from Euphrates to Jordan, from the kingdom of Mesopotamia to the Phoenician seaports on the Mediterranean and the distant Nile lands in Egypt.

Anyone nowadays wanting to follow Abraham's route requires four visas: one for Turkey, in which the site of Haran lies, one for Syria to cover the section from the Euphrates via Damascus to the Jordan, and one each for the states of Jordan and Israel, which occupy what was once Canaan. In the time of the father of the patriarchs all this was much easier. For on his long trek he had only to pass through one large stretch of national territory, the kingdom of Mari, which he was in fact quitting. The smaller city states between the Euphrates and the Nile could be by-passed. The road to Canaan lay open.

The first city of any size that Abraham must have struck on his journey is still standing today: Damascus.

To go by car from Damascus to Palestine is, particularly in springtime, an unforgettable experience.

The ancient city with its narrow streets and dark bazaar-alleys, with its mosques and its Roman remains, lies in the centre of a wide and fertile plain. When the Arabs speak of Paradise they think of Damascus. What other Mediterranean city can compare with this place, which every spring is decked with an incredible mantle of gay blossom? In all the gardens and in the hedgerows beyond the city walls apricots and almonds are a riot of pink. Flowering trees line the road which climbs gently as it heads for the south-west. Tilled fields alternate with olive groves and large mulberry plantings. High above, to the right of the road, rises the El Barada river, to which the land owes its fertility. Here mighty Hermon thrusts its steep slopes 10,000 feet into the heavens above the flat and verdant plain. From the side of this famous mountain ridge, to the south, gushes the source of the Jordan. Towering over both Syria and Palestine and visible from afar it seems to have been placed there by Nature as a gigantic boundary stone between them. Even in the blazing heat of summer its peak remains covered in snow. The effect becomes

FIG. 8.—The route taken by the father of the patriarchs from the kingdom of Mari to Canaan.

even more impressive as on the left of the road the green fields disappear. Monotonous grey-brown hills, streaked with dried up river beds, pile up towards the distant shimmering horizon where the scorching Syrian Desert begins—the home of the Bedouins. The road climbs gradually for an hour and a half. Fields and groves become rarer. The green is more and more swallowed up by the sandy grey of the desert. Then suddenly an enormous pipeline crosses the road. The oil that flows through it has already come quite a way. Its journey began in the oil wells of Saudi Arabia, over a thousand miles away, and will end in the port of Saida on the Mediterranean. Saida is the old Sidon of the Bible.

Behind a ridge suddenly appear the hills of Galilee. A few minutes later comes the frontier. Syria lies behind. The road crosses a small bridge. Under the arch a fast moving narrow current hurries on its way. It is the Jordan: we are in Palestine, in the young state of Israel.

After a few miles between dark basalt rocks the bright blue of the Lake of Galilee sparkles up at us from far beneath, It was on this lake, where time seems to have stood still, that Jesus preached from a boat off Capernaum. Here he told Peter to cast his nets and raise the great draught of fishes. Two thousand years before that the flocks of Abraham grazed on its shores. For the road from Mesopotamia to Canaan went past the Lake of Galilee.

Canaan is the narrow mountainous strip of land between the shores of the Mediterranean and the borders of the desert, from Gaza in the south right up to Hamath on the banks of the Orontes in the north.

Canaan was the "Land of Purple". It owed its name to a product of the country which was highly prized in the olden days. From earliest times the inhabitants had extracted from a shellfish (Murex), which was native to these parts, the most famous dye in the ancient world, purple. It was so uncommon, so difficult to obtain and therefore so expensive, that only the wealthy could afford it. Purple robes were throughout the Ancient East a mark of high rank. The Greeks called the manufacturers of purple and the purple-dyers of the Mediterranean Phoenicians. The country they called Phoenicia, which meant "purple" in their language.

The land of Canaan is also the birthplace of two things which have radically affected the whole world: the word "Bible" and our alphabet. A Phoenician city was godparent to the Greek word for "book": from Byblos, the Canaanite seaport, comes "Biblion" and hence, later, "Bible". In the 19th century B.C. the Greeks took over from Canaan the letters of our alphabet.

The part of the country which was to become the home of the Israelite people was named by the Romans after Israel's worst enemies: Palestine comes from Pelishtim, as the Philistines are called in the Old Testament. They lived in the southernmost part of the coast of Canaan. "All Israel, from Dan even to Beersheba" (1 Sam. 3²⁰) is how the Bible describes the extent of the Promised Land, that is, from the sources of Jordan at the foot of Hermon to the hills west of the Dead Sea, and the Negev in the south.

If we look at a globe of the world, Palestine is only a tiny spot on the earth's surface, a narrow streak. It is possible to drive comfortably in a single day round the borders of the old kingdom of Israel: 150 miles from north to south, 25 miles across at its narrowest point, 9,500 square miles in all, its size was about that of the island of Sicily. Only for a few decades in its turbulent history was it any bigger. Under its renowned kings David and Solomon its territory reached to the arm of the Red Sea at Ezion-Geber in the south, and far beyond Damascus into Syria on the north. The present state of Israel with its 8,000 square miles is smaller by a fifth than the old kingdom.

There never flourished here crafts and industries whose products were sought after by the world at large. Traversed by hills and mountain chains, whose summits rose to over 3,000 feet, surrounded in the south and east by scrub and desert, in the north by the mountains of the Lebanon and Hermon, in the west by a flat coast with no natural harbours, it lay like a poverty stricken island between the great kingdoms on the Nile and the Euphrates, on the frontier between two continents. East of the Nile delta Africa stops. After a desolate stretch of 100 miles of desert Asia begins, and at its threshold lies Palestine.

When in the course of its eventful history it was constantly being dragged into the affairs of the wider world, it had its position to thank for it. Canaan is the link between Egypt and Asia. The most important trade route of the ancient world passes through this country. Merchants and caravans, migratory tribes and peoples, followed this road which the armies of the great conquerors were later to make use of. Egyptians, Assyrians, Babylonians, Persians, Greeks and Romans one after another made the land and its people the plaything of their economic, strategic and political concerns.

It was in the interests of trade that the giant on the Nile in the third millennium B.C. was the first great power to stretch out its tentacles towards Canaan.

"We brought 40 ships, laden with cedar trunks. We built ships of cedarwood: One 'Pride of Two Lands'—ship of 150 feet: And of meru-wood, two ships 150 feet long: We made the doors of the king's palace of cedarwood." That is the substance of the world's oldest advice note from a timber importer about 2700 B.C. The details of this cargo of timber in the reign of Pharaoh Snefru are scratched on a tablet of hard black diorite, which is carefully preserved in the museum at Palermo. Dense woods covered the slopes of Lebanon then. The excellent wood from its cedars and meru, a kind of conifer, were just what the Pharaohs needed for their building schemes.

Five hundred years before Abraham's day there was a flourishing import and export trade on the Canaanite coast. Egypt exchanged gold and spices from Nubia, copper and turquoise from the mines at Sinai, linen and ivory, for silver from the Taurus, leather goods from Byblos, painted vases from Crete. In the great Phoenician dye-works well-to-do Egyptians had their robes dyed purple. For their society women they bought a wonderful lapis-lazuli blue—eyelids dyed blue were all the rage—and stibium, a cosmetic which was highly thought of by the ladies for touching up their eyelashes.

In the seaports of Ugarit (now Ras Shamra) and Tyre there were Egyptian consuls; the coastal fortress of Byblos became an Egyptian colony; monuments were erected to the Pharaohs and Phoenician princes adopted Egyptian names.

If the coastal cities presented a picture of cosmopolitan life which was busy, prosperous and even luxurious, a few miles inland lay a world which provided a glaring contrast. The Jordan mountains have always been a trouble-spot. Bedouin attacks on the native population, insurrection and feuds between towns were unending. Since they also endangered the caravan route along the Mediterranean coast, Egyptian punitive expeditions had to bring the unruly elements to heel. The inscription on the tomb of the Egyptian Uni gives us a clear picture of how one of these expeditions was organised about 2350 B.C. Uni, an army commander, received orders from Pharaoh Phiops I to assemble a striking force against Bedouins from Asia who were attacking Canaan. His report on the campaign reads as follows:

"His Majesty made war on the desert peoples and His Majesty gathered an army: in the south beyond Elephantine . . . all over the north . . . and among the Jertet-, Mazoi-, and Jenam Nubians. I was entrusted with the whole campaign." The morale of this multi-coloured fighting force comes in for high praise, and in the course of it we learn what sort of attractions Canaan offered in those days in the way of loot: "None of them stole the sandals off anyone who came their way. . . . None of them stole food from any of the cities. . . . None of them stole any goats." Uni's war-diary proudly announces a great victory and in passing gives us valuable information about the country: "The king's army returned in good order, after laying waste the country of the desert peoples, . . . after destroying their fortresses . . . after cutting down their fig-trees and vines . . . and carrying off a large number into captivity. His Majesty sent me five times to ravage the land of the desert peoples with these troops every time they revolted."

Semites thus made their first entry into the land of the Pharaohs as P.O.W.'s where they were contemptuously described as "Sanddwellers". Chu-Sebek, adjutant to King Sesostris III of Egypt, wrote in his war-diary 500 years later the following account which had been preserved at Abydos on the Upper Nile, where it was chiselled out on a monument: "His Majesty proceeded northwards to crush the Asiatic Bedouins. . . . His Majesty went as far as a place called Sekmem. . . . Sekmem collapsed together with the whole miserable country of Retenu."

The Egyptians called Palestine and Syria together "Retenu". "Sekmem" is the Biblical town of Shechem, the first town which Abraham struck on entering Canaan (Gen. 12⁶).

With the campaign of Sesostris III about 1850 B.C. we are right in the middle of the patriarchal period. Meantime Egypt had taken possession of the whole of Canaan: the country now lay under the suzerainty of the Pharaohs. Thanks to the archaeologists we possess a unique document from this epoch, a gem of ancient literature. The author: a certain Sinuhe of Egypt. Scene: Canaan. Time: between 1971 and 1928 B.C. under Pharaoh Sesostris I.

Sinuhe, a nobleman in attendance at court, becomes involved in a political intrigue. He fears for his life and emigrates to Canaan:

"As I headed north I came to the Princes' Wall, which

was built to keep out the Bedouins and crush the Sandramblers.[1]
I hid in a thicket in case the guard on the wall, who was on
patrol at the time, would see me. I did not move out of it till the
evening. When daylight came . . . and I had reached the Bitter
Lake[2] I collapsed. I was parched with thirst, my throat was red
hot. I said to myself: This is the taste of death! But as I made
another effort and pulled myself on to my feet, I heard the
bleating of sheep and some Bedouins came in sight. Their leader,
who had been in Egypt, recognised me. He gave me some water
and boiled some milk, and I went with him to his tribe. They
were very kind to me.''

Sinuhe's escape had been successful. He had been able to slip
unseen past the great barrier wall on the frontier of the kingdom
of the Pharaohs which ran exactly along the line which is
followed by the Suez Canal today. This ''Princes' Wall'' was
even then several hundred years old. A priest mentions it as far
back as 2650 B.C.: ''The Princes' Walls are being built to prevent
the Asiatics forcing their way into Egypt. They want water . . . to
give to their cattle.'' Later on the children of Israel were to pass
this wall many times: there was no other way into Egypt.
Abraham must have been the first of them to see it when he
emigrated to the land of the Nile during a famine (Gen. 12[10]).

Sinuhe continues: ''Each territory passed me on to the next. I
went to Byblos,[3] and farther on reached Kedme[4] where I spent
eighteen months. Ammi-Enschi,[5] the chief of Upper Retenu,[6]
made me welcome. He said to me: 'You will be well treated and
you can speak your own language here.' He said this of course
because he knew who I was. Egyptians[7] who lived there had told
him about me.''

We are told in great detail of the day to day experiences of this
Egyptian fugitive in North Palestine. ''Ammi-Enschi said to me:
'Certainly, Egypt is a fine country, but you ought to stay here
with me and what I shall do for you will be fine too.'

''He gave me precedence over all his own family and gave me

---

[1] ''Sandramblers'' and ''Wilderness-Wanderers'' were the favourite nicknames which the
Egyptians gave to their eastern and north-eastern neighbours, the nomads. This also
included the tribes in Canaan and Syria which had no fixed location.
[2] Still known as the ''Bitter Lakes'' on the Isthmus of Suez.
[3] Phoenician seaport north of present-day Beirut.
[4] Desert country east of Damascus.
[5] A western Semitic name, an Amorite.
[6] Name given to the hill country in the north of Palestine.
[7] Pharaoh's commissioners were at that time stationed all over Palestine and Syria.

his eldest daughter in marriage. He let me select from among his choicest estates and I selected one which lay along the border of a neighbouring territory. It was a fine place with the name of Jaa. There were figs and vines and more wine than water. There was plenty of honey and oil; every kind of fruit hung on its trees. It had corn and barley and all kinds of sheep and cattle. My popularity with the ruler was extremely profitable. He made me a chief of his tribe in the choicest part of his domains. I had bread and wine as my daily fare, boiled meat and roast goose. There were also desert animals which they caught in traps and brought to me, apart from what my hunting dogs collected. . . . There was milk in every shape and form. Thus many years went by. My children grew into strong men, each of them able to dominate his tribe.

"Any courier coming from Egypt or heading south to the royal court lived with me.[1] I gave hospitality to everyone. I gave water to the thirsty, put the wanderer on the right way, and protected the bereaved.

"When the Bedouins sallied forth to attack neighbouring chiefs I drew up the plan of campaign. For the prince of Retenu for many years put me in command of his warriors and whichever country I marched into I made . . . and . . . of its pastures and its wells. I plundered its sheep and cattle, led its people captive and took over their stores. I killed its people with my sword and my bow[2] thanks to my leadership and my clever plans."

Out of his many experiences among the "Asiatics" a life and death duel, which he describes in detail, seems to have made the deepest impression on Sinuhe. A "Strong man of Retenu" had jeered at him one day in his tent and called him out. He was sure he could kill Sinuhe and appropriate his flocks and herds and properties. But Sinuhe, like all Egyptians, was a practised bowman from his earliest days, and killed the "strong man", who was armed with shield, spear and dagger, by putting an arrow through his throat. The spoils that came to him as a result of this combat made him even richer and more powerful.

At length in his old age he began to yearn for his homeland. A letter from his Pharaoh Sesostris I summoned him to return: ". . . Make ready to return to Egypt, that you may see once more the Court where you grew up, and kiss the ground at the two

---

[1] This points to a considerable traffic between Egypt and Palestine.
[2] The bow was the typical Egyptian weapon.

great gates. . . . Remember the day when you will have to be
buried and men will do you honour. You will be anointed with
oil before daybreak and wrapped in linen blessed by the goddess
Tait.[1] You will be given an escort on the day of the funeral. The
coffin will be of gold adorned with lapis-lazuli, and you will be
placed upon a bier. Oxen will pull it and a choir will precede
you. They will dance the Dance of the Dwarfs at the mouth of
your tomb. The sacrificial prayers will be recited for you and
animals will be offered on your altar. The pillars of your tomb
will be built of limestone among those of the royal family. You
must not lie in a foreign land, with Asiatics to bury you, and
wrap you in sheepskin.''

Sinuhe's heart leapt for joy. He decided to return at once,
made over his property to his children and installed his eldest son
as "Chief of his tribe". This was customary with these Semitic
nomads, as it was with Abraham and his progeny. It was the
tribal law of the patriarchs, which later became the law of Israel.
"My tribe and all my goods belonged to him only, my people
and all my flocks, my fruit and all my sweet trees.[2] Then I
headed for the south.''

He was accompanied right to the frontier posts of Egypt by
Bedouins, thence by representatives of Pharaoh to the capital
south of Memphis. The second stage was by boat.

What a contrast! From a tent to a royal palace, from a simple
if dangerous life back to the security and luxury of a highly
civilised metropolis. "I found his Majesty on the great throne in
the Hall of Silver and Gold. The king's family were brought in.
His Majesty said to the Queen: 'See, here is Sinuhe, who
returns as an Asiatic and has become a Bedouin.' She gave a
loud shriek and all the royal children screamed in chorus. They
said to his Majesty: 'Surely this is not really he, my lord King.'
His Majesty replied: 'It is really he.'

"I was taken to a princely mansion," writes Sinuhe enthusiastically, "in which there were wonderful things and also a
bathroom . . . there were things from the royal treasure house,
clothes of royal linen, myrrh and finest oil; favourite servants of
the king were in every room, and every cook did his duty. The
years that were past slipped from my body. I was shaved and my
hair was combed. I shed my load of foreign soil[3] and the coarse

[1] Embalming.
[2] Datepalms.
[3] i.e., the dirt that came off him.

clothing of the Sandramblers. I was swathed in fine linen and anointed with the finest oil the country could provide. I slept once more in a bed. Thus I lived, honoured by the king, until the time came for me to depart this life.''

The Sinuhe story does not exist in one copy only. An astonishing number of them has been found. It must have been a highly popular work and must have gone through several "editions". Not only in the Middle Kingdom but in the New Kingdom of Egypt it was read with pleasure, as the copies found indicate. One might call it a "best-seller", the first in the world, and about Canaan, of all places.

The scholars who came across it again at the turn of the century were as delighted with it as Sinuhe's contemporaries had been 4,000 years before. They regarded it however as a well-told story, exaggerated like all Egyptian writings and completely without foundation. The Tale of Sinuhe became a mine of information for learned Egyptologists, but not for historians. They were so busy disputing about the clarification of the text, the letters, the construction and connection of the sentences that the contents were forgotten.

Meantime Sinuhe came into his own. For we now know that the Egyptian had written a factual account of Canaan at about the time that Abraham migrated there. It is to hieroglyphic texts dealing with Egyptian campaigns that we owe the first evidence we possess about Canaan. They agree with Sinuhe's description. Similarly, the Egyptian nobleman's story shows in some places almost literal correspondence with verses of the Bible which are often quoted. "For the lord thy God bringeth thee into a good land," says Deut. 8[7]—"It was a fine country," says Sinuhe. "A land," continues the Bible, "of wheat and barley and vines and fig trees. . . .'' "Barley and wheat, figs and vines were there," Sinuhe tells us. And where the Bible says: "A land of oil, olive and honey, a land wherein thou shalt eat bread without scarceness", the Egyptian text reads: "There was plenty of honey and oil. I had bread as my daily fare.''

· The description which Sinuhe gives of his way of life among the Amorites, living in a tent, surrounded by his flocks and herds, and involved in conflict with presumptuous Bedouins whom he has to drive away from his pastures and his wells, corresponds with the Biblical picture of life in patriarchal times. Abraham and his son Isaac have also to fight for their wells (Gen. 21[25], 26[15,20]).

The care and accuracy with which Biblical tradition depicts
the actual living conditions of those days is best seen when we
examine the results of sober investigation. For the variety of
recently discovered documents and monuments makes it possible
for us to reconstruct a true picture of the conditions of life in
Canaan at the time when the patriarchs entered it.

About 1900 B.C. Canaan was but thinly populated. Properly
speaking it was no-man's land. Here and there in the midst of
ploughed fields a fortified keep could be seen. Neighbouring
slopes would be planted with vines or with fig trees and date
palms. The inhabitants lived in a state of constant readiness. For
these widely scattered little townships, like veritable islands,
were the object of daring attacks by the desert nomads. Suddenly,
and when least expected, these nomads were upon them, with
indiscriminate butchery, carrying-off their cattle and their crops.
Just as suddenly they would disappear again into the vast recess
of the desert plains to the south and east. There was endless war
between the settled farmers and cattle breeders and these plundering
hordes who had no fixed abode, whose home was a goatshair
tent somewhere out under the open skies of the desert. It was
into this restless country that Abraham made his way with his
wife Sarah, his nephew Lot, his kinsfolk and his flocks.

> "And into the land of Canaan they came. And Abram
> passed through the land unto the place of Sichem, unto the
> plain of Moreh. . . . And the Lord appeared unto Abram and
> said: Unto thy seed will I give this land; and there builded
> he an altar unto the Lord, who appeared unto him. And he
> removed from thence unto a mountain on the east of Bethel,
> and pitched his tent having Bethel on the west, and Hai on
> the east: and there he builded an altar unto the Lord, and
> called upon the name of the Lord. And Abram journeyed,
> going on still toward the south" (Gen. 12$^{5-9}$).

In the twenties, remarkable sherds were found on the Nile, the
chief finds at Thebes and Saqqara. Archaeologists in Berlin
obtained some of them, others went to Brussels, and the rest
went to the great museum at Cairo. Under the careful hands of
experts the fragments were reassembled into vases and statuettes,
but the most astonishing thing about them was the inscriptions.

The writing is full of menacing curses and maledictions like:
"Death strike you at every wicked word and thought, every plot,

angry quarrel and plan''. These and other unpleasant wishes were generally addressed to Egyptian court officials and other eminent people, but also to rulers in Canaan and Syria.

In accordance with an old superstition it was believed that at the moment the vase or statuette was smashed the power of the person cursed would be broken. It was common to include within the spell the family, relatives, even the home town of the victim of the curse. The magical texts include names of cities like Jerusalem (Gen. 14^{19}), Askelon (Jud. 1^{18}), Tyre (Josh. 19^{29}), Hazor (Josh. 11^1), Bethshemesh (Josh. 15^{10}), Aphek (Josh. 12^{18}), Achshaph (Josh. 11^1) and Shechem (Sichem). Here is a convincing proof that these places mentioned in the Bible existed already in the 19th and 18th centuries B.C., since the vases and statuettes date from that time. Two of these towns were visited by Abraham. He calls on Melchizedek ''King of Salem'' (Gen. 14^{18}) at Jerusalem. Jerusalem is well enough known, but where was Sichem?

In the heart of Samaria lies a broad flat valley, dominated by the high peaks of Gerizim and Ebal. Well cultivated fields surround Ashkar, a small village of Jordan. Nearby at the foot of Gerizim in Tell el-Balata the ruins of Sichem were discovered.

It was due to the German theologian and archaeologist Professor Ernst Sellin that during excavations in 1913–14 strata from very early times came to light.

Sellin came across remains of walls dating back to the 19th century B.C. Bit by bit the picture emerged of a mighty surrounding wall with strong foundations, entirely built of rough boulders, some of them 6 feet in diameter. Archaeologists call this type a ''cyclops-wall''. The wall was further strengthened by an escarpment. The builders of Sichem fortified the 6 feet thick wall with small turrets and provided an earth wall in addition.

The remains of a palace also emerged out of the ruins. The square cramped courtyard, surrounded by a few rooms with solid walls, hardly deserved the name of palace. All the Canaanite towns whose names are so familiar, and which the Israelites feared so greatly in the early days, looked like Sichem. With few exceptions the notable building projects of that period are now known. Most of them have been excavated within the last sixty years. For thousands of years they have been buried deep in the ground, now they stand clearly before us. Among them are many towns whose walls the patriarchs had seen: Bethel and Mizpah, Gerar and Lachish, Gezer and Gath, Askelon and Jericho. Anyone who wanted to write the history of the building of fortresses and cities in Canaan, would have no great difficulty in doing so in view of the wealth of material going back to the third millennium B.C.

The Canaanite towns were fortresses, places of refuge in time of danger, whether it was from sudden attack by nomadic tribes or civil war among the Canaanites themselves. Towering perimeter walls built of these great boulders invariably enclose a small area, not much bigger than St. Peter's Square in Rome. Each of these town-forts had a water supply, but they were not towns in which a large population could have made a permanent home. Compared with the palaces and great cities in Mesopotamia or on the Nile they look tiny. Most of the towns in Canaan could have gone into the palace of the kings of Mari comfortably.

In Tell el-Hesi, probably the Eglon of the Bible, the ancient fortifications enclosed an area of just over an acre. In Tell es-Safi—formerly Gath—twelve acres; in Tell el-Mutesellim—formerly Megiddo—about the same amount; in Tell el-Zakariyah—the Biblical Azekah—less than ten acres; Gezer, on the road from Jerusalem to Jaffa, occupied just over twenty acres. Even in the more built-up area of Jericho, the inner fortified wall, the Acropolis proper, enclosed a space of little more than five acres. Yet Jericho was one of the strongest fortresses in the country.

Bitter feuds between the tribal chiefs were the order of the day. There was no supreme authority. Every chieftain was master in his own territory. No one gave him orders and he did what he pleased. The Bible calls the tribal chieftains "kings". As far as power and independence were concerned that is what they were.

Between the tribal chiefs and their subjects the relationship was patriarchal. Inside the wall lived only the chief, the aristocracy, Pharaoh's representatives, and wealthy merchants. Moreover they alone lived in strong, solid, mostly one-story houses with four to six rooms built round an open courtyard. Upper class homes with a second story were comparatively rare. The rest of the inhabitants—vassals, servants, and serfs—lived in simple mud or wattle huts outside the walls. They must have had a miserable life.

Since the days of the patriarchs two roads meet in the plain of Shechem. One goes down into the rich valley of the Jordan. The other climbs over the lonely hills southwards to Bethel, on past Jerusalem and down to the Negev, or the Land of the South as the Bible calls it. Anyone following this road would encounter only a few inhabited areas in the central highlands of Samaria and Judah: Shechem, Bethel, Jerusalem and Hebron. Anyone choosing the more comfortable road would find the larger towns and more important fortresses of the Canaanites in the lush valleys of the Plain of Jezreel, on the fertile coast of Judah and amid the luxuriant vegetation of the Jordan valley.

Abraham, as the Bible tells us, chose for his first exploration of Palestine the lonely and difficult road that points over the hills towards the south. For here the wooded hillsides offered refuge and concealment to a stranger in a foreign land, while the clearings provided pasture in plenty for his flocks and herds. Later on he and his tribe and the other patriarchs as well went back and forth along this same wretched mountain track. However tempting were the fertile valleys of the plain Abraham preferred to establish himself at first up in the hill country. For with his bows and slings he was in no condition to risk a clash with the Canaanites, whose swords and spears were more than a match for him. Abraham was not yet ready to venture out of the highlands.

Chapter 7
ABRAHAM AND LOT IN THE LAND OF PURPLE

Famine in Canaan—A Family Portrait of the patriarchal age—Permit of access to the Nile grazings—The mystery of Sodom and Gomorrah—Mr. Lynch investigates the Dead Sea—The great fissure—Did the Vale of Siddim take a headlong plunge?—Pillars of salt at Jebel Usdum.

"And there was a famine in the land: and Abram went down into Egypt to sojourn there; for the famine was grievous in the land" (Gen. 12^{10}).

We have to thank the dryness of the sands of the Egyptian desert for preserving a considerable variety of hieroglyphic texts, among which is to be found a wealth of written evidence of the immigration of Semitic families into the Nile valley. The best and clearest proof is however a picture.

Halfway between the old cities of the Pharaohs, Memphis and Thebes, 200 miles south of Cairo, there lies on the banks of the Nile amid green fields and palm groves the little settlement of Beni-Hasan. Here in 1890 a British expert, Percy A. Newberry, was given an assignment by the Cairo authorities to investigate some old tombs. The expedition was financed by the Egyptian Exploration Fund.

The tombs were located at the outer end of a desert wadi, where the remains of old quarries and a large temple also lay in peaceful seclusion. Week after week nothing but debris, rubble and the remnants of broken stone pillars streamed out of the rock-face behind which the last resting place of the Egyptian nobleman Khnum-hotpe was concealed. Hieroglyphs in a small entrance hall indicated the name of the occupant. He was the ruler of this district of the Nile, which at one time was called Gazelle Province. Khnum-hotpe lived under Pharaoh Sesostris II about 1900 B.C.

After a great deal of time and effort had been expended Newberry eventually reached a huge rock chamber. By the light of numerous torches he was able to see that there were three vaults and that the stumps of two rows of pillars protruded from the ground. The walls were bright with gorgeous coloured paintings on a thin lime-washed plaster. These depicted scenes from the life of the nobleman telling of harvest, hunting, dancing and sport. In one of the pictures on the north wall, immediately next to an over life-size portrait of the nobleman, Newberry discovered foreign looking figures. They were wearing a different type of clothing from the ordinary Egyptians, they were fairer-skinned and had sharper features. Two Egyptian officials in the foreground were obviously introducing this group of foreigners to the nobleman. What sort of people were they?

Hieroglyphs on a written document in the hand of one of the Egyptians gave the explanation: they were "Sanddwellers", Semites. Their leader was called Abishai. With thirty-six men, women and children of his tribe Abishai had come to Egypt. He had brought gifts for the nobleman, among which special mention was made of some costly stibium[1] for the nobleman's wife.

Abishai is a genuine Semitic name. After the conquest of Canaan by Joshua the name occurs in the Bible during the reign of the second king of Israel: "Then answered David and said to . . . Abishai the son of Zeruiah" (1 Sam. 26[6]). The Abishai of the Bible was the brother of King David's unpopular commander-in-chief Joab about 1000 B.C., when Israel was a large kingdom.

The artist whom Prince Khnum-hotpe entrusted with the decoration of his tomb has depicted the "Sanddwellers" with such care that the smallest detail is faithfully noted. This lifelike and unusually striking picture looks more like a coloured photograph. It gives the impression that this family of Semites had just stopped for a second, and that suddenly men, women and children would start off again and continue their journey. Abishai at the head of the column makes a slight obeisance and salutes

---

[1] Colouring for eyelashes.

the nobleman with his right hand, while his left hand holds a short cord to which a tame horned goat is attached, carrying between its horns a bent stick which is a shepherd's crook.

The shepherd's crook was so characteristic of the nomads that the Egyptians in their picture-writing used it for the name of these foreigners.

The style and colour of their clothing are faithfully reproduced. Square woollen blankets, reaching in the case of the men to the knee, in the case of the women to the calf, are caught up on one shoulder. They consist of highly coloured striped material and serve as cloaks. Does that not remind us of the famous "coat of many colours" which Jacob, much to the annoyance of his other sons, bestowed upon his favorite son Joseph (Gen. 37³)? The men's hair is trimmed into a pointed beard. The women's hair falls loosely over breast and shoulders. It is fastened by a narrow white ribbon round the forehead. The little curls in front of the ears seem to have been a concession to fashion. The men are wearing sandals, the women have dark brown half-length boots. They carry their water ration in artistically embroidered containers made of animal skins. Bows and arrows, heavy throw-sticks and spears serve as their weapons. Even their favourite instrument has been brought with them on their long journey. One of the men is playing the eight-stringed lyre. According to the instructions given in the Bible some of the Psalms of David were to be accompanied on this instrument: "To be sung to eight strings" is the heading of Psalms 6 and 12.

Since this picture dates from about 1900 B.C., which was the period of the patriarchs, we may imagine that Abraham and his family looked something like this. When he reached the Egyptian frontier a similar scene must have taken place. For the procedure for admitting foreign visitors was exactly the same at all the other frontier posts as in the case of the lord Khnum-hotpe.

FIG. 9.—A Semitic family at the time of the Patriarchs:

It was thus no different long ago from what it is now to travel in a foreign country. Certainly there were no passports but formalities and officialdom made life difficult for foreign visitors even then. Anyone entering Egypt had to state the number in his party, the reason for his journey and the probable length of his stay. All the particulars were carefully noted down on papyrus by a scribe using red ink and then sent by messenger to the frontier officer who decided whether an entrance permit should be granted. This was however not left to his own judgment. Administrative officers at the court of Pharaoh issued from time to time precise directives, even to the point of specifying which grazings were to be put at the disposal of immigrant nomads.

In times of famine Egypt was for Canaanite nomads their place of refuge and often their only salvation. When the ground dried up in their own country, the land of the Pharaohs always afforded sufficient juicy pastures. The Nile with its regular annual flooding took care of that.

On the other hand the proverbial wealth of Egypt was often a temptation to thieving bands of daring nomads who were not interested in finding pasture but were much more concerned with the bursting granaries and sumptuous palaces. Often they could only be got rid of by force of arms. As a protection against these unwelcome invaders and to keep a closer check on the frontier, the erection of the great "Princes' Wall" was begun in the third millennium B.C. It consisted of a chain of forts, watchtowers and strongpoints. It was only under cover of darkness that the Egyptian Sinuhe with his local knowledge was able to slip through unobserved. Six hundred and fifty years later, at the time of the exodus from Egypt, the frontier was also strongly guarded. Moses knew only too well that escape from the country in defiance of Pharaoh's orders was impossible. The sentries would at once have sounded the alarm and summoned the guards. Any

from a wall-painting in the prince's tomb at Beni-Hasan on the Nile.

attempt to break through would have been nipped in the bud by sharpshooters and commandos in armoured chariots and would have ended in bloodshed. That was the reason why the prophet knowing the country chose another quite unusual route. Moses led the children of Israel southwards, as far as the Red Sea, where there was no longer any wall.

After their return from Egypt Abraham and Lot separated: "For their substance was great," says the Bible, "so that they could not dwell together. And there was a strife between the herdmen of Abram's cattle, and the herdmen of Lot's cattle. . . . And Abram said unto Lot, Let there be no strife I pray thee, between me and thee, and between my herdmen and thy herdmen: for we be brethren. Is not the whole land before thee? Separate thyself I pray thee from me: if thou wilt take the left hand, then I will go to the right: or if thou depart to the right hand, then I will go to the left" (Gen. 13⁶⁻⁹).

Abraham left the choice to Lot. Lot, taking everything for granted, like so many young people, chose the best part, in the neighbourhood of the Jordan. It was "well-watered everywhere . . . as thou comest into Zoar" (Gen. 13¹⁰) and blessed with luxuriant tropical vegetation "even as the garden of the Lord, like the land of Egypt" (Gen. 13¹⁰).

From the wooded mountain chain in the heart of Palestine Lot made his way downhill to the east, wandered with his family and his flocks southwards along the Jordan valley and finally pitched his tent in Sodom. South of the Dead Sea lay an extremely fertile plain, the "Vale of Siddim, which is the salt sea"[1] (Gen. 14³). The Bible lists five towns in this valley, "Sodom, Gomorrah, Admah, Zeboiim, and Zoar" (Gen. 14²). It also knows of a warlike incident in the history of these five towns: "And it came to pass" that four kings "made war with Bera king of Sodom, and with Birsha king of Gomorrah, and with Shinab king of Admah, and Shemeber king of Zeboiim, and the king of Bela, which is Zoar" (Gen. 14²). For twelve years the kings of the Vale of Siddim had paid tribute to King Chedorlaomer. In the thirteenth year they rebelled. Chedorlaomer sought help from three royal allies. A punitive expedition would bring the rebels to their senses. In the battle of the nine kings, the kings of the five towns in the Vale of Siddim were defeated, their lands were ravaged and plundered.

[1] Dead Sea.

Among the captives of the foreign kings was Lot. He was set free again by his uncle Abraham (Gen. 14[12-16]), who with his followers dogged the withdrawal of the army of the victorious four kings like a shadow. He watches it unobserved from safe cover, makes accurate reconnaissance and bides his time. Not until they reach Dan, on the northern frontier of Palestine, does the opportunity arise for which he has been waiting. Like lightning, under cover of darkness, Abraham and his men fall on the rearguard and in the confusion that follows Lot is set free.—Only those who do not know the tactics of the Bedouins will consider this an unlikely story.

Among the inhabitants of that stretch of country the memory of that punitive expedition has remained alive to this day. It is reflected in the name of a road which runs eastward of the Dead Sea and parallel with it, traversing what was in ancient times the land of Moab and leading to the north. The nomads of Jordan know it very well. Among the natives it is called, remarkably enough, the "King's Way". We come across it in the Bible, where it is called "the king's high way" or "the high way". It was the road that the children of Israel wished to follow on their journey through Edom to the "Promised Land" (Num. 20[17,19]). In the Christian era the Romans used the "King's Way" and improved it. Parts of it now belong to the network of roads in the state of Jordan. Clearly visible from the air the ancient track shows up as a dark streak across the country.

> "And the Lord said, Because the cry of Sodom and Gomorrah is great, and because their sin is very grievous. . . . Then the Lord rained upon Sodom and upon Gomorrah, brimstone and fire from the Lord out of heaven; And he overthrew those cities, and all the plain, and all the inhabitants of the cities, and that which grew upon the ground. But his [Lot's] wife looked back from behind him, and she became a pillar of salt. . . . And lo the smoke of the country went up as the smoke of a furnace" (Gen. 18[20]; 19[24-26,28]).

The calamity which is the subject of this powerful Biblical story of divine punishment for incorrigible sin has probably in all ages made a deep impression on men's minds. Sodom and Gomorrah have become synonymous with vice and godlessness. When men have talked in terms of utter annihilation, again the fate of these cities has always sprung to their minds. Their imaginations have constantly been kindled by this inexplicable and frightful disaster, as can well be seen from the many allusions to it in ancient times. Remarkable and quite incredible things are said to have happened there by the Dead Sea, the "Sea of Salt", where according to the Bible the catastrophe must have happened.

During the siege of Jerusalem in A.D. 70 it is said that the Roman army commander Titus sentenced certain slaves to death. He gave them short shrift, had them bound together by chains and thrown into the sea at the foot of the mountains of Moab. But the condemned men did not drown. No matter how often they were thrown into the sea they always drifted back to the shore like corks. This inexplicable occurrence made such a deep impression upon Titus that he pardoned the unfortunate offenders. Flavius Josephus, the Jewish historian who lived latterly in Rome, repeatedly mentions a "Lake of Asphalt". Greeks lay stress on the presence of poisonous gases, which are reported as rising from all parts of this sea. The Arabs say that in olden times no bird was able to reach the opposite side. The creatures, as they flew across the water, would suddenly drop dead into it.

These and similar traditional stories were well enough known, but until a century ago we had no first hand knowledge of this odd mysterious sea in Palestine. No scientist had investigated it or even seen it. In 1848 the United States took the initiative and equipped an expedition to solve the riddle of the Dead Sea. One autumn day in that year the beach of the little coastal town of Akka, less than 10 miles from present-day Haifa, was black with spectators who were engrossed in an unusual manoeuvre.

W. F. Lynch, a geologist and leader of the expedition, had brought ashore from the ship which was lying at anchor two metal boats which he was now fastening on to large-wheeled carts. Pulled by a long team of horses, the trek began. Three weeks later after indescribable difficulties they had succeeded in getting the waggons over the hills of Southern Galilee. The two boats took to the water again at Tiberias. When Lynch set up his theodolite at the Lake of Galilee, the result produced the first big surprise of the expedition. To begin with he thought he had made an error of calculation, but a cross check confirmed the result. The surface of the lake, which played so notable a part in the life of Jesus, is 676 feet below the level of the Mediterranean. What then could be the height of the source of the Jordan, which flows through the Lake?

Some days later W. F. Lynch stood on the slopes of snow-capped Hermon. Among remains of broken columns and gateways lies the little village of Baniya. Local Arabs led him through a thick clump of oleanders to a cave, half choked with rubble, on the steep limestone flank of Hermon. Out of its darkness gushed a stream of pure water. This is one of the sources of the Jordan. The Arabs call the Jordan Sheri'at el-Kebire, the "Great River". This was the site of Panium where Herod built a temple of Pan in honour of Augustus. Shell-shaped niches are hewn out of the rock beside the Jordan cave. "Priest of Pan" is still clearly legible in Greek characters. In the time of Jesus the Greek pastoral god was worshipped at the source of the Jordan. There the goat-footed Pan raised his flute to his lips as if he wanted to send the Jordan on its way with a tune. Only 3 miles west of this source lay Dan, which is frequently mentioned in the Bible as the most northerly point in the country. There too is another source of the Jordan where its clear waters spring out of the southern slopes of Hermon. A third stream rushes out of a wadi higher up. The bottom of the wadi just above Dan is 1,500 feet above sea level.

When the Jordan on its way south reaches little Lake Huleh 12 miles away, the river bed is only 6 feet above sea level. Then the river rushes down the next 6 miles to the Lake of Galilee. In the course of its descent from the slopes of Hermon to this point, a distance of only 25 miles, it has dropped 2,275 feet.

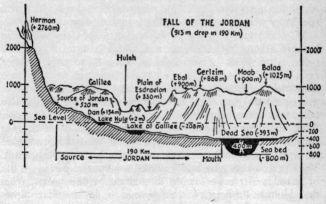

FIG. 10.—Diagram of the Jordan-drop.

From Tiberias the members of the American expedition in their two metal boats followed the endless windings of the Jordan downstream. Gradually the vegetation became sparser and the thick undergrowth extended no farther than the banks. Under the tropical sun an oasis came into view on their right—Jericho. Soon afterwards they reached their goal. There before them, embedded between almost vertical precipices, lay the vast surface of the Dead Sea.

The first thing to do was to have a swim. But when they jumped in they felt as if they were being thrown out again. It was like wearing life-jackets. The old stories were therefore true. In this sea it is impossible to drown. The scorching sun dried the men's skins almost at once. The thin crust of salt which the water had deposited on their bodies made them look quite white. No shellfish, no fish, no seaweed, no coral—no fishing boat had ever rocked on this sea. Here was neither a harvest from the sea nor from the land. For the banks were equally bare and desolate. Huge deposits of coagulated salt made the beach and the rockface above it sparkle in the sun like diamonds. The air was filled with sharp acrid odours, a mixture of petroleum and sulphur. Oily patches of asphalt—the Bible calls it "slime" (Gen. 14[10])—float on the waves. Even the bright blue sky and the all powerful sun could not breathe any life into this forbidding looking landscape.

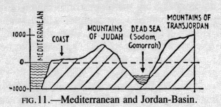

FIG. 11.—Mediterranean and Jordan-Basin.

For twenty-two days the American boats went back and forth across the Dead Sea. They tested the water and analysed it, they took innumerable soundings. The mouth of the Jordan, at the Dead Sea, lies 1,280 feet below sea level. If there were any connection with the Mediterranean, the Jordan and the Lake of Galilee, 65 miles away, would disappear. A vast inland sea would stretch almost up to the shores of Lake Huleh.

"When a storm sweeps up through this rocky basin," observed Lynch, "the waves strike the sides of the boats like blows from a hammer. But the weight of the water is such that a short time after the wind has died down the sea is calm again.''

The world learned for the first time from the report of the expedition two astonishing facts. The Dead Sea is over 1,200 feet in depth. The bottom of the sea is therefore about 2,500 feet below the level of the Mediterranean. The water of the Dead Sea contains approximately 30% of solid ingredients, most sodium chloride, i.e., cooking salt. The normal ocean has only 3.3 to 4% salt. The Jordan and many smaller rivers empty themselves into this basin of approximately 50x10 miles which has not a solitary outlet. Evaporation under the broiling sun takes place on the surface of the sea at a rate of over 230 million cubic feet per day. What its tributaries bring to it in the way of chemical substances remains deposited in this great basin's 500 square miles.

It was only after the turn of the century that, keeping pace with excavations in other parts of Palestine, interest was also awakened in Sodom and Gomorrah. Archaeologists began their quest for the vanished cities that were said to have existed in the Vale of Siddim in Biblical times. At the furthermost south-east point of the Dead Sea remains of a large settlement were found. The place is still called Zoar by the Arabs. The scientists were delighted, for Zoar was one of the five wealthy cities in the Vale of Siddim, which had refused to pay tribute to the four foreign kings. But exploratory digging which was immediately undertaken proved a disappointment. It remains uncertain, however, whether Zoar is identical with the place called Zoar in the Bible.

The date of the ruins that came to light showed it to be a town which had flourished there in the Middle Ages. There was no trace of the ancient Zoar of the king of Bela (Gen. 14[2]) or of its neighbours. Nevertheless there were plentiful indications in the environs of mediaeval Zoar that there had been a numerous population in the country in very early times.

On the eastern shore of the Dead Sea the peninsula of el-Lisan protrudes like a tongue far into the water. El-Lisan means ''the tongue'' in Arabic. The Bible expressly mentions it when the country is being divided up after the conquest. The frontiers of the tribe of Judah are being carefully outlined. In the course of this Joshua gives an unusually illuminating description of their southern limits: ''And their south border was from the shore of the Salt Sea, from the bay [lit. 'tongue'] that looketh southward'' (Josh. 15[2]).

Roman history has a story to tell of this tongue of land, which has always been wrongly regarded with considerable scepticism. Two deserters had fled to the peninsula. The legionaries in pursuit combed the ground for a long time in vain. When they eventually caught sight of the men who had given them the slip it was too late. The deserters were clambering up the rocks on the other side of the water—they had waded straight across the sea. Obviously the sea was more shallow at this spot in those days than it is today.

Unseen from the land the ground falls away here under the surface of the water at a prodigious angle, dividing the sea into two parts. To the right of the peninsula the ground slopes sharply down to a depth of 1,200 feet. Left of the peninsula the water remains remarkably shallow. Soundings taken in the last few years established depths of only 50–60 feet.

Geologists added to these discoveries and observations a fresh explanation which might clarify the occasion and the result of the Biblical story of the annihilation of Sodom and Gomorrah.

The American expedition under Lynch in 1848 produced the first information about the prodigious drop of the Jordan on its short course through Palestine. This plunging of the river bed until it is far below sea level is, as later investigation established, a unique geological phenomenon. "There may be something on the surface of another planet which is similar to the Jordan Valley, but on our planet there certainly is nothing," wrote George Adam Smith, the Scottish Old Testament scholar, in his "Historical Geography of the Holy Land". "No other part of the globe, which is not under water, lies deeper than 300 feet below sea level."

The Jordan Valley is only part of a huge fracture in the earth's crust. The path of this crack has meantime been accurately traced. It begins far north, several hundred miles beyond the borders of Palestine, at the foot of the Taurus mountains in Asia Minor. In the south it runs from the south shore of the Dead Sea through the Wadi el-Arabah to the Gulf of Aqabah and only comes to an end beyond the Red Sea in Africa. At many points in this vast depression signs of earlier volcanic activity are obvious. In the Galilean mountains, in the highlands of Transjordan, on the banks of the Jabbok, a tributary of the Jordan, and on the Gulf of Aqabah are black basalt and lava.

The subsidence released volcanic forces that had been lying dormant deep down along the whole length of the fracture. In the

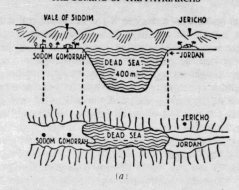

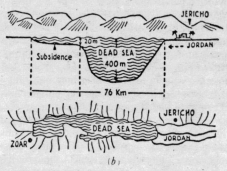

FIG. 12.—THE DEAD SEA (a) in 2000 B.C. before the end of Sodom and Gomorrah; (b) in 1900 B.C. after the disaster.

upper valleys of the Jordan near Bashan there are still the towering craters of extinct volcanoes; great stretches of lava and deep layers of basalt have been deposited on the limestone surface. From time immemorial the area around this depression has been subject to earthquakes. There is repeated evidence of them and the Bible itself records them. Did Sodom and Gomorrah sink when perhaps a part of the base of this huge fissure collapsed still further to the accompaniment of earthquakes and volcanic eruptions? And did the Dead Sea then take on a further extension towards the south as shown in Fig. 12?

And Lot's wife—"looked back from behind him and she became a pillar of salt" (Gen. 19[26]).

The nearer one gets to the south end of the Dead Sea the more wild and desolate it becomes. Landscape and mountain grow eerier and more forbidding. The hills stand there silent and everlasting. Their scarred slopes fall sheer and steep down to the sea, their lower reaches are crystal white. The unparalleled disaster which once took place here has left an imperishable and oppressive mark. Only occasionally is a band of nomads to be seen heading inland along one of the steep and rugged wadis.

Where the heavy oily water comes to an end in the south the harsh rockface on either side breaks off abruptly and gives place to a salt-sodden swamp. The reddish soil is pierced by innumerable channels and can easily become dangerous for the unwary traveller. Sweeping southwards the bogland merges into the desert Wadi el-Arabah, which continues down to the Red Sea.

To the west of the southern shore and in the direction of the Biblical "Land of the South", the Negev, stretches a ridge of hills about 150 feet high and 10 miles from north to south. Their slopes sparkle and glitter in the sunshine like diamonds. It is an odd phenomenon of nature. For the most part this little range of hills consists of pure rock salt. The Arabs call it Jebel Usdum, an ancient name, which preserves in it the word Sodom. Many blocks of salt have been worn away by the rain and have crashed downhill. They have odd shapes and some of them stand on end, looking like statues. It is easy to imagine them suddenly seeming to come to life.

These strange statues in salt remind us vividly of the Biblical description of Lot's wife who was turned into a pillar of salt. And everything in the neighbourhood of the Salt Sea is even to this day quickly covered with a crust of salt.

The question of Abraham's journeyings has not allowed scholars any peace of mind even in recent times. Abraham's sojourn in Egypt, it has been pointed out, cannot be confirmed from non-Biblical sources and even in the Bible it is merely indicated incidentally in connection with a trick to which Abraham resorted because he feared he might be killed on account of his beautiful wife.

The story in question is one of those repetitions to which we refer in the appendix to the present revised edition. It also occurs in *two* places in the Bible (1 Gen. 12, 9ff and 1 Gen. 20, 1ff), except that in the second case there is no mention at all of Egypt, but of "south country" and of Gerar which lies between Gaza and Beersheba.

In whatever way we are to interpret all this, we can scarcely be encouraged to regard the story as historical. Furthermore, the wall paintings in the grave of Khnum-hotpe at Beni-Hasan, in the light of our most recent knowledge, do not fit into the framework of the Biblical account of the patriarchs. And what is the explanation of this? As one would expect of caravan people around 1900 B.C., the caravan people depicted in the Khnum-hotpe grave had donkeys, whereas the Bible says that Abraham and his people, who according to the traditional interpretation are supposed to have lived at the same period, already possessed camels. There is a vast difference between the two animals, whether used for riding or as beasts of burden, in the distance they can travel, their cost, their mobility and consequently also in the safety of caravans equipped with one or the other of these species.

The introduction of the camel as a mount and a bearer of burdens was equal to a revolution in the organisation of transport in the Ancient East. We shall have occasion to refer to the question again.

But when did this "revolution" take place? Zoologists and Orientalists specialising in the study of domestic animals have continued to puzzle over the question, but the famous camels of the patriarchs as well as the camels belonging to those merchants who took Joseph to Egypt (we shall return to this point at the end of the next chapter) quite definitely remain problematical.

Almost more problematical than Abraham's camels, however, is the tradition concerning Sodom and Gomorrah. In particular, we must remember there can be no question that the Jordan fissure was formed before about 4000 B.C. Indeed, according to the most recent presentation of the facts, the origin of the fissure dates back to the Oligocene, the third oldest stage of the Tertiary Period. We thus have to think in terms not of thousands, but of millions of years. Violent volcanic activity connected with the Jordan fissure has been shown to have occurred since then, but even so we do not get any further than the Pleistocene which came to an end approximately ten thousand years ago. Certainly we do not come anywhere near to the third, still less the second millennium before Christ, the period that is to say, in which the patriarchs are traditionally placed.

In addition, it is precisely to the south of the Lisan peninsula, where Sodom and Gomorrah are reported to have been annihilated, that the traces of former volcanic activity cease. In short, the proof in this area of a quite recent catastrophe which wiped out towns and was accompanied by violent volcanic activity is not provided by the findings of the geologists.

But what are we to think of the incursions of the Dead Sea into the more flat area of the southern basin? During the course of its chequered history the Dead Sea or its predecessors in the Pleistocene frequently extended far across today's southern basin into Wadi el-Arabah. At times its surface lay as much as 623 feet higher than it does today. The vast sea which had collected there in those days completely filled the whole Jordan rift from Wadi el-Arabah as far as the Lake of Galilee. Then the lake diminished in size, no less than 28 ancient shore terraces bearing witness to the process. It is even possible that it dried up completely. Only at a later date did the formation of the Dead Sea of today occur, accompanied probably by violent earth tremors. This, too, took place in the Late Pleistocene when man already existed, but when there could be no question of towns. There is nevertheless the very vague possibility that the experiences of Stone Age man in this region, transmitted from generation to generation, finally took shape as the traditions of "towns" which had disappeared or even gave rise to such a tradition. This tradition appears to be very old, much older than has so far been assumed. We shall refer to it again.

Certainly earthquakes occurred in the Dead Sea area at a later date. Flavius Josephus describes the destruction caused by one which took place in 31 B.C. and there was another in Khirbet-Qumran, where the famous Dead Sea scrolls were found, which left impressive traces behind it, although there are no indications of any catastrophe which might have destroyed towns during the early part of the second millennium before Christ.

Today's place-names such as Bahr-el-hut (sea of lead, which is the Arabic name for the Dead Sea), Jebel Usdum (Mount Sodom) and Zoar do not necessarily derive from genuine, independent, direct, primary traditions parallel to the Bible. It is quite possible that they were applied to these localities subsequently and so linked to the Bible story. If so, they would merely represent a secondary tradition. We have a similar state of affairs with "Joseph's Canal" (Arabic Bahr Yusuf) in Faiyûm in Egypt to which reference will be made in the next chapter. The "Egyptian Joseph" of the Bible also makes his appearance in Islamic tradition and the name of the waterway in question could, and in all probability does, merely refer to that tradition.

It is only very recently that a great stir was caused by the excavation of Tell el-Mardikh south of Aleppo. It was here that the Italian scholars Paolo Matthiae and Giovanni Pettinato discovered Ebla, a town dating from the third millennium before Christ. The first sensational discovery was that in almost prehistoric times a high degree of culture had existed there with what was for those days an enormously differentiated social structure. The second sensation was that Ebla possessed rich archives of clay tablets. As always with archives of this nature, we are justified in having high hopes, but must be prepared to accept that opinions hitherto considered unassailable may be shown to have been built on insecure foundations. "When the texts have been studied, we shall perhaps have to forget the results of a whole century of research in the Ancient East," is how a German colleague of the Italian scholars expressed it. The third sensation and the most important in connection with the question of names is that the texts from Ebla dating from the third millennium before Christ contain names which are familiar to us from the Bible. The name of Abraham was encountered as well as those of the sinful towns of Sodom and Gomorrah, Admah and Zeboiim on the Dead Sea which were all destroyed by fire. At this point a number of fellow specialists expressed their scepticism. Had Pettinato read the texts correctly, they asked. Of course, they agreed that patriarchs' names have been found in other sources, as has already been mentioned, but did the names of Sodom and Gomorrah really occur in archives of the third millennium before Christ in Syria? Had these towns really existed as the archives said? Or do traditions concerning them go back to such early times, even earlier than the customary date accepted for the beginning of the period of the patriarchs?

A considerable period of time will elapse before all these questions are answered. In the normal way, scholars are not interested in sensations and a vast amount of work has to be done before it can be established beyond a doubt how sensational the finds at Tell el-Mardikh really are.

In the Realm of the Pharaohs from Joseph to Moses

Chapter 8
JOSEPH IN EGYPT

Had Potiphar a prototype?—The Orbiney Papyrus—Hyksos rulers on the Nile—Joseph, official of an occupying power—Corn silos, an Egyptian patent—Evidence of seven years famine—Assignments to Goshen—"Bahr Yusuf": Joseph's Canal?—"Jacob-Her" on scarabs.

"And Joseph was brought down to Egypt: and Potiphar, an officer of Pharaoh, captain of the guard, an Egyptian, bought him of the hands of the Ishmaelites, which had brought him down thither" (Gen. 39[1]).

The tale of Joseph, who was sold by his brothers to Egypt and later as grand vizier became reconciled to them, is undoubtedly one of the finest stories in the world's literature.

"And it came to pass after these things, that his master's [Potiphar's] wife cast her eyes upon Joseph; and she said, Lie with me. But he refused, and..." (Gen. 39[7-8]). When her husband came home, she said: "The Hebrew servant, which thou hast brought unto us, came in unto me to mock me" (Gen. 39[17]).

Nothing new under the sun—smirked the Egyptologists whenever they started work on the translation of the "Orbiney Papyrus". What they were deciphering from hieroglyphics was a popular story about the time of the XIX Dynasty which bore the discreet title: "The Tale of the Two Brothers". "Once upon a time there were two brothers.... The name of the elder one was Anubis, the younger was called Bata. Anubis owned a house and a wife and his younger brother lived with him as if he were his own son. He drove the cattle out to the fields and brought them home at night and slept with them in the cowshed. When ploughing time came round the two brothers were ploughing the land together. They had been a few days in the field when they ran out of corn. The elder brother therefore sent the younger one off: 'Hurry and bring us corn from the city.' The younger brother found his elder brother's wife having a hair-do. 'Up', he said, 'and give me some corn, for I have to hurry back to the field. My brother said: "Quick, don't waste any time."' He loaded up with corn and wheat and went out with his burden. . . . Then said she to him: 'You have so much energy! Every day I see how strong you are. . . . Come! Let us lie down for an hour!—It might give you pleasure, and I shall also make you fine clothes.' Then the young man was as angry as a southern panther at this wicked suggestion that had been made to him. He said to her: 'What a disgraceful proposal you have just made. . . . Never do it again and I shall say nothing to anyone.' So saying he slung his load on his back and went out to the fields. The wife began to be frightened about what she had said. She got hold of some grease paint and made herself up to look like someone who had been violently assaulted. Her husband . . . found his wife lying prostrate as a result of the outrage. Her husband said to her: 'Who has been with you?' She replied: 'No one . . . apart from your young brother. When he came to fetch the corn he found me sitting alone and said to me: "Come, let us lie down for an hour! Do up your hair." But I paid no attention to him. "Am I not your mother! and is your elder brother not like a father to you!" I said to him. But he was afraid and struck me to stop me telling you about it. If you leave him alive now I shall die.' Then his brother grew as wild as a southern panther. He sharpened his knife . . . to kill his younger brother. . . ."

We can almost see Pharaoh's courtiers whispering over it. They liked this story. Sex problems and the psychology of women interested people even then, thousands of years before Kinsey.

The story of an adulteress, in the heart of an Egyptian tale, as the prototype of the Biblical story of Joseph? Scholars argued the pros and cons based on the text of the "Orbiney Papyrus" long after the turn of the century. On the debit side, there was not the slightest trace of Israel's sojourn in Egypt apart from the Bible itself. Historians and professors of theology alike spoke of the "Legend of Joseph". Egypt was just the kind of country from which one might hope for and even expect contemporary docu-

mentation about the events recorded in the Bible. At any rate this
ought to be true as far as Joseph was concerned, for he was
Pharaoh's grand vizier and therefore a most powerful man in
Egyptian eyes.

No country in the Ancient East has handed down its history so
faithfully as Egypt. Right back to about 3000 B.C. we can trace
the names of the Pharaohs practically without a break. We know
the succession of dynasties in the Old, Middle and New Kingdoms. No other people have recorded so meticulously their
important events, the activities of their rulers, their campaigns,
their erection of temples and palaces, as well as their literature
and poetry.

But this time Egypt gave the scholars no answer. As if it were
not enough that they found nothing about Joseph, they discovered
neither documents nor monuments out of this whole period. The
records which showed hardly a break for centuries suddenly
stopped about 1730 B.C. From then on for a long time impene-
trable darkness lay over Egypt. Not before 1580 B.C. did contemporary evidence appear once again. How could this absence
of any information whatever over so long a period be explained,
especially from such a highly developed people and civilisation?

Something incredible and frightful befell the Nile country
about 1730 B.C. Suddenly, like a bolt from the blue, warriors in
chariots drove into the country like arrows shot from a bow,
endless columns of them in clouds of dust. Day and night horses'
hooves thundered past the frontier posts, rang through city
streets, temple squares and the majestic courts of Pharaoh's
palaces. Even before the Egyptians realised it, it had happened:
their country was taken by surprise, overrun and vanquished.
The giant of the Nile who never before in his history had seen
foreign conquerors, lay bound and prostrate.

The rule of the victors began with a bloodbath. The Hyksos,
Semitic tribes from Canaan and Syria, knew no pity. With the
fateful year 1730 B.C. the thirteen hundred year rule of the
dynasties came to an abrupt end. The Middle Kingdom of the
Pharaohs was shattered under the onslaught of these Asian
peoples, the "rulers of foreign lands". That is the meaning of
the name Hyksos. The memory of this political disaster remained
alive among the Nile people, as a striking description by the
Egyptian historian Manetho testified: "We had a king called
Tutimaeus. In his reign, it happened. I do not know why God

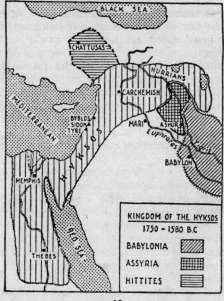

FIG. 13.

was displeased with us. Unexpectedly from the regions of the East, came men of unknown race. Confident of victory they marched against our land. By force they took it, easily, without a single battle. Having overpowered our rulers they burned our cities without compassion, and destroyed the temples of the gods. All the natives were treated with great cruelty for they slew some and carried off the wives and children of others into slavery. Finally they appointed one of themselves as king. His name was Salitis and he lived in Memphis and made Upper and Lower Egypt pay tribute to him, and set up garrisons in places which would be most useful to him . . . and when he found a city in the province of Saïs which suited his purpose (it lay east of the Bubastite branch of the Nile and was called Avaris) he rebuilt it and made it very strong by erecting walls and installing a force of 240,000 men to hold it. Salitis went there every summer partly to collect his corn and pay his men their wages, and partly to train his armed troops and terrify foreigners.''

Avaris is the town which under another name plays an important role in Biblical history. Avaris, later called Per-Ramesses, is one of the bond cities of Israel in Egypt (Ex. 1^{11}).

The Biblical story of Joseph and the sojourn of the children of Israel in Egypt probably come into this period of turbulent conditions on the Nile under the rule of the foreign Hyksos. It is therefore not surprising that no contemporary Egyptian information has come down to us. Nevertheless there is indirect proof of the authenticity of the Joseph story. The Biblical description of the historical background is authentic. Equally genuine is the colourful Egyptian detail. Egyptology confirms this from countless finds.

FIG. 14.—Installation of an Egyptian Vizier.

Spices and aromatic products are brought to Egypt by the Ishmaelites, the Arabian merchants who sell Joseph there (Gen. 37^{25}). There was a heavy demand for these things in the Nile country. They were used in religious services, where the wonderfully fragrant herbs were burned as incense in the temples. The doctors found them indispensable for healing the sick, and priests required them for embalming the bodies of the nobility.

Potiphar was the name of the Egyptian to whom Joseph was

sold (Gen. 37[36]). It is a thoroughly characteristic native name. In Egyptian it is "Pa-di-pa-rê", "the gift of the god Rê".

Joseph's elevation to be viceroy of Egypt is reproduced in the Bible exactly according to protocol. He is invested with the insignia of his high office, he receives the ring, Pharaoh's seal, a costly linen vestment, and a golden chain (Gen. 41[42]). This is exactly how Egyptian artists depict this solemn ceremony on murals and reliefs.

As viceroy Joseph rides in Pharaoh's "second chariot" (Gen. 41[43]). That could indicate the "period of Hyksos" at the earliest, for it is only during the period of the "rulers of foreign lands", or even presumably only before their expulsion and before the commencement of the "New Kingdom", that the fast war chariot reached Egypt in consequence of its being adopted by one people after another according to our most recent knowledge. The luxury model of it is the ostentatious chariot which was later used by the rulers of the "New Kingdom". Before their day this had not been the practice on the Nile. The ceremonial chariot harnessed to thoroughbred horses was in those days the Rolls Royce of the governors. The first chariot belonged to the ruler, the "second chariot" was occupied by his chief minister.

Joseph in accordance with his rank married Asenath (Gen. 41[45]) and thereby became the son-in-law of an influential man Potipherah, the priest of Heliopolis. Heliopolis is the On of the Bible and it lay on the right bank of the Nile a little to the north of present-day Cairo.

Joseph was thirty years of age when he "went out over all the land of Egypt" (Gen. 41[45]). The Bible says no more about this but there is a spot by the Nile which still bears his name.

The town of Medinet-el-Faiyûm, lying 80 miles south of Cairo in the middle of the fertile Faiyûm, is extolled as the "Venice of Egypt". In the lush gardens of this huge flourishing oasis grow oranges, mandarines, peaches, olives, pomegranates and grapes. Faiyûm owes these delicious fruits to the artificial canal, over 200 miles long, which conveys the water of the Nile and turns this district, which would otherwise be desert, into a paradise. The ancient waterway is not only to this day called "Bahr Yusuf", "Joseph's Canal", by the fellahin, but is known by this name throughout Egypt. People say that it was the Joseph of the Bible, Pharaoh's "Grand Vizier" as Arab legends would describe him, who planned it.

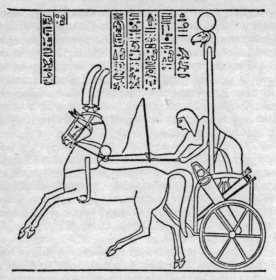

FIG. 15.—Ceremonial chariot from Thebes.

The Bible depicts Joseph as an able administrator who as grand vizier guides the Egyptian people through difficult times by his counsel and actions, making provision in years of plenty for years of want. Thus he gathers in corn and lays it up in granaries against times of need.

"And the seven years of plenteousness that was in the land of Egypt were ended. And the seven years of dearth began to come . . . and the dearth was in all lands" (Gen. 41[53,54]).

Years of drought, bad harvests and famine are well attested in the lands of the Nile. In very early times, for example at the beginning of the third millennium, there is said to have been a seven year famine according to a rock inscription of the Ptolemies. King Zoser sent the following message to the governor of the great cataracts of the Nile at Elephantine: "I am very concerned about the people in the palace. My heart is heavy over the calamitous failure of the Nile floods for the past seven years.

There is little fruit; vegetables are in short supply; there is a shortage of food generally. Everybody robs his neighbour. ... Children weep, young folk slouch around. The aged are depressed, they have no power in their legs, they sit on the ground. The court is at its wits' end. The storehouses have been opened but everything that was in them has been consumed." Traces have been found of the granaries which existed even in the Old Kingdom. In many tombs there were little clay models of them. Apparently they were making provision for possible years of famine among the dead.

"Now when Jacob saw that there was corn in Egypt, Jacob said unto his sons, Why do ye look upon one another? And he said, Behold I have heard that there is corn in Egypt: get you down thither and buy for us from thence: that we may live and not die. And Joseph's ten brethren went down to buy corn in Egypt" (Gen. 42$^{1-3}$).

This is the reason for the great journey which led to the reunion with the brother who had been sold as a slave and to the migration of the Israelites into Egypt. The viceroy brought his father, brothers and other relatives into the country: "... all the souls of the house of Jacob, which came into Egypt, were there three score and ten... and they came into the land of Goshen" (Gen. 46^{27,28}). The viceroy had obtained permission from the highest authority for his family to cross the frontier, and what the Bible records corresponds perfectly with the administrative procedure of the government.

"And Pharaoh spake unto Joseph, saying, Thy father and thy brethren are come unto thee: The land of Egypt is before thee, in the best of the land make thy father and brethren to dwell: in the land of Goshen let them dwell" (Gen. 47$^{5-6}$).

A frontier official writes to his superior on papyrus: "I have another matter to bring to the attention of my lord and it is this: We have permitted the transit of the Bedouin tribes from Edom via the Menephta fort in Zeku, to the fen-lands of the city of Per-Atum... so that they may preserve their own lives and the lives of their flocks on the estate of the king, the good Sun of every land...."

FIG. 16.—Selling corn to Semites from Canaan.

Per-Atum, that crops up here in a hieroglyphic text, is the
Biblical Pithom in the land of Goshen, later one of the bond-
cities of Israel in Egypt (Ex. 1[11]).

In cases of this sort the Egyptian frontier police, like the
higher officials, were carefully graded in a chain of command
right up to the court. The procedure to be followed was of a
standard pattern: petitioners for pasture land, refugees from
famine stricken countries, were accepted and almost always
directed into the same area. It lay on the delta, on the right bank
of the Nile in the Biblical "Land of Goshen". The seat of
government of the Hyksos rulers was also in the delta.

The children of Israel must have appreciated life in the Land
of Goshen. It was—exactly as the Bible describes it (Gen. 45[18];
46[32]; 47[3])—extremely fertile and quite ideal for cattle breeding.
When Jacob died at a ripe old age something happened to him
which was quite as unknown and uncommon in Canaan and
Mesopotamia as among his own family, who considered it a very
remarkable proceeding. His body was embalmed.

"And Joseph commanded his servants, the physicians, to
embalm his father, and the physicians embalmed Israel.[1]
And forty days were fulfilled for him: for so are fulfilled the
days of those which are embalmed" (Gen. 50[2-3]).

We can read in Herodotus, the globetrotter of the ancient
world and travel-diarist Number One, how closely this description corresponds with Egyptian practice. Later on Joseph was
buried in the same way.

Under the Egyptian Pharaohs a "Sanddweller" could never
have become viceroy. Nomads bred asses, sheep and goats and
the Egyptians despised none so much as breeders of small cattle.

[1]Jacob received from Yahweh the name Israel (Gen. 32[28]). The nation was later called the
"Children of Israel" after him.

"For every shepherd is an abomination unto the Egyptians" (Gen. 46³⁴). Only under the foreign overlords, the Hyksos, would an "Asiatic" have the chance to rise to the highest office in the state. Under the Hyksos we repeatedly find officials with Semitic names. On scarabs dating from the Hyksos period the name "Jacob-Her" has been clearly deciphered. "And it is not impossible," concludes the great American Egyptologist James Henry Breasted, "that a leader of the Israelite tribe of Jacob gained control for a time in the Nile valley in this obscure period. Such an occurrence would fit in surprisingly well with the migration to Egypt of Israelite tribes which in any case must have taken place about this time."

Like so much of what the Bible relates, the story of Joseph in Egypt has received astonishing confirmation, but this confirmation, as on so many occasions, runs into difficulties.

The confirmation

It is a fact that there were important officials in Egypt who came from Asia Minor. One of their number indeed ruled so independently that an ancient Egyptian source, referring presumably to this individual, even speaks of the "foreign rule of a Syrian".

Egypt's Pharaoh sees in a dream "well favoured kine and fatfleshed" (Gen. 41²ff and ¹⁸ff). Joseph interprets these kine as years (Gen. 41²⁶f). Egyptian inscriptions using the hieroglyphic symbol of the cow as a cryptogram, a kind of secret sign, with the meaning "years", have actually been encountered.

Joseph's "agrarian reform" did not affect the land owned by the Egyptian priests (Gen. 47²²). At least during one phase of the history of Ancient Egypt there were indeed tax reliefs for Egyptian priests. Herodotus of Halikarnassos, the Greek histori- an from Asia Minor, the "father of history", (c. 480–post 430 B.C.) is one of those who report this. Parallels to the official installation of Joseph (Gen. 41⁴²) have also been found. Paintings from the time of the New Kingdom at first led people to see correspondences, but these would not quite take us back to the time of the Hyksos, although fairly close to their period.

The difficulty

All four confirmations of the Joseph story have nothing to do with the time of the Hyksos (c. 1650–1544/41 according to von Beckerath), the time to which the Joseph episode was generally ascribed, but all, without exception, concern later phases of ancient Egyptian history.

The influential Asiatics at the Egyptian court first appear in the time of the Ramessid dynasty (13–12th century B.C.). The case of the Syrian "foreign ruler", to whom reference is made in an ancient Egyptian source, is probably that of Biya or Bai, the powerful chancellor of Queen Tewosre (c. 1200 B.C.). This source is the great Harris papyrus, which presumably, if not quite certainly, makes reference to Bai. The Harris papyrus, the statement of accounts of the reign of Ramesses III, dates from the time of Ramesses IV (12th century B.C.).

The symbol of the cow in the meaning of "year" is found only at the time of the Ptolemies (305–30 B.C.) and not earlier. It is consequently a millennium and a few centuries younger than the period of the Hyksos.

The property and tax privileges of the Egyptian priests refer only to the time of the period of the Saïtes (664–525 B.C.).

The description in the Bible of the quite special form of Joseph's installation in office with seal ring, official robe and chain has no precise correspondence, when we examine it closely, to the ancient Egyptian representations from the New Kingdom of the "investiture" and the "conferring of the gold of honour", as was first thought. The closest parallels are found at the time of Sargon II of Ashur (722–705 B.C.). This special form of investiture presumably first came to Egypt through Ashurbanipal (669/8 to about 630 B.C.) who conquered Egypt in 667–666 and in 665 B.C. made Necho, prince of Saïs, Viceroy of Egypt with appropriate ceremony. Here, too, we find express mention of the threefold investiture with ring or rings, official robe and chain.

Two questions have to be asked.

1) If the Bible story of Joseph contains elements dating from such a late period, can it then be as ancient as has been thought until now or must it not have originated much later than has hitherto been assumed?

2) If the period is not right, however, what about the authenticity of the story? And what about the genuineness of its Egyptian atmosphere?

Scholars in all parts of the world had, in fact, been more or less convinced until now of the genuine nature of the "Ancient Egyptian background" of this Biblical story. The impressive list of the reputable scholars who were not averse to regarding Joseph as a Grand Vizier during the Hyksos period almost looks

like a "Who's Who" of Egyptology according to a statement
made about ten years ago by Donald B. Redford who published a
comprehensive study of the Joseph story in 1970.

Redford and others have scrutinised the Joseph story very
closely since that time, however, with the result that considerable
doubts have arisen regarding the connection it had hitherto been
thought to have with the Hyksos period.

The merchants who bore Joseph away to Egypt had camels to
carry their wares (Gen. 37^{25}). These camels are just as much a
problem as the "camels of the patriarchs" which were discussed
in an earlier chapter in connection with Abraham. For many a
Biblical scholar they represent a stumbling-block. In short, they
are the source of argument and indicate a later period rather than
that of the Hyksos.

Let us proceed with the discussion of the various means of
transport. Many have considered the mention of the "chariot" in
the Biblical Joseph story as typical of the Hyksos period (Gen.
41^{43}). In this story what is in accordance with fact is that the
single-axled, two-wheeled chariot really reached Egypt only
during the Hyksos period. On the other hand, the chariot was not
abolished at a later date, and indeed the ancient Egyptian
pictures of chariots began only in the time of the New Kingdom.
In the famous grave of Tutankhamun, for example, Howard
Carter even found war chariots and ceremonial chariots which
had been placed in the grave with the dead king. The mention of
the chariot can consequently indicate any later period of history.

The Biblical story of Joseph obviously presupposes the knowledge and use of coins (Gen. 42^{25} and elsewhere). Principally,
however, the word for "bundle of money" (Authorised Version), "moneybag" (Gen. 42^{35}), occurs at a time when coinage
already existed. In Egypt and Palestine, this will scarcely have
been the case until the sixth century B.C.

Potiphar's title, which is usually translated as "chamberlain"
or "court official" and which in the Authorised Version appears
as "an officer of Pharaoh, captain of the guard" (Gen. 39^1),[1]
really means "eunuch". There was no such title as Potiphar's in
Egypt until the time of the Persians (525–332 B.C.).

And so it goes on. Redford enumerates no less than 23 points
which all testify against a date assigning the Joseph episode to

[1] Translator's note: The Authorised Version of the Bible gives "an officer of Pharaoh,
captain of the guard". Luther's German translation says "Pharaoh's chamberlain and
captain". I have added the precise words of the Authorised Version.

the Hyksos period, but indicate rather that it belongs to the later period of Ancient Egypt. Even a Biblical scholar like George Ernest Wright, who was so convinced of the genuineness of the ancient Egyptian atmosphere of the Joseph story, was obliged to admit in 1957 that the Egyptian names occurring in the story, and not least the name Potiphar (Pa-di-pa-Rê), had come into general use only in the time of David. The oldest Egyptian mention of the name Pa-di-pa-Rê (Potiphar) could date only from the 21st Dynasty at the earliest in the opinion of another scholar much inclined towards the "Egyptian Joseph", the Frenchman Pierre Montet. The 21st Dynasty is situated by Jürgen von Beckerath in the period 1080–946 B.C., which would, after all, be the era of David and Solomon. Yet we are still about five hundred years removed from the Hyksos period!

Whatever the question under discussion, the indications always point to phases of ancient Egyptian history later than the Hyksos period to which scholars have hitherto thought it proper to assign them. Even the pretence made by Joseph of accusing his brothers of being spies (Gen. 42⁹ and ¹⁵) has meaning only when levelled against men from Canaan, after Ashur's threat to the eastern frontier of Egypt.

And so the question remains more open today than ever whether the "Egyptian Joseph" of the Bible could be conceived as a historical personality. As things are at present, we can not accept him as the vizier of a Hyksos Pharaoh. We now have to proceed from the concept that the story about him, which reflects conditions in a later period of Ancient Egypt, comes into being very much later than many scholars have thought hitherto, unless we wish to have recourse to the idea that what is shown by direct evidence to have existed in the late period *might* naturally have existed also at an earlier time (and have been recorded exclusively in the Bible).

Chapter 9
FOUR HUNDRED YEARS' SILENCE

Reawakening on the Nile—Thebes instigates revolt—Rout of the Hyksos—Egypt becomes a world power—Indian civilisation in Mitanni—The "Sons of Heth" on the Halys—Pharaoh's widow in quest of a mate—The first non-aggression pact in the world—Hittite bridal procession through Canaan.

"And Israel dwelt in the land of Egypt in the country of Goshen: and they had possessions therein, and grew and multiplied exceedingly" (Gen. 47^{27}).

For a space of 400 years, during which, politically, the face of the "Fertile Crescent" was completely altered, the Bible is silent. In these four centuries there took place a vast rearrangement of the disposition of national groups. They interrupted the history of the Semitic kingdoms that for 1,000 years had maintained their sway on the Euphrates and the Tigris. The great island of civilisation in the Middle East was rudely dragged from its self-sufficient existence. Foreign peoples with foreign ways surged in from distant and hitherto unknown lands. For the first time it felt the clash with the outside world.

For 150 years there is also silence in Egypt. The prelude to the reawakening of the giant of the Nile opens with a remarkable motif: the roaring of hippopotami.

A papyrus fragment[1] tells how the ambassador of the Hyksos king Apophis went from Avaris to the prince of the City of the South. The City of the South was Thebes and its prince was the Egyptian Sekenenrê, who paid tribute to the foreign overlords on the upper delta. The prince in astonishment asked the emis-

[1] Papyrus Sallier I (British Museum).

97

sary of the Asiatic occupying power: "Why have you been sent to the City of the South? Why have you made this journey?" The messenger replied: "King Apophis—may he have long life, health and prosperity!—bids me say to you: Get rid of the hippopotamus pool in the east end of your city. I cannot sleep for them. Night and day the noise of them rings in my ears." The prince of the City of the South was thunderstruck because he did not know what answer to give to the ambassador of King Apophis—may he have long life, health and prosperity! At last he said: "Very well, your master—may he have long life, health and prosperity!—will hear about this pool in the east end of the City of the South." The ambassador however was not to be so easily put off. He spoke more plainly: "This matter about which I have been sent must be dealt with." The prince of the City of the South then tried in his own way to get round the determined ambassador. He was well aware of the ancient equivalent of the present day slap-up lunch as a means of creating a friendly atmosphere and goodwill. Accordingly he saw to it that the Hyksos commissioner was "supplied with good things, with meat and cakes". But his luck was out. For when the ambassador departed he had a promise from the prince in his saddle-bag, written on papyrus: "All that you have told me to do I shall do. Tell him that." Then the prince of the City of the South summoned his highest officials and his leading officers and repeated to them the message that King Apophis—may he have long life, health and prosperity!—had sent him. "Then one and all remained silent for quite a while...." At this point the papyrus text breaks off. The end of the story is unfortunately missing, but we can reconstruct the sequel from other contemporary evidence.

In the Cairo Museum lies the mummy of Sekenenrê. When it was discovered at Deir-el-Bahri near Thebes, it attracted special attention from medical men, for there were five deep sword cuts in the head. Sekenenrê had lost his life in battle.

It sounds like a fairy tale, yet it is an attractive possibility that the roaring of hippopotami at Thebes should have unseated the Hyksos rulers up in the delta. The roaring of a hippopotamus is probably the most extraordinary casus belli in world history.[1]

Beginning at Thebes the rebellion against the hated oppressors

---

[1] Apart from this literary tradition an unpublished historical text from Karnak describes the beginning of the rebellion.

spread like wildfire throughout the country. Egyptian battalions marched once more down the Nile. They were accompanied by a well-equipped fleet of galleys which headed north down the sacred river. In 1580 B.C., after years of furious attacks, Avaris, the chief fortress of the Hyksos in the delta, fell amid bloody and savage fighting. Ahmose I, son of Sekenenrê, was the glorious liberator of Egypt. A namesake of his, Ahmose, an officer in the new Royal Egyptian Navy, has left us a record of this decisive battle on the walls of his tomb at El-Kab. After a detailed description of his education he adds laconically: "Avaris was taken: I captured one man and three women, four people in all. His Majesty gave them to me as slaves."

This naval officer had also something to say about the military side of things: "Sharuhen was besieged for three years before his Majesty captured it." This was also a profitable occasion for Ahmose: "I collected two women and one labourer as my booty. I was given gold for my bravery, as well as the prisoners for my slaves."

Sharuhen was, on account of its commanding position in the Negev, an important strategic point south of the brown mountain chains of Judah. The small mound of rubble, Tell Far'a, is all that remains of it. Flinders Petrie, the famous British archaeologist, brought to light a thick wall here in 1928.

The multi-coloured army of mercenaries which the Egyptians controlled, consisting of Negroes, Asiatics, and Nubians, marched on northwards through Canaan. The new Pharaohs had learned a lesson from the bitter experience of the past. Never again would their country be taken by a surprise attack. Egypt lost no time in creating a buffer-state far in advance of its frontier posts. The remainder of the Hyksos empire was crushed and Palestine became an Egyptian province. What had once been consular stations, trading posts, and messengers' quarters in Canaan and on the Phoenician coast became permanent garrisons, fortified strong points and Egyptian fortresses in a subjugated land.

After a history of more than 2,000 years the giant of the Nile stepped out of the shadows of his Pyramids and Sphinxes and claimed the right to take an active part in affairs beyond his own border and to have some say in the outside world. Egypt matured more and more into a world-power. Previously, everyone who lived outside of the Nile valley was contemptuously described as "Asiatics", "Sandramblers", cattle-breeders—people not worthy of the attention of a Pharaoh. Now however the Egyptians

became more affable. They began communications with other
countries. Hitherto that had been unthinkable. Among the diplomatic correspondence in the archives of the palace of Mari there
is not one single item from the Nile. *Tempora mutantur*—times
change.

Their advance brought them eventually to Syria, indeed to the
banks of the Euphrates. There, to their astonishment, they came
up against people of whose existence they had no idea. The
priests searched in vain through the ancient papyrus rolls in the
temple archives, and studied without result the records of the
campaigns of earlier Pharaohs. Nowhere could they find even a
hint about the unknown kingdom of Mitanni. Its foundation is
attributed to an extremely active and creative people, the Hurrians,
named as Horites in the Bible about the time of Abraham (Gen.
14^6, etc.).

In the neighbourhood of the oil-wells of Kirkuk in Iraq, where
now derricks draw immeasurable wealth from the earth, archaeologists from U.S.A. and Iraq came across a large settlement,
the old Hurrian city of Nuzi. Stacks of tablets which have been
salvaged, and among these principally marriage contracts and
wills, contained extremely interesting information: the Biblical
Horites were not a Semitic people. Their home was among the
mountains round Lake Van. The names on many Hurrian documents indicate that at least the princely caste must be reckoned
as Indo-Aryan. It is even certain that as far as their outward
appearance was concerned they belonged to the brachycephalous
type like present day Armenians.

In the north of Mesopotamia they had built up the powerful
kingdom of Mitanni between the upper reaches of the Euphrates
and the Tigris. Their kings had collected round them an aristocracy of warlike charioteers and they bore Indo-Aryan names. The
aristocracy of the country was called Marya, which is the
equivalent of "Young Warriors". Marya is an old Indian word
and their temples were dedicated to old Indian gods. Magic
incantations from the Rigveda were intoned in front of the
images of Mithras, the victorious champion of Light against
Darkness, of Indra, who ruled the storms, and of Varuna, who
governed the eternal order of the universe. The old gods of the
Semites had crashed from their pedestals.

The Mitanni were completely devoted to their horses, they
were "horse-daft". They held the first Derbys in the world along
the banks of their great rivers. Advice on the breeding and care

of stud animals, directions for the training of cavalry horses, instructions on breaking-in young horses, regulations for feeding and training in racing stables fill veritable libraries of clay tablets. These are works on equitation which can bear comparison with any modern textbook on horse-breeding. As far as the Marya, these aristocratic charioteers, were concerned, horses were of more account than human beings.

It was with this state of Mitanni that Egypt had now a common frontier, nevertheless one on which there was to be no peace. Local feuds were unending. Raids on one side or the other constantly involved Egyptian archers in angry passages with the charioteers. In the course of these expeditions sometimes it was Egyptian striking forces, sometimes columns of Mitanni, who struck deep into the enemy's territory. The valleys of the Lebanon, the banks of the Orontes and the Euphrates were the scenes of endless battles and bloody mêlées. For almost a century the two great kingdoms were at each other's throats.

Shortly before 1400 B.C. the warlike Mitanni proposed a peaceful settlement with the Egyptians. The enemy became a friend.

What was the reason for the unexpected desire for peace on the part of the warlike Mitanni?

The impulse came from outside. Their kingdom was suddenly threatened with war on two fronts. A second powerful opponent began to storm the frontiers with his armies from Asia Minor in the north-west. This was a nation about which scholars until this century knew hardly anything, but which plays a considerable part in the Old Testament—the Hittites.

It was among the "Sons of Heth" that Abraham pitched his tent near Hebron, south of the hills of Judah, and it was from them that he bought the land where he laid his wife Sarah to rest (Gen. 23[33]). Esau, much to the distress of his parents Isaac and Rebecca, married two Hittite women (Gen. 26[34]), and King David himself took "the wife of Uriah, the Hittite" (2 Sam. 11). We are told by the prophet Ezekiel that Hittites were partly responsible for founding Jerusalem: "Thy birth and thy nativity is of the land of Canaan: thy father was an Amorite, and thy mother a Hittite" (Ezek. 16[3, 45]).

The rediscovery of the Hittite people who had sunk into complete oblivion took place in the heart of Turkey shortly after the turn of the century.

In the highlands east of Ankara, the capital, the river Halys

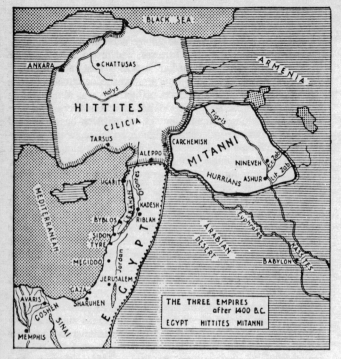

FIG. 17.

makes a huge bend on its way to the Black Sea. Almost exactly in the middle lies Boghaz-Keui: "Boghas" in Turkish means a gorge and "Keui" is a village. Near this "Village in the gorge" the German Assyriologist Professor Hugo Winckler discovered in 1905 a number of cuneiform texts, among which was also a peculiar type of hieroglyphics. They aroused tremendous interest and not only among scholars. The general public learned with amazement just what kind of people these Biblical "sons of Heth" were. The translations of the cuneiform writings brought to the notice of the world at large the hitherto unknown Indo-Germanic Hittites and their vanished empire.

Two years later a fresh expedition set out from Berlin for

Boghaz-Keui. This time it was under the direction of the President of the Archaeological Institute of Berlin, Otto Puchstein. The great pile of ruins above the village was carefully examined. This was the site of royal Chattusas, the proud capital of the Hittite empire. What remained of it was a vast ruin of walls, temples, fortified gateways—the remnants of a great city. Its walls enclosed an area of 425 acres. Chattusas was almost as big as mediaeval Nuremberg. At the city gates were life-size reliefs. It is to these effigies, carved out of black basalt as hard as iron, that we are indebted for our knowledge of the appearance of Hittite kings and warriors: their long hair hung over their shoulders like a full-bottomed wig. On top sat a high dented cap. Their short aprons were fastened with a wide belt and their shoes had pointed toes.

When Shuppiluliuma, king of the Hittites, marched south-east with a powerful army about 1370 B.C. the days of the kingdom of Mitanni were already numbered despite all their clever dynastic politics. Shuppiluliuma crushed the kingdom of the warlike charioteers, compelled it to pay tribute, and then pressed on farther to the mountains of the Lebanon in the north of Canaan. Overnight, as it were, Egypt had a new equally powerful neighbour in Syria, thirsting for victory.

A delightful document has come down to us from this period. Prince Mursilis, son of Shuppiluliuma, tells in his autobiography of an episode at the Hittite Court, which must have made such a lasting impression on him that he had it recorded.

Anches-en-Amun, the wife of Pharaoh Tutankhamun, had become a widow. She had very famous parents, Akhnaten and Nofretete. We know her from wonderful Egyptian representations as a slight young thing. But she must have been a woman who knew what she wanted and used all her natural charm to further the aims of her people in the realm of high politics. Using the inviting bed and throne of the Pharaohs as a bait—and what an attractive one—she tried to take the wind out of the sails of her powerful new neighbours by discouraging their warlike intentions. Hittite warriors had just made an attack on Amqa, the fertile country between Lebanon and Anti-Lebanon.

Mursilis dictated: ''When the Egyptians heard of the attack on Amqa they were alarmed. To make matters worse, her husband, Tutankhamun, having just died, his widow, the Egyptian queen, sent an ambassador to my father and wrote him the following letter: 'My husband is dead and I have no son. I am told that you have many sons. If you send me one of your sons he could become my husband. I do not wish to take one of my servants and make a husband of him.' When my father heard this he summoned his nobles to a council and said: 'I have never in all my life come across anything like this.' He despatched his chamberlain Hattu-Zitis: 'Go and find out if this is true. Perhaps they are trying to deceive me. There may in fact be a prince. Bring me back reliable information.' The Egyptian ambassador, the honourable Hanis, came to my father. Since my father had instructed Hattu-Zitis before he left for Egypt: 'Perhaps they have a prince of their own: They may be trying to deceive us. They may not need one of my sons at all to occupy the throne', the queen of Egypt now replied to my father in a letter: 'Why do you say, they may be trying to deceive me? If I had a son would I write to a foreign country in a manner that is humiliating both for me and my people? You do not trust me, otherwise you would not say such a thing. He who was my husband is dead and I have no sons. Am I to take one of my servants and make him into my husband? I have written to no other country, I have only written to you. They tell me you have so many sons. Give me one of your sons and he shall be my husband and king over the land of Egypt.' Since my father was so fine a king, he complied with the lady's request and sent her the son she asked for.''

Fate prevented the successful conclusion of this unusual offer of marriage. The royal throne and the bed of Anches-en-Amun both remained empty, since the candidate for both was murdered on his way to Egypt.

Seventy-five years later another offer of marriage on this same Halys-Nile axis had a happy ending, although the prelude to it, which was the din of battle and the clash of weapons, pointed to a different conclusion. Ramesses II, who was called the "Great", set out with his army for Palestine and Syria. He intended to deal with the hated Hittites once and for all.

In the valley of the Orontes, where today fields of cotton stretch far and wide and the old Crusader castle "Krak des Chevaliers" keeps an eye on the fertile plain of Bukea, there lay in those days the city of Kadesh, a little to the south of the dark green of Lake Homs. Before its walls four Egyptian armies threw themselves on the swift war-chariots and infantry of the Hittites. The battle did not, as it happened, bring Ramesses II the victory he had hoped for—he came in fact within an ace of being captured himself—but it put an end to these endless military incidents. In 1280 B.C. the Hittites and the Egyptians concluded the first non-aggression and mutual defence pact in world history. The good understanding was cemented at top level by the marriage of Ramesses II to a Hittite princess. Many lengthy inscriptions give in full and vivid detail the colourful background of what was in the circumstances an international event of the first order. Whether they are found on the walls of the temples at Karnak, Elephantine or Abu Simbel, or on the numerous monuments, they all tell the same story.

As far as self-advertisement and self-praise were concerned, Ramesses II put all his predecessors in the shade. "Then came a messenger to inform His Majesty. He said: 'Behold, even the great Prince of Hatti! Prince of the Hittites. His eldest daughter is on her way and she brings untold tribute of all kinds. . . . They have reached His Majesty's frontiers. Let the army and the dignitaries come to receive her! Then His Majesty was greatly delighted, and the palace was glad to hear these unusual tidings which were quite unheard of in Egypt. He therefore sent forth the army and the dignitaries to receive her."

A large delegation was despatched to the north of Palestine to bring back the bride. Yesterday's enemies became brothers: "So the daughter of the great Prince of Hatti came to Egypt. Whilst the infantry, charioteers and dignitaries of His Majesty accompanied them, they mingled with the infantry and charioteers from Hatti. The whole populace from the country of the Hittites was mixed up with the Egyptians. They ate and drank together, they were like blood-brothers. . . ."

The great bridal train proceeded from Palestine to the city of Per-Ramesses-Meri-Imen in the Nile delta: "Then they brought the daughter of the Great Prince of Hatti . . . before His Majesty. And His Majesty saw that she was fair of countenance like a goddess. . . . And he loved her more than anything else. . . ."

Any of the children of Israel, of their ancestors who were in Egypt at that time, could have been eye-witnesses of the ceremonial arrival of the bridal procession in the city of Per-Ramesses-Meri-Imen, which means "The House of Ramses the Beloved of Amun". As the Biblical description indicates however their presence in this city was by no means of their own accord. It is at this point also that the Bible resumes its narrative. Four hundred years which the Children of Israel had spent as immigrants in the land of the Nile have been passed over in silence. A new and significant chapter of the history of the Biblical people now begins.

To assert that the Bible remains silent concerning a period of four hundred years is correct only if the period of the patriarchs really occurred between 2000 B.C. and approximately 1800 B.C. It is precisely this, however, which recent discoveries have already obliged us to express doubts about. For example, if the legal practices of the Biblical "patriarchs" were to correspond so very exactly to those of the Hurrian town of Nuzi in Mitanni, as we noted in Book I, Chapter 5, the beginning of the patriarchal period at around 1900 B.C. becomes extraordinarily problematical.

The places, too, where the Bible speaks of Hittites appear to consign Abraham and consequently all the Biblical "patriarchs" as well to a later period. Allegedly Abraham acquired the burial-place in Hebron of his wife Sarah from Hittites (Gen. 23^{1ff}).

It is a fact that the negotiations for the sale, which are described in detail in the Bible, become clear to us today only by comparison with Hittite documents. Obviously Abraham wanted nothing but the cave and not the whole plot. Hittite documents tell us why. In accordance with Hittite customs, the plot would otherwise have been free for utilisation by the previous owner! In the end, however, agreement was reached and Abraham took not only the cave but also the field and all the trees. This, too, reminds us of Hittite documents dealing with such transactions which always state with scrupulous exactness the number of trees! This is undoubtedly another example of the surprising confirmation of details found in the Bible.

And yet we must ask what Hittites these were with whom Abraham was negotiating. Where did they come from if Abraham, as is alleged, lived at such an early date that the Hittite Empire, which according to Hittite sources was not founded until about the sixteenth century B.C., was not even in existence? And how did Hittites get to Hebron? In other words, to Southern Palestine, between the Dead Sea and the Mediterranean, and, what is more, how does it come about that the Bible (Gen. 23^7) refers to them as "the people of the land", although the southern border of the

Hittite Empire at the time of its greatest extension ran very much farther to the north, somewhat south of the modern town of Aleppo, at any rate "right up on the edge" of the maps of Palestine in current use today? And nothing else is known about any further advance southwards by Hittite settlers.

The Hittite Uriah, whom King David first cuckolded and then sent to his death (2 Sam. 11) perhaps came from one of the small early or late Hittite lands which continued to exist in Northern Syria even after the collapse of the Hittite Empire around 1200 B.C. When the Hittites are mentioned as the founders or co-founders of Jerusalem, however, this is perhaps one of those Biblical statements, according to which the "children of Heth" must have been more probably a Canaanite mountain tribe (cf. Numbers 13[29-30]). "The Amalekites dwell in the land of the south; and the *Hittites,* and the Jebusites (i.e., the original inhabitants of Jerusalem) and the Amorites dwell in the mountains; and the Canaanites dwell by the sea, and by the coast of Jordan." These inhabitants of Canaan cannot have had much to do with the Indo-European Hittites of history.

One thing is certain. The problems raised by the references to the Hittites in the Bible have not been cleared up by the discovery of the Hittite Empire in Asia Minor. On the contrary, we now have two categories of Hittites, those in the Bible and the others whose presence in Asia Minor has been proved by archaeology. The statements about the two kinds do not coincide in all respects. The difficulties have not been removed, they are just beginning! It is only the future, as we now know, that can show whether the Bible is correct in what it has to say about the Hittites.

It is necessary to add a "late news item" regarding the Hittites. Mention has already been made of the young widow of a Pharaoh who requested the Hittite King Shuppiluliuma to send her one of his sons to be her husband. Until quite recently indeed the conviction was general that this must refer to Anches-en-Amun, the widow of Tutankhamun. It is only recently that a dissenting view has been expressed, which is not yet accepted by all but appears nevertheless to be well founded, to the effect that the petitioner was not Anches-en-Amun but her elder sister Meritaton who after the death, or was it the repudiation, of her mother Nofretete, was made queen and was perhaps the last wife of her own father, Akhnaten. This deduction has been made because of the connection between the request for a bridegroom and the Egyptian-Hittite war, which took place in the time of Akhnaten and not of Tutankhamun.

Chapter 10
FORCED LABOUR IN PITHOM
AND RAAMSES

Joseph had died a long time ago—A story in pictures from a prince's tomb—Pithom labour camp in Egyptian texts—The royal seat is transferred to the delta—Ramesses II—A builder's enthusiasm and vanity lead to a fraud—Montet unearths the bond-city of Raamses—Moses wrote his name "MS"—A Mesopotamian story about a baby in the bulrushes—Moses emigrates to Midian—Plagues are no strangers to Egypt.

"Now there arose up a new king over Egypt, which knew not Joseph. Therefore they did set over them taskmasters, to afflict them with their burdens. And they built for Pharaoh treasure-cities [R. V. Store-cities], Pithom and Raamses" (Ex. 1⁸⁻¹¹).

The new king who "knew not Joseph" was most likely Ramesses II or one of his predecessors. His ignorance is understandable if Joseph lived centuries before him in the days of the Hyksos. The names of these Hyksos rulers who were so cordially detested by Egyptians have hardly been recorded, far less the names of their dignitaries and officials. Even if this pharaoh of the new dynasty, whether it was Ramesses II or a predecessor, had known of Joseph, that is as far as he would have wanted it to go. Joseph was bound to be an object of contempt to any nationally conscious Egyptian for two reasons. One, that he was an "Asiatic" and a miserable "Sandrambler", and, two, that he was the highest official of the hated occupying power. From the latter point of view any appeal to Joseph would hardly have been a recommendation for Israel in the eyes of a pharaoh.

What forced labour meant in ancient Egypt, and what the Children of Israel experienced at the great building projects on the Nile, can be gathered from a very old painting that Percy A. Newberry, the discoverer of the portrayal of the people who comprise the caravan at Beni-Hasan, found in a rock tomb west of the royal city of Thebes.

On the walls of a spacious vault there is a series of paintings from the life of a great dignitary, the vizier Rekhmirê, showing what he had done for the benefit of his country. One scene shows him in charge of public works. The detail shows the manufacture of Egyptian bricks, the most notable feature being the light-skinned workmen, who are clad only in linen aprons. A comparison with the dark-skinned overseers shows that the fair-skinned men are probably Semites, but certainly not Egyptians. "He provides us with bread, beer and every good thing." Yet despite these words of praise about the quality of the diet, there is no doubt about the fact that they are not working voluntarily but compulsorily. "The rod is in my hand," one of the Egyptian overseers is saying, according to the hieroglyphic inscription. "Be not idle."

FIG. 18.—Bricklaying with foreign labour in Egypt.

The picture is an impressive illustration of the Biblical words: "And the Egyptians made the children of Israel to serve with rigour, and they made their lives bitter with hard bondage in mortar and in bricks" (Ex. $1^{13,14}$). Israel was of shepherd stock, unused to work of any other kind, which was therefore twice as hard for them. Building and brick making were forced labour.

The painting in the rock-tomb shows a scene from the building of the Temple of Amun in Thebes. The "classical" bond-cities of the children of Israel were however Pithom and Raamses. Both names appear in slightly different form in Egyptian inventories. "Per-Itum", "House of the god Atum", is the name of a town which does not date back further than the time of Ramesses II. Per-Ramesses-Meri-Imen, which has already been mentioned, is the Biblical Raamses. An inscription of the time of Ramesses II speaks of "'PR", "who hauled the stones for the great fortress of the city of Per-Ramesses-Meri-Imen". "'Pr" is Egyptian hieroglyphics for Semites.

The question of where these bond-cities were situated remained a problem. It was known that the rulers of the New Kingdom had moved their seat from ancient Thebes northward to Avaris, which was the place from which the Hyksos had also ruled the country. The new type of international power-politics made it seem advisable to be nearer the centre of things than was the case with Thebes, which lay much farther south. From the delta they could much more easily keep an eye on turbulent "Asia", their dominions in Canaan and Syria. Pharaoh Ramesses II gave his name to the new capital. Avaris became the city of Per-Ramesses-Meri-Imen.

After a fair amount of guesswork and supposition archaeologists' picks put an end to all differences of opinion about the site of one of the bond-cities. Anyone who goes to Egypt can include a trip round its ruins in his programme. It is 60 miles by car from Cairo. About half way down the Suez Canal, where it goes through what was the Lake of Crocodiles,[1] a dried up watercourse known as Wadi Tumilat stretches westward till it strikes the easternmost arm of the Nile. There two mounds of rubble lie about 9 miles apart. One is Tell er-Retabe, which was perhaps the Biblical Pithom, the other is Tell el-Maskhuta, which many scholars consider to be Pithom, whereas others consider it to be the Biblical Succoth (Ex. 12³⁷; 13²⁰). Apart from remains of granaries, inscriptions have also been found which refer to storehouses.

If there had been patent laws 4,000 years ago, the Egyptians could have claimed exclusive rights over granaries. The silos on Canadian and American wheat farms are still built on the same principle. Admittedly Egyptian silos did not reach the same gigantic proportions, but granaries, circular buildings about 25 feet in diameter with ramps leading up to the feeder, were not uncommon on the Nile. As grand vizier Joseph built granaries (Gen. 41⁴⁸ᶠᶠ) and as slave labourers his descendants built granaries in the land of Goshen.

[1] Lake Timsah.

FIG. 19.—Corn silos in Egypt.

The search for the other bond-city, Raamses,[1] went on for a long time without success. Then nearly thirty years after the discovery of Pithom it was eventually found in 1930.

Ramesses II, the "Great", has given the archaeologists many a hard nut to crack. Apparently his vanity was even greater than his passion for building. He never hesitated to deck himself in borrowed plumes: posterity would marvel at the great builder Ramesses II! And indeed it did. The experts could hardly grasp at first how it came about that on so many temples, public buildings and in other places they came upon the cipher "Ramesses II". But when they examined the buildings a little more closely the explanation was plain. Many of these buildings must have been built centuries before Ramesses II. To pander to his own vanity however Ramesses II decided to have his monogram carved on them all.

In the delta the search for the city of Per-Ramesses-Meri-Imen led from one mound to another. One excavated site after another, throughout the Nile delta, was thought to be the one they were looking for: Pithom, Heliopolis, Pelusium and others. Guesswork came to an end only when the spade of Professor Pierre Montet of Strasbourg struck the ground near the present day fishing village of San in 1929. Thirty miles south-west of Port Said, Montet unearthed between 1929 and 1932 an unusual number of statues, sphinxes, columns, and fragments of buildings, all of them stamped with the crest of Ramesses II. This time there was scarcely any doubt that it was the remains of Per-Ramesses-Meri-Imen, the Biblical bond-city of Raamses.

[1] Per-Ramesses-Meri-Imen, probably the earlier Tanis/Avaris or Qantir, eleven miles to the south.

Just as in Pithom they found here ruins of granaries and store-houses.

The Israelites became the victims, in the truest sense of the word, of Pharaoh's lust for building. The position of their immigration area made it easier for them to be dragooned into forced labour. The Goshen of the Bible with its rich grazings began just a few miles south of the new capital and went as far as Pithom. Nothing could be simpler than to drag these foreigners who lived, so to speak, on the doorstep of these great building projects, away from their flocks and tents and force them into servitude.

The ruins at San no longer give any indication of the splendour of the former metropolis. What the columns of Israelite levies saw on their daily march to the building sites we can only gather from a contemporary papyrus letter. It is written by a schoolboy Pai-Bes to his teacher Amen-em-Opet: "I have come to Per-Ramesses of the Beloved of Amun and find it wonderful. A splendid city without a rival. Rê, the same god who founded Thebes, founded this according to the same plan. To live here is to have a glorious life. The countryside provides a wealth of good things. Every day they get fresh provisions and meat. Their pools are full of fish, their lagoons are thick with birds, their meadows are covered with green grass, the fruit from their well tilled fields has the taste of honey. Their storehouses are full of barley and corn and tower up to the sky. There are onions and chives to season the food, also pomegranates, apples, olives and figs from the orchards. Sweet wine from Kenkeme, which tastes nicer than honey. The Shi-Hor branch of the Nile produces salt and saltpetre. Their ships come and go. Everyday here there are fresh victuals and meat. People are glad to be able to live there and nobody cries: God help me! Simple folk live like great folk. Come! Let us celebrate there the festivals of heaven and the beginning of the seasons."

Years later life in the barren wilderness had blotted out the recollection of their forced labour from the minds of the children of Israel. All they remembered was the plentiful food of the delta: "Would to God we had died by the hand of the Lord in the land of Egypt, when we sat by the flesh pots and when we did eat bread to the full" (Ex. 16³). "Who shall give us flesh to eat? We remember the fish which we did eat in Egypt freely: the cucumbers, and the melons, and the leeks, and the onions and the garlic." "Who shall give us flesh to eat for it was well with us in Egypt" (Num. 11$^{4-5,18}$).

Discoveries during excavations, and contemporary texts, sometimes providing almost literal correspondence, confirm the Biblical picture. We must not think however that the academic dispute over the historicity of these events in the life of Israel is thereby settled.

Professor William Foxwell Albright of America has some sharp words to say on this subject. Since he is one of the few scholars with almost universal qualifications—as theologian, historian, philosopher, orientalist, archaeologist, and comparative philologist—they may well be cited as conclusive. "According to our present knowledge of the topography of the eastern delta the account of the start of the Exodus, which is given in Ex. 12^{37} and Ex. 13^{20}, is topographically absolutely correct." Further proofs of the essentially historical nature of the Exodus story and of the journey in the area of Sinai, Midian and Kadesh can be supplied without great difficulty thanks to our growing knowledge of topography and archaeology.

We must content ourselves here with the assurance that the hypercritical attitude which previously obtained in respect of the earlier historical traditions of Israel has no longer any justification. Even the long-disputed date of the Exodus can now be fixed within reasonable limits. . . . If we put it at about 1290 B.C. we cannot go far wrong, since the first years of the reign of Ramesses II (1301–1234) were to a large extent occupied with building activities in the city to which he has given his name— the Raamses of Israelite tradition. The striking correspondence between this date and the length of their stay given by Ex. 12^{40} as 430 years—"Now the sojourning of the children of Israel, who dwelt in Egypt, was 430 years" (Ex. 12^{40})—may be purely coincidental but it is very remarkable. According to this the migration must have taken place about 1720 B.C.

The reign of Ramesses II is the time of the oppression and forced labour of Israel, but also the time at which Moses the great liberator of his people appears.

> "And it came to pass in those days, when Moses was grown, that he went out unto his brethren, and looked on their burdens: and he spied an Egyptian smiting an Hebrew, one of his brethren. And he looked this way and that way, and, when he saw that there was no man he slew the

Egyptian and hid him in the sand. Now when Pharaoh heard this thing, he sought to slay Moses. But Moses fled from the face of Pharaoh, and dwelt in the land of Midian: and he sat down by a well'' (Ex. $2^{11,12,15}$).

Moses is a Hebrew who was born in Egypt, brought up by Egyptians, whose name can be connected with a Semitic root meaning "bring or take out, remove, extract", but can also be interpreted as Egyptian. "Moses" means simply "boy, son". A number of Pharaohs are called Ahmose, Amasis, Thutmose. And Thutmose was the name of the famous sculptor, among whose masterpieces the incomparably beautiful head of Nofretete is still the admiration of the world.

These are the facts. Egyptologists know that. But the general public picks on the famous Biblical story of Moses in the bulrushes, and it is not difficult for the eternal sceptic to produce it as an apparently valid argument against the credibility of Moses himself. "It is simply the birth-legend of Sargon"—they say. But they add mentally: "Plagiarism".

Cuneiform texts have this to say of King Sargon, the founder of the Semitic dynasty of Akkad in 2360 B.C.: "I am Sargon, the powerful king, the king of Akkad. My mother was an Enitu priestess, I did not know any father. . . . My mother conceived me and bore me in secret. She put me in a little box made of reeds, sealing its lid with pitch. She put me in the river. . . . The river carried me away and brought me to Akki the drawer of water. Akki the drawer of water adopted me and brought me up as his son. . . ."

The similarity with the Biblical story of Moses is in fact astounding: "And when she could no longer hide him, she took for him an ark of bulrushes, and daubed it with slime and with pitch and put the child therein: and she laid it in the flags by the river's brink" (Ex. 2^{3ff}).

The basket-story is a very old Semitic folk-tale. It was handed down by word of mouth for many centuries. The Sargon legend of the third millennium B.C. is found on Neo-Babylonian cuneiform tablets of the first millennium B.C. It is nothing more than the frills with which posterity has always loved to adorn the lives of great men. Who would dream of doubting the historicity of the Emperor Barbarossa, simply because he is said to be still sleeping under Kyffhäuser?

Officials everywhere and all the time enjoy the protection of

the state. So it was in the time of the Pharaohs. So it is today. It
was for this reason that Moses had no choice but to flee from
certain punishment after he had in righteous indignation killed
the guard in charge of the labour gangs.

Moses does what Sinuhe had done before him. He flees
eastward to get out of Egyptian territory. Since Canaan is
occupied by Egypt, Moses chooses for his exile the mountains of
Midian east of the Gulf of Aqabah, with which he had a remote
connection. Ketura had been Abraham's second wife, after
Sarah's death (Gen. 25[1]). One of her sons was called Midian.
The tribe of Midian is often called Kenites in the Old Testament
(Num. 24[21]). The name means "belonging to the copper-
smiths"—Qain in Arabic, Qaināya in Aramaic = a smith. This
designation connects up with the presence of metal in the
neighbourhood of the tribal territory. The mountain ranges east
of the Gulf of Aqabah are rich in copper, as the investigations of
Nelson Glueck of America have indicated.

No country will willingly part with a cheap supply of forced
foreign labour. Israel had to learn that too. Eventually we are
told that it was the occurrence of plagues that compelled the
Egyptians to give way. Whether they raged exactly at the time of
Moses can so far neither be affirmed nor denied since no
contemporary evidence on the subject has so far been found. But
plagues are neither improbable nor unusual. Indeed they are part
of Egypt's local colour. The water of the Nile "was turned to
blood". "And the frogs came up and covered the land of
Egypt." "Flies" appear, "lice", a "cattle murrain" and "boils"—
finally "hail", "locusts" and "darkness" (Ex. 7–10). These
things which the Bible describes are still experienced by the
Egyptians, as, for example, the "red Nile".

Deposits from the Abyssinian lakes often colour the flood
waters a dark reddish-brown, especially in the Upper Nile. That
might well be said to look like "blood".—At the time of the
floods "frogs" and also "flies" sometimes multiply so rapidly
that they become regular plagues on the land.—Under the
heading of "lice" would come undoubtedly the dog-fly. These
often attack whole areas in swarms, affect eyes, nose and ears,
and can be very painful.

Cattle pest is known all over the world.—The "boils" which
attack human beings as well as animals may be the so-called
"Nile-heat" or "Nile-itch". This is an irritating and stinging
rash which often develops into spreading ulcers. This horrible

skin disease is also used as a threatened punishment by Moses in the course of the journey through the desert: "The Lord will smite thee with the botch of Egypt, and with the emerods and with the scab and with the itch whereof thou canst not be healed" (Deut. 28[27]).

"Hailstorms" are extremely rare on the Nile, but they are not unknown. The season for them is January or February.— "Swarms of locusts" on the other hand are a typical and disastrous phenomenon in the countries of the Orient.—The same is true of sudden "darkness". The Khamsin, also called the Simoon, is a blistering hot wind which whirls up vast masses of sand and drives them before it. They obscure the sun, give it a dull yellowish appearance and turn daylight into darkness.—Only the death of the "first-born" is a plague for which there is no parallel (Ex. 12) and the statement in the Bible that the plague of "darkness in all the land of Egypt" affected only the Egyptians, but not the Israelites living in Egypt, is, of course, incapable of any scientific explanation. . . .

Forty Years in the Wilderness from the Nile to the Jordan

Chapter 11
ON THE ROAD TO SINAI

Departure from Raamses—Two possible sites for the "Miracle of the Sea" —Traces of fords beside the Suez Canal—Three days without water—Swarms of quails at the migration season—An expedition clears up the mystery of manna—Egyptian mining centre in Sinai—The alphabet at the Temple of Hathor.

"And the children of Israel journeyed from Rameses to Succoth (Ex. 12[37]). But God led the people about through the way of the wilderness of the Red Sea (Ex. 13[18]). And they took their journey from Succoth and encamped in Etham, in the edge of the wilderness (Ex. 13[20]). But the Egyptians pursued after them, all the horses and chariots of Pharaoh, and his horsemen and his army, and overtook them encamping by the sea, beside Pi-Hahiroth before Baal-Zephon" (Ex. 14[9]).

The first section of the route followed by the fugitives can easily be followed on the map. It is expressly noted that they did not travel in the direction of the "Way of the Land of Philistines" (Ex. 13[17]), which was the A1 route from Egypt to Asia via Palestine. This main highway for caravans and military expeditions ran almost parallel with the Mediterranean coast and was the shortest and best route, but the one which was most closely guarded. An army of soldiers and officials in the frontier posts kept a sharp watch on all traffic in both directions.

The main road was too risky. The Israelites therefore head southwards. From Per-Ramesses on the eastern branch of the delta the first stage is Succoth in Wadi Tumilat. After Etham the next stage is Pi-Hahiroth. According to the Bible this place lay "between Migdol and the sea, over against Baal-Zephon" (Ex. 14²). "Miktol" appears also in Egyptian texts; it means a "tower". A fort which stood there guarded the caravan route to the Sinai area. All that remains of it has been excavated at Abu Hasan, 15 miles north of Suez.

"And Moses stretched out his hand over the sea: and the Lord caused the sea to go back by a strong east wind all that night and made the sea dry land, and the waters were divided. And the children of Israel went into the midst of the sea upon the dry ground: and the waters were a wall unto them on their right hand and on their left" (Ex. 14²¹⁻²²).

. . . a detachment of Egyptian chariots, which was attempting to recapture the Israelites, was swallowed up by the sea, the horses and their riders were drowned.

This "Miracle of the Sea" has perpetually exercised men's minds. The difficulty which faced science and research for a long time was not to shed light on the escape itself, for which there were several real possibilities. The only dispute was about the scene of the event, and on this point it is barely possible even yet to get a clear picture.

The first difficulty is one of translation. The Hebrew words "Yam Suph" are sometimes translated as the "Red Sea", at other times as the "Reed Sea". The "Reed Sea" is frequently mentioned: "For we have heard how the Eternal dried up the water of the Reed Sea before you when you left Egypt" (Josh. 2¹⁰: Moffatt's Translation). In the Old Testament up to Jeremiah it is called the "Reed Sea". The New Testament speaks only of the "Red Sea" (Acts 7³⁶; Hebrews 11²⁹).[1]

On the shores of the Red Sea there are no reeds. The Reed Sea proper lay farther north. A reliable reconstruction of the situation that existed then is hardly possible, and that is the second difficulty. The building of the Suez Canal last century has altered the appearance of the landscape to an extraordinary degree. According to those calculations which seem to have most proba-

---

[1] Translator's Note: The German Bible uses two expressions: Ried-Meer = Reed Sea and Rotes Meer = Red Sea. The English Bible makes no distinction and uses "Red Sea" throughout. The Hebrew words Yam Suph mean Reed Sea or Papyrus Marsh as modern translations recognise.

bility, the so called "Miracle of the Sea" must have taken place
in that area. What was once Lake Balah, for example, which lay
south of the "Way of the Land of the Philistines", disappeared
when the canal was constructed and became marshland. In the
time of Ramesses II the Gulf of Suez, in the south, was
connected to the Bitter Lakes. Probably the connection extended
up to Lake Timsah, the Lake of Crocodiles. In this area there
was at one time a Sea of Reeds. The waterway to the Bitter
Lakes could be forded at several points. Fords can actually be
traced there. The flight from Egypt by way of the Sea of Reeds is
therefore perfectly credible.

In early Christian times pilgrims surmised that the flight of
Israel led them through the Red Sea. At that time they thought in
terms of the northern end of the Gulf near the town of Es-Suwez,
present-day Suez. The crossing could have taken place here too.
Occasionally strong north-west winds drive the water at the
northern extremity of the Gulf back so far that it is possible to
wade across. In Egypt the prevailing wind is from the west. The
east wind mentioned in the Bible is on the other hand typical of
Palestine.

"So Moses brought Israel from the Red Sea: and they
went out into the wilderness of Shur: and they went three
days in the wilderness and found no water. And when they
came to Marah they could not drink of the waters of Marah,
for they were bitter" (Ex. 15²²⁻²³).

"And they came to Elim where were twelve wells of
water and three-score and ten palm trees" (Ex. 15²⁷).

"And they took their journey from Elim and all the
congregation of the children of Israel came unto the wilderness of Sin, which is between Elim and Sinai. . . ." (Ex.
16¹).

The laborious journey began—a nomadic existence in a barren
scrub land that was to last for forty years.

With donkeys, goats and sheep only short stretches of about
12 miles a day could be covered. The goal each day was
invariably the next water-hole.

Forty long years the children of Israel wandered round the
edge of the desert from well to well, from water-hole to water-
hole. From the stopping places which the Bible mentions the
most important stages of the journey can be marked out.

The route is realistically and convincingly described in Numbers ch. 33. As we should expect with a mixed company of human beings and animals, they never moved far from the oases and pastures of the Sinai peninsula and the Negev.

From the Nile to the mountains of the Sinai peninsula stretches an ancient beaten track. It was the road followed by the countless labour gangs and slave gangs who had been digging for copper and turquoise in the Sinai mountains since 3000 B.C. More than once in the course of these millennia the mines had been forsaken and lapsed for centuries into oblivion. Ramesses II remembered the treasure that was lying dormant and started up the mines once more.

It was along this road to the mines that Moses led his people. It begins at Memphis, crosses the top of the Gulf, at what is now Suez, and then bends south along a waterless stretch of 45 miles, without a single oasis or spring. The Bible expressly mentions that at the beginning of their journey they wandered for three days in the desert without water, then came to a well of undrinkable water, after which they soon reached a particularly rich oasis with "twelve wells and seventy palm trees". This very exact Biblical description helped the experts to find the historical route of the Exodus.

A 45-mile trek with herds of cattle and a large contingent of people would take three days. Nomads can cope with the problem of thirst for a period of this length. They have always their "iron rations" for such an emergency, water in goatskin containers, like the patriarchal family in the mural painting at Beni-Hasan. Forty-five miles from the northern tip of the Red Sea there is still a spring called "Ain Hawarah" by the Bedouins. Nomads are very reluctant to stop here with their cattle. The water is not inviting for a long stay. It is salty and sulphurous, or "bitter" as the Bible calls it. This is Marah of olden times.

Fifteen miles farther on to the south, exactly a day's march, lies Wadi Gharandel. A fine oasis with shady palms and plenty of water-holes. That is the Biblical Elim, the second stopping place. After Elim begins the Wilderness of Sin, on the shore of the Red Sea, now known as the Plain of El Kaa. The children of Israel have come no great distance, but they are untrained and unused to privation after what was despite its rigours a well fed and well ordered life in Egypt. It is no wonder that they gave tongue to their disappointment and complaints. However they were able to augment their scanty diet with two unexpected but most welcome items.

> "And it came to pass that at even the quails came up and covered the camp: and in the morning . . . when the dew that lay was gone up, behold upon the face of the wilderness there lay a small round thing, as small as the hoar frost on the ground. And when the children of Israel saw it, they said one to another, it is manna [i.e., What is this?], for they wist not what it was. And Moses said unto them, This is the bread which the Lord hath given you to eat" (Ex. 16[13-15]).

Time and again more or less profound discussions have taken place over this question of the quails and the manna. What a vast amount of disbelief they have occasioned. The Bible is telling us about things that are miraculous and inexplicable! On the contrary quails and manna are perfectly matter of fact occurrences. We need only ask a naturalist or natives of these parts who can see the same thing happening today.

The Exodus of the Israelites began in the spring, the time of the great bird migrations. From Africa, which in summer becomes unbearably hot and dry, the birds have from time immemorial migrated to Europe along two routes. One route goes via the west coast of Africa to Spain, the other via the Eastern Mediterranean to the Balkans. In the early months of the year, quails, together with other birds, fly across the Red Sea, which they must cross on the eastern route. Exhausted by their long flight, they alight on its flat shores to gather fresh strength for the next stage of their journey over the high mountains to the Mediterranean. Josephus (*Antiquities,* III, 1, 5) describes an experience of this kind, and even today the Bedouins of this area catch the exhausted quails in spring and autumn by hand.

As far as the famous manna is concerned, we have reliable information from the botanist. To anticipate: anyone who is interested in manna will find it on the list of exports from the Sinai peninsula. Further, its supplier is registered in every botanical index of the Middle East, it is the Tamarix Mannifera, Ehr.

There is no lack of fully authenticated descriptions of its occurrence. The following eye-witness account is almost five hundred years old.

FIG. 20.—Catching quails on the Nile.

"In every valley throughout the whole region of Mt. Sinai there can still be found Bread of Heaven, which the monks and the Arabs gather, preserve and sell to pilgrims and strangers who pass that way." These words were written in 1483 by Breitenbach, Dean of Mainz, in an account of his pilgrimage to Sinai. "This same Bread of Heaven", he continues, "falls about daybreak like dew or hoarfrost and hangs in beads on grass, stones, and twigs. It is sweet like honey and sticks to the teeth. We bought a lot of it."

In 1823 the German botanist G. Ehrenberg published a paper[1] which even his colleagues received with incredulity. His explanation seemed indeed to ask people to believe too much, namely that this notorious manna is nothing more than a secretion exuded by tamarisk trees and bushes when they are pierced by a certain type of plant-louse which is found in Sinai.

A hundred years later an organised manna expedition was under way. Friedrich Simon Bodenheimer and Oskar Theodor, botanical experts from the Hebrew University at Jerusalem, set out for the Sinai Peninsula, to clear up the disputed question of the existence of manna once and for all. For several months the two scientists investigated the dry water-courses and oases in the whole area of Mt. Sinai. Their report caused a sensation. They not only brought back the first photographs of manna and fully

[1] "Symbolae Physicae".

confirmed the findings of Breitenbach and Ehrenberg, but also established the factual truth of the Biblical description of the desert migration of the people of Israel.

Without the plant-louse mentioned first by Ehrenberg there would in fact be no manna at all. These little insects live primarily off tamarisks which are a type of tree indigenous to Sinai. They exude a peculiar resinous secretion, which according to Bodenheimer is about the same shape and size as a coriander seed. When it falls to the ground it is white in colour, but after lying for some time it becomes yellowish-brown. Naturally the two scientists did not fail to taste the manna. Bodenheimer's verdict was: "The taste of these crystallised grains of manna is peculiarly sweet. It is most of all like honey when it has been left for a long time to solidify." "And it was like coriander seed, white: and the taste of it was like wafers made with honey", says the Bible (Ex. 16³¹).

The findings of the expedition likewise confirmed the other features of the Biblical description of manna. "And they gathered it every morning, every man according to his eating: and when the sun waxed hot, it melted" (Ex. 16²¹). Exactly in the same way today the Bedouins of the Sinai peninsula hasten to gather up their "Mann es-Samâ", the "Manna from Heaven", as early as possible in the morning, for the ants are keen competitors. "They begin gathering when the ground temperature reaches 21 degrees centigrade," says the report of the expedition, "which is about 8:30 a.m. Until then the insects are inert." As soon as the ants become lively, the manna disappears. That must have been what the Biblical narrator meant when he said that it melted. The Bedouins prudently do not forget to seal the manna they have collected carefully in a pot, otherwise the ants pounce on it. It was just the same in Moses' day during the sojourn in the desert: "But some of them left of it until the morning: and it bred worms. . . ." (Ex. 16²⁰).

The incidence of the manna depends on favourable winter rains and is different from year to year. In good years the Bedouins of Sinai can collect 4 pounds per head in a morning —a considerable quantity which is quite sufficient to satisfy a grown man. Thus Moses was able to order the children of Israel to "gather of it every man according to his eating" (Ex. 16¹⁶).

The Bedouins knead the globules of manna into a purée which they consume as a welcome and nourishing addition to their often monotonous diet. Manna is indeed an exportable commodity, and if it is carefully preserved, forms an ideal "iron ration" since it keeps indefinitely.—"And Moses said unto Aaron: Take a pot and put an omer full of manna therein, and lay it up before the Lord, to be kept for your generations" (Ex. 16^{33}).

"And the children of Israel did eat manna forty years, until they came to a land inhabited: they did eat manna until they came unto the borders of the land of Canaan" (Ex. 16^{35}). Tamarisks with manna still grow in Sinai and along the Wadi el-Arabah right up to the Dead Sea.

So far we have listened to science. But the question that has to be asked is whether we have not at this point crossed the frontiers of science and entered the territory of the unknown, the sphere of the miraculous? For it is clear beyond all possible doubt that the Bible does not intend us to think of this as something that happened in the normal course of events but as an act of God. The same thing is true of the quails.

"And they took their journey out of the wilderness of Sin, and encamped in Dophkah" (Num. 33^{12}).

Several hundred metres above the waters of the Red Sea lies the monotonous expanse of the Wilderness of Sin. On this torrid plateau the only things that break the bright yellow flatness of the sand are camel-thorns and sparse brushwood. Not a breath of wind or a breeze fans the traveller's brow. Anyone following the ancient beaten track to the south-east encounters an unforgettable sight: directly ahead on the horizon a jagged mountain range rises abruptly from the plateau—the Sinai massif. At closer quarters geological formations of unusual and rare ranges of colour meet the eye. Precipitous cliffs of pink and mauve granite thrust their way upwards to the blue sky. Between them sparkle slopes and gorges of pale amber and fiery red, streaked with lead-coloured veins of porphyry and dark-green bands of felspar. It is as if all the colour and beauty of a garden had been poured into this wild serrated symphony in stone. At the margin of the Wilderness of Sin the beaten track ends abruptly and is lost in a wadi.

No one knew where to look for Dophkah until the turn of the century. The only clue was contained in the name of the place itself. "Dophkah", so the subtleties of philology inform us, is related in Hebrew to the word for "smelting operations". Smelting operations take place where there are mineral deposits.

In the spring of 1904 Flinders Petrie, who had made a name for himself in England as a pioneer of Biblical archaeology, set out from Suez with a long camel caravan. A veritable mass-formation of scholars, thirty surveyors, Egyptologists and assistants accompanied him. From the banks of the Suez Canal the expedition followed the line of the Egyptian beaten track into the wilds of Sinai. Through the Wilderness of Sin as far as the mountains it followed the same route as Israel.

Slowly the caravan made its way along a wadi and round a sharp bend in the hills—suddenly time seemed to rush back three or four thousand years. The caravan was transported straight back into the world of the Pharaohs. Petrie ordered a halt. From a terrace in the rockface a temple projected into the valley. From the square columns at the gateway stared the face of a goddess with great cow's ears. A jumble of pillars with one very tall one seemed to be growing out of the ground. The yellow sand round a number of little stone altars showed unmistakable evidence of the ashes of burnt offerings. Dark caverns yawned round the cliff-face and high above the wadi towered the solid massif of Sinai.

The cries of the drivers were silenced. The caravan stood motionless as if overpowered by the almost ghostly sight.

In the ruined temple Petrie found the name of the great Ramesses II carved on the walls. The expedition had reached Serabit el-Khadem, the ancient Egyptian mining and manufacturing centre for copper and turquoise. In all probability this is where we should look for the Dophkah of the Bible.

For two long years a camp in front of the old temple brought new life into the valley. Representations of cultic acts and pictures of sacrifices on the walls of the temple indicate that this had been a centre of worship of the goddess Hathor. An almost endless confusion of half choked galleries in the neighbouring wadis bore witness to the search for copper and turquoise. The marks of the workmen's tools were unmistakable. Tumbledown settlements which housed the workers lie in the immediate neighbourhood.

The pitiless sun beat down on this cauldron of a valley, filling it with unbearable heat and making the work of the expedition doubly difficult. A worker's life in these mines in the desert must have been, above all in summer, pure hell. An inscription from the reign of Amenemhet III about 1800 B.C. told the party what it had been like.

Hor-Ur-Re, bearer of the royal seal and "Minister of Labour" under Pharaoh, is addressing the miners and slaves. He tries to cheer them on and encourage them: "Anyone should think himself lucky to work in this area". But the reply is: "Turquoise will always be in the mountain. But it is our skins we have to think about at this time of the year. We have already heard that ore has been quarried at this season. But really, our skin is not made for that sort of thing at this time of the year." Hor-Ur-Re assures them: "Whenever I have brought men out to these mines my one consideration has always been the honour of His Majesty. . . . I never lost heart at the sight of work. . . . There was no talk of: 'O for a tough skin'. On the contrary, eyes sparkled. . . ."

While the excavations in the old mines, the dwelling houses, and the temple precincts were in full swing, only a few paces from the sanctuary of the goddess fragments of stone tablets were dug out of the sand together with a statue of a crouching figure. On both the tablets and the sculpture there were unusual markings. Neither Flinders Petrie nor the Egyptologists in the party could make anything of them. They were obviously written characters of a type never seen before. Although the inscriptions give a pictographic impression—they are reminiscent of Egyptian hieroglyphics—they can hardly be said to be a picture language. There are too few different signs for that.

When all the circumstances of the find had been carefully gone into Flinders Petrie came to the following daring conclusion: "Workmen from Retenu, who were employed by the Egyptians and are often mentioned, had this system of linear writing. The inference that follows from that is extremely significant, namely that about 1500 B.C. these simple workmen from Canaan were able to write and that the type of writing is independent both of hieroglyphics and cuneiform. Further, it invalidates once and for all the hypothesis that the Israelites who came through this area from Egypt, were at that stage still illiterate."

This explanation aroused considerable attention among antiquarians, palaeographers, and historians. All existing theories about the origin and first use of writing in Canaan were at once out of date. It seemed incredible that the inhabitants of Canaan could have had their own type of script as far back as the middle of the second millennium B.C. Only from the text of the Sinai tablets could it be proved whether Petrie was actually right. Immediately on his return to England Petrie had the tablets copied.

Palaeographers from all countries pounced upon these awkward-looking scratched-out characters. No one was able to make any sense of them. It was not till ten years later that Sir Alan Gardiner, the brilliant and tireless translator of Egyptian texts, lifted the veil. He it was who first succeeded in deciphering parts of the inscriptions.

The repeated appearance of the notched "shepherd's crook" helped him along. Eventually Gardiner conjectured that a combination of four or five signs which occurred several times represented ancient Hebrew words. The five characters 1-B-'-l-t he interpreted as "(dedicated) to (the goddess) Baalath".

In the second millennium B.C. a female deity with the name of Baalath was venerated in the seaport of Byblos. It was to this same goddess that the temple at Serabit el-Khadem had been erected by the Egyptians. Only the Egyptians called her Hathor. Workmen from Canaan had dug for copper and turquoise beside her temple.

The chain of evidence was complete. The significance of the discovery at Sinai did not fully emerge until six years after Flinders Petrie's death, by which time it had had further exhaustive research and study.

Gardiner had only been able to decipher part of the strange characters. Thirty years later, in 1948, a team of archaeologists from the University of Los Angeles found the key which made it possible to give a literal translation of all the characters on the Sinai tablets. Without a doubt the inscriptions had their origin about 1500 B.C. and are written in a Canaanite dialect.

What Flinders Petrie wrested from the burning sands of Sinai in 1905 nowadays meets the eye everywhere in a different form in newspapers, magazines, books—and the keys of a typewriter. For these stones in Serabit el-Khadem provided the ancestor of our alphabet. The two primary modes of expression in the "Fertile Crescent", namely hieroglyphics and cuneiform, were already quite ancient when a third fundamental way of expressing men's thoughts was born in the second millennium B.C.—namely the alphabet. Possibly stimulated by the picture language of their Egyptian comrades, these Semitic workmen in Sinai devised their own peculiar and quite different type of script.

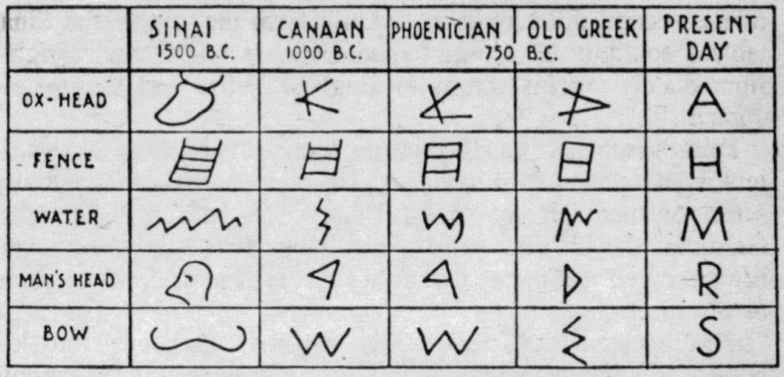

	SINAI 1500 B.C.	CANAAN 1000 B.C.	PHOENICIAN 750 B.C.	OLD GREEK B.C.	PRESENT DAY
OX-HEAD					A
FENCE					H
WATER					M
MAN'S HEAD					R
BOW					S

FIG. 21.—Development of our alphabet.

The famous Sinai inscriptions are the first stage of the North Semitic alphabet, which is the direct ancestor of our present alphabet. It was used in Palestine, in Canaan, in the Phoenician Republics on the coast. About the end of the 9th century B.C. the Greeks adopted it. From Greece it spread to Rome and from there went round the globe.

"And the Lord said unto Moses, Write this for a memorial in a book...." (Ex. 17[14]). The first time that the word "write" is mentioned in the Old Testament is when Israel reaches the next stopping place after Dophkah. Previously the word is never used. The deciphering of the Sinai tablets shows up this Biblical passage in a completely new light as a historical statement. Because we now know that three hundred years before Moses led his people out of Egypt to Sinai, men from Canaan had already been "writing" in this area, in a language which was closely related to that of Israel.

Chapter 12
AT THE MOUNTAIN OF MOSES

The "Pearl of Sinai"—Israel was 6,000 strong—Striking water from rock —Practical experience in desert life—Was the Burning Bush a gas-plant? —The valley of the monks and hermits—The great miracle.

"And all the congregation of the children of Israel journeyed from the wilderness of Sin, after their journeys, according to the commandment of the Lord, and pitched in Rephidim (Ex. 17[1]). Then came Amalek and fought with Israel in Rephidim (Ex. 17[8])."

Rephidim is now Feiran, extolled by the Arabs as the "Pearl of Sinai". Protected by the lonely but colourful rock barrier which surrounds it, this miniature paradise has presented the same appearance for thousands of years. A small grove of palm trees provides welcome shade. As they have always done since the days of their remote ancestors, the nomads bring their flocks here to drink and rest on the tiny grass carpet.

From the main camp Flinders Petrie organised parties to investigate the neighbouring territory. By dint of exhausting and difficult journeys he got to know the wadis and mountains right down to the shores of the Red Sea. He established that Feiran is the only oasis in the whole southern part of the massif. For the nomads who lived, and still live here it is essential for existence and is their most precious possession. "The Amalekites must have been trying to defend Wadi Feiran from the foreign invaders," reflected Flinders Petrie. His next thought was: "If the climate has not changed—and the proof of that lies in the fact that the sandstone pillars in Serabit el-Khadem show no sign of erosion despite the thousands of years of their existence—the population must also be numerically the same. Today at a rough estimate 5,000 to 7,000 nomads live with their flocks on the Sinai peninsula. Israel must therefore have been about 6,000 strong since the battle with the Amalekites appears to have been indecisive." "And it came to pass, when Moses held up his hand, that Israel prevailed: and when he let down his hand Amalek prevailed" (Ex. 17[11]).

Bitter fighting continued all day "until the going down of the sun", when at length Joshua won a decisive victory for Israel. Thereafter the way was open to the water supply in the oasis of Rephidim. Before that "there was no water for the people to drink" (Ex. 17[1]). In this emergency Moses is said to have taken his rod and produced water by striking a rock (Ex. 17[6]), an action which has been regarded, and not only by sceptics, as quite incomprehensible, although the Bible is merely once more recording a perfectly natural occurrence.

Major C. S. Jarvis, who was British Governor of Sinai in the thirties, has seen it happen himself. "Moses striking the rock at Rephidim and the water gushing out sounds like a genuine miracle, but the writer has actually seen this happen. Several men of the Sinai Camel Corps had halted in a dry wadi and were in process of digging about in the rough sand that had accumulated at the foot of a rock-face. They were trying to get at the water that was trickling slowly out of the limestone rock. The men were taking their time about it and Bash Shawish, the coloured sergeant, said: 'Here, give it to me!' He took the spade of one of the men and began digging furiously in the manner of N.C.O.'s the world over who want to show their men how to do things but have no intention of keeping it up for more than a couple of minutes. One of his violent blows hit the rock by mistake. The smooth hard crust which always forms on weathered limestone split open and fell away. The soft stone underneath was thereby exposed and out of its apertures shot a powerful stream of water. The Sudanese, who are well up in the activities of the prophets but do not treat them with a vast amount of respect overwhelmed their sergeant with cries of: 'Look at him! The prophet Moses!' This is a very illuminating explanation of what happened when Moses struck the rock at Rephidim."

C. S. Jarvis had witnessed a pure coincidence. For the men of the Camel Corps were Sudanese and not in any sense natives of

Sinai, who might be expected to be familiar with the technique of producing water in this way. On the journey from Kadesh to Edom Moses employed this method of striking water once more. "And Moses lifted up his hand and with his rod he smote the rock twice," as we are told in Num. 20[11]. "And the water came out abundantly and the congregation drank and their beasts also." He had obviously got to know this highly unusual method of finding water during his exile among the Midianites.

At the beginning of the Christian era many monks and hermits settled in Feiran, where Israel had had to cope with its first hostile attack under Moses. In the gullies and on the cliffs they built their tiny cells. A church was founded in Feiran and 25 miles south of the oasis a little chapel was erected at the foot of Jebel Musa.

The barbaric tribes of nomads however gave the hermits and monks of Sinai no peace. Many of them lost their lives in these repeated attacks. St. Helena, eighty year old mother of Constantine, the first Christian emperor, during a visit to Jerusalem in A.D. 327, learned of the plight of the monks of Sinai and founded a tower of refuge which was erected at the foot of the mountain of Moses.

In A.D. 530 the Byzantine emperor Justinian caused a strong defensive wall to be built round the little chapel at the mountain of Moses. Right up to the Middle Ages this fortified church at Jebel Musa was the goal of devout pilgrims who came to Sinai from every land. A legend tells how this notable spot came to be called "St. Catherine's Monastery", which is the name it bears still.

Napoleon was instrumental in saving the masonry of this isolated early Christian fortress from collapse.

In 1859 the German theologian Constantine von Tischendorf discovered in the monastery at Sinai in a good state of preservation one of the most precious parchment manuscripts of the Bible, the famous "Codex Sinaiticus". It dates from the 4th century A.D. and contains the New Testament and parts of the Old Testament.

The Czar accepted it as a gift, giving the monastery 9,000 roubles for it. Then this priceless possession found its way into the library at St. Petersburg. Finally in 1933 the British Museum bought the "Codex Sinaiticus" from the Soviet Government for £100,000.

The little chapel at the foot of Jebel Musa was built on the site where Moses according to the Bible encountered the Burning Bush: "And he looked and behold the bush burned with fire, and the bush was not consumed" (Ex. 3^2).

Different attempts have been made to find a scientific explanation of this remarkable phenomenon. An expert on the botany of the Bible, Dr. Harold N. Moldenke, director and curator of the Botanical Garden in New York, has this to say: ". . . Among the commentators who think that a natural explanation can be found, some think that the phenomenon of the bush that 'burned with fire' and yet 'was not consumed' can be explained as a variety of the gas-plant or Fraxinella, the Dietamnus Albus L. This is a plant with a strong growth about three feet in height with clusters of purple blossom. The whole bush is covered with tiny oil-glands. This oil is so volatile that it is constantly escaping and if approached with a naked light bursts suddenly into flames. . . . The most logical explanation seems to be that suggested by Smith. He puts forward the theory that the 'flames' may have been the crimson blossoms of mistletoe twigs (Loranthus Acaciae) which grow on various prickly acacia bushes and acacia trees throughout the Holy Land and in Sinai. When this mistletoe is in full bloom the bush becomes a mass of brilliant flaming colour and looks as if it is on fire."

"For they were departed from Rephidim, and were come to the desert of Sinai, and had pitched in the wilderness: and there Israel camped before the mount. And Moses went up unto God" (Ex. 19$^{2-3}$).

"So Moses went down unto the people and spake unto them. And God spake all these words saying, I am the Lord thy God. . . . Thou shalt have no other gods before me" (Ex. 19^{25}; 20$^{1-3}$).

At Sinai something happened which is unique in the history of mankind. Here lie both the roots and the greatness of a faith which was strong enough to conquer the globe.

Moses, this child of a world which believed in a host of deities and in gods of all shapes and forms, proclaimed his faith in one God alone. Moses was the herald of monotheism—that is the true greatness of this incomprehensible miracle of Sinai. Moses—this unknown son and grandson of desert nomads, brought up in a foreign land, "went down unto the people and spake unto them". Nomads in their goatshair tents, camping in the desert under the open sky, are the first to hear this astounding message, to accept it and transmit it. First of all for thirty-nine years, in the solitude of the desert, by gurgling springs, beside the still waters of shady oases, and facing the biting wind which sweeps across the sullen landscape, as they feed their sheep, their goats and their donkeys, they speak among themselves of the one great God, YHWH.

So begins the wonderful story of this world embracing faith. Simple shepherds, inured to hardship, carried the great new idea, the new faith, to their homeland, whence the message was one day to go out into the whole world and to all the peoples of the earth. The great nations and mighty empires of these far off days have long since disappeared into the dark recesses of the past. But the descendants of those shepherds who were the first to pledge their faith in one sole omnipotent God, are still alive today.

"I am the Lord thy God. Thou shalt have no other gods before me." That was a word heard for the first time since man inhabited this planet. There was no pattern for this faith, no hint of it from other nations.

We can make this assertion with confidence thanks to archaeological discoveries in Egypt, the land in which Moses grew up and received his education, as well as in other lands of the ancient East. Both the sun-worship of Akhnaten and the appearance in Mesopotamia of a blending of many deities into one sole god, Ninurta, god of war, are but vague preludes to monotheism. In all these conceptions what is lacking is the concentrated power and redemptive moral purpose rooted in the Ten Commandments, which Moses brought down from the lonely heights of Mt. Sinai into the hearts and minds of men.

It is only among the people of Israel out of the whole of the "Fertile Crescent" that there is this awakening of the new idea of God in all its clarity and purity, untainted by magic, free from a variegated and grotesque imagery, and conceived as something other than a materialistic preparation for perpetuating the self beyond the grave. Without precedent and prototype seems likewise the clear imperative of the Ten Commandments. The Israelites are bidden not to sin because they are under the obedience of Yahweh!

It was certainly possible to be quite convinced that the God-given moral law of Israel was without precedent in the Ancient East until parallels became known which show quite clearly that the Bible is certainly not alone, as seemed to be the case, in one of its most essential passages, the Ten Commandments together with Israel's other statutes. On the contrary, the Bible now proves to be completely penetrated by the spirit of the Ancient East. The Ten Commandments are thus a kind of "treaty of alliance", the "fundamental constitutional law" between Israel and its God. It is not to be wondered at, therefore, if they are in complete accordance with the treaties made with vassals in the Ancient East defining the relations between a ruler and the vassal kings he appointed to govern the peoples he had subjugated.

Such treaties began with the enumeration of the names, titles and services of the "great king". "I am the Lord thy God which have brought thee out of the land of Egypt, out of the house of bondage" (Exodus, 20^2). Here, too, we have the name (the word "Lord" according to Biblical usage in place of the real name of God, Yahweh, which it was not permitted to pronounce), the title, "God", and the essential service rendered ("which have brought you out of the land of Egypt") by the "great king", except that in this case it was Israel's heavenly "great king", the God of the Covenant. Vassals were forbidden, moreover, to enter into any relationships with foreign rulers and the commandment "Thou shalt have no other gods but me" (Ex. 20^3) corresponds to this. The imperious "thou shalt" and "thou shalt not" continually occur in the treaties with vassals. These words are consequently not by any means restricted to the Biblical Ten Commandments as many scholars have thought. One treaty with a vassal, for example, prescribes that "thou shalt not covet any territory of the land of the Hatti". Similarly the Bible prescribes that "thou shalt not covet thy neighbour's house . . ." (Ex. 20^{17}).

Other correspondences have also been noted and even include not only the safe-keeping of the tables of the law in the Ark of the Covenant in the same way that treaties with vassals were deposited in holy shrines, but also the sealing of the treaties on the one hand and the pronouncement of blessings and curses on the other. In the words of Moses (Deut. 11^{26-28}): "Behold, I set before you this day a blessing and a curse; a blessing, if ye obey the commandments of the Lord your God, which I command you this day: and a curse, if you will not obey the commandments of the Lord your God. . . ."

The well-known Catholic Bible scholar Roland de Vaux, of whom mention has already been made, discovered in a number of Hittite treaties with vassals the injunction that the text of the treaty was to be read out regularly in the presence of the vassal king and his people. And similarly with the Biblical code of laws for we read (Deut. 31[10ff]): "And Moses commanded them saying, At the end of every seven years...thou shalt read this law before all Israel in their hearing...that they may hear, and that they may learn,...and observe to do all the words of this law."

All this concerns merely the outer form of the Ten Commandments. What about the spirit? Again there is no lack of parallels. In Assyria, for example, a priest who was driving the "demons" out of a sick person, had to ask: "Has he (i.e., the sick person) offended a god? Or slighted a goddess?...Has he shown contempt to his father and mother? Or set little store by his elder sister?...Has he said 'It is' instead of 'It is not' (and vice versa)?...Has he given wrong weight? Has he broken into his neighbour's house? Has he approached too near to his neighbour's wife? Has he shed his neighbour's blood?"

Finally, two examples from Ancient Egypt where we find in "the Teachings of Amenemope" the injunction:

Remove not the boundary stone on the boundaries of the fields and displace not the measuring cord, be not covetous of a yard of ploughland and tear not down the widow's boundary.

Be not covetous of the poor man's goods and hunger not for his bread.

Set not the balance wrongly, tamper not with the weights, reduce not the portions of the corn measure.

Bring nobody into misfortune before the judges and warp not justice.

Ridicule not the blind man nor be scornful of any dwarf, render not vain the intentions of the lame.

The perfect example customarily quoted nowadays by specialists of Biblical antiquity is, however, what is known as the "negative confession" in the introduction to chapter 125 of the "Book of the Dead". According to ancient Egyptian belief, deceased persons had to make the following confession before 42 judges of the dead in a "court room".

I have not made any man sick
I have not made any man weep
I have not killed

I have not commanded any man to kill
I have not done harm to any man
I have not diminished the amount of the foodstuffs in the
    temples
I have not damaged the loaves offered to the gods
I have not stolen the loaves offered to the dead
I have not had any (illicit) sexual relations
I have not engaged in any unnatural lewdness

And so on. . . .

Elsewhere we shall see that according to our most recent knowledge the contrast between sublime monotheism on the one side and a bizarre crowd of gods on the other no longer appears so striking. At one time a "crowd of gods" certainly existed in Israel, at least in the religion of the *people* during the *early period*, but the concept of the sublime nature of royal gods was not by any means foreign to the religions of other peoples living near to the "Holy Land". So we are bound to conclude that restraint was also practised elsewhere. Responsibility, morality, law, order and ethics were all practised beyond the frontiers of Israel while the accepted norms of human behaviour which in both letter and spirit were in accordance with Israel's divine code of laws were also current elsewhere. Once again the Bible is proved right, that is to say insofar as it transmits in its legal texts, the essence of which consists of the Ten Commandments, a striking piece of cultural and moral history from the Ancient East which can be substantiated by parallels. The consequence of this renders it difficult for us today to maintain the earlier claim that the Biblical code of laws was unique. This fact may well shake the confidence of many people. We cannot remove this feeling of uncertainty. On the other hand, in consequence of confirmation from non-Biblical sources of the relevant Bible texts, Israel's relationship to the cultural and historical world around it as well as to the precepts of its neighbours now appears to us in a much clearer light.

Chapter 13
UNDER DESERT SKIES

Sinai—150 miles to Kadesh—Two springs at the chief halting-place—Scouts sent out to Hebron—The bunch of grapes was a vine—Foreign races—Peasant woman finds the Amarna Tablets—Letters from Indo-Aryan Canaanite princes—Scouts' report leads to a new decision—The "wilderness" of the Bible was steppe.

"And the children of Israel took their journeys out of the wilderness of Sinai" (Num. 10^{12}).

Israel had pledged itself to believe in one God and his laws. The portable palladium that they had constructed for him—the Ark of the Covenant—had been made out of acacia wood (Ex. 25^{10}), which is still indigenous to Sinai and widely used.

For almost a year they had lingered at Mt. Sinai. Now they set out again, heading north for Canaan. Kadesh, the next stage, which is a landmark in the long desert wanderings of the children of Israel, lies 150 miles from Sinai as the crow flies.

This stretch too can be accurately traced on the basis of the very precise topographical details given in the Bible. The route lies along the west side of the Gulf of Aqabah to the "Wilderness of Paran" (Num. 12^{16})—now Bàdiet et-Tin, i.e., "Wilderness of Loneliness"—and then continues along its eastern edge. Among the halts made on this journey (Num. 33$^{16-36}$) Hazeroth and Ezion-Geber can be identified with certainty. Hazeroth is the present-day Ain Huderah, which lies near the Gulf. Ezion-Geber lies at the topmost point of the Gulf of Aqabah and is the place which was later to become a centre for shipping and industry in the days of King Solomon (1 Kings 9^{26}).

FIG. 22.—The Ark of the Covenant with Cherubim and carrying-poles.
(Reconstruction.)

As they made their way along the shores of the Gulf the
"miracle" of the quails was repeated. Once more it was springtime, the time of bird migration, and again the description is true
to nature: "And there went forth a wind from the Lord, and brought
quails from the sea, and let them fall by the camp" (Num. 11³¹).

"And they removed from Ezion-Geber, and pitched in the
wilderness of Zin which is Kadesh" (Num. 33³⁶).

Below Hebron the hill country of Judah falls away into a fairly
flat plain, the southern part of which, towards the frequently
mentioned "Brook of Egypt", which is a ramification of wadis,
is always very poorly supplied with water (Num. 34⁵; Josh. 15⁴; 1
Kings 8⁶⁵). This is the Negev, the Biblical "Land of the South"
(Num. 13¹⁷). Amid innumerable wadis—dried-up river beds
which only run with water in the rainy season during the winter
months—lies Kadesh. The old name Kadesh is preserved in the
name of the little spring "Ain Qedeis", from which passing
Bedouins water their cattle. But this trickle of spring water can
hardly have been sufficient to provide for 6,000 Israelites and
their flocks for any length of time. Only about 5 miles to the
north-west of Kadesh, however, lies the most ample supply of
water in the whole area, "Ain el-Qudeirât". Wadi Qudeirât has
this to thank for its fertility. It was from here that the children of
Israel saw in the distance the land that had been promised to
them, of which as yet they had been able to form no clear
picture. It may be that their hasty departure from Egypt had
prevented them from finding out about it before they left.

Palestine was so well known to the inhabitants of the Nile country that anyone who was lacking in detailed knowledge of it was reckoned to be lacking in proper education. Aman-Appa, a "commissioned scribe of the army" under Ramesses II, was even ridiculed for his ignorance about Palestine. Hori, an officer of the royal stables, replies to a letter from him in an extremely satirical vein and puts his geographical knowledge to the test: "Your letter is overloaded with big words. You have asked for it and you shall have it—and more than you bargained for. What we say is: If what you say is true, come and let us test you. We shall harness a horse for you which will bring you as fast as any jackal can run. Let us see what you can do. Have you not seen the country of Upe near Damascus? Don't you know its peculiarities, or those of its river? Have you not been to Kadesh? Have you never found your way to the Lebanon where the sky is dark in broad daylight? It is overgrown with cypresses, oaks and cedars which rise sky-high. I shall also mention a mysterious city, Byblos by name. What does it look like? Tell me too about Sidon and Sarepta. They talk about another city that lies in the sea, the port of Tyre is its name. Water is carried to it by ship. If you go to Jaffa you will find that the fields are green. Go . . . and look for the pretty girl who is in charge of the vineyards. She will accept you as her mate and grant you her favours. . . . You will be drowsy and indolent. They will steal . . . your bow, your knife, your quiver. Your reins will be slashed in the darkness . . . your chariot will be smashed to pieces. But you will say: Bring me food and drink, I am happy here! They will pretend they are deaf and pay no attention. Come with me south to the region of Akka. Where is the hill of Shechem? Can this clever scribe tell me how to get to Hazor? What is special about its river? Now let me ask you about some other towns. Tell me what Kjn near Megiddo looks like, describe Rehob to me, give me a picture of Bethshan and Kiriath-El. Let me know how to get past Megiddo. How does one cross the Jordan? You see," concludes Hori, officer of the royal stables, "I have taken you through the whole of Palestine . . . have a good look at it, so that in future you will be able to describe it properly, and . . . you will . . . be made a councillor." Government officials, soldiers, merchants had at least some clear notion of Palestine. Moses, who belonged to a poor shepherd folk, had first to find out about this country. He sent out scouts.

"And Moses sent them to spy out the land of Canaan,
and said unto them, Get you up this way southward, and go
up into the mountain: and see the land, what it is; and the
people that dwelleth therein, whether they be strong or
weak, few or many" (Num. 13$^{17-18}$).

Among the twelve scouts was Joshua, a man with great gifts
as a strategist, as later became plain during the conquest of
Canaan. They chose as the best spot to spy out the land the
country round Hebron in the south of Judah. Forty days later the
men reported back to Moses. As proof that they had done their
job they brought fruit from the area they had scrutinised: figs and
pomegranates. Incredulous astonishment greeted one gigantic
bunch of grapes, cut at the "Brook of Eshcol", for "they bare it
between two upon a staff" (Num. 13^{23}). Posterity is equally
sceptical because the narrative speaks of only one cluster. Surely
it must have been a whole vine with all its fruit. The spies would
cut it down with the grapes on it to keep them fresher. At all
events the place of their origin according to the Bible is reliable.
"Brook of Eshcol" means "Valley of Grapes"; it lies south-
west of Hebron and even today this district is rich in vines. Fine
heavy bunches of from 10–12 pounds are no rarity. The scouts
made their report and described Canaan, like Sinuhe 650 years
earlier, as a land that "floweth with milk and honey", only "the
people be strong that dwell in the land, and the cities are walled
and very great" (Num. 13^{27,28}; Deut. 1^{28}).

In their recital of the different inhabitants of the country they
mention some we already know, Hittites, Amorites, Jebusites in
and around Jerusalem, Canaanites and Amalekites with whom
Israel had already come into conflict in Sinai. They also mention
the "children of Anak", which is supposed to mean the "children of the giants" (Num. 13^{22,28,33}), "Anak" might mean "long
necked", and that is as much as the experts can tell us. It has
been surmised that these "giants" are possibly survivals of
ancient pre-Semitic elements in the population but there is no
certainty in the matter.

Actually there were people from other countries living in
Canaan at that time who must have been quite unknown to
Israelites coming from Egypt. Whose "children" they were,
they intimated to posterity themselves on clay tablets which
were accidentally discovered by a peasant woman at Tell el-

Amarna[1] in 1887. Further investigation produced eventually a collection of 377 documents in all. These are cuneiform letters from the royal archives of Amenophis III and his son Akhnaten who built himself a new capital at El-Amarna on the Nile. The tablets contain correspondence from the princes of Palestine, Phoenicia and Southern Syria to the Foreign Office of both Pharaohs. They are written in Akkadian, the diplomatic language of the second millennium B.C. Most of the writings are full of typically Canaanite words, some of them are in fact written almost exclusively in this dialect. This priceless find threw light for the first time on conditions in Palestine in the 15th and 14th centuries B.C.

One of the letters runs: "To the King, my Lord, my Sun, my God, say: Thus (says) Suwardata, thy servant, the servant of the King and the dust under his feet, the ground on which thou dost tread: At the feet of the King, my Lord, the Sun of Heaven, seven times, seven times I prostrated myself, on my belly and on my back. . . ."

This is only the introduction. Nor is it in any way extravagant. On the contrary it is extremely formal, in accordance with contemporary protocol. Suwardata then comes to the matter in hand: "The King, my Lord, should know that the Habiru have risen in the lands which the God of the King, my Lord, has given me, and that I have beaten them, and the King, my Lord, should know that all my brothers have left me; and that I and Abdi-Kheba alone are left to fight against the leader of the Habiru. And Zurata, prince of Acco (Jud. 1[31]) and Indaruta, prince of Achshaph (Josh. 11[1]) were the ones who hastened to my help in return for 50 chariots of which I have now been deprived. But behold, [now] they have been fighting against me and may it please the King, my Lord, to send the Janhamu, so that we can wage a proper war and restore the land of the King, my Lord, to its old frontiers. . . ."

This letter from a prince of Canaan paints a picture which faithfully reflects the times. In these few sentences we can recognise unmistakably the intrigues and endless feuds both among the princes themselves and with the warlike nomadic tribes. The most interesting point about the letter, apart from the style and contents, is its author, Prince Suwardata. His name

[1] Middle Egypt.

shows clearly that he was of Indo-Aryan descent. Prince Indaruta whom he mentions is also an Indo-Aryan. Though it may sound extraordinary, a third of these princely correspondents from Canaan have Indo-Aryan ancestry. Biryawaza of Damascus, Biridiya of Megiddo, Widia of Askelon, Birashshena of Shechem in Samaria have all Indo-Aryan names. Indaruta, the name of the prince of Achshaph, is in fact identical with names from the Vedas and other early Sanskrit writings. Abdi-Kheba of Jerusalem, who has been mentioned, belongs to the Hurrite people often referred to in the Bible as Horites.

The reliability of this tradition has recently been illuminated by the discovery of Egyptian papyri of the 15th century B.C., in which the land of Canaan is repeatedly called "Khuru" after the Hurrites, the Horites of the Bible. According to this the Hurrites must for a time at least have been widespread throughout the whole country.

> "And all the congregation lifted up their voice, and cried: and the people wept that night . . . wherefore hath the Lord brought us into this land, to fall by the sword, that our wives and our children should be a prey?" (Num. 14$^{1-3}$).

The reports that the spies brought back telling of the strongly fortified cities of Canaan, "great and walled up to heaven" (Deut. 1^{28}), and of their superbly armed inhabitants, were not exaggerated. Turreted fortresses built of "Cyclops-walls" were to the children of Israel an unaccustomed and menacing sight. In the land of Goshen, which for many generations had been their home, there was only one fortified town, Raamses. In Canaan the fortresses were practically cheek by jowl. The country was plastered with them. Numerous strongpoints stared down from hilltops and mountain peaks, which made them look even more powerful and terrifying. Little wonder that the report of the scouts was shattering in its effect.

Israel was quite unskilled in the use and manufacture of implements of war. They had at their disposal nothing but the most primitive weapons—bows, javelins, swords, knives—to say nothing of horse-drawn chariots which the Canaanites possessed in vast numbers. Israel was still spoilt by the "fleshpots of Egypt", for which especially the older people among them were continually sighing and bemoaning their lot. Despite their new faith and the experiences of the Exodus which they had shared together, they were not yet welded into a community which would be prepared to risk a clash with superior forces.

In view of these facts Moses wisely resolved not to carry out his original intention of marching upon Canaan from the south. Neither the time nor the people was ripe for the great moment. They must begin their roaming afresh, the time of testing and proving their mettle must be prolonged in order to allow these refugees and land-hungry wanderers to develop into a tough and compact national group schooled to bear any privation. A new generation must first emerge.

We know very little about the obscure period which now follows. Thirty-eight years—almost a generation, and time enough to mould a nation. This was the duration of their sojourn in the "wilderness". Frequently associated with the "miracles" of the quails and the manna, this section of Biblical chronology and topography sounds highly improbable. And with good reason, as would appear from systematic investigations, though on different grounds from those generally supposed. Actually there never was a "sojourn in the wilderness" in the proper sense of the words.

Although the Biblical data for this period are very scanty, we can obtain a sufficiently clear picture from the few places that can be scientifically established. According to this the children of Israel with their flocks spent a long time in the Negev, near the two sources of water at Kadesh. Once they went back again to the Gulf of Aqabah into the area of Midian and the Sinai peninsula. Compared with the deadly stretches of African sand-dunes in the Sahara, this tract of land has never been a proper desert. Examination of the terrain has established the fact that since neither the irrigation nor the rainfall has altered greatly, the "wilderness" must have had at least the character of steppe country with possibilities for grazing and waterholes.

The archaeological activities of Nelson Glueck of the U.S.A. have enhanced our knowledge of the general conditions of that period. According to him these regions were inhabited about the 13th century B.C. by semi-nomadic tribes who had brisk and flourishing trading and commercial relations with both Canaan and Egypt. Among them we should include the Midianites with whom Moses lived during his exile and one of whom, Zipporah, he married (Ex. 2^{21}).

The latest Bible research proceeds somewhat differently and is not content with the demonstration that places named in the

Bible really existed and with showing that certain events related in the Bible such as the way in which Moses smote the rock causing the water to flow (Ex. 17$^{1-7}$; Num. 20$^{2-13}$; Deut. 32^{51}) or the episode of the burning bush (Ex. 3^2) might well have had a basis in fact. Such occurrences, however striking they may be, might after all provide nothing but the framework for a story which is mere invention. To give an example from the present day—it would be perfectly conceivable to write a story in which the progress of the intrigue is completely fictional although all the details, beginning with the going off of the alarm clock in the morning and proceeding with the nerve-shattering ringing of the telephone, squealing brakes, noisy tramcars, fast tube trains and so on are correct in every respect. Whether such details are described correctly or wrongly is not, therefore, fundamentally a safe indication of the truth or falseness of the story itself. And so the account of the migration of the Israelites from Egypt has been subjected to closer examination than ever before without pausing unduly to consider details.

Rather have people asked what really lies behind this story *as a whole*, the account of a migration through the desert or steppe which lasted for a generation and after which the Israelites reached their goal only by very strange detours. The result of this examination was not a world shaking discovery, nothing sensational for the press. On the contrary, it was the common and for the scientist quite unsensational realisation that things are somewhat more complicated than they appear to be at the outset. We, too, should have become accustomed by now to this fact. Thus, for example, the Bible mentions Succoth and Migdol (Ex. 13^{20} and 14^2) as places where the Israelites halted on their way out of Egypt. Obviously these places lay on a well-known escape route used by Egyptian slaves, for an ancient Egyptian reader, which was used for instruction purposes in schools and deals with the pursuit of runaway slaves (*Papyrus Anastasi* V, XIX 2–XX 6), mentions the same place-names.

Certainly it was not "the whole of Israel" which left Egypt, but only a number of groups of people who—themselves or their descendants—were later absorbed in the greatness that was Israel. The Bible itself lets us glimpse the fact that it was not "the whole of Israel" which was then migrating, for an "Israelite" was plainly not exclusively the person who arrived in the Promised Land at the end of the journey. On the contrary, there were Israelites resident there already when the migrants arrived.

Thus it came about that Joshua assembled "the whole of Israel" between the mountains of Ebal and Gerizim near Shechem and quite explicitly we are told "as well the stranger as he that was born among them" (Joshua 8³³). In other words, at the time when the Israelites took possession of the land, there must have been others who had already been living there for some time. We are left to ponder whether these people had arrived with a previous migration, or, if not, what this all indicates. . . .

Perhaps the various incidents of the migration which took place in Egypt, on the Sinai Peninsula and finally in the land on the banks of the Jordan, simply reflect different traditions of these various regions which have merely been brought into harmony with one another in the Bible and linked together to form a continuous narrative thus providing a mixture of traditions. Such a mixture is usually indicated by the repetitions which occur. And such repetitions do indeed occur here. The most obvious example is the repetition of the miracle of the sea (Ex. 14) when the Israelites cross the Jordan (Joshua 3⁴⁻¹⁷). For the second time Israel is reported to have passed dry-shod across a body of water whose waves "failed and were cut off" on the one side whereas they rose up "upon an heap" on the other. In whatever way attempts have been made to render plausible the earlier crossing of the Red Sea or rather the Reed Sea, the repetition with the crossing of the Jordan must leave us sceptical. Is it after all only fiction and not history that the writers of the Bible books are serving up to us when they relate Israel's journeyings from Egypt to the Promised Land?

Surprisingly enough quite recently we have had archaeological confirmation of two occurrences in the Biblical account of the journey through the desert which nobody would have expected in this connection. In spite of all the planning and systematic work, chance nevertheless has its part to play in archaeology and chance does not always pay any attention to what the scholars expect! In this case it enabled the Israeli archaeologist Benno Rothenberg to discover a "serpent of brass" and a tabernacle in the copper mine area of Timna (Wadi el-Arabah).

The "serpent of brass" is a serpent idol to which magical powers were attributed (Num. 21⁹). It is reported that there was a similar idol in the temple at Jerusalem which was not removed until it was broken in pieces by King Hiskia (Hezekiah) of Judah, who reigned around 700 B.C. (2 Kings 18⁴). The serpent idol naturally reminds us of the Sumerian serpent staff on a vase dedicated to the god of life Ningizidda. It reminds us, too, of the Aesculapius's staff of a later phase of Classical Antiquity as well as of the numerous serpents of Ancient Egypt. Already at the beginning of this century a German scholar, H. Gressmann, had asserted that the "brazen serpent" in the Bible must have been taken over from the Midianites with whom the Israelites were in contact during the journey through the desert.

According to the Bible, the Midianites were descended from Abraham's wife Keturah (Gen. 25$^{2-6}$) and Reuel (or Jethro), a priest of the Midianites, who was the father-in-law, adviser and co-celebrant "before the Lord" (Ex. 2^{16}; 3^1; 18^{1ff}) of Moses. The Israelites are supposed to owe the strange cult of the brazen serpent to Reuel. It is not without a touch of dramatic effect that we note that it was at an archaeological site showing signs of Midianite occupation that Benno Rothenberg found an idol in the form of a brazen serpent five inches in length and partly decorated with gold. As though this sensational confirmation of an important part of the Biblical accounts of the journey through the desert, which have been the object of so much discussion, were not enough, this small bronze serpent was found in the Holy of Holies of a tabernacle! That really was the crowning point of Rothenberg's discoveries, for the unearthing of a tabernacle was something of extraordinary importance, as ever since the nineteenth century Biblical scholars of the most varied persuasions had expressed doubts concerning the existence of the tabernacle about which the Bible has so much to say (Ex. 25–31 and 35–39). It is true that some critics had fallen silent when a very small, transportable tabernacle was discovered on a relief on the Bel Temple at Palmyra (Tadmor). At any rate the possibility of the existence of a tabernacle was no longer completely excluded, although the details of the Biblical descriptions of tabernacles were still considered to be a back projection onto the period of the wandering in the desert of conditions in the Temple at Jerusalem. In any case, the nomads' shrine on the relief at Palmyra was extremely small and strictly speaking it is rather a representation of the Ark of the Covenant than of the Tabernacle which contained the Holy Ark.

The Midianite tabernacle unearthed by Rothenberg is quite different. Its measurements bring it much closer to the tabernacle described in the Bible. It was found on the site of an older, Egyptian place of worship dedicated to the goddess Hathor. The Midianites who, following the Egyptians, were mining copper on their own account at Timna, converted this place of worship into a shrine of their own religion and covered it with an awning of which Rothenberg found not only the holes into which the posts had been rammed at an angle but even some remnants of material.

Of course, details of the interior lay-out and arrangement of the Biblical tabernacles still remain to be clarified. Thus, for example, the altar for burnt offerings is supposed to have been equipped with brass fittings and "a grate of network of brass" (Ex. 27[1-8]), but at a very much later date not even King Solomon had at his disposal craftsmen who could carry out such work. He was obliged to request them from King Hiram of Tyre (2 Chron. 2[6] and [12f]). The horns of this altar in the tabernacle, as they are called (Ex. 27[2]; 30[2f]) did not appear, according to the archaeological find in Israel, until the beginning of the time of the kings, that is to say not until the Temple had been built. It is only in connection with the time of the kings (cf. 1 Kings 1[50f]; Ps. 118 (117); Jer. 17[1]; Amos 3[14]) that the Bible mentions them again. Whatever the truth of the matter, after Rothenberg's discovery, there is now *in principle* nothing to prevent us from supposing that at quite an early date Israel possessed a tabernacle and that it was more or less like that described in the Bible.

Chapter 14
ON THE THRESHOLD OF THE
PROMISED LAND

Rise of a new generation—Change of plan—Transit permit through Edom requested—Pressing on through Transjordan—King Og's "iron bedstead" —Dolmen discovered near Amman—Moab sends its daughters—Baal worship in Canaan—Moses sees the Promised Land—Camping opposite Jericho.

"And he made them wander in the wilderness forty
years, until all the generation that had done evil in the sight
of the Lord was consumed" (Num. 32^{13}).

Not until the long years of their wanderings are approaching an end does the Bible take up the thread again of the story of the children of Israel. A new generation has sprung up and is ready to cross the threshold of the Promised Land. None of the men who led the Exodus out of Egypt will, according to the Bible, set foot in the land of promise—not even Moses himself.

The new plan of campaign is to conquer Canaan from the east, i.e., the territory east of the Jordan. Nevertheless the road to Upper Transjordan from Kadesh is blocked by five kingdoms, which occupy the broad strip of land between the Jordan valley and the Arabian desert: in the north, beginning at the spurs of Hermon is the kingdom of Bashan, then the Amorite kingdom of Sihon, next, the kingdom of Ammon, then the kingdom of Moab, on the east side of the Dead Sea, and, right in the south, Edom.

Edom is therefore the first kingdom that has to be negotiated on the way to Upper Transjordan. The children of Israel ask permission to pass through:

"And Moses sent messengers from Kadesh unto the king of Edom. . . . Let us pass, I pray thee, through thy country" (Num. 20¹⁴,¹⁷).

Main roads are the quickest roads to anywhere. In those days what corresponded to our trunk roads and motorways in the 20th century was a road that ran right through the middle of Edom. This was the old "King's Highway" which dated back to Abraham's time. "Let us pass, I pray thee, through the country", they asked; "We will go by the king's highway" (Num. 20¹⁷).

The settled population of the East always distrusts nomads, nowadays as much as long ago, even though Israel's emissaries declare expressly: "We will not pass through the fields, or through the vineyards . . . we will not turn to the right hand nor to the left, until we have passed thy borders. . . . And if I and my cattle drink of thy water, then I will pay for it" (Num. 20¹⁷,¹⁹).

In the course of an expedition which lasted several years Nelson Glueck confirmed the aptness of the Biblical description of Edom. In the southern part of Transjordan, in the territories that had once belonged to Edom and Moab, he came across numerous traces of a settlement which dated from the beginning of the 13th century. Signs of cultivated ground, which were also discovered, suggested well stocked fields. It is therefore understandable that in spite of all assurances Edom refused the children of Israel permission to use the road and pass through their country.

Their hostility compelled Israel to go a long way round. They trek northwards along the western edge of Edom towards the Dead Sea. Punon, now called Kirbet-Feinan, an old copper-mine, and Oboth, are visited for the sake of their water supplies. Then the Israelites follow the little river Sered, which marks the frontier between Edom and Moab, and reach Transjordan. They make a wide circle round Moab on the south-east side of the Dead Sea. By this time they have reached the river Arnon and the southern frontier of the kingdom of the Amorites (Num. 21¹³). Once more the Israelites ask for permission to use the "King's Highway" (Num. 21²²). Once more it is refused, this time by Sihon, king of the Amorites. A battle begins and the process of conquest by force of arms has started.

By defeating the Amorites the Israelites collect their first laurels. Conscious of their strength they push northwards over the river Jabbok and conquer the kingdom of Bashan in addition. Thus by their first determined attack they have become masters of Transjordan from the river Arnon to the banks of the Lake of Galilee.

Into the matter-of-fact description of this military offensive in Transjordan there has crept a reference to the "iron bed" of a giant, King Og of Bashan (Deut. 3^{11}), which may have puzzled many people. This mysterious and improbable sounding passage in the Bible has, however, a very natural and at the same time striking explanation. The Bible is preserving here in all faithfulness a memory which takes us back to Canaan's dim and distant past.

When the scholars were searching the Jordan country for evidence which would tie up with Biblical history, they came upon remarkable structures such as archaeologists had already encountered in other countries as well. These consisted of tall stones, built in oval formation and every now and then roofed over with a heavy transverse block—the famous Great Stone Graves. They are also called megalithic graves or dolmens, and were once used for burying the dead. In Europe—they are found in North Germany, Denmark, England and North-west France—they are called locally "Giants' Beds". Since these massive monuments are also found in India, East Asia and even the South Sea Islands, they are ascribed to a great mass migration in early times.

In 1918 Gustav Dalman, the German scholar, discovered in the neighbourhood of Amman, the modern capital of Jordan, a dolmen which aroused unusual interest because it seemed to shed light on a factual Biblical reference in quite an astonishing way. Amman stands precisely on the old site of Rabbath-Ammon. The Bible says about this giant king Og: "Behold his bedstead was a bedstead of iron; is it not in Rabbath of the children of Ammon [Rabbath-Ammon]? nine cubits was the length thereof, and four cubits the breadth of it, after the cubit of a man" (Deut. 3^{11}). The size of the dolmen discovered by Dalman corresponded approximately to these measurements. The "bed" consists of basalt, an extremely hard grey-black stone. The appearance of such a burying-place may have given rise to the Biblical description of the "iron bed" of the giant king. Further investigations have proved that dolmens are common in Palestine, principally in Transjordan above the river Jabbok, that is, in present day Ajlun. Well over a thousand of these ancient monuments are to be found among the coarse grass of the highlands. The country above the

Jabbok, so the Bible tells us, is the kingdom over which King Og of Bashan is said to have reigned, Og who alone "remained of the remnant of giants" (Deut. 3^{11}). Bashan, which was conquered by Israel, was also called "the land of giants" (Deut. 3^{13}).

West of the Jordan the only dolmens to be found are in the neighbourhood of Hebron. The scouts, whom Moses sent out from Kadesh, "ascended by the south, and came unto Hebron . . . and there we saw the giants, the sons of Anak" (Num. $13^{22,33}$). They must have seen the stone graves which have now been discovered at Hebron in the vicinity of the Valley of Grapes.

Who the "giants" really were is still quite unknown. Possibly they were a people who were much taller than the old established population around the Jordan. Clearly there was some racial memory of a taller type of man, which was enough to make a deep impression, and perhaps this is the reason why it appears in the Bible too.

These huge stone graves and the stories about giants once again bear witness to the colourful and varied history of the Land of Canaan, that narrow strip of land on the Mediterranean coast, into which from earliest times waves of alien peoples surged incessantly and left their mark behind them.

The news that Israel had conquered the whole of Jordan put King Balak of Moab into a panic. He was afraid that his own people too would be no match in physique or military skill for these tough sons of the desert. He convenes "the elders of Midian" and incites them against the children of Israel (Num. 22^4). They resolve to employ other than military measures. They will attempt to impose a check on Israel by means of magic. Incantations and curses, in the efficacy of which the peoples of the Ancient East firmly believed, will assuredly smash Israel's power. Balaam is summoned in haste from Pethor in Babylonia, where these black arts flourish. But Balaam, the great sorcerer and magician, fails. As soon as Balaam tries to utter a curse, a blessing upon Israel comes out instead (Num. 23). Then the king of Moab throws the most dangerous trump card in existence into the balance, a wicked card that is to have a lasting effect on the lives of the children of Israel.

The Bible passage which contains a description of the abominable stratagem of King Balak is felt by theologians to be embarrassing and therefore they prefer to gloss it over. The real question is, however, why such a scandalous affair appears in the

Bible at all. The answer is simple: the event was one which was of the deepest and most fateful significance for the people of Israel. That is the reason why the narrator does not maintain a modest silence but gives a frank and candid account of what actually happened.

It was in the thirties that French archaeologists, working at the Mediterranean port of Ras Shamra—the "White Haven" on the coast of Phoenicia—under the direction of Professor Claude Schaeffer of Strasbourg brought to light some evidence of Canaanite religious practices. Only then was it possible to estimate and understand what is recorded in Num. 25.

> "And Israel abode in Shittim, and the people began to commit whoredom with the daughters of Moab. And they called the people unto the sacrifices of their gods" (Num. 25[1-2]).

It is not the attractions of vice that the children of Israel are faced with. That is something that is and always had been universal. It was not professional prostitutes who led Israel astray. It was the daughters of the Moabites and the Midianites, their own wives and sweethearts. They enticed and seduced the men of Israel to take part in the rites of Baal, the fertility cult of Canaan. What Israel encountered, while still on the other side of Jordan, was the voluptuous worship of the Phoenician gods. The leaders of Israel struck swiftly and struck hard. They did not even spare their own men. Offenders were slaughtered and hanged. Phinehas, grand-nephew of Moses, who saw an Israelite taking a Midianite woman into his tent, took a javelin "and thrust both of them through, the man of Israel, and the woman through her belly" (Num. 25[8]). The people of Moab were spared since they were related to Israel—Lot, Abraham's nephew, was regarded as their ancestor (Gen. 19[37]). But against the Midianites a war of extermination was let loose, the classical "herem" or ban, as it is laid down in the Law (Deut. 7[2ff]; 20[13ff]). "Now therefore kill every male among the little ones and kill every woman that hath known man by lying with him," ordered Moses. Only the young girls were spared, everyone else was killed (Num. 31[7,17,18]).

> "And Moses went up from the plains of Moab unto the mountain of Nebo, to the top of Pisgah, that is over against Jericho. And the Lord showed him all the land" (Deut. 34[1]).

Moses had now fulfilled his heavy task. From the bond-cities of Egypt, through the years of hardship and privation in the steppes right up to that moment he had had to travel a long and bitterly hard road. He had nominated as his successor Joshua, a tried and trusted man and an unusually gifted strategist, which was what Israel was most in need of. Moses had finished the course and could take his leave of the world. He was not allowed to set foot himself on the soil of the Promised Land. But he was allowed to glimpse it from afar, from Mt. Nebo.

To visit this Biblical mountain means a journey of about 18 miles from Amman, centre and seat of government of the present kingdom of Jordan. The trip takes rather more than half an hour in a Land-Rover, crossing the hill-country on the edge of the Arabian desert, through wadis and sometimes past ploughed fields, heading straight for the south-east in the direction of the Dead Sea.

After a short climb over bare rocks we reach a broad barren plateau, 2,500 feet above sea level. On the western edge the cliffs drop sharply down to the Jordan basin. A fresh breeze blows on the summit. Under the clear blue skies there stretches into the distance in front of the enchanted visitor a unique panorama.

To the south lie the broad waters of the Salt Sea with their silvery sheen. On the far bank rises a dreary desolate scene of stone humps and hillocks. Behind it towers the long chain of brownish white limestone mountains of the Land of Judah. Just where it begins, rising sharply out of the Negev, lies Hebron. In the west, towards the Mediterranean, two tiny dots can be distinguished with the naked eye from the mountain range that stands out against the horizon—the towers of Bethlehem and Jerusalem. The eye wanders northward over the highlands of Samaria, past Galilee to the snow capped peaks of Hermon in the shimmering distance.

At the foot of Nebo narrow gorges slope downwards, brilliant with the green of their pomegranate trees and their orange coloured fruit. Then the ground sinks abruptly into the desolate steppe of the Jordan basin. A landscape of dazzling white chalk hills, almost as ghostly as the mountains of the moon and without a single blade of grass, flanks the mere 30 foot width of the river Jordan. The only comfort to the eye is a small green patch in front of the mountains that rise steeply on the west side of the Jordan—the oasis of Jericho.

This view from Nebo into Palestine was the last thing that Moses saw.

But beneath him on the broad steppe of Moab thin columns of smoke are rising heavenwards. Day and night campfires are burning among the mass of black goatshair tents. Joined to the hum of voices of all these men, women and children, the wind also carries over to the Jordan valley the bleating of grazing flocks. It is a peaceful scene. But it is only a moment of respite before the long yearned for day, the great calm before the storm which is decisively to affect the destiny of Israel and that of the land of Canaan.

The Battle for the Promised Land from Joshua to Saul

Chapter 15
ISRAEL INVADES

The world about 1200 B.C.—The weakness of Canaan—The first iron merchants—The ford across the Jordan—The stronghold of Jericho, the oldest city in the world—Scholars quarrel over broken walls—A trail of fire—Pharaoh mentions "Israel" by name for the first time—Excavations at Hazor—Graves at the Village of Joshua.

"Now after the death of Moses the servant of the Lord it came to pass, that the Lord spake unto Joshua, the son of Nun, Moses' minister, saying: Moses my servant is dead; now therefore arise, go over this Jordan, thou, and all this people, unto the land which I do give to them, even to the children of Israel" (Josh. 1$^{1-2}$).

About the same time as Israel was standing by the Jordan ready to march into the Promised Land, fate was advancing upon Mediterranean Troy and the days of the proud stronghold of King Priam were numbered. Soon the Homeric heroes of Greece, Achilles, Agamemnon and Odysseus would be arming for the fray—the hands of the timepiece of history were moving towards 1200 B.C. Israel could have chosen no better time for invasion. No danger threatened them from Egypt. Under Ramesses II Egypt had indeed known a last period of glory during which it had consolidated its power in Palestine, but even the might of Egypt crumbled in the political upheavals which marked the transition between the Bronze and the Iron Ages. Its influence in Canaan declined rapidly.

156

Torn by internal feuds between the innumerable petty king-doms and principalities of its city-states, and sucked dry by the corrupt politics of Egyptian occupation, Canaan itself had shot its bolt.

Ever since the expulsion of the Hyksos about 1550 B.C. Palestine had been an Egyptian province. Under the Hyksos a feudal system had broken up the old patriarchal social structure as it had existed in the towns of Abraham's day. Under an aristocratic ruling class, which was self-centred and despotic, the people were reduced to the level of subjects without rights, and became mere plebeians. Egypt left this feudal system in Palestine unaltered. Native princes could do as they pleased: they had their own armies, which consisted of patrician charioteers and plebeian infantry. Bloody warfare between the city-states did not worry the Egyptians. All they were interested in was the payment of tribute, which was supervised by strict and inflexible Egyptian inspectors. Garrisons and defence posts tacitly lent their activities the necessary weight. Gaza and Joppa housed the most important Egyptian administrative centres. By means of labour levies—supplied by the feudal lords—roads were built and maintained, the royal estates on the fertile plain of Jezreel south of Nazareth were managed and the glorious cedar forests of Lebanon were felled to the ground. The commissioners of the Pharaohs were corrupt. Often the troops' pay and rations were misappropriated. Whereupon they took the law into their own hands, and mercenaries from Egypt and Crete, Bedouins and Nubians plundered defenceless villages.

Under Egyptian rule the land of Canaan bled to death. The population shrank. Patrician houses of the 13th century B.C. are more primitive than they had been in earlier times, as is shown by excavations. Objets d'art and jewellery of any value are rarer, and gifts deposited with the dead in their tombs are of poorer quality. Fortress walls have lost their old solidity.

Only on the coast of Syria, protected on the landward side by the mountain ridges of the Lebanon and less affected by the quarrels of the princes, life in the maritime republics pursued its untroubled way. Whatever else happens seaports are always places where men can exchange what they have for what they want. About 1200 B.C. an entirely new metal—as valuable to begin with as gold or silver—appeared on the price lists: iron. Since it came from the Hittite country, the Phoenicians were the first to deal in this metal, which was to give its name to one of the ages of man's history. The Egyptians had known about iron for nearly 2,000 years and valued it as an extremely unusual and rare commodity. The iron they knew however did not come from our planet at all but from meteors. And the few expensive weapons that they managed to produce in this way were very properly called "Daggers from Heaven".

With the appearance of this new metal a new epoch, the Iron Age, was announced. The Bronze Age with its unique civilising achievements died away and a great epoch of the ancient world came to an end.

At the end of the 13th century B.C. a great new wave of foreign peoples surged down from the northern Aegean. By land and water these "Sea Peoples" flowed over Asia Minor. They were the fringes of a great movement of population to which the Dorian migration to Greece also belonged. The impetus of these foreigners—they were Indo-Germanic—was directed to Canaan and Egypt. For the time being Israel, waiting poised by the Jordan, had nothing to fear from them. And the Canaanites were divided and weak. Israel's hour had come. The Biblical trumpets of Jericho gave the signal.

> "... and they removed from Shittim and came to Jordan... and all the Israelites passed over on dry ground, until all the people were passed clear over Jordan... and encamped in Gilgal, in the east border of Jericho" (Josh. $3^{1,17}$; 4^{19}).

Today there is a bridge over the river at this point: the Jordan is very narrow and has always been fordable in many places. The natives know exactly where these fords are. In the dry season the dirty yellow water at Jericho is only about 30 feet wide.

When Israel reached the Jordan they found it in full spate, "for Jordan overfloweth all his banks all the time of harvest" (Josh. 3^{15}). As happened every year, the snow on Hermon had begun to melt: "... the waters which came down from above stood and rose up upon an heap" (i.e., were dammed) "very far from the city Adam... and all the Israelites passed over on dry ground, until all the people were passed clear over Jordan" (Josh. $3^{16,17}$). A much frequented ford on the middle reaches of the Jordan, el-Damiyah, recalls the "city Adam". Should there be a sudden spate it can quite easily be dammed at such a place for a short time, and while it is blocked the lower part of the river is almost dried up. (An alternative explanation is offered on p. 146.)

Considerable damming of the Jordan has however often been attested as a result of earthquake. The last thing of this kind happened in 1927. As a result of a severe quake the river banks caved in, tons of soil crashed down into the river bed from the low hills that follow the Jordan's winding course. The flow of water was completely stopped for twenty-one hours. In 1924 the same thing happened. In 1906 the Jordan became so choked up with debris as the result of an earthquake that the river bed on the lower reaches near Jericho was completely dry for twenty-four hours. Arab records mention a similar occurrence in A.D. 1267.

It is easy to see from the air why this part of the Jordan valley was so important thousands of years ago. To the east, between the river and the Arabian desert, stretches the hilly plateau of Jordan, which has always been the home of countless tribes of nomads and from which they have always been able to look across to the fertile pastures and ploughed fields of Canaan. It is a natural line of attack—the principal ford across the Jordan, easily negotiated by man and beast. But anyone trying to force his way in from the east had to face the first serious obstacle soon after crossing the river—Jericho, the strategic key to the conquest of Canaan.

> "And it came to pass, when the people heard the sound
> of the trumpet, and the people shouted with a great shout,
> that the wall fell down flat, so that the people went up into
> the city, every man straight before him, and they took the
> city. . . . And they burnt the city with fire and all that was
> therein" (Josh. 6[20,24]).

Joshua's battle for this city has made it famous. Today a battle rages round it, but it is between experts armed with spades, picks and chronological tables. According to the Bible it took Joshua seven days to subdue Jericho. The battle of the archaeologists over what is left of it has lasted—with intervals—for more than seventy years now and is by no means settled.

The exciting and dramatic excavations at Jericho are rife with remarkable finds and unexpected discoveries, with surprises and disappointments, with assertions and counter-assertions, with disputes over interpretation and chronology.

The Jordan basin has a tropical climate. The village of Eriha, the modern successor of Jericho, gives the impression of being an oasis on the edge of a barren waste of chalk. Even palm trees grow here although they are seldom found anywhere else in Palestine, except to the south of Gaza. The Bible too calls Jericho "the city of palm trees" (Jud. 3¹³). Golden red clusters of dates shimmer among the green foliage. From ancient times the spring called "Ain es-Sultan" has produced as if by magic this lush patch of vegetation. North of present day Jericho a mound of ruins is named after it, Tell es-Sultan. This is the battle ground of the archaeologists. Anyone wanting to examine it must buy a ticket. The site of the excavations lies behind a barbed wire fence.

The remains of Jericho have made Tell es-Sultan one of the most extraordinary scenes of discovery in the world, for it has long since been not merely a matter of investigating the fortress of Biblical times. In this mound, under the strata of the Bronze Age, lie traces of the Stone Age, which take us back to the earliest times of all, to the days when man first built himself settled habitations. The oldest of Jericho's houses are 7,000 years old and, with their round walls, resemble Bedouins' tents. But the art of pottery was as yet unknown among their inhabitants. In 1953 a British expedition conducted excavations here, and the director of the enterprise, Dr. Kathleen M. Kenyon declared: "Jericho can lay claim to being by far the oldest city in the world."

Shortly after the turn of the century archaeologists directed their attention to this lonely mound of Tell es-Sultan. From 1907 to 1909 picks and spades carefully felt their way through layer after layer of this massive mound of ruins. When the two leaders of the German-Austrian expedition, Professor Ernst Sellin and Professor Karl Watzinger, made known what they had discovered, they caused genuine amazement. Two concentric rings of fortification were exposed, the inner ring surrounding the ridge of the hill. It is a masterpiece of military defence made of sun-dried bricks in the form of two parallel walls about 10 or 12 feet apart. The inner wall, which is particularly massive, is about 12 feet thick throughout. The outer ring of fortification runs along the foot of the hill and consists of a 6 foot thick wall, about 25–30 feet high, with strong foundations. These are the famous walls of Jericho. The two lines of fortification, their exact historical placing, the dates of their erection and destruction have given rise to a vehement dispute among the experts who advance the pros and cons in a welter of opinions, hypotheses and arguments. It began with the first announcement by Sellin and Watzinger and has continued ever since.

FIG. 23.—The walls of the old Canaanite fortress of Jericho. (Reconstructed.)

Both discoverers arrived themselves at what they called a "considerable modification" of their first conclusion. They issued a joint statement in which they maintained that the outer wall "fell about 1200 B.C., and therefore must be the city wall which Joshua destroyed". To shed new light on the whole business a British expedition set out for Tell es-Sultan in 1930. After six years' digging further portions of the fortifications were exposed. Professor John Garstang as leader of the expedition noted every detail with the utmost precision. He described graphically the violence with which the inner circle of parallel fortifications had been destroyed: "The space between the two walls is filled with fragments and rubble. There are clear traces of a tremendous fire, compact masses of blackened bricks, cracked stones, charred wood and ashes. Along the walls the houses have been burned to the ground and their roofs have crashed on top of them."

After Garstang had consulted the most knowledgeable experts, the outcome of the second archaeological battle was that the inner ring was the more recent, therefore the one which must have been destroyed by the Israelites. But that did not settle the matter. The wrangle about the Walls of Jericho continues. Garstang dates the destruction of the inner ring about 1400 B.C. Father Hugues Vincent, a leading archaeologist and one of the most successful investigators into Jerusalem's ancient past, also studied the evidence and dated the destruction of the walls between 1250 and 1200 B.C.

Today we know that both experts were mistaken. Since their day, archaeologists have developed methods which allow us to understand excavation sites much better than was the case a few decades ago. Professor Garstang and Father Hugues Vincent both thought that walls from the *early* Bronze Age belonged to the *late* Bronze Age. Today we know that this is not so. The mistake occurred because wind and weather had largely carried away the more recent layers which covered the earliest remains. It is in one area only, at the highest place on Tell es-Sultan, on the northwest of the heap of ruins, that the remains of middle Bronze Age defence works, built on top of what is left of early Bronze Age walls, have been preserved at their full height. Scanty vestiges of late Bronze Age dwellings have been found only on the lower eastern slopes of the hill. We owe all this information to the great British archaeologist Kathleen M. Kenyon who by her extensive and successful excavations in Jericho during the fifties of the present century laid the foundations of our present-day knowledge. It was Kathleen M. Kenyon, too, who convincingly interpreted the very small amount of pottery found at Jericho. She was also able to interpret the information provided by the graves which constitute the only evidence concerning the late period of ancient Jericho.

According to her findings the walls of Jericho had to be rebuilt during the Bronze Age no less than seventeen times. The walls were repeatedly destroyed either by earthquakes or by erosion. Perhaps this weakness of the walls of Jericho found expression in the Bible account of how the children of Israel, in order to conquer Jericho, merely had to shout their war cry when the priests blew the trumpets. The middle Bronze Age city dated from the time of the Hyksos and came to an end at the same time as they, around 1550 B.C. Thereafter Jericho remained uninhabited for about a century and a half. It is only about the year 1400 B.C., as is shown by pottery, objects found in graves and the few late Bronze Age remains of dwellings on the eastern slope of the hill, that people began to settle there once more. This late Bronze Age town, of whose existence we have only such sparse evidence, was again deserted by its inhabitants, however, around 1325 B.C. Did they become the victims of conquerors of some kind who were subsequently absorbed in the melting-pot of

"Israel" and whose conquests were ultimately incorporated in the Biblical account of the settlement of the land? For if it is the case that Israelites did not come to Jericho until the time of the occupation, i.e., about the middle or towards the end of the 13th

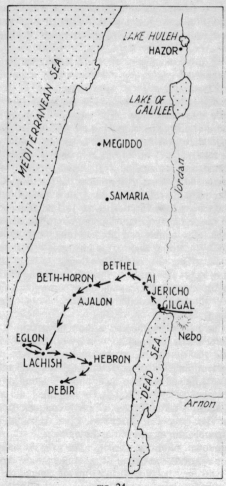

FIG. 24.

century B.C., they did not need to conquer the city for they found it uninhabited! Jericho was not rebuilt until the 9th century before Christ, in the days of King Ahab (1 Kings 16^{34}). As the Bible tells us (Joshua 6^{26}), it was as though a curse had lain on the place for centuries.

Jericho was the first strong point to be overcome on the way to the Promised Land. Archaeologists have been able on other sites to follow the further progress of the children of Israel towards their conquest of Canaan.

About 12 miles south-west of Hebron lay the Debir of the Bible. Defended by a strong enclosing wall it dominated the Negev. Excavations by W. F. Albright and M. G. Kyle of the U.S.A. in Tell Beit Mirsim since 1926 disclosed a layer of ashes and considerable destruction. The stratum of ashes contained sherds which undoubtedly date from the end of the 13th century B.C. Immediately above the burnt layer are traces of a new settlement by Israel. "And Joshua returned, and all Israel with him, to Debir, and fought against it" (Josh. 10^{38}).

Thirty miles south-west of Jerusalem the Lachish of the Bible can be identified. It must have been an extraordinarily strong fortress for Canaan. In the thirties at Tell ed-Duweir a British expedition under James Lesley Starkey measured out an area of twenty-four acres which had at one time been built up and surrounded by a strong wall. This city also fell a victim to a conflagration which destroyed everything. A bowl which was salvaged from the ruins bears an inscription giving its date as the fourth year of Pharaoh Merenptah. That corresponds to the year 1230 B.C. "And the Lord delivered Lachish into the hand of Israel" (Josh. 10^{32}).

In the Cairo Museum there is a monument from a mortuary temple near Thebes, on which the victory of Pharaoh Merenptah[1] over the Libyans is commemorated and celebrated. In order to augment his triumph, other notable victories which this ruler is said to have achieved are also mentioned. The end of the hymn of praise runs as follows: "Canaan is despoiled and all its evil with it. Askelon is taken captive, Gezer is conquered, Yanoam is blotted out. The people of Israel is desolate, it has no offspring: Palestine has become a widow for Egypt."

This triumphal hymn, written in 1229 B.C., is in more than one respect valuable and illuminating. Here for the first time in

---

[1] Acceded to the throne in 1234 B.C.

human history the name "Israel" is immortalised, and that by a foreigner and a contemporary. Israel is expressly described as a "people" and moreover in connection with Palestinian place-names—surely a proof for the most hardened sceptic that Israel was already properly settled in Canaan in 1229 B.C. and no longer completely unknown.

Shortly before 1200 B.C. Israel had reached the goal which had for so long been the object of its aspirations. It is now in Canaan, but it is not yet in full control of the country. A trail of burnt out cities marks its path and indicates an extremely shrewd strategic plan. Joshua avoided the strongest fortresses like Gezer and Jerusalem. Obviously he followed the line of least resistance. The fertile plains and river valleys are likewise still in the hands of the Canaanites and will remain so for many generations to come. Israel has neither the armour to resist the dreaded chariots, nor the technique and experience required to war against strongly fortified cities. But it has secured a foothold in the more sparsely populated areas, the hill country on both sides of the Jordan is in its hands.

About ten miles north of the Lake of Galilee lay the mighty stronghold of Hazor, which was still quite powerful, although it had had to suffer, about 1300 B.C., at the hands of conquerors, probably the Egyptians under the Pharaoh Sethos I; Joshua "took Hazor, and smote the king thereof with the sword: for Hazor beforetime was the head of all those kingdoms" (Joshua 11[10]). The word "beforetime" provides us with cause for reflection. The town, devastated probably by Sethos I, before its destruction by the Israelites, had indeed been richer and more flourishing than the Hazor they found. The more crucial event and the one which had the gravest consequences in the town's history was undoubtedly this destruction by Israel towards the end of the 13th century B.C.

The rediscovery of this royal city can be counted as one of the most surprising pieces of good fortune in recent Biblical archaeology. John Garstang, the English archaeologist, had already identified as the site of old Hazor the extensive mound of rubble Tell el-Qedah, which stands out prominently to the west of the Jordan between Lake Huleh and the Lake of Galilee. But it was not until excavations, begun in 1953 under the auspices of the Hebrew University of Jerusalem and directed by Yigael Yadin of the James A. de Rothschild expedition, had continued over several seasons that the hitherto undisturbed Tell could be awakened from its dreams and induced to part with its closely guarded secrets. Bit by bit its layers began to tell the experts the long and exciting story of the chequered fortunes of Hazor.

No fewer than twenty-one stages of development can be distinguished: twenty-one cities growing up on top of one another, each built on the rubble of past generations and each in its turn levelled to the ground, destroyed by war or fire or the force of nature. Surmounted by its citadel and fortified area the city spread its lower reaches far out into the plain. An ingenious drainage system consisting of clay pipes looked after public sanitation.

What has been discovered confirms in a striking way what the Bible has to say about the powerful role that Hazor played in Canaan at the time of the Israelite conquest. Hazor was in fact not only one of the largest settlements of the country but also one of the strongest fortresses. In the 13th century B.C. it was destroyed, as the Book of Joshua records. A layer of burnt rubble indicates a great conflagration about that time. Many scholars do not hesitate to attribute this burnt rubble to Joshua and his hosts.

With these victories and the promised occupation of Canaan, Joshua's great assignment has been fulfilled. At a ripe old age he dies and is buried, "in Timnath-Serah which is in mount Ephraim, on the north side of the hill of Gaash" (Josh. 24[30]). The Greek text (LXX 24[30b]) adds a very significant remark: "There they put with him into the tomb in which they buried him, the knives of stone with which he circumcised the children of Israel in Gilgal." In Gilgal, on the way from the Jordan to Jericho, the rite of circumcision was carried out on the men of Israel according to tradition "with stone knives". "Now all the people that came out were circumcised: but all the people that were born in the wilderness by the way as they came forth out of Egypt, them they had not circumcised" (Josh. 5[5]). Ten miles north-west of Bethel lies Kefr Ishu'a, the "Village of Joshua". In the neighbouring hillside are some rock tombs. In 1870 in one of these sepulchres a number of stone knives was found. . . .

The Biblical account of what appears in the history books as Israel's occupation of the land and the confirmation by archaeological finds of what the Bible says once again provide excellent examples of the fact that new knowledge gives rise to new problems. Hazor is a prime example. With its burnt rubble, its layer of ashes and its broken idols, it seems to support the following passage: "But the Lord thy God shall deliver them (the

Canaanites) unto thee, and shall destroy them with a mighty destruction, until they be destroyed. And he shall deliver their kings into thine hand, and thou shalt destroy their name from under heaven: there shall no man be able to stand before thee, until thou have destroyed them. The graven images of their gods shall ye burn with fire..." (Deuteronomy 7[23-25]). Hazor's late Bronze Age layer of rubble does indeed fit in chronologically very well with the beginning of Joshua's conquest towards the end of the 13th century B.C. Hazor nevertheless presents us with a problem for the king of Hazor was Jabin whom Joshua defeated "by the waters of Merom" (Joshua 11 [5ff]). According to the Book of Judges (Judges 4[2]) which deals with a later phase of Israel's history, Jabin was still ruler over the same town and Israel had been "sold into the hand of Jabin king of Canaan, that reigned in Hazor" (Judges 4[2]). It was only subsequently that Jabin was "subdued" (Judges 4[23]) by Barak, the commander of the Israelites, although it is not clear whether the decisive battle took place on the banks of the River Kishon (Judges 5[21]) or on Mount Tabor. What are we to think of this duplication? Archaeology here comes to our aid for after the catastrophe towards the end of the 13th century Hazor was by no means such an important town that it could have been considered as the residence of a "king of Canaan" into whose hands Israel was "sold". After an interlude of occupation by semi-nomads and sparse early Israelite settlement (12th–11th century B.C.), it was not until the days of King Solomon (10th century B.C.) that Hazor again became a fortified place. It seems, in consequence, that King Jabin from the period of the Judges probably never existed. He is presumably merely a literary reflection of that earlier king of Hazor of the same name during the period of the occupation of the country, that is to say, of the late Bronze Age, except that in the traditions which attached themselves to his person, late Bronze and early Iron Age elements became mingled.

Hazor is situated fairly far to the north, quite a distance north of the Lake of Galilee. Yet the Biblical accounts of a number of other sites which have been excavated in the south of the Promised Land reveal a similar mingling of Iron Age and Bronze Age traditions. Thus the town of Ai is of considerable importance among the Canaanite towns conquered by Joshua (Joshua 7[2ff] as well as 8[1-24]). According to the Bible (Joshua 12[16]) the neighbouring Beth-el is of subsidiary importance. In point of fact, a thick layer of ash and soot-covered brick rubble which covered the late Bronze Age stratum has been found in Beth-el, just as was to be expected. But what happened at Ai? Judith Marquet-Krause, who excavated there, was unable to find any stratum providing evidence of destruction in Joshua's time, the late Bronze Age. In his day Ai had long since lain in ruins and had been deserted ever since the early Bronze Age—thus justifying its name, which in Hebrew merely means "ruin", but not the detailed description of its conquest in the eighteenth chapter of the Book of Joshua! It was not until the beginning of the Iron Age that new settlers arrived, but their village was also destroyed in the end. Had Judith Marquet-Krause been mistaken? Fresh excavations directed by J. A. Callaway were intended to investigate the question. Callaway could do no more, however, than confirm that there had not been any settlement in Ai during the late Bronze Age. The Israelites, therefore, had never been able to conquer the town.

The experts racked their brains. Could the Bible have been in error to this extent? Or had the writers of the Bible confused something? Did the Biblical account of the capture of Ai really refer to the neighbouring place Beth-el which had indeed fallen into ruins at the end of the Bronze Age? Finally the idea occurred to them that all that was needed was not to cling slavishly to the hypothesis that all the events related in the Bible in connection with the occupation of the country really took place towards the end of the Bronze Age. Could the Bible perhaps be referring to the Ai of the early Iron Age? In that case, it was not only the results of excavations at Ai and the Biblical account which would correspond with one another, but a number of other sites as well such as Arad, Dibon and Gibeon which also had not yielded any traces of occupation during the late Bronze Age except for one grave in Gibeon. Even the statement that Gibeon was greater than Ai (Joshua 10^2) is correct in regard to the Iron Age settlements. Once more the Bible is right if we accept that the traditions concerning the occupation of the country mingle facts from the Bronze Age and the Iron Age.

It was in consequence of these and similar inaccuracies, however, that the specialists found themselves able to look upon the Biblical account of the occupation of the country as the condensed description of an extremely complicated and lengthy process which lasted for several centuries, but which the Bible presents to us in compressed form concentrating it all on the person of Joshua. In doing so, the Bible selects specific events and combines them to form a story in which the episodes do not always agree. Some specialists even claim that an occupation, such as is described in the Bible, never occurred and surprisingly this can be substantiated in the Bible. After his first victories in the land of the Canaanites, Joshua assembled "all Israel" by Mount Gerizim and Mount Ebal which rise above the old town of Shechem now known as Nablus. In connection with this event, the Bible expressly uses the words "all Israel . . . as well the stranger, as he that was born among them" (Joshua 8[33]). How could that be the case? Had not "all Israel" only just arrived in the Promised Land? What did this mention of those "born among them" signify? Many scholars are of the opinion that the subsequent influx of Israelites occurred in several waves. That might be the explanation—when the newcomers arrived, the others were already there. They were already residents.

There are other theories finding support in the scholarly discussions on the settlement of the land. One of them claims that what the Bible describes as an occupation was really a series of clashes between residents of the towns and the nomads or semi-nomadic inhabitants of the steppes which were brought about by social and religious motives.

Still another theory advances the idea that the occupation was really a mostly peaceful infiltration of foreign immigrants only now and then leading to tensions which worked themselves out in warlike conflicts.

Chapter 16
UNDER DEBORAH AND GIDEON

Israel settles down—Pioneering in the mountains—Peasants' huts instead of palaces—Deborah incites to revolt—Clash in the plain of Jezreel—Victory over the "chariots of iron"—Israelite crockery at Megiddo—Marauders from the desert—Traces of Abimelech's destruction of Shechem—Gideon's successful tactics—First battle in history against a camel-corps—A new breed of long-distance carriers.

"And the Lord gave unto Israel all the land which he sware to give unto their fathers: and they possessed it and dwelt therein" (Josh. 21^{43}).

Immediately after the conquest an astonishing thing happened: the tribes of Israel dug their toes into the ground they had won. They can therefore no longer have been a typical nomadic people. Canaan had experienced invasions of nomads from time immemorial but they had always been merely episodes. The tribes would graze their flocks and then one day would disappear as suddenly as they had come. Israel on the other hand became static, cultivating fields and clearing forests . . . "if thou be a great people, then get thee up to the wood country and cut down for thyself there" (Josh. 17^{15}). They gave up their tents and built themselves huts: they settled down among the ruins of the houses in the towns they had conquered. In Debir, Bethshemesh and Bethel remains of their primitive and poverty-stricken furnishings were found on top of the strata which were deposited when the towns were burned down.

This break with the past is clearly recognisable from the excavations. Where previously patrician houses and palaces of

FIG. 25.—Israelite storing-jar.

the long established feudal barons had been standing, there now
arose peasants' huts and fences. The massive defence walls show
signs of having had necessary repairs done to them. But what the
men of Israel replaced was of the thinnest masonry. The construction of a new system of strong defensive walls would have
entailed forced labour and there was nothing the Israelites hated
more. They regarded themselves as freemen, as independent
farmers. "But every man did that which was right in his own
eyes" (Jud. 17⁶). Even the word generally used in Canaan
meaning a bondsman was used by the Israelites in exactly the
opposite sense to mean a freeman. In the feudal system under the
princes of the city-states all the drudgery was done by slaves. In
the case of Israel the work of the farm was done by the freeborn
sons of the family. At their head stood the father, the patriarch.
Countless new settlements sprang into being. Archaeologists
have found traces of them throughout the highlands. But there is
very little of them left. For the first building material they used
was sun-dried mud bricks, and the buildings they put up in this
way did not last.

Real pioneer work was done by the Israelites in the mountains.
Uninhabitable areas, districts without springs or streams were
opened up. Although it sounds unbelievable, what remains of a
new technique used by their ancestors has been partly taken over
and put into commission again by the state of Israel today. They
dug cisterns in the ground to collect the rainfall, and lined the
insides with a type of limestone plaster which was hitherto
unknown. These fixtures were so solidly built that they have
been able to withstand the ravages of time for thousands of
years.

As the Book of Judges tells us, and investigation confirms, the

Israelites struck roots in their new home as settlers and farmers.
In continuous fighting with their neighbours and feuds among
themselves they gradually gained in military power and experience. The Bible mentions disputes with Moabites, Ammonites
and Aramaean tribes from the Syrian desert. It speaks of bloody
civil war, when the tribes fought against Benjamin (Jud. 20).
Bethel lay in the territory of Benjamin, and Albright, digging
there, found strata which showed that the place had been destroyed
four times between 1200 and 1000 B.C.

It was around this time too that "Abimelech fought against the
city all that day: and he took the city and slew the people that
was therein, and beat down the city, and sowed it with salt"
(Jud. 9[45]). So runs the description in the Book of Judges of the
conquest of Shechem by Abimelech, the ambitious and vindic-
tive son of Gideon who murdered all his brothers.

In 1959 at Tell el-Balata, on the site of this Biblical city which
had been the first place Abraham encountered on his arrival in
Canaan, excavations by American archaeologists from Drew
University and McCormick Theological Seminary led by Professor G. Ernest Wright, who was following the earlier investigations of Professor Ernst Sellin of Germany, were able to confirm
what the Bible has to say about the fate of Shechem. Fragments
of clay jars which were scattered about among the ruins and
could be identified as typical Israelite pottery put the date of the
destruction of Shechem towards the end of the 12th century B.C.,
that is, about the period of Abimelech. At the same time the
remains of the "tower of Shechem" were identified, as well as
the "hold of the house of the god Berith" and the "house of
Millo" which are mentioned in Jud. 9[20,46]. It does seem
however that all of these were part of a single building which
towered above the city wall and which had been built upon the
ruins of an earlier Hyksos temple.

FIG. 26.—Canaanite Prince from Megiddo seen on his throne, with harpist and
war-chariot (1200 B.C.).

These troubled years of the first colonists have found an imperishable memorial in three narratives of the Book of Judges: in the Song of Deborah, in the story of Gideon and in the doughty deeds of Samson.

The background of these "pious tales" is made up of facts, contemporary events which as a result of recent research can be dated with considerable accuracy. When Israel entered Canaan about 1230 B.C. it had to be content with the mountains... for it "could not drive out the inhabitants of the valley, because they had chariots of iron" (Jud. 1^{19}). It was not until a century later that the tide turned. It would seem that among the mountains of Galilee tribes which had settled there had to render bond-service to the Canaanites. Among them was the tribe of Issachar which is ridiculed in the Bible as "a strong ass". It is accused of "couching down between two burdens" and of becoming a "servant unto tribute" (Gen. 49^{14,15}).

Revolt broke out in Galilee in protest against this oppression. The impetus was supplied by a woman, Deborah. She summoned the tribes of Israel to fight for their freedom. It is from her that that wonderful song, which she sang to the assembled throng, has come down to us.

Barak, one of the tribe of Issachar, became the leader. Other tribes joined in and a great army was formed. Then Barak took a decisive step. He dared to do what Israel had never previously risked, he came to grips with the dreaded enemy on the plain: "So Barak went down from mount Tabor, and ten thousand men after him" (Jud. 4^{14}). The scene of the encounter was the broad and fertile plain of Jezreel between the mountains of Galilee in the north and Samaria in the south—absolute and sovereign domain of the Canaanite city princes and feudal barons. Here they awaited the dangerous fighting forces of the Canaanites ... "then fought the kings of Canaan in Taanach by the waters of Megiddo" (Jud. 5^{19}). The incredible happened—Israel won. For the first time they had succeeded in smashing and routing a force of chariots in open battle. The spell was broken: Israel had shown that it had the measure of the military technique of the Canaanites and could beat them at their own game.

Two mounds of rubble in the plain of Jezreel preserve all that is left of Taanach and Megiddo, lying about 5 miles apart. Both cities changed places several times in order of importance. About 1450 B.C. Taanach was a large city-state while Megiddo was only a small Egyptian garrison. About 1150 B.C. Megiddo was

destroyed and deserted by its inhabitants. For a long time it lay
in ruins, and was not rebuilt and inhabited until 1100 B.C. The
pottery of the new settlers there is striking. It consists of large
clay preserving jars of exactly the same type as were used at this
time by the Israelites. Archaeologists found them in all the other
settlements in the mountains of Samaria and Judaea. Taanach is
specifically mentioned in the Song of Deborah as the site of the
battle. The reference to its being "by the waters of Megiddo" is
presumably a more precise description of its situation. Megiddo
itself, whose "water" is the river Kishon, cannot at that time
have been in existence.

Archaeological discoveries and Biblical references make it
possible to date the first battle against the Canaanite chariots in
the period between the destruction and rebuilding of Megiddo,
about 1125 B.C.

The Gideon story tells of the second triumph of Israel.
Suddenly out of the East came a new, unfamiliar and sinister
threat to Israel's safety. Hordes of Midianite nomads, mounted
on camels, attacked the country, plundering, burning and
massacring . . . "for both they and their camels were without
number: and they entered into the land to destroy it" (Jud. 6[5]).
For years Israel was at the mercy of these Midianite attacks.
Then Gideon appeared as their deliverer. He adopted successfully,
as the Bible describes in detail (Jud. 7[20ff]), a new kind of surprise
tactics which routed the Midianites and apparently persuaded
them to leave the Israelites in peace from then on.

It is often the lot of peaceful inventions to be used first of all
in time of war. The new "invention" which made it possible for
the Midianites to terrorise Israel was the taming of the camel!

Tame camels are likely to have been something quite new in
the ancient world. The people of the Bronze Age probably knew
nothing of them. Egyptian texts never mention them. Even in
Mari, next door to the great Arabian desert, there is no single
reference to them in any of that vast collection of documents. We
must eliminate the camel from our conception of life in the
ancient world of the Orient. References to them in the Book of
Genesis must have crept in at a later date. The attractive scene,
for example, where we meet Rebecca for the first time in her
native city of Nahor, must make do with a change of stage props.
The "camels" belonging to her future father-in-law Abraham
which she watered at the well were donkeys (Gen. 24[10ff]).
Similarly it was donkeys that for thousands of years carried on

their backs all kinds of burdens and costly merchandise along the great trade routes of the ancient world until the tame camel saved them.

It is not quite certain when exactly the taming of the camel took place but there are some facts which point to a general conclusion. In the 11th century B.C. the camel appears in cuneiform texts and reliefs and from then on is more and more frequently mentioned. This must be about the time of the Gideon story. Doubtless such marauding attacks with animals that had until then been regarded as wild must have come as a frightful shock.

The third challenge held the greatest and deadliest danger for Israel and threatened its very existence: the clash with the Philistines.

Chapter 17
THE WARRIORS FROM CAPHTOR

Krethi and Plethi—Invasion by the "Sea Peoples"—The great trek from the Aegean—Triumphal progress with ox-waggons and ships—The Hittite empire disappears—Seaports in flames on the coast of Canaan—General mobilisation on the Nile—Pharaoh Ramesses III saves Egypt—The great land and sea engagement—Interrogation in P.O.W. camps—Life-size portraits of the Philistines.

"Have not I brought up Israel out of the land of Egypt? and the Philistines from Caphtor . . . ?" (Amos 9⁷).

The fabulous tales of the redoubtable Samson, that great bear of a man full of pranks and derring-do, herald the beginning of the great tussle.

Philistines!—This name has become common currency in so many ways. We talk of someone being "a proper Philistine", or of someone else as a veritable "Goliath". He also was one of them. We speak disparagingly of the "Cherithites and Pelethites" without realising that these terms designate "Cretans and Philistines". Who does not know the tragic love story of Samson and Delilah, the woman who betrayed him to the Philistines? Who

does not remember the superhuman strength of Samson, who could strangle lions with his bare hands, who slew 1,000 Philistines with the jawbone of an ass, and in the end, blind and deserted by the woman he loved, brought a Philistine temple crashing down about his head in the fury of his anger? Yet very few of us ever really think how little we know of these Philistines whom we talk so much about.

The Philistine people, who played a decisive role in the life of Israel, were for a long time wrapped in mystery. It is only quite recently that it has been possible to find out something about them. Bit by bit, as a result of careful examination of the fruits of scientific research, the picture has become clearer. Fragments of pottery, inscriptions in temples and traces of burnt-out cities give us a mosaic depicting the first appearance of these Philistines, which is unrivalled in its dramatic effect.

Terrifying reports heralded the approach of these alien people. Messengers brought evil tidings of these unknown strangers who appeared on the edge of the civilised ancient world, on the coast of Greece. Ox-waggons, heavy carts with solid wheels, drawn by hump-backed bullocks, piled high with household utensils and furniture, accompanied by women and children, made their steady advance. In front marched armed men. They carried round shields and bronze swords. A thick cloud of dust enveloped them, for there were masses of them. Nobody knew where they came from. The enormous trek was first sighted at the Sea of Marmora. From there it made its way southwards along the Mediterranean coast. On its green waters sailed a proud fleet in the same direction, a host of ships with high prows and a cargo of armed men.

Wherever this terrifying procession halted it left behind a trail of burning houses, ruined cities and devastated crops. No man could stop these foreigners; they smashed all resistance. In Asia

FIG. 27.—Examination of Philistine prisoners by Egyptian officers.

Minor towns and settlements fell before them. The mighty fortress of Chattusas on the Halys was destroyed. The magnificent stud horses of Cilicia were seized as plunder. The treasures of the silver mines of Tarsus were looted. The carefully guarded secret of the manufacture of iron, the most valuable metal of the times, was wrested from the foundries beside the ore deposits. Under the impact of these shocks one of the three great powers of the second millennium B.C. collapsed. The Hittite Empire was obliterated.

A fleet of the foreign conquerors arrived off Cyprus and occupied the island. By land the trek continued, pressed on into northern Syria, reached Carchemish on the Euphrates and moved on up the valley of the Orontes. Caught in a pincer movement from sea and land the rich seaports of the Phoenicians fell before them. First Ugarit, then Byblos, Tyre and Sidon. Flames leapt from the cities of the fertile coastal plain of Palestine. The Israelites must have seen this wave of destruction, as they looked down from their highland fields and pastures, although the Bible tells us nothing about that. For Israel was not affected. What went up in flames down there in the plains were the strongholds of the hated Canaanites.

On and on rolled this human avalanche by sea and by land, forcing its way all the time towards the Nile, towards Egypt. . . .

In Medinet Habu west of Thebes on the Nile stands the imposing ruin of the splendid temple of Amun, dating from the reign of Ramesses III (1195–1164 B.C.). Its turreted gateway, its lofty columns, and the walls of its halls and courts are crammed with carved reliefs and inscriptions. Thousands upon thousands of square feet filled with historical documents carved in stone. The temple is one vast literary and pictorial record of the campaigns of the Pharaohs and is the principal witness to events on the Nile at that time.

It is more than plain from these records that Egypt was then in a state of acute panic and only too conscious of the danger in which it stood. One of the texts rings with a note of anxious foreboding: ''In the eighth year of the reign of Ramesses III. . . . No country has been able to withstand their might. The land of the Hittites, Kode,[1] Carchemish . . . and Cyprus have been destroyed at one stroke. . . . They have crushed their peoples, and their lands are as if they had never been. They marched against

---

[1] The coastal area of Cilicia and Northern Syria.

Egypt.... They laid hands on every land to the farthest ends of the earth. Their hearts were high and their confidence in themselves was supreme: 'Our plans will succeed'."

FIG. 28.—The battle between Pharaoh Ramesses III and the Philistines.

Ramesses III made feverish preparations for battle and decreed a general mobilisation: "I manned my borders... and drew up my armies before them: princes, garrison commanders and warriors. I turned the river mouths into a strong defensive wall, with warships, galleys and coastal vessels... fully manned from stem to stern with brave warriors armed to the teeth. The troops were the best that Egypt could muster. They were as ready for battle as lions roaring on the mountains. The chariot detachments consisted of the swiftest runners, and every first class charioteer available. The horses flew like the wind ready to crush foreign lands under their feet...."

With an enormous fighting force and every able bodied warrior that Egypt could call on, Ramesses III advanced to engage in a great battle on land against the foreign hordes. The inscriptions have nothing very definite to say about this battle. As usual, the Egyptian war reports confine themselves in this case to singing the praises of the victor. "His troops", it is recorded of Ramesses III, "were like bulls ready for battle: his horses were like falcons amid a flock of tiny birds...." But a huge relief still portrays this terrible battle after 3,000 years: the Egyptian commandos have scurried in among the armed enemy trekkers. Fearful slaughter rages among the ponderous ox-waggons carrying the women and children. Under the hooves of the bullocks and horses the bodies of the slain lie in heaps. Victory seems to have been won already, since Egyptian soldiers are seen plundering the ox-waggons.

Egypt had won a battle of prime significance in world history. The enemy land forces had been annihilated. Ramesses III hastened to the coast in a swift chariot, since "they had entered the mouths of the river" with their ships.

This great naval battle is likewise perpetuated on a stone relief in the temple at Medinet Habu: the fleets of the two opposing forces have approached each other. Shortly before their encounter the wind must have suddenly died down, since the sails are reefed. That meant a severe handicap for the foreigners. Their ships could no longer be manoeuvred. The warriors are standing there, ready for the fray but helpless. Their swords and spears were useless except in hand to hand fighting when the ships were close enough together. The calm let the Egyptians have it all their own way. Their vessels, manned by oarsmen, approach the enemy ships at a safe distance, then the archers are given the order to fire. A murderous hail of arrows pour down upon the foreigners who provide a mass target and fall overboard in vast numbers. The bodies of badly wounded and dead men cover the water. When the enemy had been decimated and was in complete disorder, the Egyptians rowed towards them and capsized their boats. Those who escaped death by the hail of arrows or by drowning were killed or captured by Egyptian soldiers on the nearby shore.

Ramesses III had been able to ward off this deadly threat to Egypt on land and sea in these two decisive battles. There had been no victory like it in all the past history of the Nile.

After the victory a gruesome reckoning was made of dead and wounded by hacking off their hands and piling them in heaps. This was the method of counting the numbers of a defeated enemy. About what happened to the women and children of the foreigners the inscriptions tell us nothing. The reliefs show the first P.O.W. camps in history. The defeated soldiers are herded together.

The treatment which the mass of prisoners received was in principle the same as happens today. Drawn up in rank and file they squat on the ground awaiting checking. Even the much maligned questionnaire was included: Egyptian officers dictate to scribes the statements made by the prisoners. Only one matter was differently dealt with in those days. Nowadays prisoners of war have P.O.W. or K.G. painted on their tunics; the Egyptians branded Pharaoh's name on their prisoners' skins. It lasted longer.

It is to the hieroglyphics of these oldest questionnaires in the world that we owe the first historical information about the famous Philistines in the Bible.

Among these "Sea People," as the Egyptians called the foreign conquerors, one racial group assumed special importance, the Peleste or PRST. These are the Philistines of the Old Testament.

Egyptian artists were masters at depicting the physiognomy of foreign races and had an extraordinary ability to distinguish characteristic features. The reliefs at Medinet Habu indicate with this wonted accuracy the faces of the Biblical Philistines. They look like photographs carved in stone 3,000 years ago. The tall slim figures are about a head higher than the Egyptians. We can recognise the special type of dress, and weapons, and their tactics in battle. If we substitute the men of Israel for the Egyptian mercenaries we have a true-to-life picture of the battles which took place years later in Palestine and which reached the height of their fury in the reigns of Saul and David about 1000 B.C.

Chapter 18
UNDER THE YOKE OF THE PHILISTINES

Philistines on the coast—Swan pattern pottery—Beer mugs with filters—Carefully guarded iron monopoly—Philistines occupy the highlands—Traces of the burning of Shiloh—Choosing a king from dire necessity—Allenby successfully uses Saul's tactics—Surprising the Turks—Albright finds Saul's castle—Two temples in Beth-Shan—The end of Saul.

"And the children of Israel did evil in the sight of the Lord and the Lord delivered them into the hand of the Philistines forty years" (Jud. 13¹).

It was in 1188 B.C. that the Philistines suffered their severe defeat at the hands of Ramesses III. Thirteen years later they were firmly settled on the coastal plain of southern Canaan, the fertile brown plain between the mountains of Judah and the sea. The Bible lists the five cities which they possessed: Askelon, Ashdod, Ekron, Gaza and Gath (1 Sam. 6¹⁷). Each of these cities, and the land adjoining, which was cultivated by soldiers under the command of paid leaders, was ruled over by a "lord" who was independent and free. For all political and military purposes however the five city rulers always worked hand in hand. In contrast to the tribes of Israel the Philistines acted as a unit in all matters of importance. That was what made them so strong.

The Biblical narrator tells of other groups of these "Peoples of the Sea" who had arrived with the Philistines and had settled down on the coast of Canaan: "Behold I will stretch out mine hand upon the Philistines, and I will cut off the Cherethims

(Cretans) and destroy the remnant of the sea coast'' (Ezek. 25[16]).
Crete is an island in the Mediterranean which lies far removed
from Israel. Since we have learned of the historical attack of the
"Sea Peoples" on Canaan the otherwise obscure meaning of
these words has become clear. They fit exactly the situation at
that time.

When the Philistines appeared in Canaan a new and distinctive
type of pottery also made its appearance. It is easily recognisable
as different from the pottery which had previously been in use
both in the cities of the Canaanites and in the hill settlements of
the Israelites. Throughout the area occupied by the five Philistine
cities—and only there—excavations have unearthed this type of
ceramic ware. The Philistines must therefore have produced their
own pottery.

The first find of this Philistine crockery astonished the archaeologists. They had seen these shapes and colours and patterns
before. The leather coloured drinking cups and jars, with red and
black geometrical designs and swans cleaning their feathers,
were already known as coming from Mycenae. From 1400 B.C.
onwards the wonderful pottery made by Mycenaean manufacturers was greatly sought after in the ancient world and their export
trade had flooded every country with them. Shortly before 1200
B.C. with the destruction of Mycenae this import from Greece
suddenly stopped. The Philistines must have come by way of
Mycenae, and must have started up in Canaan the manufacture
of this type of ware with which they were familiar. "Have not I
brought up Israel out of the land of Egypt? and the Philistines
from Caphtor?" (Amos 9[7]). Caphtor is Crete, the great island
that lies close to Greece.

FIG. 29.—Philistine jar with swan pattern.

But Philistine pottery illustrates another interesting fact, which is also hinted at in the Bible. Many of their handsome mugs are fitted with a filter, and there can be no doubt what it was used for. They are typical beer mugs. The filter served to keep back the barley husks: they floated about in the home-brewed ale and would tend to lodge in the throat. Large numbers of wine cups and beer mugs have been found in the Philistine settlements. They must have been powerful drinkers. Carouses are mentioned in the Samson stories (Jud. 14^{10}; 16^{25}), where the fact is emphasised that the strong man himself drank no alcohol.

Beer is however no Philistine invention. The first great breweries flourished in the Ancient East. In the hostelries of Babylon there were in fact five kinds of beer: mild, bitter, fresh, lager, and a special mixed beer for export and carrying, which was also called honey beer. This was a condensed extract of roots which would keep for a long time. All that had to be done was to mix it with water and the beer was ready—an ancient prototype of our modern dry beer for use in tropical countries.

But another discovery was much more important. The Philistines were the first people in Canaan to process iron and they made the most of it. Their graves contain armour, implements and ornaments made of this rare and costly metal, as it then was. As in the case of the Mycenaean jars they manufactured their own iron. The first iron foundries in Canaan must have been built in Philistine territory. The secret of smelting iron was brought back as part of their booty as they drove through Asia Minor, where the Hittites had been the first iron-founders in the world until 1200 B.C.

This formula which they had acquired was guarded by the Philistine princes like the apple of their eye. It was their monopoly and they traded in it. Israel during this first period of settlement up on the mountains, was far too poor to be able to afford iron. The lack of iron farm implements, of iron nails for building houses and of iron weapons was a severe handicap. When the Philistines had occupied the mountains as well as the plains, they tried to prevent the making of new weapons by prohibiting the trade of smiths. "Now there was no smith found throughout all the land of Israel: for the Philistines said, Lest the Hebrews make them swords or spears. But all the Israelites went down to the Philistines, to sharpen every man his share and his coulter and his axe and his mattock" (1 Sam. 13^{19-20}).

Equipped with the most up to date weapons, tested and tried in their long experience of military campaigns, organised into a first class political system, there stood the Philistines about 1200 B.C. on the west coast hungry for conquest. They had their eye on the same goal as Israel: Canaan.

Samson's mighty deeds and his pranks are legendary tales (Jud. 14–16). But there are hard facts behind them. The Philistines were beginning to push forward and extend their territory eastwards.

Separated from each other by long valleys, lines of hills sweep up from the coastal plain to the mountains of Judah. One of these long valleys is the valley of Sorek. Samson lived in Zorah (Jud. 13²) and in Timnath, not far from it, he married a "daughter of the Philistines" (Jud. 14¹). Delilah too lived there (Jud. 16⁴). It was along this valley that the Philistines later on sent back the Ark of the Covenant which they had captured (1 Sam. 6¹²ff). This penetration of the Philistines into the hill country below the mountains of Judah was only the prelude to the great clash with Israel which followed years later.

> "Now Israel went out against the Philistines to battle, and pitched beside Eben-Ezer; and the Philistines pitched in Aphek" (1 Sam. 4¹).

Aphek lay on the northern rim of the Philistine domains. A mound of ruins, Tell el-Muchmar, conceals all that is left of this place which lay on the upper reaches of a river which flows into the sea to the north of Jaffa. From a strategic point of view Aphek was extremely favourably situated. Eastward lay the road to the mountains of central Palestine where Israel had settled. On the edge of the mountain range lay Eben-Ezer where the opposing forces met. At the first encounter the Philistines were victorious. The Israelites in dire straits sent to Shiloh for the Ark of the Covenant, their sacred talisman. In a second encounter they were completely beaten by the vastly superior force of the Philistines. The Israelite army was routed and the victors carried off the sacred Ark as the spoils of war (1 Sam. 4²⁻¹¹).

The hill country was occupied, Israel was disarmed, and garrisons were located in the tribal territories. At their first assault the Philistines had achieved their purpose, central Palestine was in their hands.

This advance of the Philistine must have gone hard with Israel, as can be judged from the contemporary evidence which has been discovered. The temple at Shiloh which Israel had built for the Ark of the Covenant was burnt to the ground. Fifteen miles south of Shechem lies Seilun which was once the flourishing town of Shiloh. On a neighbouring hill lay the sacred precincts, Israel's sanctuary and place of pilgrimage (Josh. 18[1]; Jud. 21[19ff]; 1 Sam. 3[21]). After the Old Testament period early Christian and Mohammedan memorials were erected on the site.

Between 1926 and 1929 a Danish expedition carried out excavations at this spot, under the direction of H. Kjaers. The remains of Shiloh clearly indicate that the city was destroyed about 1050 B.C. at the time of the Philistine victory over Israel. Shiloh must have stood in ruins for a long time. For 400 years after its fall the prophet Jeremiah refers to it: "But go ye now unto my place which was in Shiloh, where I set my name at the first, and see what I did to it for the wickedness of my people Israel" (Jer. 7[12]). Other places in the mountains of Judah shared the same fate as Shiloh. Archaeologists found tell-tale traces of ashes in Tell Beit Mirsim near Hebron, the Debir of the Bible, and in Beth-zur, south of Jerusalem.

About 1050 B.C. Israel's very existence was threatened. It saw itself to be on the point of losing all the fruits of its conquests and all its work of colonisation lasting almost 200 years. It was on the verge of falling under the yoke of the Philistines and facing an existence of hopeless slavery. The only way to meet this frightful peril would be to amalgamate the loosely federated tribes and form a solid united front. It was in face of this pressure from without that Israel became a nation. In those days there was only one possible form of government, a monarchy. The choice fell upon Saul, a Benjamite, a man renowned for his bravery and his great height (1 Sam. 9[2]). It was a wise choice, for Saul belonged to the weakest tribe (1 Sam. 9[21]) and the remaining tribes would therefore have no cause to be jealous.

Saul constituted his native town Gibeah as the capital (1 Sam. 10[26]; 11[4]), collected round him a small standing army and began guerrilla warfare (1 Sam. 13[1ff]). By surprise attacks he hunted the Philistine occupation troops out of the tribal territory.

That Saul was a tactician of a high order has recently, after 3,000 years, been demonstrated anew. One example, unique in its way, shows how accurate the Bible can be even in the smallest details and how reliable its dates and information.

We owe to Major Vivian Gilbert, a British army officer, this description of a truly remarkable occurrence. Writing in his reminiscences[1] he says: "In the First World War a brigade major in Allenby's army in Palestine was on one occasion searching his Bible with the light of a candle, looking for a certain name. His brigade had received orders to take a village that stood on a rocky prominence on the other side of a deep valley. It was called Michmash and the name seemed somehow familiar. Eventually he found it in 1 Sam. 13 and read there: 'And Saul, and Jonathan his son, and the people that were present with them, abode in Gibeah of Benjamin but the Philistines encamped in Michmash.' It then went on to tell how Jonathan and his armour-bearer crossed over during the night 'to the Philistines' garrison' on the other side, and how they passed two sharp rocks: 'there was a sharp rock on the one side, and a sharp rock on the other side: and the name of the one was Bozez and the name of the other Seneh' (1 Sam. 14[4]). They clambered up the cliff and overpowered the garrison, 'within as it were an half acre of land, which a yoke of oxen might plough.' The main body of the enemy awakened by the mêlée thought they were surrounded by Saul's troops and 'melted away and they went on beating down one another' (1 Sam. 14[14-16]).

"Thereupon Saul attacked with his force and beat the enemy. 'So the Lord saved Israel that day.'"

The brigade major reflected that there must still be this narrow passage through the rocks, between the two spurs, and at the end of it the "half acre of land". He woke the commander and they read the passage through together once more. Patrols were sent out. They found the pass, which was thinly held by the Turks, and which led past two jagged rocks—obviously Bozez and Seneh. Up on top, beside Michmash, they could see by the light of the moon a small flat field. The brigadier altered his plan of attack. Instead of deploying the whole brigade he sent one company through the pass under cover of darkness. The few Turks whom they met were overpowered without a sound, the cliffs were scaled, and shortly before daybreak the company had taken up a position on "the half acre of land".

---

[1] "The Romance of the last Crusade."

The Turks woke up and took to their heels in disorder since they thought that they were being surrounded by Allenby's army. They were all killed or taken prisoner.

"And so", concludes Major Gilbert, "after thousands of years British troops successfully copied the tactics of Saul and Jonathan."

Saul's successes gave Israel new heart. The pressure of the occupying power on the highlands had certainly been eased, but it was only a short respite. In the following spring the Philistines launched their counter attack.

Towards the end of the winter rainy season they gathered their fighting forces once again in Aphek (1 Sam. 29[1]). But this time they had a different plan of action. They avoided an engagement in the mountains since Israel knew that country far too well. The Philistine princes chose rather to advance northwards across the coastal plain to the Plain of Jezreel (1 Sam. 29[11]), the scene of Deborah's battle "at Taanach by the waters of Megiddo", and then eastwards almost to the banks of the Jordan.

"By a fountain which is in Jezreel" (1 Sam. 29[1])—the spring of Harod at the foot of the mountains of Gilboa—King Saul and his army ventured to meet the Philistines on the plain. The result was fatal. At the very first attack the army was scattered, the retreating troops were pursued and struck down. Saul himself committed suicide, after his own sons had been killed.

The triumph of the Philistines was complete. The whole of Israel was now occupied—the central uplands, Galilee and Transjordan (1 Sam. 31[7]). Saul's body and the bodies of his sons were impaled and exposed on the city walls of Beth-Shan not far from the battlefield. "And they put his armour in the house of Ashtaroth" (1 Sam. 31[10]), the goddess of fertility. Israel's last hour appeared to have struck. It seemed doomed to extinction. The first kingdom which began so hopefully had come to a fearful end. A free people had sunk into slavery and its Promised Land had fallen into the hands of foreigners.

The spades of the archaeologists have unearthed from among the masses of heavy black rubble silent evidence of this fateful period. The wind sweeps over the broken and crumbling masonry of the walls which saw the success and the tragedy of Israel. Ruins which witnessed Saul's happiest hours as a young king and also his shameful end.

A few miles north of Jerusalem, near the ancient road which leads to Samaria, lies Tell el-Ful, which means, literally, "hill of beans". This was once Gibeah.

In 1922 a team from the American Schools of Oriental Research began digging there. Professor W. F. Albright, who promoted the expedition, directed the operations. Remnants of walls came to light. After a long interval Albright continued his work at Tell el-Ful in 1933. A log-shaped corner turret was exposed, and then three more. They are joined by a double wall. An open courtyard forms the interior. The total area is about 40 x 25 yards. The uncouth looking structure of dressed stone gives an impression of rustic defiance.

Albright examined the clay sherds which were scattered among the ruins. They came from jars which had been in use about 1020 to 1000 B.C. Albright had discovered Saul's citadel, the first royal castle in Israel, where "the king sat upon his seat, as at other times, even upon a seat by the wall" (1 Sam. 20^{25}). It was here that Saul reigned as king, surrounded by his closest friends, with Jonathan his son, with Abner, his cousin and commander of the army, and with David, his young armour-bearer. Here he forged his plan to set Israel free and from here he led his partisans against the hated Philistines.

The other place where King Saul's destiny was fulfilled and which research has brought once more to the light of day lies about 45 miles farther north.

On the edge of the Plain of Jezreel rises the great mound of rubble called Tell el-Husn, which is visible far beyond the Jordan valley. This is the site of the ancient Beth-Shan. On the north and south slopes the strong foundation walls of two temple buildings emerge out of the piles of cleared debris.

Archaeologists of the University of Pennsylvania, led by Clarence S. Fisher, Alan Rowe, and G. M. Fitzgerald excavated them in 1921 and 1933 almost at the same time as King Saul's castle was rediscovered at Gibeah.

Religious objects found among the ruins, principally medallions and little shrines with a serpent motif, indicate that these temples were dedicated to Astarte, the Canaanite goddess of fertility, and to Dagon the chief god of the Philistines, who was half fish, half human. Their walls witnessed what the Philistines did to Saul, as the Bible records: "And they put his armour in the house of Ashtaroth; and they fastened his body to the wall of

Beth-Shan'' (1 Sam. 31^{10}). The house of Ashtaroth is the temple ruins on the south side. ''. . . and [they] fastened his head in the temple of Dagon'' (1 Chron. 10^{10}). That is the temple which has been excavated on the north slope.

When Israel Was an Empire from David to Solomon

Chapter 19
DAVID, A GREAT KING

A man of genius—From armour-bearer to monarch—Unintentional military aid for Assyria—From the Orontes to Ezion-Geber—Revenge at Beth-Shan—New buildings with casemated walls—Finding of the Pool of Gibeon—Jerusalem fell by a stratagem—Warren discovers a shaft leading to the city—The Sopher kept the "Imperial Annals"—Was David called David?—Ink as a novelty—Palestine's climate is unpropitious for keeping records.

"So all the elders of Israel came to the king to Hebron: and king David made a league with them in Hebron before the Lord. And they anointed David king over Israel...and he reigned forty years" (2 Sam. 5^{3,4}).

The new king was so versatile that it is difficult to decide which of his qualities deserves most admiration. It would be just as difficult to find as gifted and rounded a personality within the last few centuries of our own times. Where is the man who could claim equal fame as soldier, statesman, poet and musician?

Certain it is, in any case, that no people were more devoted to music than the inhabitants of Canaan. Palestine and Syria were renowned for their music as we learn from Egyptian and Mediterranean sources. Part of the essential goods and chattels which the group of members of the caravan, depicted in the wall painting at Beni-Hasan, took with them on their journey to Egypt, were musical instruments. The ordinary household instrument was the eight-stringed lyre.

The lyre travelled from Canaan to Egypt and Greece.

In the New Kingdom of Egypt (1580–1085 B.C.) inscriptions and reliefs deal with a series of themes connected with Canaanite musicians and instruments. Canaan was an inexhaustible treasure

house of musicians, from which court chamberlains and sene-
schals obtained singers and even orchestras to provide entertain-
ment for their masters on the Nile, the Euphrates and the Tigris.
Above all ladies' bands and ballerinas were in great demand.
Artists with international engagements were by no means a
rarity. And King Hezekiah of Judah knew very well what he was
doing in 701 B.C. when he sent men and women singers to
Sennacherib the formidable king of Assyria.

FIG. 30.—Captive musicians from Judah.

From the depths of despair, from their hopeless situation under
the yoke of the Philistines, Israel climbed within a few decades
to a position of power, esteem and greatness. All of that was the
work of David. He first appears, completely unknown, as Saul's
armour-bearer, becomes a condottiere, then a fierce maquis
fighter at war with the Philistines and ends up as an old man
seated on the throne of a people that had become a great power.

As happened a few centuries earlier at the time of the conquest
of Canaan, David's efforts were assisted by favourable external
circumstances. Just after the beginning of the last millennium
B.C. there was no state in Mesopotamia or Asia Minor, Syria or

Egypt, which was in a position to stop an expansion of Canaanite territory.

After the death of Ramesses XI, the last of the Ramessid dynasty, about 1080 B.C. Egypt fell into the greedy hands of a priestly clique who ruled the land from Thebes. Vast wealth had come into the possession of the Temple.

A hundred years earlier, as the Harris Papyrus informs us, 2 per cent of the population was employed as temple slaves and 15 per cent of agricultural land was temple property. Their herds of cattle amounted to half a million head. The priests had at their disposal a fleet of eighty-eight vessels, fifty-three workshops and wharves, 169 villages and towns. The pomp with which the daily ritual of the great deities was carried out beggared all description. To make the temple scales alone, on which the sacrifices at Heliopolis were weighed, 212 pounds of gold and 461 pounds of silver were used. To look after the luxury gardens of Amun in the old royal city of Per-Ramesses in the delta 8,000 slaves were employed.

We get some idea of Egypt's status in the eyes of the outside world during this priestly regime from a unique document, the travel diary of Wen-Amun, an Egyptian envoy, dating from 1080 B.C. Wen-Amun's mission was to get cedar wood from Phoenicia for the sacred barge of the god Amun in Thebes. Herihor, the high priest, furnished him with only a small amount of gold and silver but with a picture of Amun, which he obviously expected to be more effective.

The frightful experiences which Wen-Amun had to go through on his journey have left their mark in his report. In the seaports he was treated like a beggar and an outlaw, robbed, insulted and almost murdered. He, an ambassador of Egypt, whose predecessors had always been received with the greatest pomp and the utmost deference.

At last Wen-Amun, having had his money stolen on the way, reached the end of his journey. "I came to the port of Byblos. The prince of Byblos sent to me to tell me: 'Get out of my harbour'."

This went on for nineteen days. Wen-Amun in desperation was on the point of returning to Egypt "when the harbour master came to me and said: 'The prince will see you tomorrow!' When tomorrow came he sent for me and I was brought into his presence. . . . I found him seated in his upper room, with his back leaning against a window. . . . He said to me: 'What have you come here for?' I replied: 'I have come to get timber for the splendid great barge of Amun-Re, the king of the gods. Your father gave it, your grandfather gave it, and you must also give it.' He said to me: 'It is true that they gave it. . . . Yes, my family supplied this material, but then Pharaoh sent six ships here laden with the produce of Egypt. . . . As far as I am concerned I am not your servant, nor the servant of him who sent you. . . . What kind of beggar's journey is this that you have been sent on!' I replied: 'Don't talk nonsense! This is no beggar's errand on which I have been sent.' ''

In vain Wen-Amun insisted on Egypt's power and fame, and tried to beat down the prince's price for the timber. For lack of hard cash he had to bargain with oracles and a picture of the god which was supposed to guarantee long life and good health. It was only when a messenger sent by Wen-Amun arrived from Egypt with silver and gold vessels, fine linen, rolls of papyrus, cow hides, ropes, as well as twenty sacks of lentils and thirty baskets of fish, that the prince permitted the required quantity of cedars to be felled.

"In the third month of summer they dragged them down to the sea shore. The prince came out and said to me: 'Now, there is the last of your timber and it is all ready for you. Be so good as to get it loaded up and that will not really take very long. See that you get on your way and do not make the bad time of year an excuse for remaining here.' ''

David had nothing to fear from a country whose ambassador had to put up with disrespect of this sort. He advanced far into the south and conquered the kingdom of Edom, which had once refused Moses permission to pass through it on the "King's Highway" (2 Sam. 8[14]). This meant for David an accession of territory of considerable economic significance. The Arabah desert, which stretches from the south end of the Dead Sea to the Gulf of Aqabah, is rich in copper and iron, and what David needed most of all was iron ore. His most dangerous opponents, the Philistines, had a monopoly of iron in their clutches (1 Sam. 13[19-20]). Whoever controlled Edom could break the Philistine monopoly. David wasted no time: "And David prepared iron in abundance for the nails for the doors of the gates, and for the joinings: and brass in abundance without weight" (1 Chron. 22[3]).

The most important caravan route from South Arabia, the famous "Incense Road", likewise terminated in the south of Edom. By pressing forward to the shores of the Gulf of Aqabah the sea route lay open to him across the Red Sea to the remote shores of South Arabia and East Africa.

The situation was also favourable for a northward advance.

In the broad plains at the foot of Hermon and in the fertile valleys which lay in front of Antilebanon, Arab desert tribes had settled down and become static. They belonged to a race which was destined to play an important role in Israel's life, the Aramaeans, called simply Syrians in our Bible. They had founded city-states and smallish kingdoms as far down as the river Yarmuk, south of the Lake of Galilee over in Transjordan.

About 1000 B.C. they were in the process of reaching out eastward into Mesopotamia. In the course of it they came up against the Assyrians, who were within the next few centuries to become the strongest power in the ancient world. After the downfall of Babylonia, the Assyrians had subjugated Mesopotamia as far as the upper reaches of the Euphrates. Cuneiform texts recovered from palaces on the Tigris and dating from this period mention Assyria as being threatened by danger from the west. These were the Aramaeans whose thrusting attacks were made with ever increasing force.

In face of this situation David pushed north through Transjordan right up to the Orontes. The Bible says: "And David smote Hadarezer king of Zobah unto Hamath, as he went to stablish his dominion by the river Euphrates" (1 Chron. 18³). Reference to contemporary Assyrian texts shows how accurately these words in the Bible describe the historical situation. King David attacked the Aramaean king as he was on his way to conquer Assyrian territory on the Euphrates.

Without being aware of it David was aiding those same Assyrians who later wiped out the kingdom of Israel.

The frontier posts of Israel were moved forward by David to the fertile valley of the Orontes. His most northerly sentries patrolled Lake Homs at the foot of the Lebanon, where now petroleum gurgles through the great pipelines from distant Kirkuk. From this point it was 400 miles as the crow flies to Ezion-Geber on the Red Sea, the most southerly point in the kingdom.

Excavations have revealed plenty of traces of the acquisitions and expansion of the kingdom under David. There is a clear trail of evidence which accompanies his advance, including the burning of the cities of the Plain of Jezreel. Not much later than 1000 B.C. Beth-Shan, together with its pagan sanctuaries, was levelled to the ground. Archaeologists from the University of Pennsylvania dug up on these sites of ruthless fighting, shattered temples, deep layers of ashes on top of ruined walls, ritual objects and pottery belonging to the Philistines. David's vengeance administered a crushing blow to the city which had compassed the shameful end of the first king of Israel, a blow from which it did not recover for many years to come. There is no indication above the layer of ashes which points to any habitation having existed there during the centuries immediately following.

Various building projects dating from the earlier years of David's reign remain in some state of preservation, principally fortresses in Judah which had been erected for defence against the Philistines. The structures clearly reflect the pattern of Saul's stronghold in Gibeah. They have the same rough-hewn casemated walls.

Seven miles north of Jerusalem, American excavations in 1956 brought to light not only traces of the walls of the town of Gibeah, which is so frequently mentioned in the Bible, but also uncovered the scene of a bloody encounter in these olden days. As we are told in II Samuel, once upon a time on this spot there took place a murderous hand-to-hand combat between supporters of the rival generals Joab and Abner—twelve on each side, the one lot on the side of David, the other owing allegiance to the surviving son of Saul. According to 2 Sam. 2^{13}, they "met together by the pool of Gibeon". Beneath a field of tomatoes in el-Jib, as the place is now called, Professor J. B. Pritchard, of Columbia University, discovered the "Pool of Gibeon", apparently in its day a well known spot. He found a circular shaft, over thirty feet in diameter and thirty feet deep, which had been driven vertically into bed rock. A spiral path led down a ramp cut into the inside wall. Below that a winding staircase, with two openings for light and air, descended for a further forty-five feet to the reservoir itself, chiselled out of solid limestone. When the rubble which covered the whole lay-out had been cleared away, the great cistern began to fill slowly again with water from the fissures in the rock as it had done 3,000 years ago. This Biblical "Pool of Gibeon" had also provided the town with an ample supply of fresh drinking water during an emergency or in time of siege.

Valuable evidence as to the celebrated wealth of the place—"because Gibeon was a great city, as one of the royal cities" (Josh. 10^2)—was collected by the American scholars from among the rubble of the vast cistern. It is now clear that the source of

Gibeon's prosperity was a flourishing and well organised wine trade. Sixty handles belonging to clay wine-pitchers, together with the appropriate clay stoppers and fillers, were stamped in ancient Hebrew characters with firms' trade marks—among them vintners with genuine Biblical names. Repeatedly the stamp of "Gibeon" cropped up and a word that probably means "walled vineyard" and might indicate a wine of special quality. Other handles again bore the names of towns in Judah, like Jericho, Succoth and Ziph (Josh. 15^{24}) to which the various consignments were to be delivered.

Quite near the reservoir, further diggings in the winter season of 1959–60 led to the discovery of extensive wine cellars. Sixty-six almost circular cavities about six feet deep and the same in diameter had been carved out of the rock and sealed with round stone bungs. Some of these cellars had obviously been used as wine presses for trampling out the grapes; other cavities, protected by a waterproof cover, could be identified as fermentation vats. The total storage capacity so far discovered approaches 50,000 gallons.

In view of this new evidence of what was at one time a flourishing wine industry at Gibeon, a hitherto apparently insignificant point in the Biblical narrative acquires fresh significance. It concerns an incident which took place while the Israelites were bent on conquest of Canaan. We are told in Josh. 9$^{3-5}$ that "when the inhabitants of Gibeon heard what Joshua had done unto Jericho and to Ai they did work wilily . . . and took . . . wine bottles, old and rent and bound up . . . and old garments upon them". In this guise they appeared before Joshua and succeeded in hiding from him both where they came from and what a prosperous place it was.

Finally, in Jerusalem, later David's capital, the foundations of a tower and large sections of the revetment certainly point to David as the builder. "So David dwelt in the fort and called it the city of David. And David built round about. . . ."

The romantic manner in which the stoutly guarded stronghold of Jerusalem fell into David's hands was brought to light last century partly by chance and partly by the scouting proclivities of a British army captain.

On the east side of Jerusalem where the rock slopes down into the Kidron valley lies the "Ain Sitti Maryam", the "Fountain of the Virgin Mary". In the Old Testament it is called "Gihon", "bubbler", and it has always been the main water supply for the inhabitants of the city. The road to it goes past the remains of a small mosque and into a vault. Thirty steps lead down to a little basin in which the pure water from the heart of the rock is gathered.

In 1867 Captain Warren, in company with a crowd of pilgrims, visited the famous spring, which, according to the legend, is the place where Mary washed the swaddling clothes of her little Son. Despite the semi-darkness Warren noticed on this visit a dark cavity in the roof, a few yards above the spot where the water flowed out of the rock. Apparently no one had ever noticed this before because when Warren asked about it nobody could tell him anything.

Filled with curiosity he went back to the Virgin Fountain next day equipped with a ladder and a long rope. He had no idea that an adventurous and somewhat perilous quest lay ahead of him.

Behind the spring a narrow shaft led off at first horizontally and then straight up into the rock. Warren was an alpine expert and well acquainted with this type of chimney climbing. Carefully, hand over hand, he made his way upwards. After about 40 feet the shaft suddenly came to an end. Feeling his way in the darkness Warren eventually found a narrow passage. Crawling on all fours he followed it. A number of steps had been cut in the rock. After some time he saw ahead of him a glimmering of light. He reached a vaulted chamber which contained nothing but old jars and glass bottles covered in dust. He forced himself through a chink in the rock and found himself in broad daylight in the middle of the city, with the Fountain of the Virgin lying far below him.

Closer investigation by Parker, who in 1918 went from the United Kingdom under the auspices of the Palestine Exploration Fund, showed that this remarkable arrangement dated from the second millennium B.C. The inhabitants of old Jerusalem had been at pains to cut a corridor through the rock in order that in time of siege they could reach in safety the spring that meant life or death to them.

Warren's curiosity had discovered the way which 3,000 years earlier David had used to take the fortress of Jerusalem by surprise. David's scouts must have known about this secret passage, as we can now see from a Biblical reference which was previously obscure. David says: "Whosoever getteth up to the gutter and smiteth the Jebusites . . ." (2 Sam. 5[8]). The Authorised

Version translated as "gutter" the Hebrew word "sinnor", which means a "shaft" or a "channel".

Warren solved only half the problem, however, for the opening of the shaft lay outside the walls which in his day were thought to be those of the old Jebusite Jerusalem dating from before David's time. Anybody who had climbed through the shaft would still have found himself facing the Jebusite wall. It was not until the sixties of this century that the extensive excavations of Kathleen M. Kenyon cleared the matter up. The wall of what had been considered the most ancient Jerusalem was, in fact, not so old as had been thought. A much older wall was revealed which dated from before David's day and this wall ran along the slope below the opening to the entrance to the spring. David's men, who had climbed through the shaft, consequently emerged not *in front of* but a good distance *behind* what was actually Jerusalem's oldest wall; they were *right inside* the town which they were aiming to capture. This confirms the second Book of Samuel 5[8] and thus removes much of the puzzling nature of this passage.

It was in David's reign that the exact recording of Old Testament history began. "We must regard the David narratives as largely historical," writes Martin Noth, who is an extremely critical German theologian.

The increasing clarity and lucidity of contemporary records is closely associated with the gradual creation of a political system which was David's great achievement and something new for Israel. A loose federation of clans had become a nation: a settlers' colony grew into an empire which filled Palestine and Syria.

For this extensive territory David created a Civil Service, at the head of which, next to the Chancellor, stood the Sopher. "Sopher" means "writer of chronicles" (2 Sam. 8[16,17]). A writer in the second highest position in the state!

In face of the millions of secretaries and typists in the modern world, and the thousands of tons of paper that they put into their machines and cover with type every day, the legendary glory of the "scribe" has long since departed. Not even the enviable post of chief secretary to an oil magnate can be compared with that of her ancient colleague either in salary or still less in influence. It was only on the stage of the ancient orient that the scribes played the role of their profession incomparably and uniquely. And little wonder, considering how much depended on them. Mighty conquerors and rulers of great empires were their employers and they could neither read nor write!

This can clearly be seen from the style of the letters. It is not the person to whom the letter or message is sent who is addressed in the first instance. Greetings and good wishes from scribe to scribe take precedence. There is also a request to read out the contents of the letter distinctly, and, most important, correctly and under no circumstances to suppress any of it. How things were managed within this scribal sphere of authority is indicated by a vivid scene in the Foreign Office of Pharaoh Merenptah. The scribes' department is divided into three sections. In each of the two side aisles about ten secretaries sit tightly packed together. Some of them have one foot on a stool, great rolls of papyrus lie across their knees. The spacious middle section is reserved for the chief. A zealous slave keeps the troublesome flies off him with a fan. At the entrance stand two commissionaires. One is telling the other "Spray some water and keep the office cool. The chief is busy writing."

No doubt the administrative office at the court of Jerusalem was considerably less impressive. The young state of Israel was still too rustic and too poor for that. Yet David's "recorder" must have been an important and awe-inspiring official. It was his job to compile the "Imperial Annals", which doubtless were the basis of all the factual Biblical references to the administrative system and social structure under David. Among these are the great national census conducted on the approved Mari-plan (2 Sam. 24) as well as the information about his bodyguard of "Cherethites and Pelethites", a kind of Swiss guard, which consisted of Cretans and Philistines (2 Sam. 8[18]; 15[18]; 20[7]).

Undoubtedly the "Sopher" would also be the first to write down the new name of his sovereign.

FIG. 31.—A Government office on the Nile.

This name has presented a problem to the specialists, for they repeatedly came across a very similar word in texts from the Ancient East, texts from Mari; the word "dâvidum". Did this puzzling word mean "commander of an army", "supreme commander", "chief", and was David's name consequently no name at all but a title which had become a name when he mounted the throne? In addition, the Bible more than once mentions a certain Baal-hanan, the son of an Edomite king Saul (Gen. 36[38] and 1 Chron. 1[49]). On the other hand, a certain Elhanan is reported as having vanquished David's adversary Goliath and on another occasion Goliath's brother (2 Sam. 21[19] and 1 Chron. 20[5]). The names Baal-hanan and Elhanan obviously contain the names of the Canaanite gods Baal and El.

Was David's name then originally Baal-hanan or Elhanan and did he first take the name David after his accession to the throne? Thirty years ago a number of scholars were convinced of this, but since then greater caution has been shown, at least concerning the linguistic connection between the words "David" and "dâvidum", for it has become apparent that "dâvidum" does not mean "commander of an army" or anything similar, but "defeat". And nobody has ever thought of deriving the title of a commander from that word! Nor can it be accepted that personal names like Baal-hanan or Elhanan, elements of which are the names of Canaanite gods, would have met with the approval of the Biblical writers. The problem of David's name still remains unsolved.

This question of "writing" conjures up one of the arguments levelled by critics of the Bible. In Egypt waggon loads of papyrus have been found, similarly in Babylonia and Assyria mountains of cuneiform tablets—where then are the literary documents of Palestine?

Archaeologists and meteorologists may be permitted to answer this question.

About the beginning of the last millennium B.C. Canaan deserted its angular cuneiform script and the use of clumsy clay tablets in favour of a less cumbersome method of writing. Until then the text of the document had to be scratched in soft clay with a stylus. The clay had then to be baked or dried in the sun, a time-wasting procedure, before the bulk letters were ready for despatch. A new type of writing, with wavy lines, became more and more fashionable. This was the alphabet which we have already encountered in the attempts at writing made by the

Semitic miners at Sinai. Stylus and clay were clearly unsuited for these new smoothly rounded letters. So they looked for new writing utensils and found them in their baked clay tablets, inkpot and ink. Archaeologists call these little tablets with their flowing script "Ostraca". They were replaced in special cases by papyrus, the most elegant writing material of the ancient world. The Wen-Amun report shows how greatly this Egyptian export was in demand. The prince of Byblos received in return for his cedars 500 rolls of it: well over a mile of writing paper!

Palestine has a damp climate in winter on account of its rainfall. In such a climate ink is very quickly washed off hard clay, and papyrus soon disintegrates. Greatly to the distress of archaeologists, scientists and historians, all of them thirsting for knowledge, practically the sum total of Canaan's records and documents has been lost to posterity for this reason. The fact that the archaeologists were able to produce such an impressive haul from Egypt is simply the result of its proximity to the desert and the unusually dry climate.

Chapter 20
WAS SOLOMON A "COPPER-KING"?

Expedition to the Gulf of Aqabah—Iron ore and malachite—Glueck discovers Ezion-Geber—Desert storms used as bellows—The Pittsburgh of old Israel—Shipyards on the Red Sea—Hiram brought the timber—Ships' captains from Tyre—The mysterious land of Ophir—An Egyptian portrait of the queen of Punt—U.S. archaeologists buy a Tell—A model dig at Megiddo —The fateful plain of Jezreel—Royal stables with 450 stalls?

"So king Solomon was king over all Israel (1 Kings 4[1]) and Solomon had 40,000 stalls of horses for his chariots, and 12,000 horsemen" (1 Kings 4[26]).

"And Solomon built... all the cities of store... and cities for his chariots and cities for his horsemen" (1 Kings 9[17,19]).

"And king Solomon made a navy of ships in Ezion-Geber which is beside Eloth... and they came to Ophir" (1 Kings 9[26,28]).

"And all king Solomon's drinking vessels were of gold... none were of silver: it was nothing accounted of in the days of Solomon. For the king had at sea a navy... bringing gold and silver, ivory and apes, and peacocks" (1 Kings 10[2,22]).

"And the house which king Solomon built for the Lord... was... overlaid with gold" (1 Kings 6[2,22]).

"And Solomon had horses brought out of Egypt and linen yarn... and so for all the kings of the Hittites, and for the kings of Syria, did they bring them out by their means" (1 Kings 10[28,29]).

"Now the weight of gold that came to Solomon in one

year was six hundred threescore and six talents of gold" (1 Kings 10^{14}).

Doesn't it sound like a fairy tale?

Any man, even a king, about whom so much is told, is hard put to it to escape the charge of boasting. And any chronicler, telling such a story, easily gets a reputation for exaggeration. There are certainly stories in the Bible which are regarded by scholars as legends, such as the tale of Balaam the sorcerer and his talking ass (Num. 22) or the tale of Samson whose long hair gave him strength (Jud. 13–16). But this most fabulous of all stories is really no fairy tale at all.

The archaeologists dug their way to the heart of the trustworthiness of these Solomon stories—and lo and behold Solomon became their unique showpiece.

When the "fairy tale" of King Solomon—as many still believe it to be—has been stripped of its frills, there remains a framework of sober historical facts. That is one of the most exciting discoveries of recent times. It was only in 1937 that a wealth of surprising finds during excavations by two American expeditions produced proof of the truth of this Biblical story.

Packed high with the latest equipment, with drills, spades and picks and accompanied by geologists, historians, architects, excavators and the photographer who is now indispensable on a modern expedition, a caravan of camels is leaving Jerusalem. Its leader is Nelson Glueck, who like the others is a member of the famous American Schools of Oriental Research.

Soon they have left the brown mountains of Judah behind. They head south through the dreary Negev. Then the caravan enters Wadi el-Arabah, the "Valley of the Desert". The men feel as if they had been transported into some scene from a primeval world, where some Titanic power out of the depths had left its mark when it formed the earth. The "Valley of the Desert" is part of the mighty fissure which begins in Asia Minor and ends in Africa.

The scientists pay their respects to this impressive vista and then turn to the task which awaits them. Their questing eyes roam over the steep rock-face. Light and shade vary with the sun, and here and there the stone is hacked away and dented. They find that it consists of muddy yellow felspar, silvery white mica, and, where the stone shows up reddish black, iron ore and a green mineral—malachite, copper spar.

FIG. 32.—Life in a harem. "Solomon had 700 wives..." (1 Kings 11³).

Along the whole length of the wadi the American scientists come upon deposits of iron ore and copper. Wherever their tests indicate the presence of ore they find galleries let into the rock, all that remains of mines long since deserted.

At last the caravan reaches the shores of the Gulf. However invitingly the white houses of Aqabah, the Eloth of the Bible, seem to beckon them in the glaring sun, however tempting are the sounds of this busy eastern seaport after their trek through the desolate wadi, nevertheless the scientists turn their backs on this intersection of three worlds.[1] Their goal is "Tell el-Kheleifeh". This lonely mound, which seems no more than a pile of rubble, rises inland out of the shadeless plain.

Careful probing with spades prefaces the first stage of the excavation and produces unexpectedly quick results. Fish hooks come out; they are made of copper. Then tiles and remnants of walls. Some coarse looking lumps of some material in the vicinity of the Tell show traces of green. They turn out to be slag. Everywhere around them the scientists meet this sandstone with the distinctive green colour.

In his tent one evening Glueck reflects on the results of the work up to date. It has produced nothing remarkable. Meantime the whole of Transjordan is still on the programme. Glueck wants to track down the past in Edom, Moab, Ammon, even as far as Damascus. Looking through his notes, he stops and

[1] Africa, Arabia and Palestine/Syria.

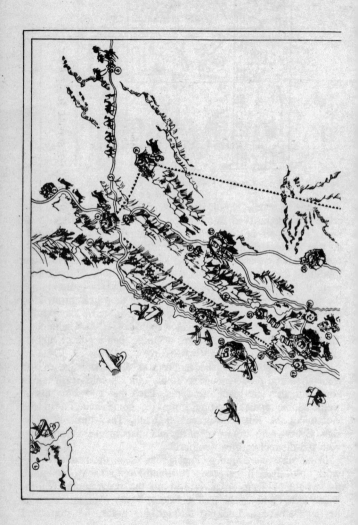

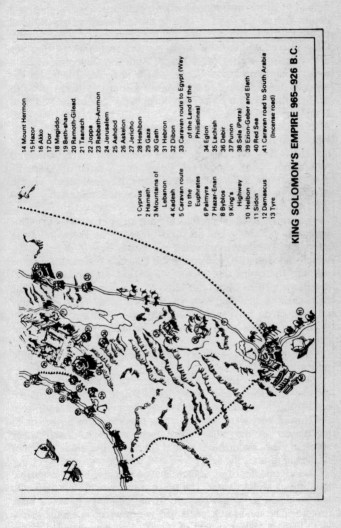

1 Cyprus
2 Hamath
3 Mountains of Lebanon
4 Kadesh
5 Caravan route to the Euphrates
6 Palmyra
7 Hazar-Enan
8 Byblos
9 King's Highway
10 Helbon
11 Sidon
12 Damascus
13 Tyre
14 Mount Hermon
15 Hazor
16 Akko
17 Dor
18 Megiddo
19 Beth-shan
20 Ramoth-Gilead
21 Taanach
22 Joppa
23 Rabbath-Ammon
24 Jerusalem
25 Ashdod
26 Askelon
27 Jericho
28 Heshbon
29 Gaza
30 Gath
31 Hebron
32 Dibon
33 Caravan route to Egypt (Way of the Land of the Philistines)
34 Eglon
35 Lachish
36 Debir
37 Punon
38 Sela (Petra)
39 Ezion-Geber and Elath
40 Red Sea
41 Caravan road to South Arabia (Incense road)

KING SOLOMON'S EMPIRE 965–926 B.C.

ponders. Iron-ore and malachite in the Arabah—and, in this
mound of debris in front of his tent, remains of walls, slag, and
copper fish-hooks—and all of it in the immediate neighbourhood
of the Gulf which the Bible calls the "Red Sea". Thoughtfully
Glueck turns up the Bible passage which mentions the Red Sea
in connection with a great king: "And king Solomon made a
navy of ships in Ezion-Geber, which is beside Eloth, on the
shore of the Red Sea, in the land of Edom" (1 Kings 9[26]). In
Biblical times Edom came right down to the gulf of the Red Sea.
Could this mound be . . . ?

It is decided to make a thorough investigation of Tell el-
Kheleifeh next day. As they dig up the material from the
test-shafts they find that at several points they come upon wall
foundations at the same level. Below that is virgin soil. Sherds
give them an indication of the date of construction of the
masonry. It is within the period of Solomon's reign, after 1000
B.C.

The time factor compelled Glueck to stop operations. This
particular expedition had other tasks ahead. But in the following
years the Americans continued the excavations in three stages,
which ended in 1940 and confirmed Glueck's theory. It appeared
that the first ruins that came to light had once been workers'
dwellings. Then came ramparts of the casemated type, the
unmistakable building style of the first Iron Age. After that
remains of an extensive settlement were excavated. The most
interesting things were casting-moulds and a vast quantity of
copper slag.

Casting-moulds and copper slag in the middle of the scorching
pitilessly hot plain?

Glueck tried to find an explanation for this strange fact. Why
did the workshops have to be located right in the path of the
sand-storms which almost incessantly sweep down the wadi from
the North? Why were they not a few hundred yards farther on in
the shelter of the hills, where there were also fresh water
springs? The astonishing answer to these questions was not
forthcoming until the last excavation period.

In the middle of a square walled enclosure an extensive
building came into view. The green discolouration on the walls
left no doubt as to the purpose of the building: it was a blast
furnace. The mud-brick walls had two rows of openings. They
were flues: a skilful system of air passages was included in the

construction. The whole thing was a proper up-to-date blast furnace, built in accordance with a principle that celebrated its resurrection in modern industry a century ago as the Bessemer system. Flues and chimneys both lay along a north to south axis. For the incessant winds and storms from the Wadi el-Arabah had to take over the role of bellows. That was 3,000 years ago: today compressed air is forced through the forge.

One question alone still remained unanswered: how was the copper refined in this ancient apparatus? Smelting experts of today cannot solve the mystery.

Earthenware smelting-pots still lie about in the vicinity: many of them have the remarkable capacity of 14 cubic feet. In the surrounding hill-slopes the multiplicity of caves hewn out of the rock indicate the entrances to the galleries. Fragments of copper sulphate testify to the busy hands that worked these mines thousands of years ago. In the course of fact-finding excursions into the surrounding country the members of the expedition succeeded in identifying numerous copper and iron mines in the wadis of the Arabah desert.

Eventually Nelson Glueck discovered in the casemated wall of the mound of rubble a stout gateway with a triple lockfast entrance. He was no longer in any doubt. Tell el-Kheleifeh was once Ezion-Geber, the long-sought vanished seaport of King Solomon: "And king Solomon made a navy of ships in Ezion-Geber which is beside Eloth. . . ."

Ezion-Geber was however not only a seaport. In its dockyards ships for ocean travel were also built. But above all Ezion-Geber was the centre of the copper-industry. Nowhere else in the "Fertile Crescent", neither in Babylonia nor in Egypt, was such a great furnace to be found. Ezion-Geber had therefore the best smelting facilities in the ancient orient. It produced the metal for the ritual furnishings of the Temple at Jerusalem—for the "altar of brass", the "sea", as a great copper basin was called, for the "ten bases of brass", for the "pots, shovels, basins" and for the two great pillars "Jachin and Boaz" in the porch of the Temple (1 Kings 7[15ff]; 2 Chron. 4). For "in the plain of Jordan did the king cast them in the clay ground between Succoth and Zarthan. . . ." (1 Kings 7[46]). One of the most recent finds in Biblical archaeology fell to the lot of a Dutch expedition which has now established the site of the former of these two places. At Tell deir Alla in Transjordan, where the river Jabbok leaves the hills six miles before it joins the Jordan, the expedition discovered traces of Succoth, the Israelite city dating from the days of Joshua.

Glueck's delight at these unparalleled finds can still be detected in the official report which gathered together the results of the researches at the Gulf of Aqabah: "Ezion-Geber was the result of careful planning and was built as a model installation with remarkable architectural and technical skill. In fact practically the whole town of Ezion-Geber, taking into consideration place and time, was a phenomenal industrial site, without anything to compare with it in the entire history of the ancient orient. Ezion-Geber was the Pittsburgh of old Palestine and at the same time its most important seaport."

FIG. 33.—Brass laver from Solomon's Temple (1 Kings 7²⁷ff; 2 Chron. 4⁶). (Reconstruction.)

King Solomon, whom Glueck describes as the "great copper-king", was on this basis reckoned among the greatest exporters of copper in the ancient world. Research on other sites completed this picture of Palestine's economy under King Solomon. South of the old Philistine city of Gaza, Flinders Petrie dug up iron-smelting installations in Wadi Ghazze. The furnaces are like those at Tell el-Kheleifeh but smaller. David had disputed the Philistines' right to their monopoly of iron and he had extracted their secret smelting process as one of the prices of their defeat. Then under Solomon the iron and copper deposits were apparently mined on a large scale and smelted.

Twenty years after Professor Glueck's first discovery of the presence of copper and slag heaps, an archaeologist, Benno Rothenberg, made a striking find in the same Wadi el-Arabah of a large copper mine dating from the same time. In the spring of 1959, twenty miles north of Ezion-Geber in Wadi Timna, Rothenberg's expedition came across extensive workings where the stone had been cut out of the rocks in thick slices and then subjected to the first process of removing the slag in basalt smelting vats.

> "For the Lord thy God bringeth thee into a good land . . . a land whose stones are iron and out of whose hills thou mayest dig brass" (Deut. 8[7-9]).

So runs part of the detailed description of the Promised Land which Moses gives the children of Israel. Copper and iron in Palestine? The work of the archaeologists has now produced evidence showing how true is this description which the Bible gives, and introduces a new factor into our picture of Old Palestine which we shall in future have to take into account, namely its remarkable industrial development.

Solomon was a thoroughly progressive ruler. He had a flair for exploiting foreign brains and foreign skill and turning them to his own advantage. That was the secret, otherwise scarcely understandable, of how the simple peasant regime of his father David developed by leaps and bounds into a first class economic organism. Here also was to be found the secret of his wealth which the Bible emphasises. Solomon imported smelting technicians from Phoenicia. Huram-Abhi,[1] a craftsman from Tyre, was

---

[1] A.V. = Hiram.

entrusted with the casting of the Temple furnishings (1 Kings 7[13,14]). In Ezion-Geber Solomon founded an important enterprise for overseas trade. The Israelites had never been sailors and knew nothing about shipbuilding. But the Phoenicians had behind them practical experience accumulated over many centuries. Solomon therefore sent to Tyre for specialists for his dockyards and sailors for his ships: "And Hiram[1] sent in the navy his servants, shipmen that had knowledge of the sea. . . ." (1 Kings 9[27]).

Ezion-Geber was the well-equipped and heavily defended export centre for the new foreign trade. From Ezion-Geber the ships set sail on their mysterious voyages to distant and unfamiliar shores. Ophir?—where was the legendary land of Ophir, the "warehouse" in which the ancient orient purchased the costliest and choicest commodities?

Many a scholarly quarrel has broken out about Ophir. Someone was always claiming to have found it. In 1871 Carl Mauch of Germany came across a large area covered with ruins in Rhodesia. Fifteen years later Steinberg of South Africa dug up, a few miles to the south, pre-Christian mining installations which were thought to be connected with the temple city. Rock-tests were supposed to show that gold and silver had at one time been quarried there. In 1910 the famous African explorer, Dr. Karl Peters of Germany, photographed carvings on this site in which experts claimed that they detected odd Phoenician characteristics.

This mysterious land of Ophir has however so far eluded the grasp of the scientists. Many indications nevertheless point to East Africa. Experts like Prof. Albright suggest that it was located in Somaliland. That would tie up very well with what the Bible says about the length of time it took to get there.

"Once in three years came the navy . . ." (1 Kings 10[22]). "The fleet may have sailed from Ezion-Geber in November or December of the first year," suggested Albright, "and returned in May or June of the third year. In this way the hot weather in summer would be avoided as much as possible. The journey in this case need have taken no more than eighteen months." Further, the nature of the merchandise "gold, silver, ivory and apes" (1 Kings 10[22]) points to Africa as the obvious place of origin.

The Egyptians were well informed about "Punt", which may be identifiable with Ophir. They must have been on the spot and

---

[1]The king of Tyre.

kept their eyes open. How otherwise could these impressive pictorial representations of "Punt" have originated, which light up the walls of the terraced temple of Deir el-Bahri? Wonderful coloured reliefs adorn this temple on the west side of Thebes, lending splendour and charm to a dusky lady—the queen of Punt—and her retinue. As usual the Egyptians have here too lavished devoted attention to the details of the costumes, the round huts, the animals and plants of "Punt". Anyone looking at them has a clear picture in his mind's eye of what this legendary Ophir looked like.

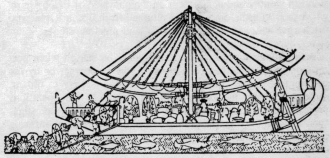

FIG. 34.—One of Queen Hatshepsut's ships returning from Punt (Ophir) with a cargo of myrrh and apes.

Inscriptions adjoining the reliefs give an account of the sensational expedition which a woman ordered to be equipped and to set out for "Punt" in 1500 B.C. On the throne of the Pharaohs at that time, as co-regent of Tutmose III, sat the famous Queen Hatshepsut, "the first great woman in history" as Breasted the Egyptologist calls her. In response to an oracle of the god Amun, which enjoined that the routes to "Punt" should be explored and that trade relations with the Red Sea ports which had been interrupted by the Hyksos wars should be resumed, the queen sent out a flotilla of five sea-going vessels in the ninth year of her reign. They were to bring back myrrh trees for the temple terraces. The fleet sailed from the Nile along a canal in the eastern part of the delta into the Red Sea and "arrived safely in Punt", where it exchanged Egyptian produce for a precious cargo of myrrh trees, ebony, gold, as well as all sorts of sweet smelling wood and other exotic articles like sandalwood, panther skins, and apes.

A display such as they had never seen before met the gaze of the Thebans as at the close of a successful trip the strange collection of dark-skinned natives of Punt made their way to the queen's palace with the marvellous products of their country. "I have made his garden into another Punt, as he commanded me . . ." says Hatshepsut exultingly, referring to the myrrh trees on the temple terraces. Egyptologists found dried up roots of myrrh in the hot yellow sand in front of the temple of Deir el-Bahri.

Like the Thebans, men and women of Israel must also have stood in wonder and amazement on the quayside of Ezion-Geber when their king Solomon's fleet returned from distant Ophir and discharged its cargo of sandalwood "and precious stones, gold, silver, ivory, apes and peacocks" (1 Kings 10^{11,22}).

Archaeological work can normally only be started when permission to excavate has been given by the landowner or by the government of the country. This is not always easy to obtain, quite apart from the fact that in the course of the operations protests or restrictions can make life difficult for the investigators. In 1925 the Americans hit upon an unusual way of ensuring that they would be left in peace to get on with the work. They bought without a moment's hesitation the mound of rubble called Tell el-Mutesellim in the Plain of Jezreel from ninety native proprietors, peasants and shepherds, lock, stock and barrel. For the Oriental Institute of the University of Chicago had in mind a model excavation for the whole of the Middle East, the most comprehensive, most painstaking, and most accurate investigation that had ever been started in Palestine.

Tell el-Mutesellim covers the site of the Megiddo of the Bible. This discovery is based on the first large-scale excavation which was undertaken on this spot by the German Oriental Society under Dr. J. Schumacher between 1903 and 1905.

Like a small edition of Table Mountain, Tell el-Mutesellim lies in the heart of a unique scenic setting. Looking down from the plateau is like looking down on a vast green lake. Into the far distance stretches the great plain, the "valley of Jezreel" (Jos. 17^{16}), in which the green meadows of the fenland and well-stocked fields of grain alternate with one another. Flocks of cranes and storks frequent the spot. Where the plain ends, the wooded hump of Carmel stands guard over the Mediterranean shore. To the north the hills of Galilee with the little village of Nazareth sweep upwards, tinted a delicate blue, and far to the right the sombre summit of Mt. Tabor bars the view into the deep cleft of the Jordan valley.

Nothing in this fertile triangle, this friendly countryside girt with gentle lines of hills, suggests that this tiny bit of land was for many thousands of years the scene of mighty battles and of momentous and decisive history.

About 1500 B.C. Pharaoh Thutmose III, riding in a "golden chariot", led his army through a narrow pass into the plain and attacked the Canaanites, who fled in terror and complete disorder to Megiddo. On the same plain the Israelites, incited by the heroic Deborah, smashed the supremacy of the Canaanite charioteers, Gideon surprised the plundering camel-borne nomads from Midian, Saul lost the battle against the Philistines, and King Josiah of Judah died about 600 B.C. as he and his men threw themselves in vain against the armed might of Egypt under Pharaoh Necho. Ruins mark the site of the Frankish castle of Faba, which the knights of St. John and the Templars occupied during the Crusades, until Saladin drove them off the plain after a frightful massacre. On the 16th April 1799 there was a battle here between the Turks and the French. With only 1,500 men Kleber, the French general, held 25,000 of the enemy at bay. The French fought like heroes from sunrise till noon. Then over a ridge to the rescue charged a troop of 600 mounted men. The officer at their head was called Napoleon Bonaparte. After the victorious "Battle of Tabor" Napoleon rode up into the hills of Galilee and ate his supper in Nazareth. In 1918 British cavalry under Lord Allenby swept through the same pass as Thutmose III and destroyed the Turkish army which was encamped on the plain.

A silent witness of all these events was Tell el-Mutesellim, where Clarence S. Fisher began operations on the model excavation in the spring of 1925.

The hill was literally cut into slices inch by inch—like cutting a cake except that the slices were horizontal ones. The centuries flashed past like a kaleidoscope. Every layer that was removed signified a chapter of world history from the 4th to the 10th century B.C.

Of the four top layers Stratum I contained ruins from the time of the Persian and Babylonian empires. Cyrus, king of Persia, destroyed the power of Babylon in 539 B.C. King Nebuchadnezzar of Babylon had conquered Syria and Palestine fifty years earlier in 597 B.C. The walls of an unusually solidly built palace still remain from that period. Stratum II provided evidence of Assyrian rule with ruins of a palace dating from the 8th century B.C. Tiglath-Pileser III subdued Palestine in 733 B.C. Stratum III and Stratum IV incorporated the Israelite period.

The most important find in this case was two seals with old Hebrew letters on them. One of them bore the inscription, "Shema, servant of Jeroboam". Jeroboam I was the first ruler of Israel after the kingdom had been divided (926–907 B.C.). A stone preserved another familiar name: Pharaoh Sheshonk I, of Egypt. The Bible calls him Pharaoh Shishak. In 922 B.C., the fifth year of King Jeroboam's reign, he attacked Palestine.

After almost ten years of toil, picks and spades had reached the layers dating from the time of King Solomon, who had died four years before the attack of Sheshonk in 926 B.C. The lowest level of rubble in Stratum IV then produced sensational surprises from King Solomon's time for the archaeologists, Gordon Loud and P. L. O. Guy, as well as for posterity.

In Solomon's day a new method of construction was adopted in the case of public buildings, defence walls, etc. Instead of the previous style of building this new type involved the introduction of smooth dressed stones at the corners and at intervals along the walls. On the lowest level of the rubble of Stratum IV ruins of a palace were exposed which displayed this characteristic feature. They are enclosed by a square wall whose sides are about 60 yards long. Additional protection was afforded by the handsome entrance gateway flanked by three pairs of close-set pillars. Archaeologists came across similar town gates with this threefold security in Ezion-Geber and in Lachish. A building with massive walls that was excavated almost at the same time turned out to be a granary, one of the "cities of store that Solomon had" (1 Kings 9[19]). Storehouses of this kind were also found at Beth-Shan and Lachish. Megiddo was the administrative centre of the 5th District in the Israel of Solomon's day. Solomon's representative in the palace, who was also responsible for the deliveries of taxes in kind to the "city of store," was "Baana, the son of Ahilud, to him pertained Taanach and Megiddo" (1 Kings 4[12]).

Although these finds were remarkable they were not sensational. The sensation was still lying untouched in the heart of Tell el-Mutesellim as if the old mound had been keeping the best to the last. In the course of the excavations there appeared among the rubble on the edge of the Tell a flat stone surface,

studded with stone stumps, ranged one behind the other in long
rows and square in shape.

Loud and Guy had at first no idea what it could have been.
There seemed to be no end to this remarkable series of flat
surfaces which emerged yard by yard out of the rubble. It
occurred to Guy that they might be the remains of stables. Did
the Bible not speak of the untold horses of King Solomon?

Amid the generally monotonous sameness of a dig that had
lasted several years with its daily stint of carrying away, empty-
ing out, sifting and arranging every fragment worth considering,
Guy's idea gave at once a new fillip to the excavations, which
even the digging gangs shared.

The archaeologists' astonishment grew with every new structure which came to light. They found that several large stables
were always grouped round a courtyard, which was laid with
beaten limestone mortar. A 10-foot wide passage ran down the
middle of each stable. It was roughly paved to prevent the horses
from slipping. On each side, behind the stone stumps, lay roomy
stalls, each of which was exactly 10 feet wide. Many of them
had still remains of feeding troughs and parts of the watering
arrangements were still recognisable. Even for present day circumstances they were veritable luxury stables. Judging by the
extraordinary care which had been lavished on buildings and
services, horses in those days were at a premium. At all events
they were better looked after than were human beings.

When the whole establishment was uncovered, Guy counted
single stalls for at least 450 horses and sheds for 150 chariots. A
gigantic royal stable indeed. "And this is the reason of the levy
which king Solomon raised: for to build . . . the wall of Jerusalem
and Hazor and Megiddo . . ." (1 Kings 9[15]). "And Solomon
gathered together chariots and horsemen: and he had a thousand
and four hundred chariots and twelve thousand horsemen, whom
he bestowed in the cities for chariots . . ." (1 Kings 10[26]). In view
of the size of the royal stable at Megiddo and the stables and
chariot sheds of similar type which have been found at Tell
el-Hesi, at Taanach and also at Jerusalem, the Biblical references
must be regarded as mere hints at the reality. These tremendous
results of the excavations give us a clear conception of the
lavishness to which old Israel was accustomed in its imperial
days.

Megiddo was after all only one of the garrisons for Solomon's new chariot corps, which formed part of the king's standing army.

In one of the ancient stable buildings which were cut deep into the rock under the high walls of the city of Jerusalem the Crusaders tethered their horses after the conquest of the Holy City by Godfrey of Boulogne almost 2,000 years after Solomon.

Horses and chariots alike were considered in Solomon's day to be worth-while trading commodities. Israel had indeed in this matter a complete monopoly (1 Kings 10[28,29]).

FIG. 35.—"And a chariot came...out of Egypt for six hundred shekels of silver" (1 Kings 10[29]).

All the important caravan routes between Egypt, Syria and Asia Minor went through Solomon's kingdom. Egypt was the chief exporter of war-chariots: "... the king's merchants received the linen yarn at a price. And a chariot came up and went out of Egypt for six hundred shekels of silver." Egyptian wheelwrights were unsurpassed craftsmen in building swift two-wheeled chariots for war and hunting. The hardwood for them had to be imported from Syria. This explains the high rate of exchange. According to the Bible one chariot was worth four horses (1 Kings 10[29]). In this connection it will not be necessary to insist on the fact that the "shekels of silver" mentioned by the Bible are an anachronism since minted coins were still unknown in King Solomon's day.

The horses came from Egypt, "and from Koa" as another

tradition tells us. "Koa" was the name of a state in Cilicia which lay in the fertile plain between the Taurus Mountains and the Mediterranean. After the destruction of the kingdom of Mitanni by the Hittites, Cilicia became the land of horse breeders and the livery stables of the ancient world. Herodotus mentions that later on the Persians fetched the best horses for their Imperial Messenger Service from Cilicia.

Israel's trading partners in the north were the "Kings of Syria and the Kings of the Hittites" (1 Kings 10[29]). This too is historically accurate. The kingdom of the Hittites had long been extinct by Solomon's day but some smaller successor states had taken its place. One of them was discovered in 1945 by Professor H. T. Bossart of Germany, although it is a century younger than Solomon. This was the royal castle in the forest of Mt. Karatepe, not far from Adana in the southeast of Turkey. Asitawanda, who built it in the 9th century B.C., was one of these "Kings of the Hittites".

The most recent researches have thrown light on Solomon, the "copper king", providing not only confirmation of statements in the Bible but also the refutation of views previously held. The Israeli professor of archaeology, Benno Rothenberg (Tel Aviv), who was born at Frankfurt am Main, has made very important contributions in this field. Mention has already been made on several occasions of his investigations at Timna in the Wadi el-Arabah area. What Rothenberg discovered there contradicts, however, the opinion held by Nelson Glueck: between the 12th century B.C. and the time of the Romans there was no extraction of copper in the "Biblical" mines at Timna. In other words, King Solomon's mines were not producing in Solomon's day, in the 10th century B.C. In fact, the Bible gives us no cause to regard Solomon as a "copper king" for there is no mention of copper exploitation at his time. On the contrary, the Bible tells us expressly that Solomon obtained the metal he required from plunder as well as from the store of his father David (1 Chron. 18[8]; 22[3,14]). Once again the Bible is right. It does not refer to copper mining in Solomon's time and it has not been possible so far to prove that any took place.

Where then does the persistent tradition about "Solomon's mines" originate? Today light has also been thrown on this question. It has nothing to do with the Bible, but a great deal with Sir Rider Haggard's novel *King Solomon's Mines* which appeared at the end of last century. Even the great Bible archaeologist Nelson Glueck, without doubt one of the most prominent figures in this field, was deceived by this pseudo-Biblical tradition of recent date.

Perhaps even greater caution than with "Solomon's mines" is required in the attempt to localise Ophir, which continues to defeat all attempts by specialists to identify it. What the German geologist Carl Mauch found in Rhodesia—and to a large extent destroyed by inexpert excavations—was Zimbabwe which was not built until some 2,000 or 2,500 years after Solomon's day, some time, therefore, between the 11th and the 15th century A.D. Zimbabwe has nothing in common with the building practices of the Phoenicians or the Arabs, nor has it any connection with the Awwam Temple of the moon god Ilumquh or Almaqah near distant Marib in Southern Arabia, a temple which, by the way, also does not date from Solomon's time but probably from the 8th or 7th century B.C. No, Zimbabwe is definitely a product of indigenous architecture, however unpleasant this fact may be for the present government of Rhodesia. The expert who made this discovery and published it, Peter S. Garlake, was deprived of his post as Curator of the Commission for Historic Monuments in Southern Rhodesia and was obliged to emigrate to a black African country. Obviously a certain amount of courage is required even today in the exercise of the archaeologist's profession and discoveries are not always followed by fame alone!

Just as it was with Solomon's copper mines, of which the Bible makes no mention, so it is with the no less famous "Solomon's stables" in Megiddo. The opinion has become more widely accepted that they date not from Solomon's time but from that of King Ahab of Israel (c. 875 to 852 B.C.), who according to the Assyrian account of the Battle of Qarqar (c. 854 B.C.) assembled 2,000 chariots, the largest force of war-chariots in the anti-Assyrian alliance. And so, basically the Biblical story has once more been confirmed, for we read (1 Kings 9[15]) merely that Solomon *fortified* Megiddo and not that he built stables there and that, speaking generally, he *had* "chariots and horsemen" (1 Kings 10[26]), but not that they were garrisoned in Megiddo.

It remains merely to add that in the view of a number of experts, among them the Israeli specialist in Biblical archaeology, Professor Yohanan Aharoni of Tel Aviv, what are reputed to be "Solomon's stables" not only date from the time of Ahab but also are not stables. It seems they are storehouses for supplies.

Similar buildings destined for the same purpose have been excavated by Yohanan Aharoni in Beersheba.

Fairly long and quite detailed passages of the Bible, chapters 6 and 7 of 1 Kings, chapters 3 and 4 of 2 Chronicles and chapters 40 to 43 of the prophet Ezekiel have received striking confirmation. These passages all refer to King Solomon's most famous building, the Temple in Jerusalem.

As excavations are impossible within the Temple area, we do not know what remains today of Solomon's construction beneath the stones of Herod the Great's temple pavement and the rock dome (Qubbet es-Sachra) built by the Omayyads, one of the most magnificent examples of Islamic architecture. Yet we know from the descriptions in the Bible as well as from parallel finds from the Canaanite-Phoenician region that this temple was a model construction such as was continually encountered in Semitic temples from the early Stone Age onwards. It consists of three connecting halls, access to each of which is possible only through the preceding one. The "small temple" of *Tell Tainat* (9th century B.C.), the late Bronze Age Canaanite temple from Layer XV in excavation section H at Hazor (13th century B.C.), and the Iron Age temple on the northwest corner of the citadel of *Tell Arad* show the closest contacts with the Biblical accounts. The latter is of particular interest as this is an Israelite sanctuary and is chronologically closest to Solomon's temple.

Connected to these three temple rooms there is first a porch (*ulam*) to which a "hall" was attached (*hekal*). The Authorised Version also refers to the *hekal* as the "greater house" or simply as the "Temple", although strictly speaking only a part of the temple complex is meant. It was this "greater house" that gave admittance to the actual sanctuary, the Holy of Holies (*debir*). The entrance to the *hekal* was flanked by two pillars, *Jachin* and *Boaz*. In fact, two stone slabs were found on *Tell Arad*, one on each side of the entrance to the *hekal*, which might well have served as the bases of pillars. The entrance to the middle room in the late Bronze Age temple of Hazor is also flanked by the bases of pillars.

Although it dates from the century *after* Solomon, the temple of *Tell Tainat* still belongs architecturally as it were to Solomon's time. It confirms the statements in the Bible concerning certain constructional details which are made mainly in connection with the building of Solomon's palace (1 Kings 7[1-12]).

According to 1 Kings 6[10] and 6[33], it appears that wood was used to cover the building both inside and out, and that wood was also used for beams and posts. Exactly the same thing occurred at *Tell Tainat*. The walls of this temple were built of bricks on a stone foundation—brick walls which were supported by wooden posts!

The temple at *Tell Tainat* was Phoenician and Solomon obtained Phoenician workmen for the construction of his Temple at Jerusalem from King Hiram of *Tyre* (1 Kings 5[32]; 2 Chron. 2[6]; 2[12f]). The interior appointments of the temple were in part Phoenician or at least influenced by the Phoenicians. In particular, this was probably so with the *cherubim* which watched over the ark in the Holy of Holies (Ex. 25[18-22]; 37[7-9]; 1 Kings 6[23-25]; 2 Chron. 3[7]; 3[10-14]). Similar carved statues providing us with an idea of the appearance of this strange creature of dual nature have been discovered in the Phoenician cultural region. The same assertion can be made regarding the ritual vessels described in the Bible which have been encountered in the Canaanite-Phoenician region and even as far away as Cyprus, which lay within the Phoenician orbit. The archaeologist can be compared to a tracker, who fits one indication in with another like a mosaic as soon as he has begun to follow a trail. In the search for models of Solomon's Temple in Jerusalem it seems that all the indications point to Canaan and Phoenicia.

Chapter 21
THE QUEEN OF SHEBA AS
A BUSINESS PARTNER

"Arabia Felix", the mysterious land—Death-march of 10,000 Romans—Number One exporter of spices—First news of Marib—Halévy and Glaser have a dangerous adventure—When the great dam burst—American expedition to Yemen—The temple of the moon in Sheba—Camels–the new long distance transport—Export talks with Solomon.

"And when the queen of Sheba heard of the fame of Solomon, she came to prove Solomon with hard questions at Jerusalem, with a very great company, and camels that bare spices, and gold in abundance and precious stones" (2 Chron. 9[1]).

For thousands of years richly laden caravans have made their way from "fortunate Arabia" to the north. They were well-known in Egypt, in Greece and in the Roman Empire. With them came tales of fabulous cities, of tombs filled with gold, tales which persisted through the centuries. The Roman Emperor Augustus determined to find out the truth about what camel drivers continually extolled in their remote country. He instructed Aelius Gallus to fit out a military expedition and to satisfy himself on the spot as to the truth of these incredible tales about south Arabia. With an army of 10,000 Roman soldiers Gallus marched south from Egypt and proceeded along the desolate shores of the Red Sea. Marib, the legendary capital city, was his goal. But he was never to reach it. For in the pitiless heat of the desert, after endless clashes with wild tribes, decimated by treacherous diseases, his army went to pieces. The few survivors who reached their native land again had no reliable factual details to add to the legendary stories of "Arabia Felix".

"In fortunate Arabia", writes Dionysius the Greek in A.D. 90, "you can always smell the sweet perfume of marvellous spices, whether it be incense or wonderful myrrh. Its inhabitants have great flocks of sheep in the meadows, and birds fly in from distant isles bringing leaves of pure cinnamon."

South Arabia was even in the ancient world export country Number One for spices and it is still so today. Yet it seemed to be shrouded in dark mystery. No man had ever seen it with his own eyes. "Arabia Felix" remained a book with seven seals. The first man in recent times to embark upon this dangerous adventure was Carsten Niebuhr, a German, who led a Danish expedition to south Arabia in the 18th century. Even he only got as far as Sana. He was still 60 miles from the ruined city of Marib when he had to turn back.

A Frenchman, J. Halévy, and an Austrian, Dr. Eduard Glaser, were the first white men actually to reach this ancient goal about a century ago. Since no foreigner, far less a European, was allowed to cross the frontier of the Yemen, and no permit could be obtained, Halévy and Glaser embarked on an enterprise which might have cost them their lives. They chartered a sailing boat and landed secretly in the Gulf of Aden disguised as Orientals. After an arduous journey of over 200 miles through parched and desolate mountain country they eventually reached Marib. Greatly impressed by what they saw they threw caution to the winds and clambered around the ruins.

Suspicious natives came towards them. The two scholars knew that it would cost them their lives if their disguise was discovered and took to their heels. At last after many adventures they reached Aden by a circuitous route. However they had been able to smuggle out copies and rubbings of inscriptions, concealed under their burnous, on the strength of which they were able to prove that Marib really existed.

Travelling merchants likewise brought inscriptions with them later on. Up to the present day their number reaches the sizeable total of 4,000. Scholars have examined and sifted the material. The script is alphabetic and therefore originated in Palestine. Dedicatory inscriptions give us information about gods, tribes and cities of a million inhabitants. And the names of four countries—"The Spice Kingdoms"—which are mentioned are: Minaea, Kataban, Hadhramaut and—Sheba.

The kingdom of Minaea lay in the northern part of Yemen and is referred up to the 12th century B.C. Writings of the 9th century B.C. mention its southern neighbour, the land of the Shebans. Assyrian documents of the 8th century B.C. likewise speak of Sheba and of close trade relations with this country whose kings were called "Mukarrib", "priest-princes".

Gradually, with the discovery of documentary evidence, this fairy-tale country of Sheba began to take definite shape.

A gigantic dam blocked the river Adhanat in Sheba, collecting the rainfall from a wide area. The water was then led off in canals for irrigation purposes, which was what gave the land its fertility. Remains of this technical marvel in the shape of walls over 60 feet high still defy the sand-dunes of the desert. Just as Holland is in modern times the Land of Tulips, so Sheba was then the Land of Spices, one vast fairy-like scented garden of the costliest spices in the world. In the midst of it lay the capital, which was called Marib. For 1,500 years this garden of spices bloomed around Marib. That was until 542 B.C.—then the dam burst. The importunate desert crept over the fertile lands and destroyed them. "The people of Sheba", says the Koran, "had beautiful gardens in which the most costly fruits ripened." But then the people turned their backs upon God, wherefore he punished them by causing the dam to burst. Thereafter nothing but bitter fruit grew in the gardens of Sheba.

In 1928 the German scholars Carl Rathjens and H. von Wissmann uncovered the site of a temple near Sana which had been first seen by their countryman Niebuhr. It was a significant start but almost another quarter of a century was to elapse before the greatest team of experts so far set out on an expedition at the end of 1951 to solve the archaeological riddle of Sheba. "The American Foundation for the Study of Man" provided the expedition with unusually large financial resources. The organiser of the enterprise was an extremely versatile palaeontologist from the University of California, Wendell Phillips, then only twenty-nine years old. After long drawn-out negotiations they succeeded in getting permission from King Imam Achmed to excavate at Marib. Marib lies at the southern tip of the Arabian peninsula about 6,000 feet up on the eastern spurs of the mountain range that skirts the Red Sea. The archaeologists started with high expectations.

A long column of jeeps and trucks rolled northwards in a cloud of dust through barren mountain country with neither roads nor paths. Suddenly like a phantom out of the shimmering yellow sand dunes there appeared before them massive ruins and columns—"Haram Bilqis". It was the ancient Ilumquh temple of Awwam, a centre of worship wrapped in legend, in the neighbourhood of Marib, the capital of the old Arabian kingdom of Sheba. Although partly covered by sand dunes as high as houses the lines of this oval-shaped temple over 300 feet long were clearly recognisable. A cursory examination of the sanctuary reveals a circular shape similar to that of the Zimbabwe ruins in Rhodesia where at one time the search for the Biblical Ophir was made. Closer investigation has shown, however, that the conformities are purely superficial. Zimbabwe, moreover, which was built between the 11th and the 15th centuries A.D., is around two thousand years younger than the old moon god sanctuary at Marib.

According to an inscription on the wall, Ilumquh, god of the moon, was worshipped in "Haram Bilqis". Masses of sand covered the temple which stood in the middle of the oval. Digging therefore began on the entrance to the great circle. The archaeologists wanted to try to approach the temple gradually from that point.

Under a boiling sun a gatehouse of surprising splendour and beauty was exposed amid understandable excitement. Wide steps covered with bronze led inside. The inner court was surrounded by a pillared hall. Stone columns 15 feet high once bore a roof which shielded it from the sun. Flanked by pillars on each side the processional way led from this point to the sanctuary of the moon god. An unusual ornamental fixture caused astonishment. From a height of 15 feet glittering fountains of water must in those days have played into this quiet courtyard. As it descended the water was caught in a narrow channel which then wound its way through the whole pillared court.

What must have been the feelings of pilgrims who made their way past these splashing sparkling fountains, fanned by the drowsy fragrance of incense and myrrh, through the pillared courts of this most marvellous edifice in old Arabia.

The digging went steadily forward until they were within a few yards of the temple. The archaeologists could see in front of them the wonderful temple gate, flanked by two slender columns—but at this point the excavation had to be precipitately abandoned. The chicanery of the governor of Marib which had been going on for weeks had now reached a dangerous point and the members of the expedition were no longer sure of their safety. They had to rise and run, leaving everything behind them. Fortunately they had some photographs among the few things they had been able to salvage on their hasty escape to Yemen.

Nearby in the Hadhramaut three digs were carried out in the following few years which were crowned with more success.

Soon after the experts had begun to evaluate the results of these four brief and somewhat dramatic expeditions, Professor W. F. Albright could say: "They are in process of revolutionising our knowledge of Southern Arabia's cultural history and chronology. Up to now the results to hand demonstrate the political and cultural primacy of Sheba in the first centuries after 1000 B.C."

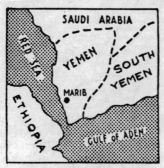

FIG. 36.—In Marib a U.S. expedition discovered the Temple of the Moon in the Kingdom of Sheba in 1951.

Just as King Solomon's ships made long sea voyages through the Red Sea to Arabia and Africa, so long distance travel began on the Red Sea coast route through the southern Sea of Sand. The new form of transport called, not unjustly, "Ships of the Desert", consisted of camels. They were able to compass distances which were hitherto reckoned impossible. An unsuspected development both in trade and transport through these vast desolate territories took place about 1000 B.C. thanks to the taming and training of these desert animals. South Arabia, which had for so long been almost as far away as the clouds, was suddenly brought into the Mediterranean world and into closer contact with the other kingdoms of the Old World. Just as with the introduction of stratosphere aircraft America was suddenly

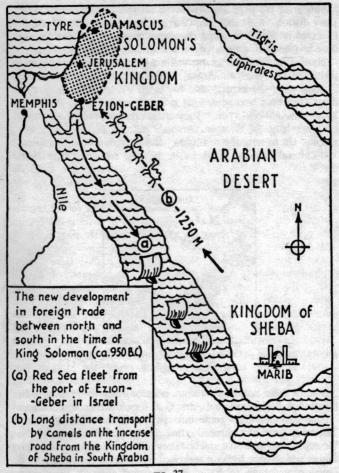

FIG. 37.

brought closer to Europe in transatlantic services, so was it also, even if on a different scale, with south Arabia and the Old World.

Previously it was by the employment of donkeys, plodding endlessly and painfully month after month, each short day's journey governed by the distance from water hole to water hole, and always in danger of attack, that the treasures of Arabia trickled northwards along the ancient Incense Road through 1,250 miles of desert. With the arrival of the new type of long-distance transport, however, a wide range of goods began to flow out of "fortunate Arabia". The new method was quicker, almost independent of water holes and therefore not tied to the old traffic routes which zig-zagged from well to well. It had also a greater capacity. The camel could carry many times the burden which an ass could carry.

The terminus of the Incense Road was Israel. Solomon's official agents, the "king's merchants," took delivery of the costly wares. It also depended on them whether the caravans would be allowed to proceed on their journey through Solomon's kingdom to Egypt, Phoenicia and Syria.

No wonder that "the fame of Solomon" came to the knowledge of the Queen of Sheba (1 Kings 10[1]). Bearing all this in mind, if we read carefully the tenth chapter of the First Book of Kings, we shall think of it no longer in terms of a "pious story" or of the Queen of Sheba as a character in a fairy tale. On the contrary the whole passage rings true and is completely intelligible. "And she [i.e., the Queen of Sheba] came to Jerusalem . . . and when she was come to Solomon, she communed with him of all that was in her heart" (1 Kings 10[2]). The queen of Sheba had assuredly quite a number of things she wanted to talk about. The head of a state whose chief export trade could only be with and through Israel, and that for unavoidable geographical reasons, would certainly have plenty to discuss with the king of that country. We should nowadays describe the affair more concretely as trade talks and should send experts minus crowns to other countries for discussions. They too would carry with them in their diplomatic bags presents which would show the respect due to the head of the state, like the queen of Sheba.

Admittedly, however vividly we are able to imagine all this, and however colourfully popular Oriental tradition embellishes the relationship between Solomon and the Queen of Sheba—throughout the East they became one of the "classical" pairs of lovers of popular tradition—the Queen of Sheba nevertheless retained a certain majestic distance.

It is a fact that popular tradition once more does indeed connect the Sheban *Awwam* temple at Marib with this "queen", but there is no doubt that this temple does not date from the time of Solomon (10th century B.C.). It was probably not built until the 8th or even the 7th century B.C. and consequently is considerably more recent than Solomon. But there are other considerations—although women such as Queen Hatshepsut and Queen Tewosre had ruled in Ancient Egypt centuries before Solomon, any non-Biblical indication of a scientifically reliable nature of a ruling princess during the time of Solomon has been denied us in southern Arabia. The Queen of Sheba, to whom we seemed already to have drawn so near, thus once again becomes inaccessible.

Chapter 22
ISRAEL'S COLOURFUL DAILY LIFE

Israel's love of ornamentation—Secrets of the boudoirs of Palestine—Sleeping with myrrh and aloes—The Balsam gardens of Jericho—Mastic, a favourite chewing gum—Perfumes of Canaan—Did the Egyptians invent the bed?—An ostracon describes a cloak being taken in pledge—Noisy flour-mills.

Amid these revelations of Egyptian, Babylonian or Assyrian splendour to which archaeology has borne witness, we have been inclined to forget until now the grey and apparently monotonous daily life of Israel. Certainly there has been nothing to record which could compare with the golden treasure of Troy, no Tutankhamun, no charming Nofretete. But was the daily life of Israel really so drab, with no colour and no sparkle?

The Israelites loved bright colours. They coloured their dress, the walls of their houses and the faces of their women. Even in the days of their patriarchs their delight in colour was apparent: "Now Israel loved Joseph more than all his children and he made him a coat of many colours" (Gen. 37³). One of the pictures in the tomb at Beni-Hasan shows this type of coat with a wonderful red and blue pattern. Red and blue were the colours for men's wear, green seems to have been reserved for women. During the desert days mention is made of "blue and purple and scarlet" (Ex. 25⁴). "Ye daughters of Israel, weep over Saul, who clothed you in scarlet..." (2 Sam. 1²⁴), cries David in his grief after the death of the first king. "And she had a garment of divers colours upon her," it is recorded of Tamar, daughter of David, "for with such robes were the king's daughters that were virgins apparelled" (2 Sam. 13¹⁸).

Nature had given the land of Canaan one of the most wonderful

painters' palettes. The children of Israel only needed to stretch
out their hands. Pomegranates and saffron yielded a lovely
yellow, madder-root and safflower a fiery red, woad a heavenly
blue: there was also ochre and red chalk. The sea donated the
queen of all dye merchants, the murex snail. Its soft colourless
body turned purple in the sunlight. That was its undoing. Vast
mountains of empty snail shells have been found at Tyre and
Sidon, which leads us to the conclusion that this was the centre
for the extraction of purple. The Phoenicians were the first to
create a proper industry for the extraction of purple in their
seaports, but later Palestine too devoted itself to the profitable
business of snail catching.

The textile town of Beth-Asbea in south Judah was famous for
byssus, the finest kind of bleached linen. "10 shirts of byssus"
are actually mentioned in an inscription of Esarhaddon, the
mighty king of Assyria. Hebron and Kirjath-Sepher had the
reputation of being important centres of the dye industry. Great
stone basins and things like cauldrons with inflow and outflow
pipes, which were dug up in these places turned out to be dyeing
vats. In Tell Beit Mirsim, the ancient Debir, they were au fait
even with the technique of cold dyes. "That saith, I will build
me a wide house," says Jeremiah (22¹⁴), "... and it is cieled
with cedar and painted with vermilion." Walls were varnished,
mosaic chips and fabrics, leather and wood were dyed, as also
were the lips, cheeks, and eyelids of beautiful women. "Thy lips
are like a thread of scarlet ... thy temples are like a piece of
pomegranate ...", "... the hair of thy head like purple ...",
"... how much better ... the smell of thine ointments than all
spices" (Song of Songs 4³; 7⁶; 4¹⁰), sings King Solomon himself
in his Song of Songs, one of the most beautiful love songs in the
world.

FIG. 38.—Stone dyeing plant in ancient Israel.

In highly poetic language it refers to Israel's delight in adornment and discreetly deals with the secrets of the beauty-parlour. These perfumes and paints, ointments and hair dyes, choice and expensive, manufactured with the best ingredients that the world could provide would still do credit to the much lauded cosmetics industry of Europe and overseas.

Sweet smelling perfumes have always been highly prized; aromatic resins were not only primarily esteemed as incense in the ritual of the temple, but they had also their place in everyday life, in the home, in clothing, on the hair and in divans and beds.

"I have decked my bed with coverings of tapestry . . . of Egypt. I have perfumed my bed with myrrh, aloes and cinnamon" (Prov. 7^{16}), runs the warning against the artful wiles of the adulteress. "All thy garments smell of myrrh, and aloes and cassia, out of the ivory palaces, whereby they have made thee glad" is the song of praise in Ps. 45^8.

Botanists have investigated these stories that often sound like fairy tales, and have hunted up the ingredients of perfumes and the suppliers of dyes. They found them among delicate flowers and herbs, in the sap of shrubs and blossoms. Many came from foreign lands, but many still grow in Palestine today.

From India came cassia (Cinnamomum Cassia), a tree with a cinnamon-like bark, and calamus (Andropogon Aromaticus), also called ginger-grass. They came across the Indian Ocean in the course of foreign trade to the packing stations for spices in South Arabia and made their way from there by caravan to the Mediterranean countries.

Cinnamon had a world tour behind it. Originally it came from China, then on to Persia, thence to India, where it became indigenous and was exported to Arabia.

Incense was obtained from the Boswellia bush. Its home is in Arabia and Somaliland, like the Commiphora Myrrha, the myrrh tree. The cradle of the aloe is the island of Socotra at the lower end of the Red Sea, whence comes its name Aloe Succotrina.

There was many a dispute about the origin of balsam. The Bible seemed to be really in error, for botanists know very well that the balsam bush (Commiphora Opobalsamum) grows only in Arabia. How could Ezekiel (27^{17}) claim that Judah and Israel had sent to Tyre "wax, honey, oil and balsam" (Moffatt)?

The botanists and Ezekiel are both right. The botanists had merely forgotten to look up Josephus, the great Jewish historian, where he tells us that there has been balsam in Palestine since the time of Solomon. The bushes were cultivated principally in the neighbourhood of Jericho. Josephus also answers the question as to how they got there. They were reared from seeds which had been found among the spices which the Queen of Sheba brought as gifts.

That seems a daring assertion.

But there is a further bit of evidence. When the Romans entered Palestine, they actually found balsam plantations in the plain of Jericho. The conquerors prized the rare shrub so highly that they sent twigs of it to Rome as a sign of their victory over the Jews. In A.D. 70 Titus Vespasian put an imperial guard in charge of the plantings to protect them from destruction. A thousand years later the Crusaders found no trace of the precious bushes. The Turks had neglected them and allowed them to die.

Mastic, which Ezekiel also mentions, is still found in Palestine. These are the yellowish-white transparent globules from a pistachio-bush (Pistacia Lentiscus). They are greatly valued for their perfume and are used medicinally. Children gladly surrender their last baksheesh for a few drops of this native chewing-gum, which was wisely extolled in ancient times as being good for teeth and gums.

In the Promised Land the following aromatic resins are indigenous: Galbanum from a parsley-shaped plant (Ex. 30^{34}), Stacte from the Storax bush (Ex. 30^{34}), Ladanum from the rock-rose and Tragacanth (Gen. 37^{25}) from a shrub of the clover family. Botanists found all the Biblical spices.

The receptacles for these often expensive items have been found by archaeologists under the debris of walls, among the ruins of patrician houses, and in royal palaces. Bowls of limestone, of ivory and sometimes of costly alabaster, with little pestles, were used for mixing the aromatic ingredients of the finest unguents. The recipes of experts in ointments were greatly sought after. Tiny bottles of burnt clay were used for keeping perfumes. In larger jars and jugs the scented spices were replaced with olive oil. Oil was well known for keeping hair and skin in good condition. Even poor folk rubbed it into their hair and skin, without the scented and generally very expensive ingredients. They got plenty of oil from their olive groves.

Washing in water was a daily necessity and was done as a matter of course. They washed before and after meals, washed the feet of their guests and washed themselves each evening. Stone basins, foot baths and clay bowls found throughout the whole country during excavations confirm the numerous Biblical

FIG. 39.—Stone footbath, with heel-rest, handles and waste-pipe.

references to this practice. (Gen. 18^4; 19^2; 24^{32}; Song of Songs 5^3; Job 9^{30}; Luke 7^{44}; Mark 7^3, etc.) Lyes from plants and minerals provided lotions and soap (Jer. 2^{22}; Job 9^{30}).

"A bundle of myrrh is my well beloved unto me: he shall lie all night betwixt my breasts" (Song of Songs 1^{13}). This is a transference of ideas referring to the discreet practice whereby women carried a small bag containing myrrh under their dresses. Neither curling pins, nor hair pins, nor mirrors—brightly polished metal discs—failed to find a place on the dressing table. These important items of beauty culture counted as luxury imports from the Nile, where they had been regarded as indispensable by the wives of the Pharaohs for many dynasties.

However much the prophets railed against it they were never able to drive the ancient equivalents of rouge and mascara completely out of the boudoirs of the wealthy.

Women were fond of decorating their hair with delicate yellow sprays of the lovely Loosestrife bush. But they were even more fond of a yellowish red powder which was extracted from the bark and from the leaves of the same shrub. The Arabs call it Henna. With this henna they dyed their hair, their toe nails and their finger nails. Astonished archaeologists found nail varnish of this bright red hue on the hands and feet of Egyptian mummies. Cosmetic laboratories and factories still use henna despite all recent developments. Eyebrows and eyelashes were tinted with Galena, powdered Lapis-lazuli gave the desired shadows on the eyelids. Dried insects provided, as in the modern lipstick, the necessary carmine for a seductive mouth.

In view of the dainty perfume flasks, the ivory ointment boxes, the mixing jars and rouge pots, which have been salvaged from the ruins of Israelite cities, we can well imagine how harsh the threats of the prophet Isaiah sounded in this world which cared so much for colour, cosmetics and perfume: "And it shall come to pass, that instead of sweet smell there shall be stink; and instead of a girdle, a rent; and instead of well-set hair baldness; and instead of a stomacher a girding of sackcloth; and burning instead of beauty'' (Is. 3^{24}).

In the Old Testament there is certainly mention of sitting at table on couches but no one goes to bed in our sense. The bed is a rare de luxe item of furniture.

FIG. 40.—Spice-mill (left) and stone grater for grinding corn.

The question whether the bed was invented in the Nile region is one that we cannot answer with certainty. Naturally beds were to be found in all the countries of the Ancient East and one has even been found in a middle Bronze Age grave (grave H 18) at Jericho. Together with other items this grave also contained a table. It can nevertheless be stated without fear of contradiction that beds were more common in Egypt than elsewhere. With great delight Sinuhe on his return observes: "I slept on a bed once more." But even 500 years later a bed was still a novelty. For when the Princess of Mitanni, Taduchepa, presumably afterwards Queen Nofretete, was married into the Egyptian royal family, she brought bedspreads as her dowry, admittedly expensively woven, but only bedspreads. The royal palace in her home country did not know what a bed was—everybody slept on the floor.

In Israel too only court circles and the well-to-do possessed so expensive an item. The plain man's bed was his cloak. At night

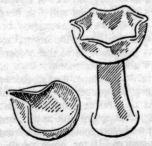

FIG. 41.—Simple oil lamp and seven-pointed candlestick.

he wrapped himself in it (Ex. 22^{27}). The law made allowance for
this in that while it declared that a man's "bed" could be taken
in pledge, that was only permissible during the day. At night he
had to have it back again (Ex. 22^{26}). A lucky chance led to the
discovery in 1959 among the ruins of Yavne Yam, eight miles
south of Tel Aviv, of a unique document which records an actual
case of a cloak being taken in pledge. In a letter of the 7th
century B.C., the text of which is clearly written in ink on a
fragment of pottery, an "ostracon", a peasant from whom such a
cloak had been taken in pledge, defends himself against the
charge of being in debt. The archaeologists could make out
distinctly . . . "And he took thy servant's cloak after I had brought
in the harvest . . . and all my brothers will testify truthfully on my
behalf that I am not in his debt." The "cloak" was in reality
only a woollen cover and seems to have been designed for any
emergency. As well as keeping out the cold in our sense and
serving as a bed it was also used as a carpet (2 Kings 9^{13}; Matt.
$21^{7,8}$).

The bed was never regarded as the ideal place to rest either in
Israel or in the Ancient East in general. It was a rare luxury and
always remained so. Its cousin the divan, however, likewise a
product of the "Fertile Crescent", became famous for its comfort and its cushions. With its arrangement of pillows during the
day which were spread out at night, it was the prototype of our
modern variety. What even bombed-out Central Europe and the
smallest 20th-century households have been able to afford was
the last word in furniture 3,000 years ago. The divan was also
known in Israel. "And satest upon a stately bed, and table
prepared before it . . ." (Ezek. 23^{41}).

We are prone to thunder against the nerve shattering noise of
our machine age and often wish the good old days of peace and
quiet would come back again. Was Israel any better off?

Instead of the blaring of loudspeakers, from daybreak onwards
houses and tents echoed to the sound of stone hand-mills. At
crack of dawn began the grinding of the corn and pounding it
into flour. This was as much the woman's job as grinding coffee
today. Only grinding flour was incomparably harder and heavier
work. It often took two of them to turn the heavy stone.

The threat of a thorough going anti-noise campaign which is
often talked about nowadays would have meant something frightful in those circumstances. If the noise of the mill stopped,
hunger crept over the land. Jeremiah had a vision of this as he

foretold what would happen during the Exile in Babylon: "Moreover I will take from thee the voice of mirth . . . the sound of the millstones and the light of the candle, and this whole land shall be a desolation. . . ." (Jer. 25[10,11]).

VI

Two Kings—Two Kingdoms from Rehoboam to Jehoiachin

Chapter 23
THE SHADOW OF A NEW WORLD POWER

The Empire splits—Frontier posts between Israel and Judah—Napoleon reads Shishak's report on Palestine—Samaria, the northern capital—Traces of Ahab's "ivory palace"—A mysterious "third man"—Arabs blow up victory monument in Moab—Mesha the mutton-king's song of triumph—Assyria steps in—The black obelisk from Nimrud—King Jehu's portrait in Assyria—Consignments of wine for Jeroboam II—Uzziah's palace—The prophet Amos warns in vain—The walls of Samaria are strengthened to 30 feet.

"So Israel rebelled against the house of David unto this day...there was none that followed the house of David, but the tribe of Judah only" (1 Kings 12^{19,20}).

Solomon the Great died in 926 B.C. The dream of Israel as a great power was buried with him for ever. Under the leadership of two unusually gifted men—David and Solomon—this ambitious dream had been built up stone by stone for two generations. But at the very moment of Solomon's passing, the old tribal dissensions broke out again and the empire of Syria and Palestine was shattered as the inevitable end of the quarrel. Two kingdoms took its place—the kingdom of Israel in the north, the kingdom of Judah in the south. A new chapter in the history of the people of the Bible had begun.

It was the Israelite people themselves that gnawed away their own foundations and destroyed their empire. It became only too plain what road they proposed to follow slowly until the bitter

239

end when the inhabitants of Israel fell a prey to the Assyrians, and the inhabitants of Judah a prey to the Babylonians. Divided among themselves, what happened to them was worse than simply sinking back into obscurity. They were caught between the millstones of the great powers which were in the following centuries to dominate the world stage. Israel and Judah collapsed amid a welter of dispute and barely 340 years after Solomon's death both kingdoms were no more.

Solomon's last wish was certainly carried out: his son Rehoboam sat on the throne at Jerusalem for a short spell as ruler of all the tribes. The endless quarrelling of the tribes among themselves hastened the end of the empire, since this resulted in civil war. Ten tribes in the north seceded. Jeroboam, who had lost no time in returning from exile in Egypt, assumed the crown in 926 B.C. and became king of Israel in the north. The remainder stayed faithful to Rehoboam, and formed Judah in the south with its capital Jerusalem (1 Kings 12[19,20]).

There was no harmony between Judah and Israel. They shed each other's blood in feud after feud. Time and again fighting broke out on the question of frontiers. "And there was war between Rehoboam and Jeroboam all their days" (1 Kings 14[30]). It was no different under their successors. "And there was war between Asa and Baasha king of Israel all their days" (1 Kings 15[16]). Judah built the fortress of Mizpah on the main strategic route from Jerusalem to the north, farther to the east they strengthened Geba "... and king Asa built with them Geba of Benjamin and Mizpah" (1 Kings 15[22]). That was the final frontier.

FIG. 42.—Border stronghold of Mizpah between Judah and Israel.
(Reconstruction.)

From 1927–35 an American expedition from the Pacific School of Religion, under the direction of William Frederick Bade, excavated abnormally massive stonework at Tell en-Nasbe, 7 miles north of Jerusalem. It was the remains of the old frontier fortress of Mizpah. The enclosing wall was 26 feet thick. This tremendous defensive wall shows how hard and bitter was the civil war that raged between north and south.

Israel was hemmed in on both sides: by Judah on the south, who even summoned the hated Philistines to help to keep Israel in check, and in the north by the kingdom of the Aramaeans, whose powerful aid had been secured by Judah through an alliance (1 Kings 15[18ff]).

Centuries passed, centuries of endless conflict with this vastly superior power which was the deadly enemy. The continuous sequence of wars did not end until the new world power Assyria had crushed the Aramaeans. But with the emergence of Assyria Israel's days, indeed the days of both kingdoms, were numbered.

Over and above all this, just after the civil war had started the country suffered unexpectedly the first foreign invasion for generations. Shishak[1] of Egypt attacked with his armies and marched through the country, plundering as he went. His greatest haul was from the old capital Jerusalem, ". . . and he took away the treasures of the house of the Lord, and the treasures of the king's house; he even took away all: and he took away all the shields of gold which Solomon had made" (1 Kings 14[25,26]). The Temple and the House of Lebanon, as the Bible calls the royal palace, had hardly been standing twenty years, and already these proud tokens of Solomon's greatness were robbed of their glory. Instead of the golden shields which had been plundered "king Rehoboam made in their stead brazen shields" (1 Kings 14[27]). It was an ill-omened act.

The first European of note to stand in front of a large document of the Pharaoh whom the Bible calls Shishak was Napoleon Bonaparte. He was not aware of it however since at that time no one had as yet deciphered hieroglyphics. It was in 1799 that he wandered, deeply impressed, with a company of French scholars, through a vast Egyptian temple area at Karnak on the east side of Thebes. In the middle of this, the greatest temple area ever constructed by human hands, 134 columns up to 75 feet high support the roof of a colossal court. On the outer

[1]Pharaoh Sheshonk I.

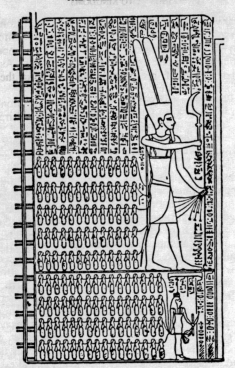

FIG. 43.—Victory relief of Pharaoh Sheshonk I (the ''Shishak'' of the Bible) in the Temple at Karnak.

wall, on the south side, an imposing relief which perpetuates the marauding expedition of this Pharaoh stands out boldly in the bright sunshine of the Nile.

The god Amun, holding in his right hand a sickle-shaped sword, brings to Pharaoh Sheshonk I 156 manacled Palestinian prisoners who are attached by cords to his left hand. Every prisoner represents a city or a village. Some of them have Biblical names such as ''the Father of Arad'' (Josh. 12[14]; Jud. 1[16]) and ''the Field of Abraham''. The fortified city of Megiddo is among those represented, and in the ruins of Megiddo the name of Sheshonk I has been found.

Sheshonk's campaign was for a long time the last. Not for

more than 300 years was Egypt again in a position to enforce its ancient claim to the suzerainty of the Syrian-Palestine territories.

The deadly danger that faced Israel came from the north—Assyria. During the reign of King Omri (882–871 B.C.) Assyria prepared to pounce. As if in a practice manoeuvre for the real thing it tried a thrust westwards from Mesopotamia.

"From Aleppo I launched the attack and crossed the Orontes." This sentence from a cuneiform inscription of Ashurnasirpal II rings out like an opening fanfare of trumpets. It had taken Assyria over 200 years to dispose of its enemies inside and outside Mesopotamia. From the ancient city of Ashur on the Tigris, which bore the name of their chief god, the Semitic race of Assyrians, eager for conquest and skilled in administration, had extended their dominion over all the peoples of Mesopotamia. Now their eyes were fixed on the conquest of the world. The prelude to that had to be the possession of the narrow coastal strip of Syria and Palestine which barred the way to the Mediterranean, as well as the occupation of the important seaports, the control of the chief caravan routes and of the only military road into Egypt.

When Assyria set itself this target the fate of Syria and Palestine was sealed.

The report of Ashurnasirpal indicates briefly what was also in store for Israel and Judah. "I marched from the Orontes . . . I conquered the cities . . . I caused great slaughter, I destroyed, I demolished, I burned. I took their warriors prisoner and impaled them on stakes before their cities. I settled Assyrians in their place. . . . I washed my weapons in the Great Sea."

As unexpectedly as the Assyrians had appeared, so with equal abruptness they departed, laden with "silver, gold, lead, copper", the tribute of the Phoenician cities of Tyre, Sidon and Byblos.

King Omri of Israel heard of all this with dark foreboding. This former army officer however still showed his outstanding flair for soldiering now that he had become king. In the heart of the Samarian highlands he bought a hill on which he built a new capital for Israel, the stronghold of Samaria (1 Kings 16²⁴). He was certain that Israel would need it, and need it badly.

The choice of a site revealed the expert who was guided by strategic considerations. Samaria lies on a solitary hill, about 300 feet high, which rises gently out of a broad and fertile valley and is surrounded by a semi-circle of higher mountains. A local spring makes the place ideal for defence. The view westwards from the summit extends as far as the Mediterranean.

King Omri made an impression on the Assyrians. A century after his dynasty had crashed, Israel was still officially called "The House of Omri" in cuneiform texts.

Eighteen years after Omri's death what they had dreaded actually happened. Shalmaneser III fell upon Carchemish on the Euphrates and was on his way to Palestine.[1]

Ahab, Omri's son who succeeded him on the throne, guessed what a violent clash with the rising world-power of Assyria would mean and did the only proper thing in the circumstances. He had recently beaten his old enemy Benhadad of Damascus, king of the Aramaeans. Instead of letting him taste to the full the victor's power, he handled him with unwonted magnanimity, he "caused him to come up into the chariot", called him "my brother", made "a covenant with him and sent him away" (1 Kings 20[33,32,34]). So he made an ally out of an enemy. His people misunderstood his policy and one of the prophets took him to task. Only the future would show how well he had known what he was doing. War on two fronts had been avoided.

"In sheepskin boats I crossed the Euphrates in flood," runs the cuneiform report of Shalmaneser III, king of Assyria. His sappers knew how to make a pontoon bridge out of inflated animal skins.

In Syria he was met by an opposing coalition from Syria and Palestine, and he took careful note of how the army was made up. Apart from the troops of the Biblical Benhadad of Damascus and another Syrian prince, there were "2,000 chariots and 10,000 horses belonging to Ahabbu the Sirilaean". Ahabbu the Sirilaean, who provided the third strongest army, was king of Israel.

The alliance between Israel and Damascus did not last long. Hardly had the Assyrians left the country when the old enmities broke out again and Ahab lost his life fighting the Aramaeans (1 Kings 22[34-38]).

The Bible devotes six chapters to the life of this king. Much of it has been dismissed as legend, such as "the ivory house which he made" (1 Kings 22[39]), or his marriage to a Phoenician princess, who brought with her a strange religion, "... he took to wife Jezebel the daughter of Ethbaal king of the Zidonians,

---

[1] 853 B.C.

and went and served Baal and worshipped him ... and made the Asherah ..." (1 Kings 16[31,33]—R.V.) or the great drought in the land, "And Elijah ... said unto Ahab: As the Lord, the God of Israel liveth, before whom I stand, there shall not be dew nor rain these years, but according to my word" (1 Kings 17[1]).

None the less they are historical facts.

Two great assaults have been made on the old ruined mound of Samaria. The first campaign was led by George A. Reisner, Clarence S. Fisher, and D. G. Lyon of the University of Harvard from 1908–10, the second excavation by an Anglo-American team under the British archaeologist J. W. Crowfoot from 1931–1935.

The foundations of Israel's capital rest on virgin soil. Omri had in fact acquired new land.

During the six years when he reigned there this otherwise peaceful and lonely hill must have been one great bustling building site. The huge blocks of the strong fortifications make the strategic intention of the builder plain. The walls are 15 feet thick. On the acropolis on the west side of the hill foundations and walls of a building were exposed. This enclosed a wide courtyard and was the royal palace of the northern kingdom of Israel.

After Omri, Ahab his son, the new king, lived here. He continued building in accordance with his father's plans. The construction was carried out with remarkable skill, nothing but these huge carefully dressed limestone blocks being used.

As the rubble was being carted off the diggers very quickly noticed the innumerable splinters of ivory that it contained. Finds of ivory itself are nothing unusual in Palestinian excavation. On almost every site this expensive material is encountered, but always in isolated pieces, yet in Samaria the ground is literally covered with them. At every step, every square yard, they came across these yellowish brown chips and flakes, as well as fragments which still showed the marvellous craftsmanship of these elegant reliefs carved by Phoenician masters.

There was only one explanation of these finds: this palace was the famous "ivory house" of King Ahab (1 Kings 22[39]).

Obviously this monarch did not build his entire palace of ivory. Since this has however generally been assumed, the veracity of the Biblical passage has been questioned. It is now quite clear what happened: Ahab had the rooms of the palace

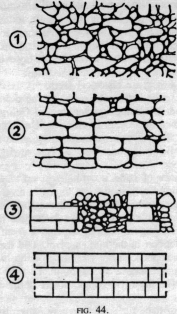

FIG. 44.
1. "Cyclops" wall at Jericho (patriarchal age).
2. Wall of Saul's royal castle at Gibeah (1020 B.C.).
3. Wall of Solomon's "chariot city" of Megiddo (950 B.C.).
4. Wall of King Ahab's palace in Samaria (850 B.C.).

decorated with this wonderful material and filled them with ivory furniture.

The proofs of the historical basis for the drought and for Ahab's father-in-law Ethbaal of Sidon were provided by Menander of Ephesus, a Phoenician historian. The Ethbaal of the Bible was called Ittobaal by the Phoenicians and in Ahab's day he was king of the port of Tyre.[1] Menander records the catastrophic drought which set in throughout Palestine and Syria during the reign of Ittobaal and lasted a whole year.

Under King Jehoram, Ahab's son, Israel suffered an invasion which had terrible consequences and resulted in a considerable loss of territory.

[1] The Biblical historians often used the term Sidonian to mean Phoenicians generally.

The Aramaeans attacked them and besieged Samaria. A frightful famine racked the inhabitants. Jehoram, who held the prophet Elisha responsible for it, wanted to have him put to death. Elisha however prophesied that the famine would end on the following day. As the Bible records, "a lord, on whose hand the king leaned" (2 Kings 7²), doubted this prophecy.

This "lord" has given rise to great discussions. His function appeared to be extremely mysterious. Nothing was known of any office of this sort. Biblical commentators sought in vain for some explanation. Eventually philologists found a slight clue. The Hebrew word "shalish", which has been translated as "lord", comes from the word for "three". But there was never a third-class officer. When Assyrian reliefs were examined more closely the true explanation was found.

Every chariot was manned by three men: the driver, the fighter, and a man who stood behind them. With outstretched arms he held on to two short straps which were fastened to the right and left sides of the chariot. In this way he protected the warrior and the driver in the rear and prevented them from being thrown out during those furious sallies in battle when the open car passed over dead and wounded men. This then was the "third man". The inexplicable "lord, on whose hand the king leaned" was the strap-hanger in King Jehoram's chariot.

Under Jehoram Israel lost a large slice of territory east of the Jordan. Moab in Transjordan was a tributary of Israel. There is a detailed account of a campaign against Mesha, the rebellious "Mutton-King": "And Mesha, king of Moab, was a sheepmaster, and rendered unto the king of Israel a hundred thousand lambs, and a hundred thousand rams, with the wool. But it came to pass, when Ahab was dead, that the king of Moab rebelled against the king of Israel" (2 Kings 3⁴,⁵). Israel summoned to her aid the southern kingdom, Judah, and the land of Edom.

They decided to make a joint attack on Moab from the south. This meant going round the Dead Sea. Relying on the prophecy: "Ye shall not see wind, neither shall ye see rain: yet that valley shall be filled with water, that ye may drink, both ye, and your cattle and your beasts" (2 Kings 3¹⁷), the allies venture to march through that desolate country. "And they fetched a compass of seven days' journey: and there was no water for the host, and for the cattle that followed them." On the advice of the prophet Elisha they made the valley "full of ditches". "And it came to pass in the morning ... behold there came water by the way of

Edom, and the country was filled with water.'' This was seen by spies from Moab, who "saw the water on the other side as red as blood'' (2 Kings 3[9,16,20,22]) and thought that the enemy were fighting among themselves.

The allied forces were successful in Moab, they laid waste the land, "they beat down the cities, and on every good piece of land cast every man his stone, and filled it: and they stopped all the wells of water, and felled all the good trees: only in Kir-Haraseth left they the stones thereof'' (2 Kings 3[25]).

Oddly enough the end of this successful campaign was "that they departed from him and returned to their own land'' (2 Kings 3[27]).

It seemed impossible to check up on the accuracy of this Biblical story.

In 1868, F. A. Klein, a missionary from Alsace, was visiting Biblical sites in Palestine. The route he followed took him through Transjordan, through Edom and eventually to Moab. As he was riding in the neighbourhood of Diban, the ancient Dibon on the middle reaches of the Arnon, his attention was particularly aroused by a large smooth stone. The yellow sand had almost completely drifted over it. Klein jumped from his horse and bent over the stone curiously. It bore unmistakably ancient Hebrew writing. He could hardly believe his eyes. It was as much as he could do in the heat of the mid-day sun to stand the heavy basalt stone upright. It was three feet high and rounded on top. Klein cleaned it carefully with a knife and a handkerchief. Thirty-four lines of writing appeared.

He would have preferred to take the stone document away with him there and then, but it was far too heavy. Besides, in no time a mob of armed Arabs was on the spot. With wild gesticulations they surrounded the missionary, maintaining that the stone was their property and demanding from him a fantastic price for it.

Klein guessed that his discovery was an important one and was in despair. Missionaries never have much money. He tried in vain to make the natives change their minds. There was nothing for it but to mark the site carefully on his map. He then gave up the idea of continuing his journey, hurried back to Jerusalem and from there straight home to Germany to try to collect the necessary money for the Arabs.

But in the meantime other people got busy, which was a good

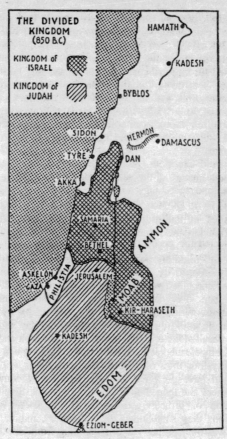

THE DIVIDED
KINGDOM
(850 B.C.)

KINGDOM of
ISRAEL

KINGDOM of
JUDAH

HAMATH

KADESH

BYBLOS

SIDON

HERMON

DAMASCUS

TYRE

DAN

AKKA

SAMARIA

AMMON

BETHEL

ASKELON

PHILISTIA

JERUSALEM

MOAB

GAZA

KIR-HARASETH

KADESH

EDOM

EZION-GEBER

FIG. 45.

thing. Otherwise an extremely valuable piece of evidence for
Biblical history might well have been lost for ever.

A French scholar, Clermont-Ganneau, who was working in
Jerusalem, had heard of the German missionary's discovery and
had at once set out for Diban. It needed all his powers of
persuasion to get the suspicious Arabs even to allow him to
examine the writing on the basalt stone. Surrounded by the

hostile eyes of the natives, Clermont-Ganneau took a squeeze of the surface. Months later, when Parisian scholars had translated the text, the French government sanctioned the purchase without hesitation. But judge the Frenchman's disappointment when he reached Diban, equipped with a caravan and the necessary sum of money, and found that the stone had disappeared. Only a patch of soot indicated the spot where it had been. The Arabs had blown it to pieces with gunpowder—from avarice. They hoped to do a more profitable trade with Europeans whose obsession with antiquity would make them willing to buy individual pieces.

What could Clermont-Ganneau do but set out on the trail of the individual pieces of the valuable document. After a great deal of trouble and searching, and after endless haggling, he was successful in retrieving some of the broken fragments. Two larger blocks and eighteen smaller pieces were reassembled and completed in accordance with the squeeze, and before Klein had even collected the necessary money, the impressive stone from Diban was standing among the valuable recent acquisitions in the Louvre in Paris.

This is what it says: "I am Mesha, son of Chamosh, king of Moab. . . . My father was king of Moab for thirty years and I became king after my father: and I built this sanctuary to Chamosh[1] in Qerihoh,[2] a sanctuary of refuge: for he saved me from all my oppressors and gave me dominion over all my enemies. Omri was king of Israel and oppressed Moab many days, for Chamosh was angry with his land. And his son succeeded him and he also said, I will oppress Moab. In my days he said this: but I got the upper-hand of him and his house: and Israel perished for ever. . . . I have had the ditches of Qerihoh dug by Israelite prisoners. . . ."

This Moabite victory message aroused considerable interest in learned circles. Many scholars did not conceal their suspicion that it was a forgery. International experts scrutinised the stone and its inscription. All the tests made it plain beyond doubt that this was in fact a historical document, a contemporary record of the King Mesha of Moab who is mentioned in the Bible.

It is also Palestine's oldest written document, dating from

---

[1] God of Moab, worshipped also in Jerusalem among other foreign deities in the time of Solomon.
[2] The capital of Moab: the Kir-Haraseth of the Bible (2 Kings 3[25]).

about 840 B.C. in Moabite dialect, which is closely related to Biblical Hebrew. That caused a real sensation.

Audiatur et altera pars—There are always two sides to a story! If we want an objective picture it is always advisable to study the war-diaries of both opponents. There is more likelihood of getting a clearer picture of the real situation. In this particular case, as it happens, the Biblical description and the Moabite text supplement each other admirably. The Mesha-stele[1] adds the necessary colour to the Biblical narrative and illumines its obscurity. The stele and the Bible agree on the decisive point, namely that the campaign ended with the defeat of the Israelite king. The Bible describes at length the initial success of Israel, which King Mesha passes over in silence. The unfortunate outcome of the campaign is only briefly hinted at in the Bible, whereas the Moabite king revels in his victory. Both are telling the truth.

As far as the "bloody water" is concerned, which saved the allies from dying of thirst on their march through this barren country, a geologist found a natural explanation. If trenches are dug in the tufa beside the Dead Sea, they fill up with water at once, which seeps through from the high plateau and owes its reddish colour to the character of the soil. To this day shepherds in Transjordan often manufacture water holes in exactly the same manner.

"And Israel perished for ever," says the Mesha stele triumphantly. By this is meant the bloody extirpation of the dynasty of Omri from the throne of Israel. Jehoram was killed. Not one member was spared of the ruling house which had propagated the hated worship of Baal in Israel through King Ahab's marriage to the Phoenician princess Jezebel (2 Kings 9^{24ff}; 10^{11ff}).

Information about King Jehu's reign is scanty: "In those days the Lord began to cut Israel short: and Hazael smote them in all the coasts of Israel" (2 Kings 10^{32}). The total extent of the losses in men and material first becomes plain in a passage about the reign of Jehoahaz, son of Jehu:[2] "Neither did he leave of the people to Jehoahaz but fifty horsemen, and ten chariots, and ten thousand footmen: for the king of Syria had destroyed them and had made them like the dust by threshing" (2 Kings 13^7). Ahab's

---

[1] A "stele" in archaeology is an independent upright column or pillar, also tombstone.
[2] 818–802 B.C.

proud chariot-corps was reduced from 2,000 to ten. How could that have happened?

A young Englishman, Henry Layard, a lawyer by profession and attaché-elect at Constantinople, had an incredible stroke of luck as a novice in archaeology in 1845. With literally only £50 in his pocket he had set out to excavate an old mound on the Tigris, Tell Nimrud. On the third day he came upon remains of a palace. He dug a trench, but nothing but masses and masses of sand came out of it. When the trench was 20 feet deep Layard had to stop work, to his great disappointment, as his money had run out.

He was feeling depressed as he loaded his few tools on to the packmules, when excited cries from the natives made him pause. One of them ran up to him and got him to go and look at the end of the trench where something dark was showing up against the golden yellow sand. Digging was hastily resumed and produced a huge pure black stone in the shape of an obelisk. Layard tenderly cleaned the ancient dust and dirt off his find. And now he could see reliefs, pictures and inscriptions in cuneiform writing on all four sides.

Well wrapped up and guarded like the apple of his eye the black stone sailed up the Tigris in one of the fragile river-boats to be presented to the more than somewhat astonished officials of the British Embassy in Constantinople. A meagre £50 had produced unexpected dividends indeed. Never again in the history of archaeology would such a valuable find result from such a small investment.

Proudly the technicians cleared a fitting site for the stone in the British Museum. Thousands of Londoners and European scholars marvelled at this ancient piece of evidence from the distant east. The tip of the 6 foot obelisk of black basalt is in the shape of a three-tiered temple tower. Visitors gazed in astonishment at the wonderful reliefs displayed in five rows round the column.

Magnificently attired royal personages are chiselled out as in real life: some of them prostrate themselves with their faces to the ground in front of a commanding figure. Long columns of bearers are laden with costly treasures, such as ivory tusks, bales of fringed fabrics borne on poles, pitchers and baskets full to the brim. Among the animals included can be observed an elephant with remarkably small ears: there are camels with two humps, apes, antelopes, even a wild bull and a mysterious unicorn.

Anyone trying to interpret the meaning of the reliefs was thrown back on pure conjecture. For at that time no one in the world could read cuneiform script. The stone remained dumb. Even the scholars learned no more about the Assyrians than the Bible told them. At the beginning of the 19th century even the names Sumerian and Akkadian meant nothing. "One box, not more than three feet square," wrote Layard, "fitted with little inscribed cylinders, seals and textual fragments, which could not even be systematically arranged, were at that time all that London knew of the early period of Mesopotamian history."

It was only later, when the text had been translated, that it transpired that the black obelisk was a victory monument by the Assyrian king, Shalmaneser III,[1] contemporary and adversary of King Ahab of Israel. It celebrates an endless succession of bloody campaigns.

FIG. 46.—Tribute of King Jehu to Shalmaneser III.

The enumeration of them contains an extremely interesting cross-reference to the Biblical tradition dealing with the period.

Three times, in the sixth, eleventh, and fourteenth year of his reign, the Assyrian came up against a coalition of kings of Syria and Palestine during his victorious incursions into the West. In the campaign in the eighteenth year of his reign however only one king opposed him in this territory. The Assyrian texts name as the adversary only King Hazael of Damascus, whom the Bible also mentions.

But the victory monument gives ample information about the former ally of the king of Damascus, Jehu of Israel.

[1] 858–824 B.C.

The second row of the relief shows a long queue of heavily laden envoys in richly ornamented tunics and peaked caps. The relevant text reads: "Tribute of Jaua of Bit-Humri: Silver, gold, a golden bowl, golden goblets, a golden beaker, pitchers of gold, lead, sceptres for the king and balsam-wood I received from him."

"Jaua of Bit-Humri" is none other than King Jehu of Israel. The Assyrians called Israel "Bit-Humri", which means "House of Omri".

This hint from the royal palace on the Tigris provides the key to our understanding of the losses which the northern kingdom of Israel sustained during the reign of Jehu.

Tribute is only paid by those who voluntarily surrender: a vanquished enemy supplies loot. Jehu had been disloyal to Damascus and had brought gifts to the Assyrians. For his faithlessness towards his old ally, for deserting Damascus, Jehu and his son Jehoahaz and most of all the people of Israel had to pay a bitter price. Hardly had the Assyrians turned their backs on Syria than Hazael of Damascus began to make a destructive onslaught on Israel in revenge. The result of it is described in the Bible: "In those days the Lord began to cut Israel short: and Hazael smote them in all the coasts of Israel . . . and made them like the dust by threshing" (2 Kings 10³²).

"That lie upon beds of ivory, and stretch themselves upon their couches, and eat the lambs out of the flock, and the calves out of the midst of the stall: that chant to the sound of the viol, and invent to themselves instruments of music, like David; that drink wine in bowls and anoint themselves with the chief ointments. . . ." (Amos 6⁴⁻⁶).

The fact that Assyria had, after Shalmaneser III, a succession of weak kings, allowed both kingdoms, Israel and Judah, another respite, which, however, meant only a postponement. Since Assyria was occupied with unrest in its own territory, Israel and Judah were able to enjoy a spell of peace from 825 to 745 B.C.

For forty years Uzziah, the leper, reigned as king of Judah. Israel was governed by Jeroboam II.[1] Under his long rule Israel flourished again, became rich, wallowed in luxury, and the aristocracy lived for themselves and for the moment, effete, corrupt and vicious. The prophet Amos raised his voice in warning. He lashed out at their unbridled love of pleasure.

[1] 787–747 B.C.

Archaeological reports and dry accounts of expeditions shed a powerful light upon these prophetic warnings. In Israel, in and around the old mound of ruins that represented ancient Samaria, evidence was lying dormant which would indicate this materialism and luxury in the soil strata from the decades following 800 B.C. in the reign of Jeroboam II. The royal palace of Samaria contained a considerable number of elegant clay tablets inscribed with ink and paint. On sixty-three of these invoices for wine and oil which had been delivered at the Court the senders are the managers of the crown lands of Jeroboam II, farmers and their employees, whose handwriting is extremely good.

From the same period comes a number of beautifully carved ivories, some of which are expensively embellished with gold and semi-precious stones and ornamented with colourful powdered glass. They show mythological motifs borrowed from Egypt, like Harpocrates on the lotus flower or figures of gods like Isis and Horus or cherubs. At that time all over Israel granaries and storehouses were being built to hold goods of all descriptions whose supply exceeded demand.

What was the reason for this sudden change? To what did they owe their new found riches?

A few decades previously things had looked black for Israel. A sentence from the record of the forty-one-year reign of Jeroboam II contains the clue to the problem: "He restored the coast of Israel from the entering of Hamath unto the sea of the plain" (2 Kings 14[25]). The "sea of the plain" is the Dead Sea. Once again the kingdom stretched into Transjordan and—as in David's and Solomon's time—up to Syria.

About 800 B.C. the conquest of Damascus by the Assyrians

FIG 47.—Nobleman's house at Megiddo during the monarchy. (Reconstruction.)

had broken the power of the Aramaeans and thereby—it sounds as if fate were being ironical—cleared Israel's arch-enemy out of the way. Israel seized the opportunity to reconquer long-lost territory, exploited the situation to its own advantage and the tribute exacted from Transjordan proved a source of new wealth for Israel.

Evidence of a similar period of peace and prosperity in the southern kingdom of Judah has since come to hand. Professor Michael Evenari, vice-president of the Hebrew University, discovered in 1958 traces of several Judaean farms equipped with cisterns, irrigation systems, and fortifications, far south in the arid Negev near Mizpeh Ramon. The finds date from the reign of Uzziah, king of Judah. We are specifically told in 2 Chron. 26[10] that this king "built towers in the desert and digged many wells; for he had much cattle...."

In 1959 Professor Aharoni of the Hebrew University was the first to discover a Judaean palace two miles south of Jerusalem. On Rachel's hill on the road to Bethlehem, at the spot where, according to tradition, Mary and Joseph on their way to Bethlehem "to be taxed" refreshed themselves at the spring, the site of a large castle was excavated, 250 feet by 150 feet square, and dating from the 8th century B.C. It had been surrounded by a casemated wall like that of King Ahab in Samaria and had a triple gate in the style of Solomon's day. Three sides of the courtyard were surrounded by buildings, two sides residential and the third for stores. When the excavators asked themselves the question as to who could have been the builder and first tenant of this lordly rural demesne they were given only one hint: "And Uzziah the king was a leper unto the day of his death, and dwelt in a several house, being a leper; for he was cut off from the house of the Lord" (2 Chron. 26[21]).

Individual items removed from the palace rubble indicate how right the prophets were in their condemnation. Several symbols of Astarte witness to the "idolatry" that went on in this princely home (2 Kings 15[4]).

Harsh and full of foreboding in these days of pseudo-prosperity ring out the prophetic words of Amos: "Woe... to them, that trust in the mountain of Samaria... ye that put far away the evil day and cause the seat of violence to come near.... Therefore now shall they go captive with the first that go captive and the banquet of them that stretched themselves shall be removed" (Amos 6[1,3,7]). But in vain—they fall upon deaf ears. Only King

Jeroboam cannot have had much faith in the peace, perhaps because the words of the prophet found an echo in his heart. At all events he feverishly set about strengthening the defences of the royal city of Samaria, which were in any case sufficiently forbidding.

J. W. Crowfoot, the English archaeologist, found what Jeroboam in his wisdom and foresight had achieved. Samaria had been surrounded with a double wall and the existing walls which were already massive had been further strengthened. In the northern section of the acropolis, where Samaria must have been most vulnerable, Crowfoot exposed a titanesque bastion. He measured it and was certain he must have made a mistake. He measured it carefully once more. No doubt about it, the wall—solid stone through and through—was 30 feet thick.

Chapter 24
THE END OF THE NORTHERN KINGDOM

Pul the soldier becomes Tiglath-Pileser III—King Pekah mentioned at Hazor —Assyrian governors over Israel—Samaria's three-year defiance—Consul Botta looks for Nineveh—The bourgeois king opens the first Assyrian museum— Searching for evidence by moonlight—The library of Ashurbanipal—Deportation of a people.

"And Pul the king of Assyria came against the land" (2 Kings 15^{19}).

Concise, sober and dispassionate, these words announce the end of the northern kingdom. The death of Jeroboam II introduced the last act. In the same year 747 B.C. the leprous king Uzziah of Judah also died. In the short intervening period during which anarchy reigned Menahem made himself king at Samaria. In 745 B.C. a former soldier by name Pulu had ascended the throne of Assyria, and from then on was known as Tiglath-Pileser III.[1] He was the first of a succession of brutal tyrants who conquered what was so far the greatest empire of the Ancient East. Their goal was Syria, Palestine, and the last cornerstone of the old world, Egypt. That meant that both Israel and Judah were caught between the pitiless millstones of a military state, for which the word peace had a contemptible sound, whose despots and cohorts had only three values: marching, conquering, oppressing.

From North Syria Tiglath-Pileser III swept through the Mediterranean countries, and forced independent peoples to become

[1] 745–727 B.C.

provinces and tributaries of the Assyrian Empire. Israel at first submitted voluntarily: "And Menahem gave Pul[1] 1,000 talents of silver, that his hand might be with him, to confirm the kingdom in his hand. And Menahem exacted the money of Israel, even of all the mighty men of wealth, of each man fifty shekels of silver, to give to the king of Assyria. So the king of Assyria turned back, and stayed not there in the land" (2 Kings 15[19,20]). "I received tribute from Menahem of Samaria," notes Tiglath-Pileser III in his annals.

One thousand talents correspond to 6 million gold sovereigns, 50 shekels per head from the "men of wealth" amounted to 100 gold sovereigns each. Economists and statisticians will gather that there must have been 60,000 well to do people in Israel.

King Menahem entertained the illusion that a pact with the tyrant and voluntary tribute would be the lesser of two evils. But the result was bad blood among his own people. Anger at the Assyrian taxes found an outlet in conspiracy and murder. Pekah, an army officer, murdered Menahem's son and heir and ascended

FIG. 48.—Tiglath-Pileser III (with bow and sword) besieging a fortress. Battering-rams pound the walls. Impaled victims in background.

[1] Tiglath-Pileser III.

the throne. From then on the anti-Assyrian party was the determining factor in the policy of the Northern Kingdom.

Rezin, king of Damascus, powerfully grasped the initiative. Under his leadership the defensive league of the Aramaean states against Assyria came to life again. Phoenician and Arab states, Philistine cities and Edomites joined the alliance. Israel too took its place in the federation. Only King Ahaz of Judah remained obstinately outside. Rezin and Pekah tried to force Judah into the league violently. "Then Rezin, king of Syria, and Pekah son of Remaliah king of Israel, came up to Jerusalem to war: and they besieged Ahaz, but could not overcome him" (2 Kings 16[5]).

In dire straits the king of Judah sent out an S.O.S. "So Ahaz sent messengers to Tiglath-Pileser king of Assyria, saying, I am thy servant, and thy son: come up and save me out of the hand of the king of Syria, and out of the hand of the king of Israel, which rise up against me. And Ahaz took the silver and gold that was found in the house of the Lord, and in the treasures of the king's house, and sent it for a present to the king of Assyria" (2 Kings 16[7,8]).

"I received tribute from Jauhazi [Ahaz] of Judah," observes the Assyrian once more.

Now events took their disastrous course. For our knowledge of further developments we are indebted to two great historical records. Firstly, the Bible and secondly the cuneiform tablets of stone and clay, on which—over 600 miles from where the terrible events took place—the military developments were officially recorded. For more than two and a half millennia these documents lay in the magnificent palaces on the Tigris until scholars ran them to earth and translated them into our tongue. They make it plain once more in quite a unique way how true to history are the contents of these Biblical stories.

The Bible and the Assyrian monuments are in entire agreement in their description of these events which were fatal for the Northern Kingdom. The Old Testament historian notes down the facts soberly, the Assyrian chronicler records every brutal detail:

Second Book of Kings	*Cuneiform Text of Tiglath-Pileser III*
"The king of Assyria went up against Damascus, and took it, and carried the people of it cap-	"His noblemen I impaled alive and displayed this exhibition to his land. All his gardens

tive to Kir, and slew Rezin"
(2 Kings 16⁹)

and fruit orchards I destroyed.
I besieged and captured the native city of Reson (Rezin) of
Damascus. 800 people with
their belongings I led away.
Towns in 16 districts of Damascus I laid waste like mounds
after the Flood."
(From: Western Campaign
734–733 B.C.)

Second Book of Kings	*Cuneiform Text of Tiglath-Pileser III*
"In the days of Pekah king of Israel came Tiglath-Pileser king of Assyria and took . . . Hazor and Gilead and Galilee, all the land of Naphtali, and carried them captive to Assyria" (2 Kings 15²⁹)	"Bet-Omri (Israel) all of whose cities I had added to my territories on my former campaigns, and had left out only the city of Samaria. . . . The whole of Naphtali I took for Assyria. I put my officials over them as governors. The land of Bet-Omri, all its people and their possessions I took away to Assyria." (From: Western Campaign and Gaza/Damascus campaign 734–733 B.C.)
"And Hoshea . . . made a conspiracy against Pekah . . . and slew him and reigned in his stead" (2 Kings 15³⁰)	"They overthrew Pekah their king and I made Hoshea to be king over them." (From: Gaza/Damascus campaign.)

Sombre evidence of the capture of Hazor by Tiglath-Pileser
III, king of Assyria (2 Kings 15²⁹), has been supplied by a layer
of rubble at Tell el-Qedah in Israel. In the course of more recent
excavations by archaeologists from the Hebrew University, traces
came to light of the shattered Israelite fortress which had been
rebuilt during the monarchy for defence purposes by Solomon
and Ahab on the site of the old Canaanite fort which had been
conquered by Joshua. The strength of the keep with its six-foot

thick walls was such that it was only surpassed by the famous royal palace at Samaria, now likewise rediscovered.

The apartments in the castle at Hazor were covered by a layer of ashes three feet thick, the stones were blackened with smoke, charred beams and fragments of what had been at one time panelled ceilings lay scattered about the ground. By exercising the utmost care the archaeologists were able to salvage from the piles of rubble some precious examples of the arts and crafts of northern Israel: a statuette of a well-groomed young woman and a marble incense-spoon. The greatest thrill was to find among the fragments of broken pottery the name of King Pekah himself, written in old Semitic script. This was the first written evidence of an Israelite king in Galilee.

When the armed hordes of Assyrians withdrew from Palestine they left Israel mortally wounded, smashed to the ground, decimated by deportation, beaten back into a tiny corner of the northern kingdom. With the exception of Samaria all its cities had been annexed and the country had been divided into provinces over which Assyrian governors and officials exercised strict control.

All that was left of Israel was a dwarf state, a tiny pinpoint on the map: the mountain of Ephraim with the royal city of Samaria. There lived King Hoshea.

The southern kingdom of Judah still remained free from foreign domination—for the time being. But it had to pay tribute to Tiglath-Pileser III.

The warlike Assyrian colossus had enclosed in his mighty grip the whole of the "Fertile Crescent" from the shores of the Persian Gulf, from the mountains of Persia to Asia Minor, from the Mesopotamian plain through Lebanon and Antilebanon as far as Palestine. Alone, away to the south-west, the 20 acre royal city of Samaria with its few square miles of hinterland, providing it with corn and barley, was unsubdued.

From this corner a gauntlet of defiance flew through the air to land at Assyria's feet.

After the death of Tiglath-Pileser III Hoshea conspired with Egypt. He refused to pay his annual tribute to Assyria. Shalmaneser V,[1] the successor of Tiglath-Pileser III, at once struck back. For when he "found conspiracy in Hoshea: for he had sent messen-

[1] 727–722 B.C.

gers to So[1] king of Egypt, and brought no present to the king of Assyria, as he had done year by year: therefore the king of Assyria shut him up and bound him in prison" (2 Kings 17[4]). Part of the organisation of the hated reign of terror—even in those days—was a widespread net of informers and spies.

With the fall of Samaria the last remnant of the Northern Kingdom of Israel suffered the fate of Damascus, ". . . in the ninth year of Hoshea the king of Assyria took Samaria and carried Israel away into Assyria" (2 Kings 17[6]).

For three years the little mountain fortress withstood the deadly pressure of superior forces with the courage of a lion (2 Kings 17[5]).

Cuneiform texts record that Shalmaneser V died unexpectedly during the siege of Samaria. His successor Sargon II[2] nevertheless continued the attack. "In the first year of my reign," boasts Sargon in his annals, "I besieged and conquered Samaria. . . . I led away into captivity 27,290 people who lived there."

The discovery of the Sargon inscriptions over 100 years ago is like a romantic tale from the fabulous land of the caliphs. None the less it is a milestone in our knowledge of the ancient world. For it marked the birth of Assyriology, which by its sensational discoveries has for the first time given many Biblical narratives a genuine historical content.

The motor car had not been invented: electric light was still unknown: no steel frames of derricks towered out of the sandflats by the Tigris: Mosul still wore the colourful variegated garb of a city from the Arabian Nights. Bazaars, harems, and a real live caliph were all there. It was the heart of the ancient orient and the year was 1840.

Summer lay like a red-hot breath over the city with its elegant white minarets and its narrow dirty muddy alleyways.

For a European the heat was enervating and unbearable. Paul Emile Botta, the new French consular agent, escaped from the incubator as often as he could to take a ride by the Tigris and breathe fresher air. But soon certain desolate mounds on the other side of the river began to fascinate him more. Admittedly they had nothing to do with the routine duties of a consular agent, but M. Botta was a scholar. He had been carefully following an

---

[1] So = Sewe, ruler of Egypt, called Sib'e by the Assyrians.
[2] 721–705 B.C.

academic dispute which had broken out over the Biblical name Nineveh. No one could say with any certainty where this city lay in olden times. It was a case of one surmise being as good as another. One suggestion pointed in the direction of Mosul. In the course of his wanderings among the yellow brown sandhills on the far side of the river Botta had repeatedly noticed fragments of bricks. They were only plain looking uncommunicative fragments. Nevertheless he mentioned them in a letter to Paris. In reply came a letter from M. Mohl, secretary of the Société Asiatique. It encouraged him to examine the terrain a little more closely.

Botta hired a bunch of natives out of his own pocket. In the typical round Tigris-boats they headed up river towards the mounds and prepared to excavate.

This first attempt of a modern European to come to grips with ancient Nineveh and wrest its secrets from it failed to achieve the desired result. Botta ordered digging to begin on several slopes. Some weeks flashed past as the work went busily on. But the result was precisely nothing. Botta saw his money being expended to no purpose and brought his private expedition which had been started with such enthusiasm to a disappointing end.

Perhaps he might have kept his hands off any further researches in this area except that he heard something which spurred him to new activity. In the village of Khorsabad, 7 miles to the north, Arabs working in the fields were said to have found great pillars.

In the early part of March 1842 Botta and his workers were on the spot. They began to excavate, and on the same day they struck stonework, apparently the inner wall of a large building.

Botta was highly delighted although at that moment he had no idea that he was responsible for a historic event of the greatest importance for scholarship. The stonework was part of the first of the gigantic Assyrian palaces which after lying dormant for thousands of years were now to come to light. It was the birth of Assyriology. And the first thing that this new science got itself involved in was—as we shall see in a moment—an erroneous idea.

Once again French scholarship displayed in this case sound judgement. The Académie des Inscriptions, which Botta informed at once, saw to it that the government placed funds at his disposal. It was to begin with no vast amount of money but gold francs were still worth something in the East. The sultan gave the required permission for excavation.

But on the site itself Botta had to endure unimaginable difficulties due to the extremely underhand dealings of the local authorities in Mosul. At one moment the trenches came under suspicion as being military defences; at another the primitive shelters of the members of the excavations were suspected of being army bivouacs. It seemed that by every possible means the great excavation was to be thwarted. More than once Botta had to send an S.O.S. to Paris and invoke the aid of the French diplomatic service.

Despite all this, sections of a huge palace were liberated from the sand at Khorsabad.

Eugène N. Flandin, a well-known Paris artist, who had specialised in antiquities, had been given the assignment by the Louvre which nowadays falls on the official photographer of any expedition. His pencil reproduced accurately on paper all that the ground yielded up. The drawings were collected into a handsome folio and the large volume was adorned with the proud title "Le Monument de Ninive". For Botta was convinced that he had found the Biblical city of Nineveh at Khorsabad. And that was where he was wrong.

If he had only dug a few inches deeper into the mounds opposite Mosul, where two years earlier he had given up the apparently hopeless task in disgust, he would in fact have made the discovery of his life. As it happened the credit for discovering Nineveh went to Henry Layard, who at the instigation of the British Government commenced digging in 1845 at the very spot where Botta had given up.

At the first spadeful, so to speak, he came upon the walls of one of the great palaces of Nineveh.

What Botta had excavated at Khorsabad was the great castle of Sargon, the home of Sargon II, king of Assyria. But that did not emerge until later. If Botta had been able to read the tablets which were salvaged at Khorsabad he would never have made his mistake. "Dur-Sharrukin", Castle of Sargon, was written there in cuneiform, which at that time, 1842, had not yet been completely deciphered. The key to its translation was not agreed on until fifteen years later.

In 1857 Rawlinson and Hincks in England and Oppert in France independently of each other produced translations of a piece of text which corresponded exactly. With that the correct interpretation of Assyrian script was assured.

In October 1844 the tablets salvaged by Botta containing

FIG. 49.—Ruins of the royal homes of Assyrian monarchs on the Tigris.

reliefs and historical texts, as well as statues and sections of pillars, started out on an adventurous journey. From Khorsabad the precious cargo rocked its way down the Tigris on skiffs and rafts. At Basra on the Persian Gulf the valuable freight was transferred to the "Cormoran", which conveyed it to Europe. It made a great sensation in Paris and evoked as lively an interest among the general public as among the scholars.

On 1st May 1847 in the splendid galleries of the Louvre designed by Percier and Fontaine, Louis Philippe, the bourgeois king, handed over to the public with impressive ceremony this collection, which contained the earliest evidence from the realm of Biblical story. With that the first Assyrian museum in the world had been founded.

The mounds of old Nineveh provided the new world with its most extensive collection of information about ancient times.

The story of the discovery of this left a bitter taste in French mouths. When the British began their diggings, the French had also staked a claim on a section of the mounds.

In the British excavation area a vast palace had come to light which had been identified as the historic Nineveh of the Bible. But what might still be lying hidden over there in the French sector? Rassam, one of the members of the British party, decided to take time by the forelock. He took advantage of the absence of his chief, Rawlinson, leader of the expedition, and of the presence of a full moon to make a purposeful excursion into the

French reservation. At the first stroke he came upon the palace of Ashurbanipal with the famous library belonging to that monarch, which was indeed the most famous in the whole of the ancient orient. Twenty-two thousand cuneiform tablets found their way into the British Museum.

They contained the essential material for understanding the historical and intellectual background of Mesopotamia, its peoples, its kingdoms with their arts and crafts, cultures and religions. Among them were the Sumerian flood story and the Epic of Gilgamesh.

What had been until then a mysterious sealed chapter of our world's history was suddenly opened and page after page was turned over. Rulers, cities, wars and stories which people had only heard about through the Old Testament revealed themselves as real facts.

We must include among these the city of Erech which is described in the tenth chapter of Genesis as part of the kingdom of Nimrod, the "mighty hunter before the Lord". About fifty miles to the north-west of Ur of the Chaldees, Professor H. J. Lenzen was the director of excavations which from 1928 onwards provided valuable information. From a pile of ruins, which the Arabs call Warka, he would produce impressive evidence of the ancient city of Uruk, as Erech is styled in the cuneiform texts, including written tablets which go back to the fourth and third millennium B.C. In the course of his investigations the German archaeologist came across the remains of walls which could be credited to the legendary king Gilgamesh. Over five miles in length they afforded their protection to this ancient Biblical city.

Meantime the original starting point of all these exciting investigations and discoveries had long been forgotten. But if it had not been for the Bible perhaps the quest would never have begun.

About the middle of last century, Nineveh, Sargon's castle, and, at Tell Nimrud, the Calah of Genesis which Nimrod built (Gen. 10[11]) were all discovered. But it was several decades before the enormous quantity of cuneiform texts was deciphered, translated, and made available to a wider circle. It was not until the turn of the century that several comprehensive scholarly works appeared, containing translations of some of the texts, including the annals of Assyrian rulers well known to readers of the Old Testament, Tiglath-Pileser or Pul, Sargon, Sennacherib, and Esarhaddon.

Since then they have become essential features of all national libraries, as well as of universities and colleges. A unique mine of information eagerly studied and used by historians, Assyriologists and theological students—all of them people with a professional interest. But who else reads them or knows about them? Yet they could easily, even taking the reliefs alone, provide a large clear illustrated commentary on the Bible.

The Assyrian documents contain a wealth of interesting and informative details which corroborate the historical truth of the Bible.

Botta found in Sargon's castle at Khorsabad his reports on his campaigns in Syria and Palestine, and his capture of Samaria in Israel.

"... in the first year of my reign I besieged and conquered Samaria." Sargon II reigned from 721 to 705 B.C. According to that the northern kingdom of Israel collapsed in 721 B.C. (2 Kings 17[6]).

"People of the lands, prisoners my hand had captured, I settled there. My officials I placed over them as governors. I imposed tribute and tax upon them, as upon the Assyrians." So reads the account of the conquest of Samaria in the annals. The Old Testament describes the uprooting tactics employed in this case too by ruthless dictators, the first large scale experiment of its kind in the world made by the Assyrians: "And the king of Assyria brought men from Babylon, and from Cuthah, and from Ava, and from Hamath, and from Sepharvaim, and placed them in the cities of Samaria, instead of the children of Israel: and they possessed Samaria, and dwelt in the cities thereof" (2 Kings 17[24]).

Tens of thousands of human beings were violently driven from their homeland, deported to foreign lands, and their places filled by others dragged from different areas.

The aim of this was clear: national consciousness, and with it the will to resist, was to be broken. The "Fertile Crescent" was ploughed up, its peoples tossed about hither and thither. Instead of a varied range of races and religions existing side by side the result was a jumble.

Samaria shared this fate. Its motley collection of inhabitants became known as "Samaritans". "Samaritans" became a term of abuse, an expression of abhorrence. They were despised not only on religious grounds but also as individuals: "For the Jews have no dealings with the Samaritans" (John 4[9]). It was only when

Jesus told the story of the "Good Samaritan" that he turned this term of abuse into a byword for practical Christian charity (Luke 10[3ff]).

The people of the Northern Kingdom and their kings with them disappeared, were absorbed into the population of these foreign lands, and never emerged again in history. All investigation into what became of the ten tribes who had their home there has so far come to nothing.

Chapter 25
JUDAH UNDER THE YOKE OF ASSYRIA

Hopes aroused by Sargon's death—A fig poultice cures King Hezekiah—A well-tried Ancient Eastern remedy—Merodach-Baladan: gardener and rebel —Secret armaments in Judah—Aqueduct through the rocks of Jerusalem— Inscription describes Hezekiah's tunnel—The fate of Lachish in stone relief —Traces of Assyrian battering-rams in the ruins—A puzzling retreat—Herodotus' story of the king with the mouse—Starkey finds a plague-grave—Sennacherib describes the siege of Jerusalem.

"Therefore I will wail and howl, I will go stripped and naked: I will make a wailing like the dragons, and mourning as the owls. For her (i.e., Samaria's) wound is incurable: for it is come unto Judah: he is come unto the gate of my people, even to Jerusalem" (Micah 1⁸⁻⁹).

In Judah there may have been some who rejoiced at the downfall of their hostile brother. The prophet Micah however was overwhelmed with grief and filled with deep anxiety at the news. He guessed that the blow that had crushed Samaria would one day strike the people of Judah and the city of Jerusalem. At that time Hezekiah was king of Judah,[1] "and he did that which was right in the sight of the Lord" (2 Kings 18³). Since the father of Hezekiah had voluntarily submitted to Tiglath-Pileser III in 733 B.C., Judah had been a dependent vassal-state, whose deliveries of tributes were carefully noted in Nineveh. Hezekiah was not prepared to follow in his father's footsteps. The reaction set in when he came to the throne. "He rebelled against the king of Assyria" (2 Kings 18⁷).

[1] 725–697 B.C.

Hezekiah was no hothead, but a clever, cool, calculating and farsighted man. He knew very well that what he was about was a highly dangerous and risky business for himself and his people. Only 30 miles from Jerusalem the Assyrian governor of Samaria was sitting eyeing him with suspicion. One careless step, a nod to Nineveh, and Hezekiah would find himself off his throne and clapped in irons. He merely held the throne in fee. Hezekiah proceeded with the utmost caution, "and he prospered, whithersoever he went forth" (2 Kings 18[7]).

In the Philistine city-state of Ashdod, which was oppressed in the same way, anti-Assyrian riots broke out. That brought into being a league against the tyrant on the Tigris.[1] Hezekiah saw a chance to further his plan. He showed his sympathy but remained officially aloof, and intrigued behind the scenes.

Jerusalem had at this time visitors from overseas, tall personages from "beyond the rivers of Ethiopia" (Is. 18[1]). These were Ethiopian envoys. The king of Egypt at that point was Shabaka, a Pharaoh from Ethiopia. The Assyrians replied to the riots in Ashdod with armed force. A "turtanu", a field-marshal, appeared on the scene with an army. "In the year that Tartan came unto Ashdod [when Sargon the king of Assyria sent him] and fought against Ashdod and took it. . . ." (Is. 20[1]).

On the walls of Sargon's castle the court chroniclers describe the carrying out of this punitive expedition as follows: "Ashdod . . . I besieged and conquered . . . its gods, its women, its sons, its daughters, its goods and chattels, the treasures of its palace, and all the people of its territory I counted as plunder. I settled those cities anew. . . ."

The anti-Assyrian league had gone to pieces on the approach of the Assyrians. Ashdod's territory became an Assyrian province.

Nothing happened to Hezekiah, although his name was on the black list. Assyrian informers had seen through his game and had given Sargon II full details of Hezekiah's secret dealings with Egypt, as can be seen from the text of a fragment of a prism:

"Philistia, Judah, Edom and Moab, who planned hostilities, infamies without number . . . who, in order to prejudice him against me and make him my enemy, brought gifts in homage to Pharaoh, king of the land of Egypt . . . and begged him to form an alliance. . . ."

In 705 B.C. news spread like wildfire, raising at once fresh

[1]713 B.C.

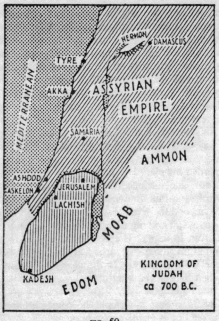

FIG. 50.

hopes of liberation from the Assyrian yoke: Sargon had been murdered! All over the "Fertile Crescent", in the Assyrian provinces and in the vassal states, conspiracies, discussions and intrigues began.

"In those days was Hezekiah sick unto death" (2 Kings 20^1).

Happening precisely at this moment of feverish political activity it was a grave handicap. For many states in Syria and Palestine were looking expectantly to the able king of Judah.

How could Hezekiah be cured of his serious illness? "And Isaiah said, Take a lump of figs, And they took and laid it on the boil, and he recovered" (2 Kings 20^7).

The course of history is often rich in remarkable parallels and associations. So it is in the case of this Biblical therapy.

In the north Syrian harbour of Ras Shamra, French excavators in 1939, digging among the ruins of the Phoenician seaport of Ugarit, came upon fragments of an old book of veterinary science, which contained prescriptions for the treatment of sick and ailing horses. The captain of the household cavalry of the king of Ugarit had, about 1500 B.C., entered in it tried remedies of this sort: "If a horse has a swollen head or a sore nose, prepare a salve from figs and raisins, mixed with oatmeal and liquid. The mixture should be poured into the horse's nostrils."

FIG. 51.—King Sargon II of Assyria with his Tartan (relief from Khorsabad).

For every kind of sickness there is a very detailed prescription. The chief medicaments are plants and fruit, like mustard and liquorice juice. Advice is even given on how to deal with horses that bite and neigh too much. Does any modern breeder or owner of horses know how to cure that? In those days a neighing horse could in certain circumstances be fatal. Horses were used exclusively for fighting and hunting. A troop of chariots, however well hidden in an ambush, could be betrayed by a sudden loud neighing. It was the same with hunting.

These recognised cures have been tried out successfully from time immemorial by the peoples of the ancient orient. They are nature's remedies which can also be profitably used in the case of human beings. One of them, which is particularly commended in the veterinary manual, is "Debelah", a sort of poultice of compressed figs. It was a "Debelah" that the prophet prescribed for Hezekiah's abscess. It worked, and he was all right again in three days.

Many of these tried remedies dating back to Biblical times,

and largely consisting of ingredients supplied by Mother Nature, have been either lost or forgotten in the whirligig of time. Many of them on the other hand have been quietly passed on from generation to generation. This prescription for figs is one of them. Swiss doctors still prescribe finely chopped up figs steamed in milk, for certain kinds of abscesses. An Arabic remedy reminds us of the "Debelah". A thick sticky liquid made from grape-juice is called "Dibis" in the native tongue.

"At that time Berodach-Baladan,[1] the son of Baladan king of Babylon, sent letters and a present unto Hezekiah: for he had heard that Hezekiah had been sick" (2 Kings 20[12]).

This was the traditional practice in court circles and was part of the royal etiquette in the ancient East. Presents were sent and enquiries made about the health of "our brother". The clay tablets of El-Amarna mention the habit frequently.

Merodach-Baladan[2] however found Hezekiah's illness a convenient pretext for making contact with him. The real reason for his polite courtesies lay in the field of high level politics.

"Merodach-Baladan, king of Babylon", was for a long time a mysterious personage both to readers of the Bible and to scholars. It is now quite certain that he was in his own day an extremely important person. We even know something about his private habits. He was for example a great gardener, not in the sense of being keen to lay out handsome royal parks, but with a real down to earth interest in the vegetables and fruit of Mesopotamia, whether it was endives, beetroot, cucumbers, thyme, coriander, saffron, peaches or medlars. He described the various types of plants and how to cultivate them, and was in fact the author of a practical handbook on vegetable gardens, as archaeologists discovered with no little astonishment.

Apart from his private hobby of gardening, Merodach-Baladan both as a king and as a Babylonian was the most bitter and determined opponent of Nineveh. No other monarch in the "Fertile Crescent" attacked the Assyrians so vigorously over many years, engaged them in so many heated battles, or intrigued so unremittingly against the tyrants of the Tigris, as he did.

The assassination of Sargon brought Merodach-Baladan into the field. It was at this point that his ambassadors visited

[1] Here wrongly spelt Berodach-Baladan. Isaiah (39[1]) spells it correctly Merodach-Baladan.
[2] = Marduk-Aplaiddin in Babylonian.

Hezekiah. What was in fact discussed on the occasion of the official visit during the convalescence of Hezekiah can be read between the lines: "And Hezekiah hearkened unto them, and showed them all the house of his precious things . . . and all the house of his armour" (2 Kings 20¹³), Judah's arsenal. Secret armaments and feverish preparations for D-day, the great showdown with Assyria which they saw to be imminent, were in full swing. "Also . . . he built up all the wall that was broken, and raised it up to the towers, and another wall without, and repaired Millo in the city of David, and made darts and shields in abundance" (2 Chron. 32⁵).

Jerusalem's defences were overhauled and strengthened for a long siege, the old perimeter wall was renewed, breaches repaired, and turrets erected. On the north side of the city, its most vulnerable point, a second outer wall was added. Hezekiah even pulled down houses to make room for it (Isa. 22¹⁰). But that did not exhaust his precautions. "And the rest of the acts of Hezekiah, and all his might, and how he made a pool, and a conduit, and brought water into the city, are they not written in the book of the Chronicles of the kings of Judah?" (2 Kings 20²⁰).

The Chronicler completes the story: "This same Hezekiah also stopped the upper water course of Gihon, and brought it straight down to the west side of the city of David. . . ." (2 Chron. 32³⁰).

Jerusalem, the old city of David, has many mysterious corners. Pilgrims from all over the world, travellers of three faiths, Christians, Jews, Mohammedans, come to pay homage at its holy places. Seldom does one of these endless visitors stumble upon the dark depressing spot outside the walls, far below the noisy streets of the city, which bears eloquent testimony to one of the most dire moments in its ancient story, to a time fraught with fear and menace. This spot had sunk into oblivion. In 1880 it was discovered by a fluke. It still bears as plain as day all the marks of feverish haste.

Outside the city, where its southeastern slopes sweep gently down to the Valley of the Kidron, lies a small still sheet of water, enclosed by walls, the Pool of Siloam. Two Arab boys were playing there—one of them fell in. Paddling for all he was worth, he landed on the other side, where a rock wall rose above the pool. Suddenly it was pitch black all round him. He groped about anxiously and discovered a small passage.

The name of the Arab boy was forgotten but not his story. It was followed up and a long underground tunnel was discovered.

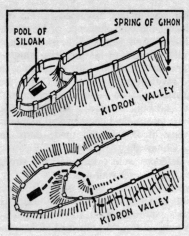

FIG. 52.—King Hezekiah's great Tunnel of Siloam in Jerusalem.

A narrow passage about 2 feet wide and barely 5 feet high had been cut through the limestone. It can only be negotiated with rubber boots and a slight stoop. For about 500 yards the passage winds imperceptibly uphill. It ends at the Virgin's Fountain, Jerusalem's water supply since ancient times. In Biblical days it was called the Fountain of Gihon.

As experts were examining the passage they noticed by the light of their torches old Hebrew letters on the wall.

The inscription, which was scratched on the rock only a few paces from the entrance at the Pool of Siloam, reads as follows: "The boring through is completed. And this is the story of the boring: while yet they plied the pick, each toward his fellow, and while yet there were three cubits to be bored through, there was heard the voice of one calling to the other that there was a hole in the rock on the right hand and on the left hand. And on the day of the boring through the workers in the tunnel struck each to meet his fellow, pick upon pick. Then the water poured from the source to the pool twelve hundred cubits, and a hundred cubits was the height of the rock above the heads of the workers in the tunnel."

The Turkish government had the inscription prized out before the First World War. It is now exhibited in the museum at Istanbul.

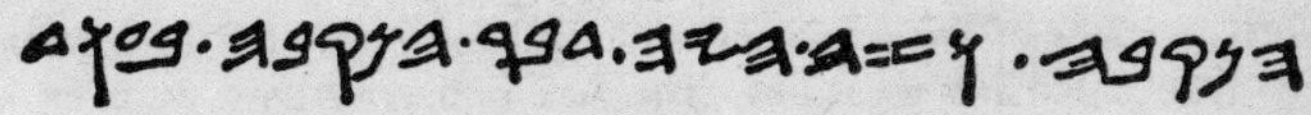

אׁ7ׁ0ׁ9ׁ·ׁׁ39ׁ9ׁ7ׁאׁ·ׁׁ9ׁ9ׁאׁ·ׁׁ3ׁזׁאׁ·ׁ3ׁ=ׁ7ׁ ·ׁׁ39ׁ9ׁ7ׁ3

FIG. 53.—"The boring through is completed. And this is the story of the boring:
while yet . . ." (Beginning of the Siloam inscription.)

It was Hezekiah's aqueduct.

During a siege the Number One problem is that of providing drinking water. The founders of Jerusalem, the Jebusites, had sunk a shaft down through the rock to the Fountain of Gihon. Hezekiah directed its water, which would otherwise have flowed into the Kidron valley, through the mountain to the west side of the city. The Pool of Siloam lies inside the second perimeter wall which he constructed.

There was no time to lose. Assyrian troops could be at the gates of Jerusalem overnight. The workmen therefore tackled the tunnel from both ends. The marks of the pickaxes point towards each other, as the inscription describes.

Oddly enough the canal takes an S-shaped course through the rock. Why did the workmen not dig this underground tunnel the shortest way to meet each other, that is, in a straight line? The wretched job would have been finished quicker. Seven hundred feet of hard work would have been saved out of the total 1,700 feet.

Locally, there is an old story which has been handed down which claims to explain why they had to go the long way round. Deep in the rock, between the spring and the pool, are supposed to lie the graves of David and Solomon.

Archaeologists took this remarkable piece of folk-lore seriously and systematically tapped the walls of the narrow damp tunnel. They sank shafts into the rock from the summit and R. Weill actually came across cavities cut in the rock, which were perhaps graves, but which had obviously been despoiled in early times. Were these perhaps the graves of David's line? Kathleen M. Kenyon, one of the most prominent Biblical archaeologists of recent years, does not think so. Others, however, are of a different opinion. We shall probably never know what these "royal graves" really were. . . .

"Now in the fourteenth[1] year of king Hezekiah did Sennacherib king of Assyria come up against all the fenced cities of Judah and took them" (2 Kings 18[13]).

---

[1] Biblical chronology is out here by ten years. It was the twenty-fourth year.

The states of Syria and Palestine had four years left in which to take defensive measures. The Assyrian governors were expelled. A strong league was formed. The kings of Askelon and Ekron joined up with Hezekiah, and Egypt promised help in case of military developments.

Naturally the new Assyrian ruler Sennacherib[1] was not unaware of all this. But his hands were tied. After the assassination of his predecessor Sargon, the eastern part of his empire revolted. The leading spirit in this was Merodach-Baladan. As soon as Sennacherib was once more in control of the situation in Mesopotamia, by the end of the year 702 B.C., he set out for the west and smashed the rebellious little countries in one single campaign. A similar fate overtook the Egyptian army which Pharaoh Shabaka had sent under the command of his nephew Taharka against the Assyrians. The Second Book of Kings and the Book of Isaiah confer upon the latter, a future pharaoh, who was also related to the Ethiopian dynasty, distinction which was still to come, in that they described him even in those troubled times as "Tirhakah, king of Ethiopia" (2 Kings 19[9]; Isa. 37[9]). The whole of Judah was occupied by Sennacherib's troops, Hezekiah was shut up in Jerusalem. Among the frontier fortresses Lachish alone still offered resistance. Sennacherib deployed his storm-troopers against this unusually strong fortified city.

Anyone who wishes to re-live the frightful battle of Lachish, vividly and dramatically to the smallest detail, must pay a visit to the British Museum. It is here that the massive relief, which eye-witnesses created on the orders of Sennacherib 2,650 years ago, have found a resting place. Sir Henry Layard salvaged this precious object from the ruins of Nineveh.

On the turrets and breastwork of the stronghold of Lachish with its stout high walls the Judahite defenders fought with clenched teeth. They showered a hail of arrows on the attackers, hurled stones down upon them, threw burning torches—the fire-bombs of the ancient world—among the enemy. The faces, curly hair, and short beards are easily recognisable. Only a few wear any protection for head or body.

At the foot of the wall the Assyrians are attacking with the utmost violence and with every type of weapon. Sennacherib had deployed the whole range of approved assault-tactics. Every Assyrian is armed to the teeth: each one wears shield and helmet.

[1] 705–681 B.C.

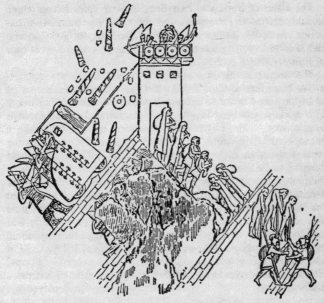

FIG. 54.—Assyrians storming Lachish 701 B.C.

Their engineers have built sloping ramps of earth, stones and
felled trees. Siege-engines, the first tanks in history, push forward up the ramps against the walls. They are equipped in front
with a battering ram which sticks out like the barrel of a cannon.
The crew consists of three men. The archer shoots his arrows
from behind a sheltering canopy. A warrior guides the ram, and
under its violent blows stones and bricks crash down from the
walls. The third man douses the tanks with ladlefuls of water,
extinguishing the smouldering fire-bombs. Several tanks are
attacking at the same time. Tunnels are being driven into the rock
beneath the foundations of the walls. Behind the tanks come the
infantry, bowmen, some of them kneeling, some stooping, protected
by a shield-bearer. The first captives, men and women, are being
led off. Lifeless bodies are hanging on pointed stakes—impaled.

James Lesley Starkey, a British archaeologist, dug up the ruins
of the walls of the fortress of Lachish. The holes and breaches
made by the Assyrian tanks can be seen to this day.

Amid the confusion of the battle and the din of the siege around the frontier fortress of Judah an order went out from Sennacherib: "And the king of Assyria sent Tartan, and Rabsaris and Rab-Shakeh from Lachish to king Hezekiah with a great host against Jerusalem" (2 Kings 18[17]).

That meant attack on Jerusalem.

The historians of the Assyrian king have preserved a record of what happened next. A hexagonal prism from the rubble heaps of Nineveh says: "And Hezekiah of Judah who had not submitted to my yoke . . . him I shut up in Jerusalem his royal city like a caged bird. Earthworks I threw up against him, and anyone coming out of his city gate I made to pay for his crime. His cities which I had plundered I cut off from his land. . . ."

Surely now must come the announcement of the fall of Jerusalem and the seizing of the capital. But the text continues: "As for Hezekiah, the splendour of my majesty overwhelmed him . . . 30 gold talents . . . valuable treasures as well as his daughters, the women of his harem, singers both men and women, he caused to be brought after me to Nineveh. To pay his tribute and to do me homage he sent his envoys."

It is simply a bragging account of the payment of tribute—nothing more.

> "And the king of Assyria appointed unto Hezekiah king of Judah three hundred talents of silver and thirty talents of gold" (2 Kings 18[14]).

The Assyrian texts pass on immediately from the description of the battle of Jerusalem to the payment of Hezekiah's tribute. Just at the moment when the whole country had been subjugated and the siege of Jerusalem, the last point of resistance, was in full swing, the unexpected happened: Sennacherib broke off the attack at five minutes to twelve. Only something quite extraordinary could have induced him to stop the fighting. What might it have been?

Whilst the Assyrian records are enveloped in a veil of silence, the Bible says: "And it came to pass that night, that the angel of the Lord went out, and smote in the camp of the Assyrians an hundred fourscore and five thousand: and when they arose early in the morning, behold, they were all dead corpses. So Sennacherib, king of Assyria departed, and went and returned, and dwelt at Nineveh" (2 Kings 19[35,36]).

Herodotus of Halicarnassus, the most famous traveller in the ancient world, historian and author of an early Baedeker, helped to solve the puzzle. This friend of Pericles and Sophocles, who was born about 500 B.C., had a definite flair for finding out strange facts about people and nations. Like a personified questionnaire he extracted from his contemporaries on his travels through the Ancient East information on all sorts of things which he thought were worth knowing or were unknown to him. In Egypt he had a long conversation with a temple priest who imparted a strange story to the inquisitive Greek.

It happened that at the very time that Sennacherib the Assyrian marched against Egypt with a large armed force, there was a priest-king on the throne of Egypt who treated the army as a contemptible profession. The Egyptian warriors, who had been so disdainfully dealt with, refused to take the field. Thereupon the priest-king hurried to the temple in deep despair. There he was told that the god would help him. Relying upon this, the king, who had actually no soldiers behind him but only shopkeepers, tradesmen and market folk, went to meet Sennacherib. At the narrow entrances into the country "an army of field-mice swarmed over their opponents in the night... gnawed through their quivers and their bows, and the handles of their shields, so that on the following day they fled minus their arms and a great number of them fell. Hence," concludes Herodotus' story, "this king still stands in Hephaistos' temple with a mouse in his hand, and with the following inscription: 'Look on me and live in safety'."

However obscure the meaning of this religious legend may be its core is historical.

For the peoples of the ancient world—as also for the Bible (1 Sam. 6⁴)—the mouse was what the rat was for the people of the Middle Ages. It was the symbol of plague.

On the edge of the city of Lachish, Starkey, the archaeologist, found possible confirmation of the story in 1948: a mass grave in the rock with 2,000 human skeletons, unmistakably thrown in with the utmost haste. If these were the remains of the victims of an epidemic, then its effects must have been devastating.

The drama of the campaign had been unfolded and once more Jerusalem had escaped. But all round it the land of Judah presented a pitiable spectacle: "The daughter of Zion is left as a cottage in a vineyard," laments the prophet Isaiah, "as a lodge in a garden of cucumbers." The "country is desolate", the

FIG. 55.—King Sennacherib seated on his throne in front of the vanquished city of Lachish. (Detail of a campaign relief.)

"cities are burned with fire . . . and it is desolate as overthrown by strangers" (Isa. 1⁸,⁷).

Only the thought of the marvellous deliverance of the city of David gives the sorely tried people new hope and courage. Undaunted, they bend all their energies to rebuilding, which, without interference from Nineveh, goes quickly forward. Sennacherib never came back. For the next twenty years the tyrant devoted himself to campaigns and battles in Mesopotamia. Then Sennacherib, like his father Sargon, fell by an assassin's hand. "And it came to pass, as he was worshipping in the house of Nisroch his god, that Adrammelech and Sharezer his sons smote him with the sword: and they escaped into the land of Armenia. And Esarhaddon his son reigned in his stead" (2 Kings 19³⁷). So runs the brief account of the event in the Bible.

FIG. 56.—Assyrian encampment in Sennacherib's day—a relief from Nineveh.

Esarhaddon himself, the successor to the throne, describes in vivid detail these turbulent days in Nineveh: "Disloyal thoughts inspired my brothers.... They rebelled. In order to exercise royal authority they killed Sennacherib. I became a raging lion, my mind was in a fury...."

Despite the intense cold and amid snow and ice he set out without delay to destroy his enemies in the eleventh month of the year 681 B.C. "These usurpers...fled to an unknown land. I reached the quay on the Tigris, sent my troops across the broad river as if it were a canal. In Addar[1]...I reached Nineveh well pleased. I ascended my father's throne with joy. The south wind was blowing...whose breezes are propitious for royal authority....I am Esarhaddon king of the world, king of Assyria...son of Sennacherib."

[1] Twelfth month.

Chapter 26
THE SEDUCTIVE RELIGIONS
OF CANAAN

The "abominations of the heathen"—Harsh words from the prophets—Philo of Byblos: a witness—Eusebius, the Christian Father, finds no one to believe him—Ploughman stumbles upon Ugarit—A powerful seaport disappears—Schaeffer digs at the "Head of Fennel"—The library in the priest's house—Three scholars decipher an unknown alphabet.

"Manasseh was twelve years old when he began to reign, and reigned fifty and five years in Jerusalem.... And he did that which was evil in the sight of the Lord, after the abominations of the heathen, whom the Lord cast out before the children of Israel" (2 Kings 2[1,2]).

"Abominations of the heathen," says the official report. Isaiah, the great prophet who was contemporary with King Manasseh,[1] puts it more plainly when he complains bitterly: "How is the faithful city become a harlot" (Isa. 1[21]).

All the other prophets through the centuries constantly utter the same harsh and unambiguous accusation, which seems so monstrous to readers of the Bible.

The charge runs like a red thread through many books of the Old Testament, accompanying the chances and changes of Israel's history.

It rings out from the time when Israel after its long desert wanderings reached the Jordan about 1230 B.C. (Num. 25[1,3]). We hear it in the time of the Judges (1 Sam. 2[22]). It echoes

[1] 696–642 B.C.

through the two kingdoms, Judah (1 Kings 14^{23,24}) as well as Israel (Hosea 4^{13,14}). Even in the years of captivity by the waters of Babylon in the 6th century B.C. it is not silent (Ezek. 16^{15ff}).

For 1,500 years after the books of the Bible had made their way into Europe, their contents were communicated to the people exclusively by priests and monks. For they were written in Greek, Latin and Hebrew. It was only at the Reformation, when the first translations had been printed and could be obtained by everyone, that as more and more people came to read the Bible for themselves they came across passages which startled them. The Bible spoke about harlots. It is understandable that people whose houses and dwellings lay close in the shadow and protection of cathedrals and churches which pointed them heavenwards, found difficulty in comprehending this fact.

What did the European, for whom God was "a safe stronghold", know about the religions of the land in which the Bible was first written?

The prophets and chroniclers tended to be thought of as men who, in their zeal for Yahweh and their anger against foreign religions, had probably gone too far. This objection was levelled at the Bible right up to the present day.

There is secular evidence for what the Bible calls "the abominations of the heathen". Philo of Byblos, a Phoenician scholar, who lived 100 years before Christ, had collected abundant material from his native land and had written a history of Phoenicia, the "Phoinikika". It deals with historical events in the seaports and maritime republics of Canaan from earliest times, and describes the Phoenician gods, mythologies and religious practices. As a reliable source for his work Philo of Byblos cites the Phoenician priest Sanchuniathon, who has been already referred to, and who lived in the 6th or 7th century B.C. When, as the result of an earthquake, the inscribed pillars in the temple of Melkart at Tyre crashed to the ground, Sanchuniathon is said to have copied the ancient inscriptions.

Bishop Eusebius of Caesarea in Palestine discovered the writings of Philo of Byblos in A.D. 314 and gave an account of them. Much of what they recorded, particularly as regards mythology and religion, seemed quite incomprehensible.

At the head of the baals of Canaan was the god El. His wife was Asherah, a goddess who is also mentioned in the Bible. El married his three sisters, one of whom was Astarte. She is frequently referred to in the Old Testament as Ashtaroth (Judges 10[6], etc.). El not only kills his brother but also his own son: he cuts off his daughter's head, castrates his father, castrates himself and compels his confederates to do the same.

Little wonder that people in the Christian era were not prepared to believe stories of enormities of this sort.

With us it is accepted as a matter of course that every half civilised community controls the morality of its citizens. But in Canaan in those days the cult of sensuality was regarded as the worship of the gods, men and women prostitutes ranked as "sacred" to the followers of the religion, the rewards for their "services" went into the temple treasuries as "offerings for the god".

The last thing the prophets and chroniclers did was to exaggerate. How well founded their harsh words were has only become fully understood since the great discoveries of Ras Shamra.

On the north coast of Syria exactly opposite the east tip of Cyprus lies Mînet El-Beidâ, the "White Haven". The Mediterranean waves break here on dazzling snow white limestone rocks in a wonderful display of colour, changing from light green to deep violet. Inland, great banks of clouds surrounded the lonely mountain top of "Jebel Aqra". The natives say that long ago it was the dwelling-place of the gods of their ancestors.

Near the sea in 1928 a peasant who was ploughing discovered a long underground passage. Initial investigation showed that it led to a tomb. It was a sepulchral vault in the style of Mycenae.

When the discovery was announced France, which as mandatory power was in control of Syria, reacted with its customary alacrity. M. Dussaud, curator of oriental antiquities in the Louvre, despatched Professor Claude F. A. Schaeffer with some other experts to the "White Haven". Exciting discoveries awaited them.

Half a mile from the shore and the old Mycenae grave rose an artificial hill. Round its base flowed a pleasant rippling brook. It had always been called by the natives Ras es Shamra, "Head of Fennel". Fennel was actually growing on the old heap of ruins which concealed the remains of the Phoenician royal city of Ugarit. More than 3,000 years ago it had been wiped out for good by the onslaught of the Sea Peoples.

Schaeffer had incredible luck with his excavations on the "Head of Fennel". For here at last the long-sought information

about the religions of Canaan came to light. Between two
temples, one of them dedicated to the god Baal and the other to
the god Dagon, he found among the houses of rich merchants the
house of the High Priest of Ugarit, who owned a handsome
library, as is clear from the large number of inscribed tablets
which were found there. Schaeffer's trained eye recognised at
once that the writer must have been using a hitherto unknown
Phoenician alphabet. It was surprisingly quickly deciphered in
1930 by three scholars—Professor H. Bauer, of the University of
Halle, Germany, and C. Virolleaud and E. Dhorme of France.
The bilingual documents—one of the languages is an ancient
Canaanite dialect, which is something like pre-Mosaic Hebrew—
are exclusively concerned with the gods and religions of old
Canaan, with which Israel on entering the Promised Land had its
first fateful encounter.

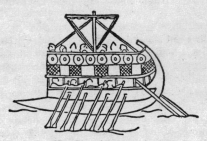

FIG. 57.—Phoenician merchantman.

The myths and practices described in this unique collection of
documents, abounding in barbaric activities of gods and demi-
gods, indicate the particular significance which was attached to
the rites of the goddesses of fertility in Canaan.

The forms of worship which Canaan connected with fertility
extended to everyday life. Under each of the houses which were
excavated was found a burial vault in which the inhabitants of
Ugarit buried their dead. Oddly shaped clay funnels were sunk
into the ground through which water, wine, oil and the flesh and
blood of animal sacrifices were offered to the dead. The fertility
cults did not hesitate to penetrate even the world beyond death.
The feeding-funnels leave us in no doubt about that. They are
decorated with the appropriate symbols.

Mandrakes played a large part in the ritual of the living.

Ancient Canaanites and Phoenicians ascribed aphrodisiac properties
to these fleshy roots. They were supposed to be able to stimulate
passion and cure barrenness.

Gruesome and ferocious are Astarte and Anath, goddesses of
fertility and of war alike. The Baal-epic of Ugarit depicts the
goddess Anath: "With her might she mowed down the dwellers
in the cities, she struck down the people of the sea-coasts, she
destroyed the men of the east." She drove the men into her
temple and closed the doors so that no one could escape. "She
hurled chairs at the youths, tables at the warriors, footstools at
the mighty men." "She waded up to the knees, up to the neck in
blood. Human heads lay at her feet, human hands flew over her
like locusts. She tied the heads of her victims as ornaments upon
her back, their hands she tied upon her belt." "Her liver was
swollen with laughing, her heart was full of joy, the liver of
Anath was full of exultation." "When she was satisfied she
washed her hands in streams of human blood before turning
again to other things."

Anath is the sister and wife of Baal, the god of storm and rain.
His symbol is a bull's head. Baal fertilises the cattle in the
meadows with rain to make them fat. He is also concerned with
their propagation. When he dies at the turn of the seasons,
overpowered "like the bull under the knife of the sacrificer", his
son takes over his duties. "And the children of Israel did evil in
the sight of the Lord and served Baalim" (Jud. 2[11]). Quite
recently an image of one of these gods was recovered on Israeli
territory at Hazor. It was found in one of the heathen shrines
which according to the Bible the Israelites erected in many
places for the worship of strange gods. In the centre of an area
encircled with flat stones, with two altars for burnt offerings
dating from the days before the monarchy, stood some weapons
and a clay jar. It contained, together with other bronze votive
figures, an image of a seated god—a "baal".

Professor Schaeffer also found in Ugarit small images and
amulets of Astarte. They are made of clay and gold and the
goddess is naked. Snakes and pigeons, renowned in the Ancient
East for their fertility, are her symbols.

The goddesses of fertility were worshipped principally on hills
and knolls. There their votaries erected for them Asherim, set
out "sacred pillars", trees, under which the rites were practised,
as the Bible repeatedly points out: "For they also built them high

FIG. 58.—Gold plaquette of a naked goddess of fertility.

places and pillars, and Asherim on every high hill and under every green tree" (1 Kings 14²³—R.V.).

It is only since the results of scientific investigation into Canaanite gods and Phoenician religions have come to light that we can properly gauge the intensity of the moral struggle that the people of Israel had to face.

What temptation for a simple shepherd folk, what perilous enticement! More than once the Baal religions got a firm foot-hold and penetrated right into the temple of Yahweh, into the Holy of Holies.

Without its stern moral law, without its faith in one God, without the commanding figures of its prophets, Israel would never have been able to survive this struggle with the Baals, with the religions of the fertility goddesses, with the Asherim and the high places.

That was the reason for the "objectionable passages". In the interests of truth the matter could not be passed over in silence.

If we look at these things with "Biblical eyes", as it were, then such is undoubtedly the impression we receive. Intensive study of the archaeological finds at Ugarit, particularly of the clay tablets, has revealed not only contrasts but also remarkable correspondences between Biblical and old Canaanite religious conceptions.

The Bible continually gives us glimpses of a state of affairs which presumably was quite different from what it appears to have been at first glance. For example, the authentic people's religion of the "children of Israel" as it was actually practised over wide areas must have been very different from what the authors of the Biblical writings would have liked to see.

The prophets continually found cause for anger and the Bible authors complained increasingly about "the worship of idols" and "golden calves". Such statements are in themselves of necessity an indication that cults must have been practised to which a part of the population obviously clung, but which were not in accordance with the norm regarded as valid by the Biblical authors and were consequently condemned.

A few examples will show what the real state of affairs must have been. Mention has already been made in another connection of the way in which Rachel, the wife of the Biblical "patriarch" Jacob, stole the "images" (*teraphim*) of her father, Laban (Gen. 31[19ff]). A brazen serpent idol from the early nomadic period (Numbers 21[9]) was worshipped in the Temple at Jerusalem until the time of King Hezekiah of Judah, around 700 B.C. (2 Kings 18[4]). Even Solomon, the builder of the Temple, incurred the wholehearted disapproval of the Biblical writers by allowing the ladies of his harem to adhere to gods and cults with which they considered it a grave mistake to have contact.

He not only allowed "high places" to these gods to be built on the Mount of Olives (1 Kings 11[1-8]; 2 Kings 23[13]) but himself took part in such cults. Almost all the Israelite and Jewish rulers after him acted in the same way. Even a fanatic like the cruel Jehu of Israel (842/1–815/4 B.C.) who was responsible for the dreadful slaughter of the worshippers of Baal (2 Kings 10[18-28]) was said to have taken part in unorthodox cults (2 Kings 10[29]). Among the "children of Israel" naked figures of "Astarte" were quite common. Even "in the shadow of the Temple", so to speak, of Solomon's Temple in Jerusalem, the British archaeologist Kathleen M. Kenyon excavated a room which pillars for the cult showed to be a heathen place of worship. Popular religion as practised by the "children of Israel", then, was in reality rather different from what the Bible would have us believe. The Bible itself allows us far too many glimpses of this.

Whilst on the one hand things were occurring in the "Holy Land" which were not all in accordance with the Biblical conception of worship, there was no lack on the other hand, among Israel's neighbours, who are often under such heavy

attack in the Bible, of divine personifications of moral principles. The Canaanites were also acquainted with the "Biblical"
concept of the kinghood of God, which was consequently not
confined to the Bible. Now that texts from Ugarit have made us
better acquainted with ancient Canaanite gods like El and Baal,
we can only be amazed at the extent to which these gods gave
expression to religious concepts which we later encounter in the
Bible. This goes so far that even the God of the Bible is the
"King above all Gods" (Psalms 95[3]; 96[4]; 97[7,9]), which naturally
only means anything if people believe in other gods as well. Like
the Ugaritic Baal, the Biblical King of Gods has his "mountain
of holiness" in the north (Psalm 48[3]). It is thanks to the Biblical
scholar Otto Eissfeldt of Halle that we know which mountain
was meant—the 1,770 metre-high Zaphon or Mons Casius which,
visible from afar and frequently shrouded by rain clouds, is
today known as Jebel al-Aqra, and lies 30 kilometres north of
Ras Shamra on the Mediterranean coast of northern Syria.
And just as Baal, the storm god, rides on the clouds, so the
God of the Bible rides on the clouds and winds (Psalm
104[3]).

In spite of all the continual disapproval of the prophets, El and
Baal personified moral values. El was "holy" and Baal, like the
God of the Covenant, acted as "judge" and ensured justice. The
Bible has thus received confirmation and elucidation from a
quarter from which it was least to be expected. The despised and
accursed religion of ancient Canaan has helped us to reach a new
understanding of Biblical statements about the "religion of the
fathers". And when the Biblical fathers called upon *El-Elyon*
(the "all highest"), *El-Olam* (the "ancient of ancients", "the
eternal"), *El-Roy* ("he who appears", "he who sees me") and
El-Shaddai ("the highest" or "almighty"), their prayers were
directed, as many scholars believe, to the chief Canaanite god El
in one of his local variants.

El and Baal were the divine kings of the Canaanite Pantheon.
They were later replaced by Yahweh, the god of the "chosen
people" of the Bible. Yet there were certain differences. El was
static, at rest, unapproachable, while Baal, in contrast, was
dynamic, active, actual.

One thing is clear—a royal god such as the God of the Bible,
beside whom there was no place for other gods even in a
subservient rôle, was naturally incompatible with a myth which

included other gods—the exuberant growth of a myth of this kind endowed the ancient gods of Canaan with features which we find bizarre—for such a myth would have implied adherence to the belief in other gods. . . .

Chapter 27
THE END OF NINEVEH AS A WORLD POWER

Ashurbanipal plunders Thebes—An empire stretching from the Nile to the Persian Gulf—The "great and noble Asnapper"—Big game hunting with bow and arrow—Assyria's strength is exhausted—Crushed between two powers—Medes and Chaldeans arm—Scythian hordes in Palestine—Nineveh sinks in ruins—The "Fertile Crescent" breathes again—A Biblical slip of the pen—Gadd's discovery in London—Nebuchadnezzar, crown prince of Babylon.

"Art thou better than populous No, that was situate among the rivers, that had the waters round about it. . . . Ethiopia and Egypt were her strength and it was infinite. . . . Yet was she carried away, she went into captivity: her young children also were dashed in pieces at the top of all the streets . . ." (Nahum 3$^{8-10}$).

In 663 B.C. the Assyrians celebrated the greatest triumph in their whole history. King Ashurbanipal conquered the capital of Upper Egypt No-Amun, which the Greeks called Thebes. According to Homer it had 100 gates and until then it had been regarded as impregnable. It was an event which caused an enormous stir in the world of the ancient orient, in the "Fertile Crescent" itself and as far as Greece. The Assyrians plundered the metropolis, whose temples contained boundless wealth. "I conquered the whole city . . . silver, gold, precious stones, the whole contents of its palace, coloured vestments, linen, magnificent horses, slaves, both men and women, two great obelisks of shining bronze weighing 2,500 talents; I took the temple gates from their place

293

and brought them to Assyria. Enormous spoils of priceless worth did I take with me from Thebes," exulted Ashurbanipal.

The Assyrian war machine had made a tabula rasa of the far famed temple-city on the Nile. Excavations fully confirm the description of the catastrophe given by the prophet Nahum and by the victor himself. The capital of Upper Egypt never again recovered from this blow.

After this victorious expedition the world of those days lay at Assyria's feet. From the upper reaches of the Nile to the mountains of Armenia and the mouth of the Euphrates the nations were under its yoke, their peoples reduced to vassals.

But scarcely had Assyria reached the pinnacle of its might when the power of the empire began to wane. Ashurbanipal was not a conqueror or war lord of the calibre of his father Esarhaddon, to say nothing of his prodigious grandfather Sennacherib.

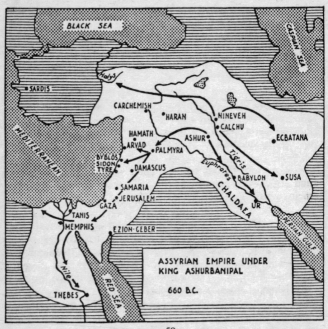

FIG. 59.

Ashurbanipal, the "great and noble Asnapper" (Ezra 4¹⁰), had already developed other interests.

After the long succession of bloodstained tyrants this one Assyrian did the world an inestimable service. He ordered the transcription of the masterpieces of Akkadian literature, including the Babylonian Creation story: he commissioned the production of dictionaries and grammars of the various languages which were spoken in his colossal empire. The library which he built up in Nineveh was by far the largest and most important in the Ancient East. Without this precious collection mankind would have been infinitely poorer in its knowledge of the thought and literature of the "Fertile Crescent" from earliest times.

Nevertheless the wild streak in this last important scion of the race of Assyrian rulers was not completely tamed. As well as being a lover of art and literature he loved hunting. Ashurbanipal was a big game hunter in the proper sense of the word, and his successors in this pursuit can hardly compete with him. It was not with planes and armour-plated jeeps at 60 miles an hour, not with elephant-howdahs equipped with telescopic sights which enable the fatal shot to be fired from a safe distance where there is no threat of slashing paws or snapping teeth, that this big game hunter of the ancient world set out to attack his prey. On these wonderfully vivid large reliefs which were found in his palaces on the Tigris he hunts in a light two-wheeled hunting car or on horseback—with bow and arrow or javelin. "30 elephants, 257 wild beasts, 370 lions," according to the cuneiform texts, made up the splendid total of Ashurbanipal's bag.

"Woe to the bloody city! . . . There is a multitude of slain and a great number of carcases, and there is none end of their corpses. . . ." (Nahum 3¹,³).

So the prophet Nahum announces the end of Nineveh, the end of its world empire and centuries of bloody tyranny.

With the death of Ashurbanipal¹ the sudden and rapid collapse began. The new great powers of Indo-Aryans and Semites gripped the gigantic structure between them like a vice, crushed it and divided the colossal spoil between them.

To the north-east the kingdom of the Medes in the mountains

¹ 626 B.C.

of Iran had come into being. Then "Cyaxares came to power,"
writes Herodotus, "and united all Asia beyond the Halys under
him. Then he gathered together all his peoples and marched
against Nineveh to take the city."

In the south-east of Mesopotamia a second adversary had
sprung up whom the Assyrians had to take seriously. From the
fringe of civilisation south of the estuary of the Euphrates, where
"Ur of the Chaldees" was also situated, Semitic tribes had
pushed their way inland and had imported new vigour into the
old kingdom of Babylon. They called themselves "Chaldeans".
Merodach-Baladan, who a century before had made a name for
himself and had plagued Assyria for many years, was one of
them.

Meantime his countrymen had succeeded in penetrating the
whole country in a series of waves of invasion. In 625 B.C. a
Chaldean assumed control over South Mesopotamia. Nabopolassar
became king and founder of the Neo-Babylonian Empire. The
Chaldeans likewise had only one end in view, the destruction of
Assyria.

At the same time as the two powers, north and south, were
lying in wait to administer the death blow to Assyria, a wild
horde burst out of the Caucasus into the "Fertile Crescent",
penetrated into Media and inundated the Assyrian empire. These
were the Scythians. Looting and burning, they forced their way
from Mesopotamia through Palestine to the very frontiers of
Egypt.

Through the maritime plain by the Mediterranean stormed this
unruly mob of Scythian horsemen. Fearful and frightening rumours
heralded their approach. The inhabitants of Judah must have seen
them as they looked down from the mountains; the prophet
Zephaniah foresees with horror what will happen. "For Gaza
shall be forsaken, and Ashkelon a desolation: they shall drive out
Ashdod at the noonday and Ekron shall be rooted up. . . . In the
houses of Ashkelon shall they lie down in the evening. . ."
(Zeph. 2⁴˒⁷).

"They headed for Egypt," Herodotus relates, "and while they
were in Palestinian Syria, Psammitichus,[1] king of Egypt, went to
meet them and persuaded them with gifts and pleas to go no
further. And while the Scythians on their way back were in the

Syrian city of Ashkelon a few of them remained behind and plundered the temple of Aphrodite Urania. Those Scythians who had plundered the temple in Ashkelon together with their descendants for ever were smitten by the goddess with a gynaecological ailment.''

Within ten years the Asiatic horsemen had disappeared again like an evil apparition.

In Palestine the name of a city kept the memory of the Scythians green. Beth-Shan was re-named Scythopolis. It is not known, however, how the town acquired this name. There are no traces of occupation by the Scythians nor of occupation by a garrison of Scythian mercenaries which would also be conceivable as the origin of the place-name. Scythopolis thus remains one of the many points of disagreement among experts who have specialised in the archaeology of the Holy Land.

Then the Medes and the Neo-Babylonians bore down upon the Assyrians on two fronts. They attacked from north and south at the same time. Ashur, the great city and fortress on the Tigris, was the first to fall in 614 B.C. ''The king of Babylon and his army, which had set out to assist the Medes, did not arrive in time for the battle. The king of Babylon and Cyaxares[1] met each other among the ruins of the city,'' says a Neo-Babylonian chronicle, ''and pledged themselves to friendship and confederacy. . . . They took vast quantities of booty in the city and reduced it to a heap of rubble and ruins.''

In 612 B.C. the alliance of Medes and Neo-Babylonians achieved its aim. After a ''violent battle the city was taken'': Nineveh was destroyed. ''And he will stretch out his hand against the north and destroy Assyria: and will make Nineveh a desolation, and dry like a wilderness.'' Zephaniah had prophesied this (Zeph. 2[13]) and now it had happened:—the nerve-centre of Assyrian power destroyed and reduced to ashes, the Nineveh which for centuries with its armies of conquest and occupation, with torture, terror and mass deportations had brought nothing but blood and tears to the ancient world.

The ''Fertile Crescent'' breathed again. Jubilation filled its afflicted peoples—new hope began to spring up, in which Judah shared.

After the death of Ashurbanipal, when the hated Assyrian

[1] King of the Medes.

colossus was shaken by the first signs of ultimate collapse, King Josiah[1] had without hesitation banned the practice of foreign religions in Jerusalem. There was more to that than merely religious objections. It clearly signified· the termination of the state of vassalage, of which the gods of Nineveh, imported by compulsion, were symbolic. Together with these compulsory deities, Josiah expelled all the Mesopotamian "workers with familiar spirits, and the wizards, and the images and the idols" (2 Kings 23[24]). He also cleared out all the Canaanite religious practices (2 Kings 23[7]).

Josiah's reforms paved the way for a renewed religious and national vitality which developed into a regular frenzy when news of the fall of Nineveh confirmed their freedom.

Meantime something quite unexpected happened which threatened to ruin everything. . . . "Pharaoh-Nechoh king of Egypt went up against the king of Assyria to the river Euphrates: and king Josiah went against him, and he slew him at Megiddo, when he had seen him" (2 Kings 23[29]). This passage from the Bible is a perfect example of how a single word can completely change the meaning of a narrative. In this case the wrong use of the little word "against" brands Josiah as the accomplice of the hated tyrant. At some point or other the word translated "against" has been wrongly copied. In reality Pharaoh Necho went to the aid of Assyria, i.e., "towards". It was only through a chance discovery that the Assyriologist C. I. Gadd found out this historical slip of the pen.

The place of discovery was quite outside the normal archaeological pattern—it was a museum. In 1923 Gadd was translating a badly damaged fragment of cuneiform text in the British Museum which had been dug up in Mesopotamia many years previously.

It read as follows: "In the month of Du'uz [June-July][2] the king of Assyria procured a large Egyptian army and marched against Harran to conquer it. . . . Till the month of Ulul [August-September] he fought against the city but accomplished nothing."

The "large Egyptian army" was the forces of Pharaoh Necho.

After the fall of Nineveh what remained of the Assyrian forces had retreated to Northern Mesopotamia. Their king embarked upon the forlorn hope of reconquering from there what he had lost. It was for this purpose that Pharaoh Necho had hastened to

[1] 639–609 B.C.
[2] 609 B.C.

his aid. But when after two months of fighting not even the town of Harran had been recaptured, Necho retired.

It was the appearance of Egyptian troops in Palestine that decided Josiah to prevent the Egyptians at all costs from rendering military aid to the hated Assyrians. So it came about that the little army of Judah marched against the far superior Egyptian force, with the tragic ending at Megiddo. "Neko," writes Herodotus, "also defeated the Syrians[1] in a land engagement at Magdolus."[2]

On the way back to Egypt Pharaoh Necho assumed the role of overlord of Syria and Palestine. He made an example of Judah, so as to leave it in no doubt on whom the country now depended. Jehoahaz, Josiah's son and successor, was stripped of his royal dignities and taken as a prisoner to the Nile (2 Kings 23[31-34]). In his stead Necho placed another son of Josiah upon the throne, Eliakim, whose name he changed to Jehoiakim (2 Kings 23[34]).

Egyptologists have not been able so far to produce any hymns of triumph of Pharaoh Necho. Herodotus learned from Egyptian priests a century and a half later that he had presented to the temple of Apollo in Miletus "the garb in which he had accomplished these deeds" in thank-offering for the participation of Greek mercenaries in his expedition. In the land he conquered he left nothing but a stele. It bears his name in hieroglyphic script. Its fragments were left lying in Sidon.

Four years later—605 B.C.—Necho's dream of suzerainty over "Asia", as his predecessors had always called it, was at an end.

Even while he was collecting tribute in Palestine, decisions were being taken about his "conquest" elsewhere. After their joint victory the Medes and the Neo-Babylonians had divided the empire of Assyria between them. The Medes annexed the north and north-east; Babylon the south and south-west. Syria and Palestine thus fell to King Nabopolassar. But in the meantime he had grown old and was no longer fit for the fray. He therefore sent the crown prince of Chaldea, his son Nebuchadnezzar, to take possession of the new territories.

Necho made an attempt to repulse him but failed miserably. Near Carchemish, in the same region where four years previously he had endeavoured to assist the last king of Assyria, he suffered

[1] Judah.
[2] Megiddo.

total defeat at the famous passage across the Euphrates from Mesopotamia to North Syria (Jer. 46[2]).

Necho fled through Palestine followed by the jeers of the prophet Jeremiah: "Pharaoh king of Egypt is but a noise: he hath let the appointed time pass by. . . . The sound thereof shall go like the serpent. . . ." (Jer. 46[17,22]—R.V.).

After this shameful flight Judah saw no more of Necho. "And the king of Egypt came not again any more out of his land: for the king of Babylon had taken, from the river of Egypt unto the river Euphrates, all that pertained to the king of Egypt" (2 Kings 24[7]). The crown prince of Chaldea was not able to exploit his victory at Carchemish. In the course of the battle news of the death of his father overtook him, and he had perforce to return to Babylon. After Nebuchadnezzar[1] had acceded to the throne more important affairs of state kept him in his own country for the next few years. Judah was spared a fresh occupation for a time and was left to itself.

There are no contemporary records giving us the details of what happened in Judah around the turn of the 6th century. The Bible gives no clear picture of when, for example, the Chaldeans made their first appearance in the country, or of when they started to demand tribute. The Neo-Babylonian kings, unlike their predecessors the Assyrians, left no informative annals behind them. Inscriptions on buildings which have been preserved merely indicate historical events.

[1] 605–562 B.C.

Chapter 28
THE LAST DAYS OF JUDAH

First deportation—King Jehoiachin in Babylonian court records—Discovery in the basement of the Berlin Museum—Nebuchadnezzar on the conquest of Jerusalem—Second punitive campaign—Despatches on clay—Starkey's tragic death—Incendiary technique of Babylonian engineers—A clean slate for the archaeologists.

"In his days Nebuchadnezzar king of Babylon came up, and Jehoiakim became his servant three years" (2 Kings 24[1]).

About the turn of the 6th century there took place the calamitous event which in a few years was to blot out Judah for ever as a nation with a place in the history of the ancient orient. Events now began to close in with frightening speed upon the tiny vassal-state on the Jordan and its inhabitants, which were to result in Judah's most grievous hour of affliction. They ended with the road to exile and forcible removal to Babylon.

It began with refusal to pay tribute, and rebellion against the new feudal lord. In 598 B.C. open revolt broke out in Judah. King Jehoiakim "... turned and rebelled against him" (2 Kings 24[1]).

At first Nebuchadnezzar did not intervene in person. Perhaps he did not think it sufficiently important: in a great empire local rebellions are no rare occurrence. He was content to leave it, to begin with, to troops from Moab, Ammon and Syria, strengthened by Chaldean regulars. They do not appear to have taken control of the situation however, whereupon Nebuchadnezzar himself hurried to Judah.

He was already on his way to Palestine with a considerable force when Jehoiakim unexpectedly died. It appears that so far he is the only king of Judah of whom we have a portrait. In Ramath-Rahel near Jerusalem, where a royal citadel from the time of Jehoiakim was found, a sherd with a line drawing on it was recently unearthed. This is thought to represent Jehoiakim. His son followed him upon the throne: "Jehoiachin was eighteen years old when he began to reign, and he reigned in Jerusalem three months.... And Nebuchadnezzar king of Babylon came against the city and his servants did besiege it.... And he carried away all Jerusalem.... And he carried away Jehoiachin to Babylon" (2 Kings 24$^{8-15}$).

In 597 B.C., as the Bible says, King Jehoiachin and his family were deported to Babylon as prisoners. But after 2,500 years who could hope to check up on the reliability of this factual statement? Nevertheless, shortly before the beginning of the 20th century an opportunity came the way of the archaeologists to find out something definite about the destination of the royal family of Judah.

In 1899 the German Oriental Society equipped a large expedition under the direction of Professor Robert Koldewey, the architect, to examine the famous ruined mound of "Babil" on the Euphrates. The excavations, as it turned out, took longer than anywhere else. In eighteen years the most famous metropolis of the ancient world, the royal seat of Nebuchadnezzar, was brought to light, and at the same time, one of the Seven Wonders of the World, the "Hanging Gardens", loudly extolled by Greek travellers of a later day, and "E-temen-an-ki", the legendary Tower of Babel. In the palace of Nebuchadnezzar and on the Ishtar Gate, which was situated beside it, countless inscriptions were discovered.

Nevertheless the scholars were conscious of a certain disappointment. In contrast to the detailed records of Assyrian rulers, in which the names and fortunes of the kings of Israel and Judah were frequently given a historical setting, the Neo-Babylonian records hardly mentioned anything apart from the religious and architectural events of their day. They contained for example no corroboration of the fate of Judah.

Thirty years later, when the great finds at "Babil" had long since found their way into archives and museums, there emerged a number of unique documents from the immediate neighbourhood of the Ishtar Gate—in Berlin!

On Museum Island, in the middle of the Spree in the heart of the German capital, the wonderful Ishtar Gate from Babylon had been reconstructed in the great Central Court of the Kaiser-Friedrich Museum. Menacing and sinister, the bright yellow bodies of the long row of lions stood out against the deep blue of the glazed tiles on the Processional Way of Marduk.[1] As it had done by the Euphrates, so now it led astonished citizens of the 20th century to the splendid gate dedicated to the goddess Ishtar, with its dragons and wild oxen.

While deeply impressed visitors from all over the world stood in the Central Court upstairs in front of the lofty and brilliantly coloured twin-gate, and, as Nebuchadnezzar had done long ago, turned under its arch on to the Processional Way, 300 cuneiform tablets lying in the basement rooms of the museum were waiting to be deciphered.

Koldewey's team had rescued them from the outbuildings of Nebuchadnezzar's palace near the Ishtar Gate, had numbered them and packed them in boxes. Together with masses of brightly glazed tiles, bearing reliefs of lions, dragons and wild oxen, they had made the long journey to Berlin, where, as luck would have it, the old tablets were lying in their packing-cases by the Spree, almost exactly as they had been in Babylon, only a few yards under the Ishtar Gate.

After 1933 E. F. Weidner, the Assyriologist, took in hand to look through the tablets and sherds in the basement rooms of the Kaiser-Friedrich Museum. He then translated them one by one. They contained nothing but court inventories, receipted accounts from the royal commisariat, book-entries of ancient bureaucrats, nothing but ordinary everyday matters.

Despite that, Weidner stuck it out manfully day after day in the basement under the Ishtar Gate and worked at his translations tirelessly.

Then all of a sudden his monotonous job came unexpectedly to life. Among this dull administrative rubbish Weidner suddenly found some priceless relics of red tape in the ancient world.

On four different receipts for stores issued, among them best quality sesame oil, he came upon a familiar Biblical name: "Ja'-u-kinu"—Jehoiachin!

There was no possibility of his being mistaken, because Jehoiachin was given his full title: "King of the [land of]

[1] Babylonian god.

Judah". The Babylonian clay receipts moreover bear the date of the thirteenth year of the reign of King Nebuchadnezzar. That means 592 B.C., five years after the fall of Jerusalem and the deportation. In addition the Babylonian steward of the commissariat has mentioned in three cases five of the king's sons, who were in charge of a servant with the Jewish name of "Kenaiah".

Other personnel on the ration-strength of Nebuchadnezzar's stores are noted as "eight persons from the land of Judah", who possibly belonged to the retinue of King Jehoiachin, among them a gardener by the name of "Salam-ja-a-ma".

Jehoiachin, the deposed king of Judah, lived with his family and his retinue in the palace of Nebuchadnezzar in Babylon. We may conclude from Weidner's discovery that the Biblical account in the Second Book of Kings may be thus supplemented: "And for his diet, there was a continual diet given him of the king of Babylon, every day a portion, until the day of his death, all the days of his life" (Jer. 52³⁴).

A sensational addition to the account of these events was made in 1955 through the examination of 2,500-year-old cuneiform tablets which had long lain in peaceful oblivion in the British Museum. D. J. Wiseman was engaged in deciphering these tablets when to his great surprise he came across the following entry in the official records of the Babylonian royal house:

"In the seventh year, in the month Chislev, the king assembled his army and advanced on Hatti-land [Syria]. He encamped over against the city of the Judaeans and conquered it on the second day of Adar [16th March 597]. He took the king [Jehoiachin] prisoner, and appointed in his stead a king after his own heart [Zedekiah]. He exacted heavy tribute and had it brought to Babylon."

Here we have the original account in Babylonian chronicles of the first conquest of Jerusalem by Nebuchadnezzar as it has been preserved for us in the Bible in the 24th chapter of the Second Book of Kings.

> "And it came to pass in the ninth year of his reign, in the tenth month, in the tenth day of the month, that Nebuchadnezzar, king of Babylon, came, he and all his host, against Jerusalem. . . . And the city was besieged unto the eleventh year of king Zedekiah" (2 Kings 25¹,²).

Eleven years had gone by since the capture of Jehoiachin and the first deportation to Babylon. The time had now come for Judah's fate to be sealed.

The last scene in the tragedy of this tiny nation provides a classic example of how Biblical narratives and archaeological discoveries illuminate the same event from different points of view, and how accurate are the statements of the prophet alongside the official account in the Second Book of Kings and in Chronicles. Jeremiah sketches with swift strokes of his brush scenes taken from the exciting and anxious events of the last days, which through discoveries in Palestine in our own day are confirmed as being startling in their accuracy and historically genuine.

After the first conquest in 597 B.C. Nebuchadnezzar allowed Judah to continue its existence as a vassal-state. The successor to the throne, after Jehoiachin had been led off into captivity, was his uncle Mattaniah, who was renamed Zedekiah by the Chaldean king. As we may conclude from Jer. 13[19] the territory of Judah was reduced: "The cities of the south shall be shut up and none shall open them" (Jer. 13[19]).

The deportation of their kinsmen before their very eyes, the bitter experiences of a century and a half, the miserable fate of the northern kingdom, still only too fresh in their memories, nevertheless did not extinguish the will to resist.

Soon indeed voices were being raised, denouncing Babylon, and demanding the recovery of all that had been lost (Jer. 28[1-4]). The prophet Jeremiah raised his voice in warning but it was the anti-Babylonian group which was more and more heeded. They egged the people on and eventually got the upper hand of the spineless and vacillating king. Alliances were struck with the bordering vassal-states. There was a meeting of "messengers" from Edom, Moab, and Ammon as well as from the seaports of Tyre and Sidon in the presence of King Zedekiah in Jerusalem (Jer. 27[3]).

The fact that in 588 B.C. a new Pharaoh, Apries,[1] ascended the throne had clearly a decisive influence on the decision to revolt (Jer. 44[30]). The new ruler of Egypt must have given Judah assurances of armed help, for "Zedekiah rebelled against the king of Babylon" (2 Kings 24[20]).

---

[1]558–568 B.C. Jeremiah calls him "Hophra".

In the "tenth month" (2 Kings 25[1]) of the same year 588
B.C.—it was "the ninth year" of King Zedekiah—Nebuchadnezzar
arrived with a strong army from Babylon. With the speed of
lightning the punitive campaign against rebellious Judah was
unfolded.

The Chaldean divisions of infantry, fast cavalry and charioteers
smashed all resistance and conquered city after city. Except for
the capital, Jerusalem, and the frontier fortresses of Lachish and
Azekah in the south, the whole land was finally subdued.

Jerusalem, Lachish and Azekah were determined to fight to
the end: "When the king of Babylon's army fought against
Jerusalem and against all the cities of Judah that were left,
against Lachish and against Azekah: for these defenced cities
remained of the cities of Judah" (Jer. 34[7]).

Impressive and enduring evidence of the last phase of this
hopeless struggle lies before us.

Twenty miles south-west of Jerusalem the green valley of Elah
pushes its way far into the mountains of Judah. This was the
scene of the duel between young David and Goliath the Philistine
giant (1 Sam. 17[19f]).

FIG. 60.—Fortress of Lachish in Judah with double walls and triple gate.
(Reconstruction.)

The little brook out of which David gathered "five smooth
stones" for his sling still runs and burbles between its oak trees
(1 Sam. 17[40]).

From the river bed the hill slopes gently upwards to a height
of 1,000 feet. From the top the cornfields and olive groves of the
old plain of Philistia can be seen stretching away to the far
horizon where they meet the silvery sparkle of the Mediterranean. On this spot Dr. Frederick J. Bliss, the British archaeologist, identified a fort with eight stout towers as ancient Azekah,
one of the frontier fortresses which, as we have seen, remained
unconquered. Just about 12 miles to the south the ruins of

Lachish were found to contain valuable evidence. J. L. Starkey, the archaeologist, disinterred them in the thirties when the Wellcome–Marston expedition from the U.K. investigated the ruins of the great city gate, where the battle was fiercest. Eighteen ostraca, inscribed clay sherds, contained information about forward posts, observation posts and strong points held by Judahite troops which had not yet been overwhelmed. These despatches on clay had been sent to "Jaosh", the "commandant of the fort of Lachish", during that fateful "tenth month" of the year 558 B.C. The messages, scratched out in haste, indicate with every line the frightful tension that existed just before the collapse. One of the last of these eye-witness reports reads: "May Yahweh grant that my lord should hear good tidings ... we are watching for the signal stations of Lachish, according to the signals which my lord has given ... we are no longer receiving signals from Azekah." This message told Jaosh, the commanding officer at Lachish, that Azekah had fallen. Nebuchadnezzar could now withdraw his engineers for the attack on the last fortress but one.

British archaeologists with the Wellcome–Marston expedition obtained information about the terrible end of Lachish in 1938 after six strenuous seasons of excavating.

It was the last success that was to crown the career of James Lesley Starkey, the famous excavator of Lachish. During the Palestinian troubles which had broken out he was shot by Arabs at the age of forty-three in the neighbourhood of Hebron on the road from Lachish to Jerusalem. His death was a tragic case of mistaken identity. In the course of the protracted excavations he had grown a beard and the Arabs took him for a Jew.

In 701 B.C. the storm troops of Sennacherib, king of Assyria, had rushed the walls of Lachish with "tanks" fitted with battering rams. Nebuchadnezzar's special detachments adopted an entirely different technique to force the city to surrender.

Investigation of the stratum which marked the Babylonian work of destruction produced, to Starkey's astonishment, ashes. Ashes in incredible quantities. Many of the layers are several yards thick and are still—after 2,500 years—higher than the remains of the solid walls of the fortress. Nebuchadnezzar's engineers were specialists in the art of incendiarism, past masters at starting conflagrations.

Whatever wood they could lay hands on they dragged to the

spot, stripped the whole area around Lachish of its forests and thickets, cleared the hills of timber for miles around, piled the firewood as high as a house outside the walls and set it alight. Countless olive-groves were hacked down for this purpose: the layer of ashes contains masses of charred olive stones.

Day and night sheets of flame leapt sky high, a ring of fire licked the walls from top to bottom. The besieging force piled on more and more wood until the white-hot stones burst and the walls caved in.

So Lachish likewise fell and only Jerusalem still offered resistance. The whole weight of the Babylonian war machine could now be directed against it. It was impossible to use the new incendiary technique in this case, for the forests around Jerusalem had, since the time of the patriarchs and of Joshua's conquest, been reduced to miserable little plantings and under-growth (Josh. 17[15,18]). They therefore preferred to storm Jerusalem with the approved technique of battering rams and siege engines. For eighteen months Jerusalem was besieged and heroically defended: "And the city was besieged unto the eleventh year of king Zedekiah" (2 Kings 25[2]).

What made the defenders hold out, despite the fact that famine had long been raging in the city and was taking a heavy toll, was a desperate hope that Egypt might come to their assistance.

It seemed that this hope was to be fulfilled, for the Babylonians suddenly withdrew. "Then Pharaoh's army was come forth out of Egypt: and when the Chaldeans that besieged Jerusalem heard tidings of them, they departed from Jerusalem" (Jer. 37[5]). An army did in fact at that time come up from the Nile under Pharaoh Apries, as Herodotus also mentions. Its destination was however not Jerusalem. Apries was making an attack by land and sea against the Phoenician ports.

Archaeologists have found evidence on fragments of Egyptian monuments of Pharaoh's presence in Tyre and Sidon at that time.

So it came about as Jeremiah had prophesied: "Behold, Pharaoh's army, which is come forth to help you, shall return to Egypt unto their own land" (Jer. 37[7]). After a few days the enemy was back in front of Jerusalem, the siege continued with the utmost fury, and the end could no longer be delayed.

> "And the city was broken up, and all the men of war fled
> by night, by the way of the gate between two walls which is
> by the king's garden" (2 Kings 25[4]).

Thanks to the result of excavations, the route taken by the defenders in their flight can now be reconstructed without difficulty.

King Hezekiah had strengthened the old fortifications of the city of David by a second wall on the south side (2 Chron. 32⁵). There is still no certainty as to the line it followed.

The moment the enemy entered the city through a breach in the walls the defenders retreated in the first instance behind the double walled southern part of the fortifications and only with the onset of darkness did they escape through an outer gate into freedom and then over the hills to Jericho. In the process King Zedekiah was taken. His children were "slaughtered" before his eyes, he himself had his eyes put out (2 Kings 25⁷)—the harsh Babylonian martial law for traitors. This cruel punishment by blinding is frequently attested on pictorial reliefs.

Jerusalem was given over to plundering: the royal palace and the temple were set on fire, the city walls and fortifications were razed to the ground. The order to destroy was given to "Nebuzar-Adan, captain of the guard" (2 Kings 25⁸), a grand vizier who appears in the Babylonian list of court officials as "Nabu-Seri-Idinnam". Once more in 587 B.C. part of the population was deported (2 Kings 25¹¹). Nebuchadnezzar erased the royal house of David, which had reigned without interruption for 400 years. The land of Judah became a Babylonian province. Those who were left waged a maquis type of war from their hide-outs in the mountains and claimed as their victim Gedaliah, who had been appointed governor by the Babylonians. There are those who believe that the third and last deportation was in reprisal for this (Jer. 52³⁰). Little groups of Judahites were able to escape it by fleeing to Egypt (2 Kings 25²⁶; Jer. 43⁷). The curtain of history was lowered on an empty land. The tribes of Israel were scattered to the four winds.

Scholars like S. A. Cook and C. C. Torrey have denied the truth of the Biblical tradition of this carrying off into exile. In their view there was never a mass deportation from Judah, at the most some of the nobility were imprisoned in Babylon.

On the other hand, Professor Albright in his writings never tires of emphasising the severity and the extent of the devastations in Judah, so that one is more inclined to believe that the Babylonians made a clean sweep in Judah as the Bible indicates. What was the real state of affairs? One year after the first edition of the present work, a publication appeared which earned a doctorate for Enno Janssen, a Protestant theologian, at the

FIG. 61.

University of Kiel. With great diligence he had assembled all the available results of the investigations of modern research and all the views expressed by experts on the situation in the devastated kingdom of Judah at the time of the Babylonian exile. Janssen did not by any means demolish what Albright insisted upon so emphatically. Systematically, painstakingly, almost pedantically, he listed the towns which had been worst hit, he assembled the information on how extensive the destruction had been in the towns which had been less affected—insofar as that can be ascertained today—and the places which continued to be inhabited during the period of exile. His results may surprise many who find it difficult to free themselves from the idea that the towns of Judah had been completely laid waste.

Certainly the destruction was great and the human losses through war, deportations and executions were not small, yet there were still people, including priests, even in Jerusalem, who lamented the destruction of the Temple and went about earning their living. Land was distributed among people of the poorer classes by the Babylonians and those who were better off were not completely liquidated or deported.

It can be deduced from certain statements in the Bible that there apparently still were comparatively well-to-do people who had managed to survive the catastrophe in their ''wainscotted houses'', or at least had once again been able to acquire ''wainscotted houses'' in Judah during the period of exile. The governor, appointed by the Babylonians, was a Jew named Gedaliah and the Bible mentions his father as a friend and protector of the prophet Jeremiah. When Jeremiah escaped the deportation, he went to Gedaliah in Mizpa where the remnants of the Jewish upper classes had assembled. As has already been mentioned, Gedaliah was finally assassinated by a Jewish nationalist, but the mere fact that there was a governor indicates that something was left to administer, or to put it in other words, that people were still living in Judah. The fact that Gedaliah lived in Mizpa, which is situated to the north of Jerusalem, tells us that Mizpa was still functioning tolerably well as a community.

Certainly we do not wish to minimise what had happened to Judah. Perhaps we may refer to the experience of towns and cities throughout the world which in our own day have been reduced to rubble, which despite devastation, despite all the horrors of war, despite the deportation of their inhabitants and all the risks and uncertainties brought about by warfare, were far from being completely depopulated. Moreover, our interpretation of the past depends at least as much on how we experience the present as on what actually happened in the past. In 1945 nobody would have raised any objections if a writer had described cities such as Coventry, Hiroshima, Stalingrad, Dresden or Berlin as "completely destroyed". When we read in Jeremiah 34²²: "Behold . . . saith the Lord, . . . I will make the cities of Judah a desolation without an inhabitant", these words may well express what Judah's inhabitants felt but perhaps even more what was felt by those people carried off into Babylonian exile, for they probably thought all hope lost of ever seeing Ancient Israel rise again to its former greatness. The end of the Kingdom of Judah marked the end of the history of Ancient Israel; the history of the Jews now began.

VII

From the Exile to the Maccabean Kingdom from Ezekiel to John Hyrcanus

Chapter 29
EDUCATION THROUGH EXILE

Good advice from the prophet Jeremiah—The firm of Murashu and Sons, Nippur—Interest 20 per cent—Farmers and shepherds turned traders—Koldewey excavates Babylon—A town plan like New York—The greatest city in the ancient world—Tower of Babel 300 feet high—Chamber of Commerce on the Euphrates.

"Build ye houses, and dwell in them: and plant gardens, and eat the fruit of them . . . that ye may be increased there and not diminished. And seek the peace of the city whither I have caused you to be carried away captives" (Jer. 29⁵⁻⁷).

So wrote the prophet Jeremiah from Jerusalem to the elders, priests, prophets and to the whole nation that at Nebuchadnezzar's bidding had been carried off to Babylon. Following his well-considered advice, they sought and found "the peace of the city", and did not fare at all badly. The Exile in Babylon was not to be compared with the harsh existence of the children of Israel on the Nile, in Pithom and Raamses in the days of Moses. Apart from a few exceptions (Is. 47⁶) there was no heavy forced labour. Nowhere is there any mention of their having to make bricks by the Euphrates. Yet Babylon ran what was probably the greatest brick-making industry in the world at that time. For never was there so much building going on in Mesopotamia as under Nebuchadnezzar.

Anyone who took Jeremiah's advice as his guide got on well,

some indeed very well. One family which had made the grade
has left to posterity its dust-covered business documents on clay.
"Murashu and Sons"—International Bank—Insurance, Convey-
ancing, Loans—Personal and real estate—Head office: Nippur—
Branches everywhere—a firm with a reputation throughout the
world, the "Lloyd's" of Mesopotamia.

The Murashus—displaced persons from Jerusalem—had done
well for themselves in Nippur since 587 B.C. They were an old
established office. Their firm still stood for something in
Mesopotamia even in the Persian era. The "books" of "Murashu
and Sons" are full of detailed information about the life of the
exiles, such as their names, their occupations, their property.

Scholars from the University of Pennsylvania discovered some
of the Jewish firm's deeds stored in its former business premises
in Nippur. They were in great clay jars, which, in accordance
with security precautions in those days, had been carefully sealed
with asphalt. It was not only Assyriologists who read the
translations of these documents with delight.

The offices of Murashu and Sons were a hive of activity. For
150 years they enjoyed the confidence of their clients, whether it
was a matter of conveyance of large estates and sections of
the canals or of slaves. Anyone who could not write, when he
came eventually to add his signature, put, instead of his name,
the print of his finger-nail on the documents. It corresponded to
putting a cross, in the presence of witnesses, as in the case of
illiterates today.

One day three jewellers called on Murashu and Sons . . . "Elil-
aha-idinna and Belsunu and Hatin said to Elil-nadin-sum, son of
Murashu: In the case of this emerald ring, we give a twenty-
years guarantee that the stone will not fall out of the gold. If the
emerald falls out of the ring before the expiry of twenty years,
Elil-aha-idinna, Belsunu and Hatin undertake to pay damages to
Elil-nadin-sum amounting to 10 Minas of silver." The document
is signed by seven people. Before the lawyer's name the clay
bears the imprint of three finger-nails. These are the signatures
of the three jewellers who were unable to write.

An exiled Jew, Mannudannijama, came to Murashu and Sons,
because he wanted to arrange a deed of conveyance with a
Babylonian concerning an important herd of cattle: "13 old
rams, 27 two year old rams, 152 lambing ewes, 40 year old
rams, 40 year old ewe-lambs, an old he-goat, a two year old
he-goat . . . a total of 276 white and black, large and small sheep

and goats . . . cash on delivery. . . . Mannudannijama to be responsible for pasture, feeding, and safe custody. . . . Nippur, the 25th of Ulul . . . Signed: Fingernail of Mannudannijama.''

Securities for those imprisoned for debt were deposited with the bank. There were special departments for all eventualities of life.

The rate of interest was 20 per cent, not introduced by Murashu, let it be said. That was the normal rate in those days.

"Murashu and Sons" may serve as an example of the profession, which since the days of the Exile has been associated with the children of Israel. It became for them the profession par excellence and has remained so until now: that of merchant and trader. In their homeland they had only been peasants, settlers, cattle breeders and tradesmen. The law of Israel had made no provision for commerce: it was an alien occupation. The word "Canaanite" was for them synonymous with "shopkeeper", "merchant", people whom the prophets had vigorously castigated for their sins. "He is a merchant, the balances of deceit are in his hand: he loveth to oppress" (Hos. 12[7]; Amos 8[5,6]).

The switchover to this hitherto forbidden profession was extremely clever—a fact that is seldom properly understood. For it proved to be in the last resort, when added to a tenacious attachment to their old faith, the best guarantee of the continuance of Israel as a people. As farmers and settlers scattered throughout a foreign land they would have intermarried and interbred with people of other races and in a few generations would have been absorbed and disappeared. This new profession demanded that their houses should be in more or less large societies, within which they could build themselves into a community and devote themselves to their religious practices. It gave them cohesion and continuity.

The Israelites could have chosen no better training college. Babylon as an international centre of trade, industry and commerce was the great school for the cities and capitals of the whole world, which from then on were to become the home of the homeless. The metropolis, whose ruins after 2,500 years still betray its ancient power and glory, had no equal in the ancient world.

Sixty miles south of busy Bagdad the desert is churned up, scarred and furrowed. As far as the eye can see, there stretches a maze of trenches, rubble heaps, and pits which bear witness to the efforts of German archaeologists, over a period of eighteen years. As a result of this prolonged campaign[1] Professor Robert Koldewey has been able to bring to light the fabulous Babylon of the Bible.

Scarcely forty years after the excavations the site presented a dismal and chaotic appearance. Wind and desert sand were slowly but relentlessly covering up again the gigantic skeleton of the old metropolis. Only on one side a few block-like towers stood out with sharply defined silhouette against the sky. Their brick walls, once brightly tiled, were bleak and bare. Here at the Ishtar Gate began the long Processional Way. Where it ended, a massive hump on the other side of the city proclaimed the presence of one of the greatest edifices of the ancient world, the Tower of Babel.

The pomp and glory, the power and might of the city which "sinned against the Lord" (Jer. 50[14]) were all destroyed and disappeared. It was never again inhabited. Could the oracle of the prophet Isaiah have been more completely fulfilled?

> "And Babylon, the glory of kingdoms, the beauty of the Chaldeans' pride shall be as when God overthrew Sodom and Gomorrah. It shall never be inhabited, neither shall it be dwelt in from generation to generation.... But wild beasts of the desert shall lie there: and their houses shall be full of doleful creatures: and ostriches shall dwell there.... And wolves shall cry in their castles and jackals in the pleasant palaces" (Is. 13[19-23]—R.V.).

It is a long time now since the site was deserted by jackals and owls and more so by ostriches. Even the mighty Euphrates has turned its back on it and has chosen a new bed. Once upon a time the arrogant walls of the city and the lofty Tower were reflected in its waters. Now a silhouette of palm trees in the distance indicates its new course. The little Arab settlement of "Babil" preserves in its name the memory of the proud city: but it lies some miles north of the ruins.

"Babylon Halt" is written in Arabic and English on the signboard of the station on the Bagdad railway which lies a few hundred yards from the mounds and allows the visitor, a rare

[1] 1899–1917.

occasion these days, to make a tour of the desolate yellowish-brown ruins. Here he is surrounded by the silent stillness of utter solitude.

The ruins preserved as their most precious treasure documents of incomparable value: it is thanks to them that we are able today to reconstruct an accurate picture of the time of the Jewish exile which was also the period of Babylon's greatest prosperity.

"Is not this great Babylon, that I have built for the house of the kingdom, by the might of my power, and for the honour of my majesty" (Dan. 4³⁰). These words which Daniel puts into the mouth of King Nebuchadnezzar do not exaggerate. Hardly any other monarch in the past was such an assiduous builder. There is scarcely any mention of warlike activities, conquests and campaigns. In the forefront there is the constant building activity of Nebuchadnezzar. Hundreds of thousands of bricks bear his name, and the plans of many of the buildings have been preserved. Babylon in fact surpassed all the cities of the ancient orient: it was greater than Thebes, Memphis and Ur, greater even than Nineveh.

"The centre of the city, which is full of three and four-storied buildings, is traversed by dead straight streets not only those that run parallel to the river but also the cross streets which lead down to the water side." So Herodotus described what he himself had seen. The town plan of Babylon is reminiscent of the blueprints for large American cities.

Coming from Palestine, even from proud Jerusalem, the exiles had only known narrow twisting streets, little better than alleys. In Babylon however they made the acquaintance of streets as broad as avenues and as straight as if they had been drawn with a ruler. Every one of them bore the name of one of the gods in the Babylonian pantheon. There was a Marduk street and a Zababa street on the left bank of the river. In the right-hand corner of the city they crossed the streets of the moon god Sin and of Enlil, the "Lord of the World". On the right bank Adad street ran from east to west, and intersected the street of the sun-god Shamash.

Babylon was not only a commercial but a religious metropolis as can be seen from an inscription: "Altogether there are in Babylon 53 temples of the chief gods, 55 chapels of Marduk, 300 chapels for the earthly deities, 600 for the heavenly deities, 180 altars for the goddess Ishtar, 180 for the gods Nergal and Adad and 12 other altars for different gods."

Polytheism of this kind with worship and ritual which extended to public prostitution must have given the city, in terms of the present day, the appearance of an annual fair.

"But the most vicious practice of the Babylonians is the following," writes Herodotus in shocked astonishment (I, 199). "Every woman in the country must take her seat in the shrine of Aphrodite, and once in her life consort with a stranger.... And only when she has been with him, and done her service to the goddess, is she allowed to go home: and from then on no gift is great enough to tempt her. All the women who are tall and beautiful are quickly released: but the unattractive ones have to wait for a long time before they can fulfil the law: some of them have to wait three or four years."

The abominable temptations and enticements which were part of everyday life in Babylon remained indelibly fixed in the minds of the exiled Jews. Through the centuries until the time of Christ the brilliant metropolis was for them: "Babylon the Great, the mother of harlots and abominations of the earth" (Rev. 17⁵). The idea of Babylon as a cesspool of vice is rooted in the vocabulary of every modern language.

The German archaeologists had to clear away over a million cubic feet of rubble before they had exposed part of the temple of Marduk on the Euphrates, which had been rebuilt under Nebuchadnezzar. The structure, including its out-buildings, measured approximately 1,500 feet by 1,800 feet. Opposite the temple rose the Ziggurat, the tower of Marduk's sanctuary.

"Go to, let us make brick, and burn them thoroughly. And they had brick for stone, and slime had they for mortar. And they said, Go to, let us build us a city, and a tower whose top may reach unto heaven: and let us make us a name...." Gen. 11³,⁴).

The bricklaying technique described in the Bible at the building of the Tower of Babel corresponds with the findings of the archaeologists. As the investigations confirmed, actually only asphalted bricks were used in the construction, especially in the foundations. That was clearly necessary for the security of the structure in accordance with building regulations. In the neighbourhood of the river the regular rise in the level of the water and the constant dampness of the ground had to be borne in mind. Foundations and stonework were therefore made water-proof and damp-proof with "slime", i.e., asphalt.

The beginning of the building of the Tower of Babel is described in the Book of Genesis and comes before the days of the patriarchs. Abraham lived, as we can gather from what has been discovered at Mari, in the 19th century B.C. Is this a contradiction? The history of the tower, "whose top may reach unto heaven", points back into the dim past. More than once it had been destroyed and rebuilt. After the death of Hammurabi the Hittites tried to raze the mighty structure to the ground. Nebuchadnezzar merely had it restored.

Seven stages, "seven squares", rose one above the other. A little tablet belonging to an architect which was found in the temple expressly mentions that length, breadth and height were equal and that only the terraces had different measurements. The length of the sides at the base is given as being rather more than 290 feet. The archaeologists measured it as 295 feet. According to that the tower must have been almost 300 feet high.

The Tower of Babel was also involved in dubious religious rites. Herodotus describes them: "On the topmost tower there is a spacious temple, and inside the temple stands a couch of unusual size richly adorned, with a golden table by its side. There is no statue of any kind set up in the place, nor is the chamber occupied at nights by anyone but a single native woman, who, as the Chaldeans, the priests of this god, affirm, is chosen for himself by the deity out of all the women of the land. They also declare—but I for my part do not believe it—that the god himself comes down into the temple and sleeps upon the couch. This is like the story told by the Egyptians of what takes place in Thebes, where a woman always sleeps in the temple of the Theban Zeus. . . ."

On the streets and squares between the temples, the chapels and the altars, trade and commerce flourished. Solemn processions, heavily laden caravans, traders' barrows, priests, pilgrims, merchants surged to and fro, colourful and noisy. Religious life and business life were so closely associated in Babylon's everyday affairs that they often dovetailed into each other, as they did in the temples. What else could the priests do with all the sacrificial animals, all the "tithes" that were presented daily on the altars, many of them quickly perishable, apart from turning them into money as soon as possible? Just as in Ur, the temple authorities in Babylon ran their own department stores and warehouses. They also ran their own banks to invest their revenues to the best advantage.

Outside the double walls of the city, which were broad enough "to allow a four-horse chariot to turn on them",[1] lay the "Chambers of Commerce". It was on the river-bank that prices were fixed and exchange rates established for the commodities that arrived by boat. "Karum", "quay", was the name the Babylonians gave to what we now call the Exchange. As well as taking over the Quay, or Exchange, from the Babylonians the old world has also taken over its system of weights and measurements.

However much the Jews may have sought "the peace of the city" and found it; however much they may have learned in the cities of Babylonia which would profit future generations, broaden their own outlook and raise their standard of living, all of which would benefit future generations in many ways—nevertheless their heart-yearnings for their distant little homeland on the Jordan left them no inward peace. They could not forget the city of David, their beloved Jerusalem. "By the rivers of Babylon, there we sat down; yea, we wept, when we remembered Zion" (Ps. 137). These were no empty words. For thousands of them set out on the difficult journey home. They rebuilt their shattered city and the temple of Yahweh. Without a passionate longing for the homeland they had lost, that would never have happened.

[1] Herodotus.

Chapter 30
SUNSET IN THE ANCIENT ORIENT

The old world about 500 B.C.—Last spasms before the end—Escape into the past—Nabonidus restores ancient buildings—First museum in the world at Ur—Semitic empires make their exit—The birth of the west.

"Behold evil shall go forth from nation to nation and a great whirlwind shall be raised up from the coasts of the earth" (Jer. 25^{32}).

The hands of the cosmic clock are approaching 500 B.C. The ancient orient carries more than 3,000 years on its shoulders. The nations in the "Fertile Crescent" and on the Nile have grown old, their creative impulse is exhausted, they have fulfilled their task, and the time is drawing near for them to step off the stage of history.

The sun of the ancient orient is setting and its peoples are vaguely conscious of the approaching night.

Yet there is to be a last flicker of life among these weary nations: they summon up enough strength for one last effort. From Egypt to the lands on the Euphrates and the Tigris it is as if there is to be one final attempt to rise before sinking into insignificance. Were they looking back and thinking of the leading role they had played on the world's stage? It would almost seem as if they were. Their monarchs look back to the great symbols of their glorious past. They believe that with a new display of strength they can delay the inevitable.

Pharaoh Necho and Pharaoh Apries made great efforts to reconquer Syria and Palestine. The Old Kingdom with its "campaigns against Asia'' became the ideal of the 26th dynasty.[1] Large navies were built and an attempt was made to restore the old canal between the Nile and the Red Sea.

Even if the new manifestations of strength bore no fruit, and success eluded their military exploits, nevertheless the example of the great days of the builders of the Pyramids lent vitality in other directions. Painters and sculptors copied the works of their great predecessors. Names of Pharaohs of the third millennium were engraved on new scarabs. Ancient official titles and court titles were revived, the civil service was, as it were, antiquarianised.

The same thing happened on the Mediterranean coast in Phoenicia. In 814 B.C. according to tradition, but somewhat later according to the results of archaeological research, Carthage was founded as a North African colony of the city of Tyre. By this time the power of these Phoenician merchant sailors had reached its limit. From the Black Sea to the Straits of Gibraltar they had trading posts and bases along the shores of the Mediterranean. A century later the Greeks had inherited their world trade. Sanchuniathon, the priest, wrote the history of Phoenicia. He was commissioned by a king to copy old inscriptions and texts which Philo of Byblos was to use much later as the source for his history.

With Ashurbanipal[2] the Assyrian Empire reached the zenith of its power. It stretched from the Persian Gulf to Upper Egypt. The tiger of the ancient orient had eaten his fill, and the ruler of the most powerful of all conquering nations allowed himself to be painted in an arbour of grape-vines, reclining on soft cushions and being handed a goblet of wine. Collecting old books was his hobby and he had the biggest library in the ancient world. On his instructions the repositories of old temples were ransacked in a search for lost documents. His scribes made copies of thousands of tablets from the reign of the great Sargon I (2350 B.C.). The hobby of his brother Shamash-Shumukin of Babylonia went even further. He had the events of his day written up in the ancient language of Sumeria.

Nebuchadnezzar too,[3] the last great ruler on the throne of Babylon, was afflicted with this longing for old forgotten far-off things. His court chroniclers had to compose inscriptions in Old

[1] 663–525 B.C.
[2] 669–626 B.C.
[3] 605–562 B.C.

Babylonian, which nobody could either speak or read. Architecture and literature flourished once again among the Chaldeans.

Observing the sky in the interests of astrology led to undreamt of advances. They were able to predict eclipses of the sun and moon. In the Babylonian School of Astronomy about 750 B.C. observations of heavenly bodies were recorded and continued without interruption for over 350 years, the longest series of astronomical observations ever made. The accuracy of their reckoning exceeded that of European astronomers until well into the 18th century.

Nabonidus[1] may well have been the first archaeologist in the world. This monarch, the last of the Babylonian rulers, caused ruined shrines and temples to be excavated, old inscriptions to be deciphered and translated. He restored the staged tower at Ur which had been weakened by age, as was shown by the finds at Tell al-Muqayyar.

Princess Bel-Shalti-Nannar, sister of the Belshazzar in the Bible, had the same interests as her father Nabonidus. Woolley discovered in an annexe to the temple in Ur, where she had been priestess, a regular museum with objects which had been found in the southern states of Mesopotamia—probably the earliest museum in the world. She had actually carefully catalogued her collection piece by piece on a clay cylinder. This is, in Woolley's words, the "oldest museum catalogue known".

One people alone—broken up into many parts and at that time scattered far and wide throughout the "Fertile Crescent"—did not succumb to surfeit or slackness: the children of Israel, descendants of the patriarchs, were filled with eager hope and had a definite end in view. They did not disappear: they found the strength to preserve themselves for new millennia—up to the present day.

For 1,500 years mankind's biggest light had come from the "Fertile Crescent," the oldest centre of civilisation since the Stone Age. About 500 B.C. darkness fell, imperceptibly but irresistibly, over the lands and peoples who had within them the seed of all that would come after them—but in other lands.

A new light was already shining from the mountains of Iran: the Persians were coming. The great Semitic states and Egypt had fulfilled their assignment in history: the most significant and decisive part of man's early existence had helped to prepare the

[1] 555–538 B.C.

ground for the Indo-Germanic kingdoms which gave birth to Europe.

From the extreme south-eastern tip of the continent the light travelled farther and farther west. From Greece to Rome, across the barrier of the Alps, across Western Europe and up to Scandinavia and the British Isles. Light from the East!

On its way, within a few centuries, new civilisations would appear, art would reach unimagined heights of beauty and harmony, the human mind in the philosophy and science of the Greeks would soar to pinnacles denied to the ancient orient.

On its way the light would also bring the varied colourful legacy of the ancient orient, from a practical system of weights and measures to astronomy, it would bring writing, the alphabet and—the Bible.

Chapter 31
CYRUS, KING OF PERSIA

Two famous dreams—Cyrus unites Media and Persia—The Writing on the Wall—Belshazzar was merely crown prince—Peaceful entry into Babylon—Persian toleration.

"Thus saith the Lord to his anointed, to Cyrus, whose right hand I have holden, to subdue nations before him; and I will loose the loins of kings, to open before him the two leaved gates; and the gates shall not be shut" (Is. 45¹).

Seven years after Nebuchadnezzar's death, Nabonidus, the "first archaeologist", ascended the throne of Babylon in 555 B.C. He was to be the last ruler from Mesopotamia. For events in the highlands of Iran suggested that world history was quickly heading for a great revolution.

Five years after the accession of Nabonidus the new era began with the Persians' rise to power.

The Medes—who since the fall of Nineveh in 612 B.C. had shared the stricken Assyrian empire with the Babylonians—were unexpectedly overcome by their neighbours and vassals, the Persians. Astyages, king of the Medes, was beaten by his own grandson, Cyrus.

In the ancient world great men were wont to herald their arrival in extraordinary ways; often the remarkable circumstances of their birth took them outside the normal framework of the lives of their contemporaries. Two unusual dreams are said to have decided the destiny of Cyrus. They were gossiped around the whole of the ancient orient and in this way came to the ears of Herodotus, who recounts them:

"Astyages . . . had a daughter who was named Mandane. He dreamt that from her such a stream of water flowed forth as not only to fill his capital but to flood the whole of Asia. This vision he laid before such of the Magi as had the gift of interpreting dreams, who expounded its meaning to him in full, whereat he was greatly terrified. On this account, when his daughter was of marriageable age, he would not give her to any of the Medes lest the dream should be accomplished, but married her to a Persian by name Cambyses. . . .

"When Mandane was living with Cambyses, Astyages in the very first year saw another vision. He fancied that a vine grew from the womb of his daughter and overshadowed the whole of Asia. After this dream, which he submitted also to the interpreters, he sent to Persia and fetched away Mandane, who was now with child, and was not far from her time. On her arrival he set a watch over her, intending to destroy the child to which she should give birth: for the Magian interpreters had expounded the vision to foreshow that the offspring of his daughter would reign over Asia in his stead. To guard against this, Astyages, as soon as Cyrus was born, sent for Harpagus, a man of his own house and the most faithful of the Medes . . . and addressed him thus: '. . . Take the child born of Mandane: carry him with thee to thy home and slay him there. . . .' "

Harpagus found that he had no heart to carry out this murderous command of the child's grandfather. No more had a shepherd to whom he deputed the task. So Cyrus remained alive.

It was not only the birth and boyhood of Cyrus that were wrapped in legend. This Persian king's son, descended from the royal race of Achaemenes, has, more than any other prince of the ancient world, caught the imagination and evoked the admiration of all nations. Xenophon, the Greek, celebrated the foundation of his empire in a complete romance, the "Cyropaedia".

The Bible remembers him as an enlightened monarch. His unparalleled, swift and brilliant rise to power was marred by no deed of violence. His able and humane policy made him one of the most attractive figures in the ancient orient. The most repugnant feature of oriental monarchs before him, despotic cruelty, was foreign to this Persian.

The figure of Cyrus became a hard fact of history in 553 B.C. In that year he captured Ecbatana, capital of the kingdom of Media. His royal grandfather Astyages was banished. Cyrus amalgamated Media with the Persian kingdom. Babylonia, Lydia in Asia Minor and Sparta formed an alliance against the conqueror. Croesus king of Lydia—his name is still proverbial for great riches—attacked the Persians. Cyrus took Sardis,[1] his capital, and defeated him.

The way to Babylonia was open and Babylon lay invitingly before him. Against the background of such a situation a strange and mysterious story got about which, since it has been recorded in the Bible, has gripped the imagination of the western world:

"Belshazzar the king made a great feast to a thousand of his lords, and drank wine before the thousand. . . . They drank wine, and praised the gods of gold, and of silver, of brass, of iron, of wood and of stone. In the same hour came forth fingers of a man's hand, and wrote over against the candlestick upon the plaister of the wall of the king's palace. . . . Then the king's countenance was changed, and his thoughts troubled him, so that the joints of his loins were loosed, and his knees smote one against another. . . . And the king spake and said to the wise men of Babylon, Whosoever shall read this writing, and shew me the interpretation thereof, shall be clothed with scarlet, and have a chain of gold about his neck, and shall be the third ruler in the kingdom" (Daniel $5^{1, 4-7}$). "Mene, Mene, Tekel, Upharsin" were the words on the wall which have become famous. They mean: "God hath numbered thy kingdom". "Thou art weighed in the balances and art found wanting". "Thy kingdom is divided and given to the Medes and Persians" (Dan. 5^{25-28}).

When Joseph in Egypt was able to interpret Pharaoh's dreams of the seven fat kine and the seven lean kine and of the ears of corn, he was made second man in the kingdom, grand vizier.

What was the meaning of the promised reward for guessing the meaning of the mysterious writing to be "the third ruler in the kingdom"?

This Biblical statement was unintelligible and was only explained with the help of archaeology.

Who Belshazzar was has now been established by cuneiform texts from his own father. He was not, in fact, as the Book of Daniel says (5^2), the son of Nebuchadnezzar, but of Nabonidus, who says in an inscription: "And put into the heart of Belshazzar, my first born son, the fruit of my loins, fear of thy sublime divinity, that he commit no sin, and that he may have fulness of life."

[1] Fifty miles east of Izmir.

Thus it is clear that Belshazzar was crown prince, therefore the second man in Babylonia. He could only therefore hold out a promise of third highest place in the kingdom.

The story of Belshazzar's Feast and the Writing on the Wall reflects through the eyes of the prophets a contemporary political situation. In 539 B.C. Cyrus turned his attack against Nabonidus, and the Babylonian army was defeated. With that the hours of the last great Mesopotamian empire were numbered.

"Come down, and sit in the dust, O virgin daughter of Babylon: there is no throne, O daughter of the Chaldeans" (Is. 47[1]).

A year after the battle Cyrus, king of Persia, made his triumphal entry into conquered Babylon.

Hittites, Kassites, Assyrians had at various times threatened the great city with the same fate. This conquest however did not follow the normal pattern: it was without a parallel in the military practice of the ancient orient. For this time there were no columns of smoke rising from behind shattered walls, no temples or palaces razed to the ground, no house plundered, no man was butchered or impaled. The clay cylinder of Cyrus narrates in Babylonian script what took place:

"As I entered Babylon in peace, and established my royal residence in the palace of the princes amid jubilation and rejoicing, Marduk, the great lord, warmed the hearts of the Babylonians towards me, while I for my part devoted myself daily to do him reverence. My troops wandered peacefully widespread throughout Babylon. In all Sumer and Akkad I let no man be afraid. I concerned myself with the internal affairs of Babylon and all its cities. The dwellers in Babylon.... I freed from the yoke that ill became them. I repaired their houses, I healed their afflictions... I am Cyrus, king of all, the great king, the mighty king, king of Babylon, king of Sumer and Akkad, king of the four corners of the earth...."

The last sentences almost suggest that the Biblical Chronicler had known the text of the clay cylinder. "Thus saith Cyrus, king of Persia, All the kingdoms of the earth hath the Lord God of heaven given me...." (2 Chron. 36[23]).

That rulers should make tolerance, including religious tolerance, their motto was uncommon, and marked the Persian king out from the first.

After the entry into Babylon Cyrus at once had the images and shrines of the local gods set up again. He was concerned with "the daily worship of the chief god of the city Marduk". In the city of Ur he did the same. On a broken cylinder which was preserved among the ruins Cyrus himself says: "Sin, the light of heaven and earth, with his favourable omens gave into my hands the four corners of the earth. I brought the gods back into their sanctuaries."

His tolerance was also to the advantage of the Jews. After these many years of exile their dearest wish was now to find fulfilment.

Chapter 32
RETURN TO JERUSALEM

The edict of Cyrus—The trek of the 42,000—A caravan of fateful significance —Starting work on the ruins—A lonely grave in Pasargadae—Rebuilding the Temple—The Persian Empire: from the Nile to India—Duncan finds Nehemiah's work—The secret of the "thick water"—A theocratic state—Judah coins stamped with the Athenian owl—A Persian province for two centuries.

"In the first year of Cyrus the king, the same Cyrus the king made a decree concerning the house of God at Jerusalem, Let the house be builded, the place where they offered sacrifices, and let the foundations thereof be strongly laid: the height thereof threescore cubits, and the breadth thereof threescore cubits" (Ezra 6³).

This meant permission for them to return to Jerusalem. The text of the royal decree is in imperial Aramaic, the new official language of the Persian government. Archaeology has been able to establish the authenticity of this permit, which has been incorporated in chapter six of the Book of Ezra.

It was a matter of reparation. It is clear from the terms of the enactment that the Persians regarded themselves as successors of the Babylonians: ". . . let the expenses be given out of the king's house. And also let the golden and silver vessels of the house of God, which Nebuchadnezzar took forth out of the temple which is at Jerusalem, and brought into Babylon, be restored and brought again unto the temple, which is at Jerusalem, every one to his place, and place them in the house of God" (Ezra 6⁴,⁵).

The carrying out of the order was entrusted by Cyrus to Sheshbazzar,[1] the governor (Ezra 5[14]), a prince of Judah, and probably a member of the house of David.

It is understandable that fifty years after the deportation not everyone would take advantage of this permission to return to the land of their fathers. In any case it was a risky business to leave this wealthy country of Babylon where they had established themselves and where most of them had grown up and to set out on the difficult road back to the ruins of a ravaged land. Despite this, in the spring of 537 B.C., after long preparations a lengthy caravan set out on the trail towards the old homeland. "The whole congregation together was forty and two thousand three hundred and threescore. Besides their servants and their maids, of whom there were seven thousand three hundred thirty and seven, and there were among them two hundred singing men and singing women. Their horses were seven hundred thirty and six: their mules two hundred forty and five, their camels four hundred thirty and five, their asses six thousand seven hundred and twenty" (Ezra 2[64-67]).

Whether this list of people returning to their homeland really is that of the members of a mighty trek from the Euphrates to Judah is debatable. It is all repeated in Nehemiah almost word for word except that the number of singing men and singing women is not quite the same as there is a difference of 45. In this instance, however, the list is of a population census, a register of the Persian satrapy which Judah had become under Persian rule. However this may be and whatever the number of people who did, in fact, return to Judah after the long years in exile, we can vividly imagine their journey into the land west of the Jordan.

Almost 800 miles have to be covered between Babylon and distant Jerusalem, with the clouds of dust churned up by the caravan as a faithful companion throughout the whole journey. One day they would pass the site of old Mari. They would reach the spot where, on the opposite side of the river, the Balikh, on whose lower reaches Haran was situated, enters the Euphrates.

From then on the returning exiles were following the same track which had been taken by Abraham 1,400 years earlier, when he left the land of his fathers to go to Canaan, via Damascus and along the foot of Hermon to the Lake of Galilee.

[1] It is thought that Sheshbazzar is the same as Shenazar, the fourth son of King Jehoiachin (1 Chron. 3[18]).

Then came the day when from among the brown peaks of the mountains of Judah the desolate ruins of the city of Zion rose before their eyes—it was Jerusalem.

What fateful significance this journey had for the generations that were still to come!

"The future of the world lay in this procession to Jerusalem," says the American scholar and educationist Mary Ellen Chase, who lectured in universities on "The Bible as Literature" from 1926 onwards. "It rested with it whether we should have a Bible at all as we know it—the Bible, the Jewish faith, Christianity and many centuries of western culture. If there had been no return to Jerusalem, Judah would assuredly have shared by and large the fate of Israel, become intermingled with the east and eventually been lost as a united people."

Soon after their arrival in Jerusalem the foundations of the new Temple were laid amid great enthusiasm. But then the work slackened off (Ezra 5^{16}). The great enthusiasm of the returned settlers quickly waned: life was too hard and barren in this depopulated land, where dilapidated houses provided the scantiest of shelter. Added to this was the problem of making a living, as Haggai said "ye run every man unto his own house" (Haggai 1^9). Everyone was too concerned with his own problems.

The rebuilding advanced but slowly. The first settlers were poor, and as the remains of their household belongings indicate, few in number. The objects which have been discovered clearly reflect the harshness of that first early stage.

Cyrus, the liberator, died on an expedition to the east in 530 B.C. and was buried in the royal palace of Pasargadae near Persepolis.[1] His palace was built in the form of individual pavilions: each one lay in the centre of a magnificent garden: the whole area was enclosed by a high wall.

On the southern slopes of a long range of hills there still stands among the rough grass of the highlands a small unpretentious stone building dating from the time of Cyrus. Six square blocks form the steps which lead up to a small chamber, above the entrance to which there could at one time be read the following plea: "O man, whoever you are and whenever you come, for I know that you will come—I am Cyrus, who gave the Persians their empire. Do not grudge me this patch of earth that

---

[1] Thirty miles north-east of Shiraz in Southern Iran, famous in modern times as a centre of carpet weaving.

FIG. 62.—Mausoleum of Cyrus.

covers my body.'' Alas, the small stone chamber in which a
golden sarcophagus enclosed the mortal remains of the great
Persian is now as empty as the place above the entrance which
bore the inscription. Occasionally shepherds with their flocks
pass unconcernedly by this forgotten spot, as they did in olden
times, across the wide plateau where the lion is still lord of the
chase.

Cyrus was followed by his son Cambyses II.[1] With the conquest of Egypt Persia became under him the greatest empire that
the world had ever seen: it stretched from India to the Nile.

It was not until the reign of his successor Darius I[2] that the
rebuilding of the Temple in Jerusalem was finally taken in hand.
Almost twenty years had passed since the foundations had been
laid. At the request of the official responsible for the administration
of Judah, the Satrap of Transeuphrates, Darius I expressly
confirmed the permit issued by Cyrus. The official exchange of
letters with the Persian court on this matter can be found in the
Book of Ezra (5[6]–6[12]).

Many experts are convinced of the historicity of these documents although others are doubtful. If they are not genuine,
however, they are very clever imitations both as to form and
content. The Bible here even uses the Aramaic of the empire, the
commercial language of the Achaemenide Empire. Numerous
other contemporary texts confirm, moreover, the extent to which
Darius fostered the indigenous cults of the peoples incorporated
in his empire, not only in Palestine, but also in Asia Minor and
Egypt.

[1] 530–522 B.C.
[2] 522–486 B.C.

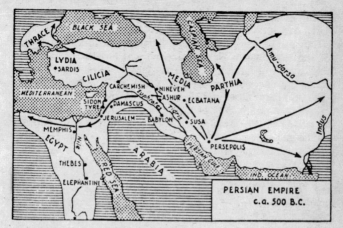

FIG. 63.

For example the inscription of Usahor, an Egyptian doctor, runs as follows: "King Darius—may he live for ever—commanded me to go to Egypt . . . and make up once more the number of the holy scribes of the temple and bring new life into what had fallen into decay. . . ."

Darius wrote to Gadata, the steward of his demesnes, in no uncertain manner. He took him sharply to task for his attitude to the priesthood of the temple of Apollo in Magnesia: "I hear that you are not carrying out my instructions properly. Admittedly you are taking trouble over my estates, in that you are transferring trees and plants from beyond the Euphrates to Asia Minor. I commend this project and the Court will show its gratitude. But in disregarding my attitude to the gods you have provoked my displeasure and unless you change your tactics you will feel its weight. For you have taken away the gardeners who are sacred to Apollo and used them for other gardening jobs of a secular character, thereby showing a lack of appreciation of the sentiments of my ancestors towards the god who has spoken to the Persians. . . ."

The efforts of the returned exiles were for many years confined exclusively to rebuilding the Temple at Jerusalem. Building

operations started in October–November 520 B.C. and by 12
March 515 B.C. they were completed.[1]

They had to wait for the city wall until the next century. It was
not until the time of Nehemiah, who was installed as independent governor of Judah by King Artaxerxes I[2] of Persia in 444 B.C.,
that they began work on the wall, which was finished in record
time. "So the wall was finished . . . in fifty and two days" (Neh.
6[15]). A new wall in fifty-two days—impossible! Nehemiah himself tells us of "the walls of Jerusalem which were broken down,
and the gates thereof were consumed with fire" (Neh. 2[13]). The
walls were thus merely repaired. And that must have happened
in a hurry. For the neighbouring tribes, above all the Samaritans,
wanted to stop the refortification of Jerusalem by every means in
their power. The Jews had to be constantly on the lookout:
"everyone with one of his hands wrought in the work, and with
the other hand held a weapon" (Neh. 4[17]).

It is no different today in the case of the building operations of
farmers, workers and shepherds in the modern state of Israel.

The speedy filling up of holes and patching up of gaps in the
walls reflect the pressure of the time factor and the feverish
anxiety with which the work went forward. The British archaeologist J. Garrow Duncan dug up parts of the wall on the little
hill to the south-east above the Gihon spring. In his report he
says: "The stones are small, rough, irregular and unequal. Some
of them are unusually small and seem to be merely chips broken
off from bigger stones, just as if they were using any kind of
material that came to hand. The large holes and hollow spaces
are filled up with a haphazard mixture of clay plaster mixed with
tiny chips of stone. . . ."

During the time that Nehemiah was governor of Jerusalem we
are told how the holy fire of the Temple was rediscovered. The
first two chapters of 2 Maccabees tell how Nehemiah "sent in
quest of the fire the descendants of the priests that hid it". They
"had found no fire but thick water". When at Nehemiah's
command they poured this thick water over "the wood and the
things laid thereupon", "there was kindled a great blaze so that
all men marvelled" (2 Macc. 1[21-22]). Nobody paid much attention

---

[1] Zech. 1[1]—the eighth month of the second year of Darius = Oct.–Nov. 520 B.C.
(Start of building operations).
Ezra 6[15]—the third day of the month of Adar, (Babylonian: Addaru) in the sixth year of
Darius = 12 March 515 B.C. (Completion of Temple).
[2] 465–424 B.C.

FIG. 64.—Stamp on Judahite pitcher bearing the inscription "Jerusalem".

to the observation that followed: "And Nehemiah and they that were with him called this thing Nephthar" (2 Macc. 1³⁶). Yet this passage in the Bible contains a very clear hint regarding a quite specific mineral product which must have been well known to the Israelites, and it is only very recently that this was recognised. In the new state of Israel petroleum, or naphtha—the word is of Babylonian derivation—has in fact been found. Since 1953, drilling near the Dead Sea, in the Negev and in the neighbourhood of Askelon has led to the successful opening of Israeli oil wells.

The rebuilding of the Temple and of the old city of David after the return from exile in Babylon make it abundantly clear that Israel knew full well that the days of the monarchy had gone for ever and that only the inward solidarity of a religious community could guarantee the further existence of the tiny state in face of what political developments might be in store for them. With this end in view they made the holy city the centre of Jewry, both for those Jews who lived in the homeland of Judah and for those who were scattered throughout the world. The High Priest of the new Temple at Jerusalem became head over all Israel. The little theocracy in Palestine took no noteworthy part in the affairs of the world during the subsequent centuries. Israel turned its back on politics.

With Persian approval the Law of God became the law of Israel, indeed of Jews everywhere, as the Book of Ezra clearly indicates (Ezra 7²³⁻²⁶).

The Biblical passage is convincingly borne out by another document from the same period.

In 1905 three papyrus documents were discovered on the palm-covered island of Elephantine, which lies beside the first cataract of the Nile near the Aswan dam. They are written in imperial Aramaic and date from the year 419 B.C. One of them is an Easter message from King Darius II of Persia containing instructions as to how the Feast of the Passover is to be celebrated. The recipients of the letter were the Jewish military colony in Elephantine. The sender signs himself Hananiah,

FIG. 65.—Coin from Judah with Zeus and the Athenian owl (Persian period).

"agent for Jewish affairs at the court of the Persian governor of Egypt".

For two centuries the Persians were liege lords of Jerusalem. The history of Israel during this period seems to have been subjected to no violent variations. The Bible makes no mention of it, nor have the layers of rubble anything significant to tell us of this long space of time. At all events there is a complete absence of large buildings, or objects of art and craft, among the archaeological trophies recovered from the appropriate layer. Fragments of simple household utensils prove how miserably poor life in Judah must have been at that time.

Coins certainly occur in the course of the fourth century B.C. They bear the proud legend "Yehud", "Judah". Apparently the Persians had granted the high priest the right to mint silver coins. Following the example of the Attic drachma, they are decorated with the portrait of Zeus and the owl of Athens, testimony to the way in which Greek trade and influence had been able to penetrate everywhere in the Orient long before the days of Alexander the Great.

Chapter 33
UNDER GREEK INFLUENCE

Alexander the Great in Palestine—Causeway forces capitulation of Tyre—Siege towers 160 feet high—Alexandria: the new metropolis—Ptolemies occupy Judah—Seventy-two scholars translate the Bible—Pentateuch in Greek—The Septuagint came from Pharos—A stadium below the Temple—High Priest in "gaming house"—Jewish athletes give offence.

"And it came to pass, after that Alexander the Macedonian, the son of Philip, who came out of the land of Chittim,[1] and smote Darius king of the Persians and Medes, it came to pass, after he had smitten him, that he reigned in his stead, in former time, over Greece. And he fought many battles, and won many strongholds...." (1 Maccabees 1[1]—R.V.).

In the 4th century B.C. the centre of political power gradually shifted from the "Fertile Crescent" to the West. The prelude to this development, which was of decisive importance for the whole world, had been two famous battles in the previous century, in both of which the Greeks called a halt to any further Persian advance. At Marathon in 491 B.C. they defeated the Persian armies of Darius I. At Salamis, off Athens, they smashed the Persian fleet eleven years later in 480 B.C.

With the victory of Alexander the Great[2] over Darius III,[3] king of Persia, in 333 B.C. at Issus, near the present day seaport of

[1] Greece.
[2] 336–323 B.C.
[3] 336–331 B.C.

Alexandria in North Syria, the Macedonians arrogated to themselves the leading role among the nations of the world.

Alexander's first target was Egypt. With a picked force of 32,000 infantry and 5,000 cavalry he marched south at the age of twenty-four, accompanied off shore by a fleet of 160 ships. Twice he was held up on the coast of Syria and Palestine.

The first occasion was at Tyre. This Phoenician city, heavily fortified and protected by stout high walls, was built on a small island which guarded the coastline. Alexander performed here a miracle of military ingenuity by building a 2,000 foot mole in the sea out to the island city. To safeguard the operations, mobile protective shields, so-called "tortoises," had to be employed. Despite this the construction of the causeway was greatly hindered by an incessant hail of missiles. Meantime his engineers were on shore building veritable monsters: "Helepoleis". These were mobile protective towers many stories high, which held the detachments of bowmen and light artillery. A drawbridge on the front of the towers enabled a surprise attack to be made on the enemy's walls. They were the highest siege towers ever used in the history of war. Each of them had twenty stories and the topmost platform towered at a height of over 160 feet far above the highest city walls.

When after seven months preparation these monsters, bristling with weapons, slowly and clumsily rolled towards Tyre, the fate

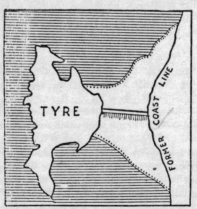

FIG. 66.—Alexander the Great built a 650 yard causeway across to Tyre.

of the maritime stronghold, which was considered to be impregnable, was sealed.

"And Tyrus did build herself a stronghold and heaped up silver as the dust and fine gold as the mire of the streets. Behold, the Lord will cast her out and he will smite her power in the sea; and she shall be devoured with fire" (Zechariah 9[3-4]). This is the Bible's comment on Alexander's conquest. It was incorporated in the Book of Zechariah, in the later, second part. Today nobody has any doubts about the authenticity of these words as a genuine commentary by the Jewish community of Alexander's day on the events of the year 332 B.C.

". . . Gaza shall . . . be very sorrowful," we read in the following verse (Zechariah 9[5]) which deals with this year in Alexander's life. It was indeed the old Philistine town of Gaza which brought the Macedonian king to a halt for the second time. But this siege lasted only two months, and then the road to the Nile lay open.

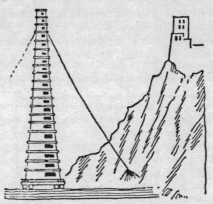

FIG. 67.—Alexander's mobile siege-towers were 160 feet high.

The siege of Gaza in south-west Palestine especially must have made some impact on the Jews. The noise of troops marching down the coast below them and camping there must have been heard on their hills above. Yet the Bible has as little to say about these events as indeed about the whole period of Greek supremacy for almost 150 years. Its historians do not take us beyond the end of the kingdoms of Israel and Judah and the creation of the theocracy under Persian sovereignty. It is only with the beginning of the Maccabean wars that it embarks once more upon detailed history.

But Flavius Josephus, the Jewish historian, gives an account which is not found in the Bible of the campaign of the victorious Greek through Syria and Palestine at this time. After the capture of the fortress of Gaza, he says, Alexander the Great came to Jerusalem. The people and Jaddua the High Priest received him with great ceremony. Alexander offered sacrifices in the Temple and granted the people favours.

Alexander can hardly have found time for a trip to Jerusalem, since he had already been held up for nine months by the resistance of Tyre and Gaza. After the fall of Gaza he hurried on by the quickest road to Egypt, leaving the conquest of the territory inland to his general Parmenion, who had no difficulty in subduing the country. Only Samaria, the seat of the governor of the province, had to be forcibly brought to heel. As a punishment it had a colony of Macedonians settled in it.

Jerusalem and the province of Judah seems to have submitted to their new masters without more ado. At all events no contemporary source has so far suggested that there was any resistance from the theocracy.

The visit of Alexander to Jerusalem is probably only a legend which nevertheless contains a grain of truth. It bears eloquent witness to the fact that the Greek conqueror too tolerated the way of life of the theocracy of Judah. It was left unmolested as a religious community.

This is quite in accord with what archaeology has been able to establish. There are no traces of either a Greek conquest or a Greek occupation of Judah at that time.

Only in the neighbouring city of Samaria a strong Greek fortress came into existence about 322 B.C. Excavations disclosed a whole series of round towers. They lean against the old casemated wall which was built in the days when Samaria was still the capital of the kingdom of Israel.

Alexander remained in Egypt, which welcomed him as a liberator, during the winter of 332–331 B.C. On the outermost tip of the Nile delta he founded the city of Alexandria, which was destined for the role of the metropolis of the new age. It quickly blossomed into the centre of a new intellectual life which attracted the best minds of the Greek and oriental world within its orbit.

At its foundation Alexander issued instructions which were to be of the highest significance in future days. He guaranteed to the Jews—descendants of the refugees in the Babylonian era— the same rights as were accorded to his own countrymen. This provision, carried on by the successors of the great Macedonian, led to Alexandria becoming subsequently one of the great reservoirs of Jewish life and culture.

The name of the city founded by Alexander does not appear in the Bible earlier than the Book of Acts: "And a certain Jew named Apollos, born at Alexandria, an eloquent man and mighty in the scriptures, came to Ephesus" (Acts 18[24]).

On the way to one of the greatest and most successful military expeditions known to history, Alexander marched once more through Palestine. Every country in the Ancient East fell before him. He pressed on to the Indus, almost to the foot of the Himalayas. On the way back he was attacked by a fever. Alexander died in Babylon at the age of 33 on the 13th of June 323 B.C.

In view of the fact that, long before Alexander, the Greeks had been stretching out their feelers in a thousand ways in the direction of Mesopotamia and Egypt, we can only shake our heads in amazement at Jewish ignorance of the ways of the world. Time seems to have been standing still in the little theocracy and the life of its tiny religious community appears to have been influenced only by the Torah, the Law of God.

A long way back there had been Greek mercenaries in the armies of Pharaoh Psamtik II and Nebuchadnezzar, king of the Chaldeans. It was also a long time since the first Greek forts and trading stations had started to spread along the coast of Syria and Palestine. In the 5th century B.C. there were already highly educated Greeks travelling and studying in all countries of the ancient Orient: Herodotus and Xenophon, Hecataeus and Ctesias.

Were these men in their theocratic community no longer able to recognise or understand the signs of the times? Or did they intentionally shut their eyes and blindly hope to keep the future at bay?

If so they must have had all the ruder awakening when they came face to face with Greece but a few steps from the sanctuary of the Temple and could disguise from themselves no longer that

FIG. 68.

Jewish youth had fallen completely for the sport of throwing the discus, which had been imported from Greece. Athletic contests on the Greek pattern quickly found an enthusiastic response among the young people.

Greece was not a danger to the Jews by reason of its growing ascendancy, or militarism, or seductive temptations. The danger lay far more in the freer atmosphere of a fabulous modern world. Hellas, with its Pericles, Aeschylus, Sophocles, Euripides, with its Phidias and Polygnotus, its Plato and its Aristotle, had climbed up to a new stage in human development.

Undisturbed by the new era of mankind the tiny theocracy went on obstinately in its own way, held tenaciously and inflexibly to its traditions and to the past. Despite all this it was forced to join issue with the new ideas. But there was still time enough before the 2nd century B.C.

> "So Alexander . . . died. And his servants bore rule every
> one in his place. And after his death they all put crowns
> upon themselves: so did their sons after them many years:
> and evils were multiplied in the earth" (1 Macc. 1$^{7-9}$).

The idea behind the struggle for power of Alexander's captains—the Diadochi—is not unknown even in 20th century politics. In its original form it was no more of an advertisement for the profession of army commanders. Alexander's generals had no scruples about getting rid of his whole family by murdering them: Philip Arrhidaeus his half brother, his mother Olympia, his widow Roxana and his posthumous son. The conflict came to a head in the division of the empire into three kingdoms.

The kingdom of Macedonia in Northern Greece.

The kingdom of the Seleucids, which extended from Thrace through Asia Minor and Syria to the border of India. Antioch, in the north of Syria, situated on the lower reaches of the Orontes, was founded as capital of this second and by far the largest of the successor states. Thereafter almost all the Seleucid monarchs added to their own names the name of this city: Antiochus.

The third was the Ptolemaic kingdom on the Nile with Alexandria as its capital. It was ruled by a dynasty whose last representative, Cleopatra, has ever since enjoyed a certain amount of fame for having so successfully turned the heads of her distinguished contemporaries Julius Caesar and Mark Antony.

Ptolemy I was the first ruler of this dynasty.

Two unusually far-sighted rulers, Ptolemy I and his son Ptolemy II Philadelphus, developed their capital city of Alexandria into a nursery of Hellenistic culture and learning, whose fame extended far beyond the borders of their own kingdom and made it a radiant centre of attraction for emigrants from Judah among others. In this crucible they steeped themselves in the beauty of the Greek language, the only means of tasting the delights of the prodigious advances of the human mind and the human spirit. It was the international language of learning and of commerce, the language of tens of thousands of Israelites who knew no other home.

The rising generation no longer knew Hebrew as their mother tongue. They could no longer follow the sacred text in the services of the synagogue. Thus it came about that the Jews in Egypt decided to translate the Hebrew scriptures. About 250 B.C. the Torah was translated into Greek, a fact of immeasurable import for Western civilisation.

The translation of the Bible into the Greek tongue was for the Jews in Egypt such an incredible step forward that legend took hold of it. The story is told in an apocryphal letter of Aristeas of Alexandria.

Philadelphus,[1] the second of the Ptolemaic dynasty, took great

---

[1] 285–246 B.C.

pride in the fact that he possessed a collection of the finest books in the world. One day the librarian said to the monarch that he had brought together in his 995 books the best literature of all nations. But, he added, the greatest books of all, the five books of Moses, were not included among them. Therefore Ptolemy II Philadelphus sent envoys to the High Priest to ask for a copy of these books. At the same time he asked for men to be sent who could translate them into Greek. The High Priest granted his request and sent together with the copy of the Torah 72 learned and wise scribes. Great celebrations were organised in honour of the visitors from Jerusalem, at whose wisdom and knowledge the king and his courtiers were greatly astonished. After the festivities they betook themselves to the extremely difficult task which had been assigned to them, and for which there was neither prototype nor dictionary. They set to work out at sea, on the island of Pharos off Alexandria, at the foot of one of the seven wonders of the world—the 300 feet high lighthouse which Ptolemy II had erected as a warning for shipping far and near. Each of them worked in a cell by himself. When the scholars had completed their work and the translations were compared with one another all seventy-two are said to have corresponded exactly, word for word. Accordingly the Greek translation of the Bible was called the "Septuagint", meaning "the Seventy".

What had previously been made known only in the sanctuary, only in the old tongue, and only to the one nation was now all at once available and intelligible for people of other tongues and other races. The hitherto carefully guarded door was thrown wide open.

Judah's attachment to the kingdom of the Ptolemies lasted for more than 100 years. Then the Seleucids of Antioch forced their way southwards, an expansion for which they had long been striving. After a victorious battle against Ptolemy V at the sources of the Jordan, Antiochus III, called the Great, took over Palestine in 195 B.C., and Judah thereby once more came under a new sovereignty.

Gradually the foreign seed began to sprout even in the theocracy. The manifold and enduring influence of the Greek attitude of mind, which had been infiltrating since Alexander's victorious campaigns, became more and more apparent.

When "Antiochus surnamed Epiphanes . . . reigned in the hundred and thirty and seventh year of the kingdom of the Greeks" (1 Macc. 1[10]) and "Jason . . . laboured underhand to be high priest... he forthwith brought his own nation to the Greekish fashion.... For he built gladly a place of exercise under the tower itself, and brought the chief young men under his subjection.... Now such was the height of Greek fashions, and increase in heathenish manners through the exceeding profaneness of Jason, that ungodly wretch and no high priest; that the priests had no courage to serve any more at the altar, but despising the temple, and neglecting the sacrifices, hastened to be partakers of the unlawful allowance in the place of exercise, after the game of Discus called them forth" (2 Macc. 4[7-14]).

This "place of exercise"—Luther even translated it as a "gaming-house"—was nothing more or less than a stadium. Why then so much excitement over a sports ground? Gymnastics in Jerusalem—discus throwers and sprinters in the holy city—it sounds perhaps unusually progressive, but why should Yahweh be displeased at it, how could a High Priest be denounced as ungodly on that account?

Between the method of playing games today and playing games in those days there is a slight but very essential difference. It has nothing to do with the exercises themselves, which have remained practically the same for over 2,000 years. The difference lies in dress. True to the Olympic pattern, games were played completely naked. The body could only be "covered" with a thin coat of oil!

Nakedness itself must have been regarded by all orthodox believers in Judah as a challenge. They firmly believed in the corruption of human nature from youth onwards and in the sinfulness of the body. It is impossible that athletics in full view of the Temple, only a few steps from the Holy of Holies, should not have been regarded as an outrageous insult or that it should not have given rise to vigorous opposition. According to contemporary sources the High Priest, Jason, had located the stadium in the heart of Jerusalem, in the valley[1] which bordered the Temple hill.

But that was not the end of the scandal. It was not long before Jewish athletes were guilty of a serious crime against the Law, they "made themselves uncircumcised" (1 Macc. 1[15]).

The Greek conception of beauty and the circumcision of Jewish athletes displayed in full view of the public eye were two irreconcilable things. Jewish teams—not in Jerusalem among

---

[1] Josephus calls it the "Tyropoeon"—"(Valley) of the cheesemakers".

their own people naturally—met with scorn and ridicule, and even aversion, as soon as they appeared in contests away from home. The Bible speaks of "the game that . . . every fifth year was kept at Tyrus" (2 Macc. 4[18]), although this does not refer to a Jewish team but to a ceremonial delegation whose duty was confined to the presentation of gifts.

Many of them must have suffered so much from the disgust which they encountered that they sought a remedy. Other translations refer to a surgical operation which restored the natural state (see Kautzsch on 1 Macc. 1[15]).

Nakedness had come for a second time to be Judah's great temptation. Nakedness had been the outstanding characteristic of the fertility goddesses of Canaan, nakedness was now paraded by the athletes in the sports grounds which had sprung up all over the country. In those days a much deeper significance was attached to athletics than to sport in the modern sense. They were religious exercises, dedicated to the foreign Greek gods Zeus and Apollo. The reaction of orthodox Judaism to this revival of a real threat to their religion could only be uncompromising.

Their new overlords, the Seleucids, gave them all too soon every reason to be so.

Chapter 34
THE BATTLE FOR RELIGIOUS LIBERTY

Tax official plunders Jerusalem—Worship of Zeus in the Temple—The revolt of the Maccabees—The Battle of the Elephants at Bethlehem—Americans find Beth-Zur—Coins from Antioch among the rubble—Canteen supplies from Rhodes—Pompey storms Jerusalem—Judah becomes a Roman province.

"And taking the holy vessels with polluted hands, and with profane hands putting down the things that were dedicated by other kings to the augmentation and glory and honour of the place he gave them away" (2 Macc. 5^{16}).

King Antiochus IV,[1] called Epiphanes, plundered and desecrated the Temple in Jerusalem in 168 B.C. Plundering temples was his speciality, so his contemporaries tell us. Polybius, the Greek historian, observed in his forty-volume "History of the World" that Antiochus IV had "despoiled most sanctuaries".

However, the treasures of the Temple were not enough for the Seleucid king. He sent in addition his chief tax collector Apollonius with an armed force to Jerusalem. This man, "when he had taken the spoils of the city, [he] set it on fire, and pulled down the houses and walls thereof on every side. But the women and children took they captive, and possessed the cattle" (1 Macc. 1$^{29-32}$; 2 Macc. 5^{24ff}).

Throughout the chances and changes of its history Israel had been spared none of the horror and ignominy which could befall a nation. But never before, neither under the Assyrians nor under the Babylonians, had it received such a blow as the edict issued

[1] 175–163 B.C.

by Antiochus Epiphanes by which he hoped to crush and destroy the faith of Israel.

> "And the king sent letters by the hand of messengers unto Jerusalem and the cities of Judah, that they should follow laws strange to the land" (1 Macc. 1[44]).

The worship of Olympian Zeus was set up in the Temple of Yahweh. For taking part in any Jewish religious ceremonies, the traditional sacrifices, the sabbath or circumcision, the penalty was death. The holy scriptures were destroyed. This was the first thoroughgoing religious persecution in history.

But Israel gave the world an example of how a nation that refuses to be untrue to itself can and must react to a violation of its conscience of this kind.

There were of course even in those days weak characters who chose the way of least resistance. Nevertheless many ". . . chose rather to die, that they might not be defiled . . ." (1 Macc. 1[63]). But it was the resolute and fervent faith of an old man which first kindled the torch of revolt in the land.

Modin was the name of a small village, 20 miles from Jerusalem on the western fringe of the highlands of Judah. Today it is the market town of el-Medieh. Here lived the priest Mattathias with his five sons. When Antiochus' officers came to Modin to force the inhabitants to "forsake the law", to offer sacrifices and to burn incense, Mattathias steadfastly refused to obey the order, and when he saw one of his countrymen offering a sacrifice he could not "forbear to show his anger according to judgement: wherefore he ran and slew him upon the altar. Also the king's commissioner, who compelled men to sacrifice, he killed at that time, and the altar he pulled down" (1 Macc. 2[1-25]). This act was the signal for open resistance, for a life and death struggle for religious freedom—the "Wars of the Maccabees".

Mattathias and his sons escaped. In their secret haunts in the mountains and in caves they gathered round them a band of those who shared their beliefs and with their assistance waged bitter guerrilla warfare against the occupying power. After the death of the old priest his son Judas, whose surname was Maccabaeus,[1] became the leader.

It was in the highlands of Judah that the rebels achieved their

---

[1] i.e., "Hammer".

first successes. Their achievements were indeed remarkable. This small untrained and badly equipped band mastered the well-drilled and numerically superior occupation troops. Beth-Horon, Emmaus and Beth-Zur were captured. The Seleucids had to retreat until reinforcements arrived from Antioch. Judas Maccabaeus liberated Jerusalem in 164 B.C. and restored the old order in the Temple. The altar was rebuilt and sacrifices to Yahweh were offered as in former times (1 Macc. 4[36ff]).

In the course of military expeditions which took him more and more across the frontiers of the province of Judah, Judas Maccabaeus entered Galilee and Transjordan and wherever there were Israelites who remained true to the old faith. On the way to Idumaea, the old town of Hebron in Southern Judah was besieged and destroyed. This continuing good fortune of Judas Maccabaeus in battle compelled King Antiochus V Eupator,[1] son of Epiphanes, to intervene with a large armed force. In the decisive battle, which took place a few miles south-west of Bethlehem near Beth-Zachariah,[2] the Seleucids employed elephants, flanked by detachments of cavalry. The Maccabeans were unable to cope with this colossal superiority and were defeated. Dissension amongst themselves drove the victors to make peace with surprisingly favourable terms for the vanquished. The decrees of Antiochus IV Epiphanes of 167 B.C. were rescinded, liberty of worship was guaranteed and the religious community at Jerusalem was once more recognised (1 Macc. [30ff,58ff]).

The aims of the Jewish rebellion had been achieved.

Not content with that, the Maccabees wanted political independence as well as freedom of religion. The successors of Judas Maccabaeus, his brothers Jonathan and Simon, began the struggle anew. It ended in 142 B.C. under Simon, with Syria granting them also political freedom (1 Macc. 15[1ff]).

A fortress which was in the midst of the struggle and changed hands several times was Beth-Zur.[3] The results of excavation correspond to the historical circumstances described in the First Book of the Maccabees.

"Khirbet et-Tubeka" is the modern name of this once hotly contested spot. It controls the old road from Jerusalem to Hebron on the frontier between Judah and Idumaea which lies to the south of it. In 1931 the American archaeologist W. F. Albright

---

[1] 163–162 B.C.
[2] Now Bet-Iskarje.
[3] Or Beth-Sur.

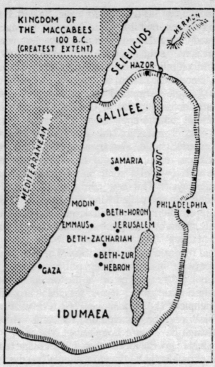

FIG. 69.

and O. P. Sellers found here a large collection of coins. One
hundred and twenty-six out of a total of over 300 were stamped
with the names of Antiochus Epiphanes and Antiochus Eupator.

The hill still bears the foundations of a powerful fortress in
which three stages of construction can be clearly distinguished.
Only fragments remain of the lowest and oldest. They date from
Persian times. The next stage above it is of oriental character.
This is the work of Judas Maccabaeus dating from the first
period of his successful revolt. "And they set there a garrison to
keep it, and fortified Bethsura to preserve it: that the people
might have a defence against Idumaea" (1 Macc. 4[61]).

After the Battle of the Elephants near Beth-Zachariah, Antiochus

V Eupator occupied this border fortress: "So the king took Bethsura, and set a garrison there to keep it" (1 Macc. 6[50]).

The troops of the Seleucids likewise have left unmistakable traces of their stay. As the archaeologists were able to establish, these consisted of relics of their catering arrangements, which were found among the ruins of the walls erected by Judas Maccabaeus. Part of the rations of these soldiers was wine of excellent quality from the hills of Greece. From the handles of the jars, which lay about among the mass of broken earthenware, Albright and Sellers were even able to tell where the wine came from. A wine merchant in Rhodes must have been the army's principal supplier.

That was in 162 B.C. A year later the Seleucids fortified Beth-Zur anew. A new citadel, with characteristic Hellenistic masonry, arose upon the ruined Maccabean walls. Their general Bacchides "repaired the strong cities in Judah. . . . He fortified also the city Bethsura . . . and put forces in them and provision of victuals" (1 Macc. 9[50,52]).

The Biblical record ends with the murder of Simon, brother of Judas Maccabaeus. The spiritual and political leadership of Judas was transferred, with the office of High Priest, to Simon's son John. He was called John Hyrcanus. "John, the High Priest, and the Jewish people" and "John the High Priest, Head of the Jewish people" are the inscriptions on coins which he had minted and which have since been found.

We are indebted to Flavius Josephus' careful account of the history of the period for accurate information about this Maccabean and his successors.[1] By dint of incessant and purposeful fighting the frontiers of Judah were extended farther and farther. Under Alexander Jannaeus[2] they enlarged their territories until they almost covered the area previously occupied by the kingdoms of Israel and Judah.

As time went on the Seleucids became less and less serious adversaries. They lacked the strength to cope with the Maccabeans when Rome—now, having overthrown Hannibal of Carthage,[3] undisputed mistress of the Western Mediterranean—had expanded its sovereignty beyond Greece into Asia Minor.

[1] Josephus calls them "Hasmoneans" from the name of their ancestor the father of Mattathias ("Wars of the Jews", I, 1. 3).

[2] 103–76 B.C.

[3] At the battle of Zama in 202 B.C.

Pompey, the Roman general, marched through the kingdom of the Seleucids into Palestine. After a three months' siege Roman legions entered Jerusalem in 63 B.C. Judah became a Roman province.

With this event the political independence of Israel came to an abrupt end.

DIGGING UP
THE NEW TESTAMENT

I
Jesus of Nazareth

Chapter 35
PALESTINE ON MARE NOSTRUM

A Province of the Roman Empire—Greek cities on the Jordan—The New Testament—The governor appears in history—A census every fourteen years.

"But when the fulness of the time was come God sent forth his son. . . ." (Gal. 4[4]).

In the wide circle of countries which surround Mare Nostrum,[1] from North Africa and Spain to the shores of Asia Minor, the will of Rome, now mistress of the world, reigned supreme. After the disappearance of the great Semitic empires of the "Fertile Crescent", Palestine was drawn into the new world and shared its destinies. Roman occupation troops enforced the will of Rome in a land which was ruled and exploited by men who were likewise nominees of Rome.

Life in the Roman Empire took on more and more the stamp of Greece: Roman civilisation was to a large extent Greek civilisation: Greek was the world language which united all the subject peoples of the East.

Anyone wandering through Palestine at the turn of the eras might have imagined he was in Greece. Across the Jordan lay out and out Greek cities. The "Ten Cities"[2] of the gospels (Matt. 4[25]; Mk. 5[20]) took Athens as their model: they had temples which were sacred to Zeus and Artemis, they had their theatre, their pillared forum, their stadium, their gymnasium and their baths. Greek in architecture as well as in the habits of their citizens were likewise Caesarea, the seat of Pilate's government, which lay on the Mediterranean south of Carmel, Sepphoris and

---

[1] The Roman name for the Mediterranean.
[2] Greek: Dekapolis.

Tiberias, which lay a few miles north of Nazareth on the Lake of Galilee, Caesarea Philippi, built at the foot of Hermon, and likewise Jericho. Only the many small towns and villages in Galilee, as in Judah, had retained their Jewish style of architecture. It was in these genuine Jewish communities that Jesus lived and worked, and nowhere do the Gospel writers speak of his ever having lived *in* one of the Greek cities but only in their neighbourhood (Mark 7[31]).

Nevertheless Greek dress and much of the Greek way of life had long before Jesus' day penetrated into the purely Jewish communities. Natives of Galilee and Judah wore the same sort of clothes as were worn in Alexandria, Rome or Athens. These consisted of tunic and cloak, shoes or sandals, with a hat or a cap as head covering. Furniture included a bed and the Greek habit of reclining at meals was generally adopted.

The Old Testament covers a period of nearly 1,200 years if we reckon from the Exodus from Egypt under Moses, or nearly 2,000 years if we reckon from the time of the patriarchs. The New Testament on the other hand covers a period of less than 100 years. From the beginning of the ministry of Jesus to the end of the Acts of the Apostles is only a little more than thirty years. The Old Testament largely reflects the varied history of the people of Israel; the New Testament is concerned with the life and sayings of a few individuals: it revolves exclusively round the teaching of Jesus, round his disciples and the apostles.

Archaeology cannot produce extensive evidence from the world of the New Testament. For the life of Christ offers nothing that would leave any material traces on this earth: neither royal palaces nor temples, neither victorious campaigns nor burnt cities and countrysides. Jesus was essentially a man of peace, he taught the Word of God. Archaeologists have recognised their task to be that of reconstructing his environment and rediscovering the villages and cities where he lived, worked and died. Yet for this purpose they have been given a unique guide. No event out of the whole of Graeco-Roman history, no manuscript of any classical author has come down to posterity in anything like so many ancient copies as the scriptures of the New Testament. They can be numbered in thousands, and the oldest and most venerable among them are only a few decades removed from the time of Christ.

A manuscript containing part of St. John's Gospel, for example, the famous Papyrus Bodmer II, comes from the time of Trajan, the Roman emperor who reigned from A.D. 98–117. This precious document in Greek script, so far probably the oldest New Testament writing, was discovered by a lucky chance in Egypt in 1935.

"And it came to pass in those days that there went out a decree from Caesar Augustus that all the world should be taxed. (And this taxing was first made when Cyrenius was governor of Syria.) And all went to be taxed every one into his own city. And Joseph also went up from Galilee, out of the city of Nazareth, into Judaea, unto the city of David, which is called Bethlehem (because he was of the house and lineage of David) to be taxed with Mary his espoused wife..." (Luke 2$^{1-5}$).

The census is by no means the invention of modern statisticians. Practised in ancient times, it fulfilled then as now two extremely reasonable purposes. It provided the relevant information firstly for calling up men for military service and secondly for taxation purposes. In subject countries it was the second of these that mostly concerned the Romans.

Without exacting tribute from its foreign possessions, Rome would never have been able on the strength of its own resources to afford the luxury of its much admired magnificent buildings and pleasances, its extravagant way of living, or its expensive system of administering its empire. Roman emperors were able to guarantee their people "Panem et Circenses", "bread and circuses", on a grand scale at no cost to themselves. Egypt had to provide the corn for the free bread. And the great arenas for the games were built by slaves with money derived from tribute.

The census, which was its official name in Rome, was originally held every five years. This five year period even entered the literature of Rome as the "lustrum" and this word enjoyed great favour among Roman writers and in formal speech. Changes in the economy as well as in the constitution, the introduction of immunity from taxation for Roman citizens and the troubles of the later Republican period led to the gradual abandonment of the census. Especially in the later Republican period there was no longer any question of a regular five yearly census. It is true that Augustus revived the census, particularly in the provinces, but even he did not reintroduce it on the old five year basis. It is important to remember this for the dating of the birth of Jesus depends upon it to some extent.

"Cyrenius the governor" was the senator P. Sulpicius Quirinius, who is otherwise known to us from Roman documents. The Emperor Augustus rated highly the outstanding ability of this social climber both as soldier and administrator. He was born in modest circumstances near Tusculum in the Alban hills, a place which was reckoned among the favourite resorts of the noble Roman families.

In A.D. 6 Quirinius went as legate to Syria. Coponius was sent with him from Rome to be the first Procurator of Judaea. Between A.D. 6 and 7 they carried out a census. Can this refer, however, to the census mentioned by St. Luke? In the first place, Luke speaks of an Imperial decree "that all the world should be taxed", i.e., the whole Roman empire. But the census taken in the years 6 and 7 A.D. was merely a provincial one and, secondly, Jesus would then have been born around 7 or 6 B.C. as many believe. According to the Biblical account, the census decreed by Caesar Augustus took place about the year Christ was born. There is no record of a general census throughout the empire in the years 7 and 6 B.C.

Is it possible that St. Luke made a mistake?

For a long time it seemed as if he had. It was only when a fragment of a Roman inscription was discovered at Antioch that the surprising fact emerged that Quirinius had been in Syria once before on a mission from the Emperor Augustus in the days of Saturninus the pro-consul.

At that time his assignment had been purely military. He led a campaign against the Homonadenses, a tribe in the Taurus mountains in Asia Minor. Quirinius established his seat of government as well as his headquarters in Syria between 10 and 7 B.C.

Chapter 36
THE STAR OF BETHLEHEM

A suggestion by Origen—Halley's comet over China—Kepler's observations in Prague—Astronomical tablets found at Sippar—Babylonian astronomers' records—Modern astronomical calculations—December frost in Bethlehem.

"Now when Jesus was born in Bethlehem of Judaea, in the days of Herod the king, behold, there came wise men from the east to Jerusalem, saying, Where is he that is born king of the Jews? for we have seen his star in the east, and are come to worship him" (Matt. 2[1,2]).

International expeditions of astronomers have been regarded as a matter of course for a long time now. Scientists from all countries, laden with special instruments and measuring apparatus, stream into every corner of the globe when there is a total eclipse or some other important astronomical phenomenon to be observed.

For centuries St. Matthew's story of the Messianic star has exercised men's imaginations. Laymen and experts alike have aired their views on the subject and these have found expression in a considerable volume of literature. Anything that has ever moved across the canopy of heaven, as well as much that has only existed in men's imaginations, has been dubbed the "Star of Bethlehem".

That this is a case of a phenomenon in the sky of quite an unusual type is indicated by the Bible in unmistakable terms. Astronomers are the experts in these matters of heavenly phenomena and we should therefore expect from them an explanation which would fit in with modern scientific knowledge.

If we think of a sudden bright light in the sky, we can only reckon with two types, apart from shooting stars: either a comet or an exploding star, technically known as a "nova".

Conjectures of this kind were expressed in early times. Origen, one of the Christian Fathers, who lived in Alexandria about A.D. 200, wrote as follows: "I am of the opinion that the star which appeared to the Wise Men in the east was a new star which had nothing in common with those stars which appear either in the firmament or in the lower levels of the atmosphere. Presumably it belonged to the category of these heavenly fires which appear from time to time and have been given names by the Greeks depending on their shape, either comets, or fiery beams, or starry hosts, or starry tails, or vessels or some such name."

Bright comets, with tails often stretching half across the sky, have always made a deep impression on men's minds. They were held to portend special events. Is it surprising that this most magnificent of all stellar spectacles should be associated with the idea of the star of the Wise Men of the East? Artists seized upon this attractive motif: in many popular representations of the crib in pictures of the birth of Christ a radiant comet shines over the manger bed of Bethlehem.

Excavations and ancient writings which have come to light have produced astonishingly detailed information about astronomical occurrences stretching back over thousands of years. We now possess notes and observations from Greek, Roman, Babylonian, Egyptian and Chinese sources.

After the assassination of Caesar, shortly after the Ides of March in 44 B.C., a brilliant comet was seen. Seventeen years before the turn of the eras, another extremely bright comet appeared suddenly, and was observed for a whole night in Mediterranean countries. The next dazzling comet to be reported was in the year A.D. 66, shortly before Nero committed suicide.

Between these two there is another account with most precise details, this time from Chinese astronomers. Their observations are recorded in the Wen-hien-thung-khao encyclopaedia of the Chinese scholar Ma Tuan-lin: "In the first year of [the Emperor] Yuen-yen, in the 7th month, on the day Sin-ouei [25 August] a comet was seen in the region of the sky known as Toung-tsing [beside the Mu of the Gemini]. It passed over the Ou-tschoui-heou [Gemini], proceeded from the Ho-su [Castor and Pollux] in a northerly direction and then into the group of Hien-youen [the head of Leo] and into the house of Thaiouei [tail of Leo]. . . . On the 56th day it disappeared with the Blue Dragon [Scorpio]. Altogether the comet was observed for 63 days.''

This very full account from ancient Chinese sources contains the first description of the famous Halley's comet, that great trailing star which always reappears close to the sun after an interval of seventy-six years. The last time it was seen was between 1909 and 1911. The strange display will be seen again in 1986. For the comet keeps to a strict time schedule on its tremendous elliptical course through space. But it is not always visible and not equally visible everywhere. Thus in the year 12 B.C. in China it was an astral phenomenon which could be accurately observed in all its phases. Whereas in the Mediterranean countries, in Mesopotamia and Egypt, there is no mention whatever at that time of a heavenly body of such striking and impressive brilliance.

The same is true of "new stars". These "Novae" are constellations in space which suddenly burst asunder in an atomic explosion of colossal magnitude. Their radiance, which outshines the light of all other stars, is so noticeable and so unusual that it is always remarked upon. About the turn of the eras the blazing light of a new star is only twice mentioned, in 134 B.C. and A.D. 173. None of the old sources and traditions says anything about a bright comet or a new star in the Mediterranean world about the year A.D. 1.

Shortly before Christmas 1603, on December 17th, the Imperial Mathematician and Astronomer Royal Johannes Kepler was sitting through the night high above the Moldava in the Hradçyn in Prague, observing with his modest telescope the approach of two planets. "Conjunction" is the technical name for the position of two celestial bodies on the same degree of longitude. Sometimes two planets move so close to one another that they have the appearance of a single larger and more brilliant star. That night Saturn and Jupiter had a rendezvous in space within the constellation of Pisces.

Looking through his notes later Kepler suddenly remembered something he had read in the rabbinic writer Abarbanel, referring to an unusual influence which Jewish astrologers were said to have ascribed to this same constellation. Messiah would appear when there was a conjunction of Saturn and Jupiter in the constellation of Pisces.

Could it have been the same conjunction at the time of the birth of Christ as Kepler had observed at Christmastide in 1603?

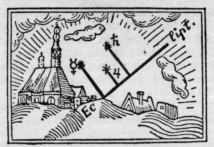

FIG. 70.—Conjunction of Mercury, Jupiter and Saturn in December 1603 according to Kepler.

Had it announced, as Kepler wrote later, the coming of the real "Star of Bethlehem"? Or was this constellation perhaps itself the "Christmas Star" as some people believed at a still later date with Kepler as their authority?

Kepler checked his calculations again and again. He was a mixture of scholar and quack, astronomer and astrologer, a disciple of those doctrines which had been put in the same class as mixing poisons as far back as the Code of Justinian. The result was a three-fold conjunction within the space of a year. Astronomical calculations gave the year as 7 B.C. According to astrological tables it must have been 6 B.C. Kepler decided in favour of 6 B.C. and dated the conception of Mary consequently 7 B.C.

His fascinating discovery was published in a number of books, but this enlightened genius who established the planetary laws named after him eventually steeped himself overmuch in the realm of mysticism. Consequently Kepler's hypotheses were for a long time rejected and finally disregarded. It was not until the 19th century that astronomers remembered them again.

Finally in 1925 the German scholar P. Schnabel deciphered the "papers" in Neo-Babylonian cuneiform of a famous professional institute in the ancient world, the School of Astrology at Sippar in Babylonia. Among endless series of prosaic dates of observations he came across a note about the position of the planets in the constellation of Pisces. Jupiter and Saturn are carefully marked in over a period of five months. Reckoned in our calendar the year was 7 B.C.!

Archaeologists and historians have to reconstruct their picture of a bygone age with enormous effort, from monuments and documents, from individual discoveries and fragments. It is simpler for the modern astronomer. He can turn back the cosmic clock at will. In his planetarium he can arrange the starry sky exactly as it was thousands of years ago for any given year, any month, even any day. The position of the stars can be calculated backwards with equal precision.

In the year 7 B.C. Jupiter and Saturn did in fact meet in Pisces and, as Kepler had already discovered, they met three times. Mathematical calculations established further that this threefold conjunction of the planets was particularly clearly visible in the Mediterranean area.

The time-table of this planetary encounter when it is presented in the prosaic dating system of modern astronomical calculations looks something like this:

About the end of February in 7 B.C. the clustering began. Jupiter moved out of the constellation Aquarius towards Saturn in the constellation of Pisces. Since the sun at that time was also in the sign of Pisces its light covered the constellation. It was not until April 12th that both planets rose in Pisces heliacally with a difference of 8 degrees of longitude. "Heliacal" is the word used by astronomers to indicate the first visible rising of a star at daybreak.

On May 29th, visible for fully two hours in the morning sky,

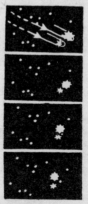

FIG. 71.—Third conjunction of Jupiter and Saturn on December 4th in 7 B.C. in the constellation of Pisces.

the first close encounter took place in the 21st degree of Pisces
with a difference of 0 degrees of longitude and of 0.98 degrees
of latitude.

The second conjunction took place on October 3rd in the 18th
degree of the constellation of Pisces.

On December 4th for the third and last time a close encounter
of the planets Jupiter and Saturn took place. This time it was in
the 16th degree of Pisces. At the end of January in the year 6
B.C. the planet Jupiter moved out of Pisces into Aries.

"We have seen his star in the east" (Matt. 2^2), said the Wise
Men, according to the A.V. The translation is however incorrect,
for the words "in the east" are in the original "En té anatolé"—
the Greek singular—but elsewhere "the east" is represented by
"anatolai"—the Greek plural. The singular form "anatolé"
has, it is maintained, quite a special astronomical significance, in
that it implies the observation of the early rising of the star, the
so-called heliacal rising. The translators of the Authorised Version could not have known this.

When "en té anatolé" is translated properly, Matt. 2^2 reads as
follows:

"We have seen his star appear in the first rays of dawn." That
would have corresponded exactly with the astronomical facts, if
the constellation under discussion, and this, of course, is the big
question, was the Star of the Wise Men, the Star of Bethlehem,
the Christmas Star. Perhaps the following considerations will
help us.

But why this ancient learned expedition of the three Wise Men
to Palestine when, as we know, they could see the occurrence
just as well in Babylon?

The skygazers of the East in their capacity as astrologers
attached a special significance to each star. According to the
Chaldeans, Pisces was the sign of the West, the Mediterranean
countries: in Jewish tradition it was the sign of Israel, the sign of
the Messiah. The constellation of Pisces stood at the end of the
sun's old course and at the beginning of its new one. What is
more likely than that they saw in it the sign of the end of an old
age and the start of a new one?

Jupiter was always thought of by all nations as a lucky star
and a royal star. According to old Jewish tradition Saturn was
supposed to protect Israel: Tacitus equates him with the god of
the Jews. Babylonian astrology reckoned the ringed planet to be
the special star of the neighbouring lands of Syria and Palestine.

Since Nebuchadnezzar's time many thousands of Jews had lived in Babylon. Many of them may have studied at the School of Astrology in Sippar. This wonderful encounter of Jupiter with Saturn, guardian of Israel, in the constellation of the "west country", of the Messiah, must have deeply moved the Jewish astrologers. For according to astrological ways of thinking it pointed to the appearance of a mighty king in the west country, the land of their fathers. To experience that in person, to see it with their own eyes, that was the reason for the journey of the wise astronomers from the East.

This is what may have happened: on May 29th in the year 7 B.C. they observed the first encounter of the two planets from the roof of the School of Astrology at Sippar. At that time of year the heat was already unbearable in Mesopotamia. Summer is no time for long and difficult journeys. Besides that, they knew about the second conjunction on October 3rd. They could predict this encounter in advance as accurately as future eclipses of the sun and moon. The fact that October 3rd was the Jewish Day of Atonement may have been taken as an admonition, and at that point they may have started out on their journey.

Travel on the caravan routes even on camels, the swiftest means of transport, was a leisurely affair. If we think in terms of a journey lasting about six weeks, the Wise Men would arrive in Jerusalem towards the end of November.

"Where is he that is born King of the Jews? for we have seen his star in the east, and are come to worship him." "When Herod the king had heard these things, he was troubled, and all Jerusalem with him" (Matt. 2^{2-3}). For these Eastern astronomers that must have been the first and obvious question, which would however arouse nothing but startled concern in Jerusalem. They knew nothing about schools of astrology in the Holy City.

Herod, the hated tyrant, was alarmed. The announcement of a new-born king brought his sovereignty into question. The people on the other hand were pleasurably startled, as appears from other historical sources. About a year after this conjunction of planets which has just been described, a strong Messianic movement came into being. Flavius Josephus, the Jewish historian, records that about this time a rumour went around that God had decided to bring the rule of the Roman foreigners to an end and that a sign from heaven had announced the coming of a Jewish king. Herod, who had been appointed by the Romans, was in fact not a Jew but an Idumaean.

Herod did not hesitate. He "gathered all the chief priests and scribes of the people together" and "demanded of them where Christ should be born". They searched through the ancient sacred scriptures of the nation and found the allusion which is contained in the book of the prophet Micah, who had lived 700 years before in the kingdom of Judah: "But thou, Bethlehem Ephratah, though thou be little among the thousands of Judah, yet out of thee shall he come forth unto me that is to be ruler in Israel..." (Micah 5^2).

Herod therefore summoned the Wise Men and "sent them to Bethlehem" (Matt. 2^{4-8}). Since Jupiter and Saturn came together for the third time in the constellation of Pisces on the 4th December, "they rejoiced with exceeding great joy" and set out for Bethlehem "and lo, the star, which they saw in the east, went before them" (Matt. $2^{10,9}$).

On the road to Hebron, 5 miles from Jerusalem, lies the village of "Bet Lahm", which was the old Bethlehem of Judah. The ancient highway, which Abraham had once passed along, lay almost due north and south. At their third conjunction the planets Jupiter and Saturn appeared to have dissolved into one great brilliant star. In the twilight of the evening they were visible in a southerly direction, so that the Wise Men of the East on their way from Jerusalem to Bethlehem had the bright star in front of their eyes all the time. As the gospel says, the star actually "went before them".

Every year millions of people all over the world hear the story of the Wise Men of the East. "Star of Bethlehem", a symbol which is always associated with Christmas, impinges on life in other ways. In biographical dictionaries and on tombstones it has its place beside the date of birth.

Christendom celebrates Christmas from December 24–25. Astronomers and historians, secular and ecclesiastical, are however unanimous that December 25 of the year one was not the authentic date of the birth of Christ, neither as regards the year nor the day. The responsibility for this lies at the door of the Scythian monk Dionysius Exiguus, who made several mistakes and miscalculations. He lived in Rome, and in the year 533 he was instructed to fix the beginning of the new era by working backwards. But he forgot the year zero which should have been inserted between 1 B.C. and A.D. 1. He also overlooked the four years when the Roman emperor Augustus had reigned under his own name Octavian.

The Biblical tradition gives us this clear indication: "Now when Jesus was born in Bethlehem of Judaea, in the days of Herod the king..." (Matt. 2[1]). We know from numerous contemporary sources who Herod was and when he lived and reigned. In 40 B.C. Herod was designated king of Judaea by the Romans. His reign ended with his death in 4 B.C. Jesus must therefore have been born before 4 B.C. if Matthew's statement is correct.

December 25 is referred to in documents as Christmas Day in A.D. 354 for the first time. Under the Roman emperor Justinian[1] it was recognised as an official holiday. An old Roman festival played a major part in the choice of this particular day. December 25 in ancient Rome was the "Dies Natalis Invicti", "the birthday of the unconquered", the day of the winter solstice and at the same time, in Rome, the last day of the Saturnalia, which had long since degenerated into a week of unbridled carnival, and therefore a time when the Christians could feel most safe from persecution.

Meteorologists as well as historians and astronomers have something of importance to contribute to this question of fixing the date of the birth of Jesus. According to St. Luke: "And there were in the same country shepherds abiding in the field, keeping watch over their flock by night" (Luke 2[8]).

Meteorologists have made exact recordings of the temperature at Hebron. This spot in the southern part of the highlands of Judah exhibits the same climatic conditions as Bethlehem, which is not far distant. The temperature readings show over a period of three months that the incidence of frost is as follows: December —2.8°; January—1.6°; February—0.1°. The first two months have also the greatest rainfall in the year: approximately 6 inches in December, and nearly 8 inches in January. According to all existing information the climate of Palestine has not changed appreciably in the last 2,000 years, consequently modern accurate meteorological observations can be taken as a basis.

At Christmas-time Bethlehem is in the grip of frost, and in the Promised Land no cattle would have been in the fields in that temperature. This fact is borne out by a remark in the Talmud to the effect that in that neighbourhood the flocks were put out to grass in March and brought in again at the beginning of November. They remained out in the open for almost eight months.

[1] A.D. 527–565.

Around Christmas-time nowadays both animals and shepherds are under cover in Palestine.

What St. Luke tells us points therefore to the birth of Jesus as having taken place before the onset of winter, and the description of the brilliant star in St. Matthew's gospel points to the year 7 B.C.

In recent years, several publications dealing with the life of Christ have appeared. They have attracted a good deal of attention although some of them are not from the pens of professional Biblical specialists. We cannot merely disregard them, as some of them provide us with thoroughly prepared collections of material while also presenting us with a reliable assessment of the opinions of the specialists. These publications have not actually produced any new facts, although they have sometimes shed new light on already published material. Yet, in fact, this new light is not really new, for these views have for long been under discussion among the experts. The public has been made aware of these questions, however, by these publications and this is a sufficient reason for not neglecting them.

It will probably not be generally realised that Johannes Kepler himself did not consider the conjunction of the planets Mercury, Jupiter and Saturn, which he had calculated, as the actual "Star of Bethlehem", the "Christmas Star", but merely as its forerunner. For his part he still remained convinced that Jesus was born *later* and not as early as 7 or 6 B.C. Of course, nobody can guarantee that in the days of Jesus people saw any connection between him and the heavenly phenomenon calculated by Kepler and observed in Babylon. Everything else that can be deduced and has actually been deduced from this heavenly phenomenon and from the fact that it was also noticed in Mesopotamia may indeed be very ingenious, but it remains mere speculation, however brilliant, which in itself lacks all conclusiveness and would require convincing proof in order to be unreservedly accepted as correct.

For the problem of the "assessment" mentioned in Luke 2^{1-5} still remains. It is a historical fact that it was made in the year 6/7 *after* Christ's birth, although with the reservation that during the year in question no general census throughout the empire was made, as Luke asserts, but merely a limited provincial one.

In consequence of all these facts and considerations, the views expressed today in regard to the date of the birth of Jesus are much more restrained than was the case a few years ago. The period between the year 7 B.C. (if Kepler's conjunction of planets is to be connected in any way with the birth of Jesus) and the year A.D. 7 (on account of the population census by Quirinius) is the time span in question. Jesus must have been born during this period. It is not possible today to be more specific . . .

One thing is remarkable. Towards the end of Herod's reign, about the year 6 B.C., a Messianic dispute between Herod, who regarded himself as a kind of Messiah, and the Pharisees who had other notions about the Messiah, became so acute that the Pharisees predicted Herod's early death, whereupon Herod had the ringleaders executed. This was about the time of Kepler's conjunction of the planets. We naturally do not know whether there were people who believed in the stars and who actually ascribed some Messianic interpretation to this conjunction and whether it was this, among other things, which inflamed people's minds and feelings. That would, however, be a possibility. It would also be possible that the action taken by Herod against his opponents in the Messianic quarrel was the reason why the Evangelist Matthew portrays Herod as a pitiless persecutor of the Messiah who did not even shrink from the Massacre of the Innocents at Bethlehem (Matthew 2[16]).

Chapter 37
NAZARETH IN GALILEE

Death of King Herod—"The most cruel tyrant"—Unrest in the land—Checking Jerusalem's finances—Sabinus steals the Temple treasures—Varus crucifies 2,000 Jews—"Nazarene" or "Nazarite"?

"But when Herod was dead, behold, an angel of the Lord appeareth in a dream to Joseph in Egypt, saying, Arise, and take the young child and his mother, and go into the land of Israel: for they are dead which sought the young child's life. . . . But when he heard that Archelaus did reign in Judaea in the room of his father Herod, he was afraid to go thither" (Matt. 2^{19,20,22}).

Herod died at the age of seventy in 4 B.C., thirty-six years after Rome had made him king. It is said that immediately after his death there occurred an eclipse of the moon which modern astronomers reckon to have happened on March 13th.

Flavius Josephus passes harsh judgement on him when he comes to write about Herod a few decades later: "He was no king but the most cruel tyrant who ever ascended the throne. He murdered a vast number of people and the lot of those he left alive was so miserable that the dead might count themselves fortunate. He not only tortured his subjects singly but ill treated whole communities. In order to beautify foreign cities he robbed his own, and made gifts to foreign nations which were paid for with Jewish blood. The result was that instead of their former prosperity and time honoured customs the people fell victim to utter poverty and demoralisation. Within a few years the Jews suffered more misery through Herod than their forefathers had done in the long period since they left Babylon and returned under Xerxes."

In thirty-six years hardly a day passed without someone being sentenced to death. Herod spared no one, neither his own family nor his closest friends, neither the priests nor least of all the people. On his list of victims stand the names of the two husbands of his sister Salome, his wife Mariamne and his sons Alexander and Aristobulus. He had his brother-in-law drowned in the Jordan and his mother-in-law Alexandra put out of the way. Two scholars who had torn down the golden Roman eagle from the gateway of the Temple were burned alive. Hyrcanus the last of the Hasmoneans was killed. Noble families were exterminated root and branch. Many of the Pharisees were done away with. Five days before his death the old man had his son Antipater assassinated. And that is only a fraction of the crimes of this man who "ruled like a wild beast".

The Massacre of the Innocents at Bethlehem, which the Bible lays at his door (Matt. 2^{16}), fits in perfectly with this revolting picture of his character.

After the murder of Antipater, Herod on his death bed made a will in which he nominated three of his younger sons as his successors. Archelaus was to succeed to the kingdom, Herod Antipas and Philip were to be tetrarchs, rulers of Galilee and Peraea, part of Transjordan, and the territory north-east of the Lake of Galilee. Archelaus was acknowledged as king by his family and was acclaimed by Herod's mercenaries—Germans, Gauls and Thracians. But throughout the country the news of the despot's death brought uprisings of a violence which had seldom been seen in Jewry. Their burning hatred of the house of Herod was mingled with their loathing of the Romans.

Instead of lamenting the death of Herod they proclaimed their grief over the deaths of his innocent victims. The people demanded that the learned Jehuda ben Saripha and Mattathias ben Margoloth, who had been burned like torches, should be atoned for. Archelaus replied by sending his troops to Jerusalem. Three thousand people were butchered on one day alone. The courts of the Temple were strewn with corpses. This first act of Archelaus revealed at one stroke the true character of the man—Herod's son yielded nothing to his father in cruelty and injustice.

However, the will had to be approved by the Emperor Augustus. Archelaus and Herod Antipas accordingly set out for Rome one after the other. At the same time fifty of the elders representing the people of Israel hastened to Augustus to beseech him to rid them of this "monarchy". In the absence of the Herodians the unrest assumed more serious proportions. As a security measure a Roman legion was despatched to Jerusalem. Right in the midst of this turmoil, as luck would have it, there arrived one of the hated Romans in the person of Sabinus, agent of the Imperial Treasury. Disregarding all warnings he took up his abode in Herod's palace and proceeded to audit the taxes and tribute of Judaea.

Masses of pilgrims were streaming into the Holy City for the Feast of Weeks. Bloody clashes ensued. Bitter fighting broke out in the Temple area. Stones were thrown at the Roman troops. They set fire to the arcades, then rushed into the Temple and pillaged all they could lay hands on. Sabinus himself relieved the Temple treasury of 400 talents. At which point he had to retreat precipitately to the palace and barricade himself in.

Revolt spread from Jerusalem through the country like wildfire. The royal palaces of Judaea were plundered and set ablaze. The governor of Syria hastened to the scene with a powerful Roman army strengthened with troops from Beirut and Arabia. As soon as the marching columns appeared in sight of Jerusalem the rebels fled. They were pursued and captured in droves.

Two thousand men were crucified.

The Roman governor of Syria who issued this order wrote his name in the history books through a decisive defeat which he suffered in A.D. 9. He was Quintilius Varus, who was posted from Syria to Germany, and lost the battle of the Teutoburgian Forest.

This was the terrifying situation when Joseph, on his way back from Egypt, "heard that Archelaus did reign in Judaea in the room of his father Herod". It was for this reason that "he was afraid to go thither".

King Herod is one of those figures in world history whom we know only from what their adversaries said about them. The impression created is correspondingly sinister. It is confirmed by the account of the Massacre of the Innocents at Bethlehem (Matthew 2¹⁶). At the same time, however, it must be remembered that we have here an example of the widespread literary motive of the chosen child, who for that very reason is exposed to danger—a motive that was attached to a number of prominent figures in antiquity, to Sargon of Akkad, Moses, Cyrus the Great and even to the Emperor Augustus as well as to such mythical characters as Oedipus whom his father Laius maimed and rejected.

We have consequently become much more cautious nowadays in regard to our views on the historicity of the Massacre of the Innocents at Bethlehem. Today we look upon the doubtful story rather as an attempt, prompted by the mentality of those days and using the methods current at the time, to emphasise the importance of Jesus. In so doing, matters such as the historicity of the measures taken by Herod in his quarrel with the Pharisees concerning the Messiah form an additional factor (cf. the end of the preceding chapter). Furthermore, the story of the Massacre of the Innocents linked Jesus with Moses who, as the Bible tells us, miraculously escaped from similar persecution by the Pharaoh of Egypt (Exodus 1^{15}-2^{10}). Herod's persecution of Jesus fits in very well with the flight of Joseph, Mary and the child to Egypt, for which the Evangelist gives as the real reason: ". . . that it might be fulfilled which was spoken of the Lord by the prophet, saying, Out of Egypt have I called my son" (Matthew 2^{15}; cf. also Hosea 11^1). This constitutes another reference to Moses whose name can mean "son" in Egyptian. On the other hand, there is absolutely no historical or archaeological proof of the flight to Egypt any more than there is for Jesus' stay in Nazareth.

Strictly speaking, the term "Nazarene" is capable of more than one interpretation. Although it means "man from Nazareth", there may also be a punning intention on the Hebrew word *nezer* which means "twig" or "rod" (cf. Isaiah 11^1: ". . . a rod out of the stem of Jesse"). The word "Nazarene" occurs in Matthew in connection with a promise: ". . . that it might be fulfilled which was spoken by the prophets, He shall be called a Nazarene" (Matthew 2^{23}). This does not make matters any easier, for to which words Matthew is referring, if not to the words quoted from Isaiah, is not clear. Perhaps a certain echo of the appellation *Nazarite* ("consecrated by or dedicated to God") is intended, although this presents certain philological difficulties. *Nazarite* is a descriptive term, earlier applied to Samson (Judges $13^{5,7}$, also 16^{17}) which demanded of him who claimed to be one, a certain asceticism, such as the observance of a number of taboos. Again there is uncertainty and it cannot be denied that more than one specialist considers the statements in the Gospels regarding the birth-place of Jesus as emanations from the fantasy of the Gospel writers who, not properly understanding the word, simply changed it to Nazarene. Mark Lidzbarski has even asserted that a place called Nazareth did not exist in the time of Jesus. It can be objected, however, even if we do not know what Nazareth was called in Jesus' day, that occupation of this spot, if by "occupation" we mean living in wretched caves, was continuous from about 900 B.C. to about A.D. 600, as has been shown by the unearthing of small objects among which are a number dating from the time of King Herod the Great (40 or 37–4 B.C.). The somewhat deprecatory words of Nathanael (John 1[46]): "Can there any good thing come out of Nazareth?" may well refer to the wretchedness of the place in those days, although the Bible calls it a "town". There is no reference to Jesus, Mary or Joseph. The spring in Nazareth where women still draw water in pitchers as they did in the time of Jesus is not on record under the name "Mary's spring or fountain" before the 11th century . . .

Chapter 38
JOHN THE BAPTIST

The witness of Josephus—A forbidden marriage—Herod Antipas orders an arrest—The castle of Machaerus in Moab—The dungeon of death—Princess Salome—Capernaum "on the sea"—Ruins in a eucalyptus grove—The place where Jesus taught.

"Then cometh Jesus from Galilee to Jordan, unto John, to be baptised of him" (Matt. 3^{13}).

This was the event which took Jesus for the first time from his Nazareth home. After the years of childhood and youth, about which we are told almost nothing, he stepped on to the stage for his public ministry. "And Jesus himself, when he began to teach, was about thirty years of age" (Luke 3^{23}—R.V.).

John preached and baptised in the Jordan valley south of Jericho, where the river is crossed by the well-known ford. He was therefore in the territory of Herod Antipas, the tetrarch appointed by Rome.

Apart from his baptism of Jesus, it is principally through his tragic end that John has become known throughout the world. He was beheaded.

Specialists are puzzled by many questions concerning him. What was his attitude towards the Essenes who left behind them the famous Dead Sea scrolls in Qumran? Was he perhaps a Nazarite, as the Old Testament calls the sort of person, like the hero Samson, who had dedicated himself entirely to God and as a sign of this observed certain taboos? And was he really the forerunner of Jesus as the New Testament describes him? What part did he play in the Messianic movements of his day? Did he consider himself, or did people consider him perhaps as a kind of Messiah? Was he perhaps, as has been suggested, a sort of rival to Jesus whom the Jesus tradition has appropriated and remodelled as the forerunner of Jesus?

Did the godly Baptist, who appears at the decisive turning point in Jesus' life, exist at all? His contemporary, Josephus, tells us that John was a high-minded man "who urged the Jews to strive towards perfection and exhorted them to deal justly with one another and walk humbly with God and to present themselves for baptism. As they flocked to him from all directions Herod Antipas began to be alarmed lest the influence of such a man might lead to disturbances. In consequence of Herod's suspicions John was put in chains, sent to the castle of Machaerus and there beheaded."

"For Herod had laid hold on John, and bound him and put him in prison for Herodias' sake . . ." (Matt. 14[3]; Mark 6[17]; Luke 3[19]). According to the Gospels this was the reason for John's arrest. Josephus has some more background detail to offer:

In the course of a trip to Rome Herod Antipas, a son of Herod the Great got to know Herodias, his brother's wife, and was so much attracted by her that he ventured a proposal of marriage. Herodias agreed and brought with her into the marriage her daughter Salome.

According to Mosaic law marriage with a sister-in-law was forbidden and—according to the Gospels—John the Baptist denounced it, an offence which in the eyes of the enraged Herodias could only be expiated by his death.

Josephus puts the event in a concrete historical setting, the castle of Machaerus, one of the numerous strongholds which Herod the Great had built in Palestine.

Machaerus, the place where John forfeited his life, lies in dark and rugged country on the east side of the Dead Sea. No road links this isolated spot with the outside world. Narrow paths lead up from the valley of the Jordan into the bare and desolate mountains of what was once Moab. In the deep wadis a few Bedouin families wander with their flocks over the scanty rough grass.

Not far from the river Arnon one lofty peak rises above the round humps of the other mountains. Its summit, which is swept by chill winds, is still crowned with ruins. "El Mashnaka", "The Hanging Palace", is what the Bedouins call this deserted place. This was the fortress of Machaerus. Far to the north can

be seen with the naked eye the part of the Jordan valley where
John baptised the people and where he was arrested.

So far no excavations have been carried out among the ruins of
"El Mashnaka" and few have visited the lonely spot at all.
Below the summit the rock-face is at one point hollowed out to a
considerable depth. Narrow passages lead into a large vaulted
chamber which from time to time provides shelter for nomads
and their flocks when sudden storms take them by surprise
among the mountains of Moab. From the carefully shaped walls
it is obvious that this was once the castle dungeon. This gloomy
vault sheltered John the Baptist after his arrest. It is probable that
he was beheaded here, if the statement of Josephus is correct, for
according to Mark 6[17ff] the execution evidently took place in
Galilee, presumably in the new palace which had recently been
constructed by Herod Antipas at Tiberias on the Lake of Galilee.

Anyone who has heard of the beheading of John associates
automatically with it the name of Salome, and thinks at once of
the daughter of Herodias who at her mother's behest is said to
have asked for the head of John as a reward for her dancing. This
Salome has taken her place in the literature of the world. Oscar
Wilde wrote a play "Salome", Richard Strauss made the story
of this Jewish princess the theme of his famous opera "Salome",
even Hollywood has used the story of Salome as the subject of
one of its epoch-making films.

But in the New Testament we may search in vain for the name
of this princess. The Bible makes no mention of Salome. In the
story of John the Baptist she is simply called the "daughter of
Herodias" (Mark 6[22]).

It is Josephus who has told us the name of this "daughter of
Herodias". A small coin has preserved her appearance for
posterity. She is depicted on it with her husband Aristobulus.
The coin bears the inscription "King Aristobulus–Queen Salome".
Salome must have been still a girl when John the Baptist was
beheaded—about nineteen years old.

"Now when Jesus had heard that John was cast into
prison he departed into Galilee: and leaving Nazareth, he
came and dwelt in Capernaum, which is upon the sea coast,
in the borders of Zabulon and Nephthalim" (Matt. 4[12,13]).

During the short course of Jesus' ministry, which according to
the evangelists Matthew, Mark and Luke cannot have lasted more

than a year and a half, one place always takes priority. Matthew indeed on one occasion calls it "his own city" (Matt. 9¹): Capernaum on the Lake of Galilee.

At the north end, not far from the spot where the fast running waters of the Jordan pour into the lake, the shore curves into a small bay. Out of the dark greenness of eucalyptus bushes comes a glint of white stone flags with four pillars rising out of them. Tufts of grass sprout from between the paving stones of the courtyard, shattered columns and blocks of basalt with carved ornamentation lie strewn around. All that remains of what was once the entrance are the broad steps of a staircase, the last remnants of a one-time splendid synagogue.

That is all that is left to bear witness to ancient Capernaum.

In 1916 the German archaeologists H. Kohl and C. Watzinger discovered hidden under rubble and overgrown with grass the fragmentary remains of this edifice. Franciscans rebuilt part of the old façade out of the ruins. The walls of the original building consisted of white limestone: on three sides it was surrounded by rows of tall pillars. The interior, measuring 80 × 50 feet, was decorated with sculptures of palms, vine branches, lions and centaurs. From there the view through a large window ranged southwards over the broad surface of the lake to where Jerusalem lay behind the pale blue outlines of distant hills.

Both archaeologists were convinced that they had found the synagogue of Capernaum dating from the time of Christ. But in the whole of Palestine there is not one synagogue left from those days. When the Romans in two bloody wars razed Jerusalem to the ground and the inhabitants of the ancient country were scattered to the four winds, their sanctuaries also fell a prey to destruction.

This building came into being for the first time about A.D. 200 on top of the ruins and foundations of the synagogue in which Jesus often stood and taught on the Sabbath day: "And they went into Capernaum; and straightway on the sabbath day he entered into the synagogue and taught" (Mark 1²¹).

Most of the inhabitants of the little town of Capernaum lived on the natural riches of the lake: huts and houses in large numbers nestled quietly on the gentle slopes or surrounded the synagogue. On the day when Jesus came from Nazareth to Capernaum he took the first decisive step towards proclaiming his message: "Now as he walked by the sea of Galilee, he saw Simon and Andrew his brother, casting a net into the sea; for they were fishers. And Jesus said unto them: Come ye after me, and I will make you fishers of men'' (Mark 1$^{16-17}$). He met another pair of brothers, James and John, as they were mending their nets. The first people to listen to his words, to accept his teaching and to become his disciples, were simple men, fishermen of Galilee.

Jesus often wandered up from the lake into the Galilean hills, and preached in many of the towns and villages, but always returned to the little fishing town: it remained the main centre of his mission. And when one day he left Capernaum and set out with twelve disciples for Jerusalem, it was his last journey.

Chapter 39
THE LAST JOURNEY, TRIAL AND CRUCIFIXION

Detour through Transjordan—The tax-collector of Jericho—View from the Mount of Olives—Arrest on the Mount of Olives—The "clubs" of the high priests—The Procurator Pontius Pilate—Vincent discovers the "Pavement"— Scourging in the courtyard of the Antonia—"The most cruel form of execution"—A crown of Syrian Christ-thorn—A drink to stupefy—Heart failure as the cause of death—Crurifragium hastens the end—A solitary tomb under the Church of the Holy Sepulchre—Tacitus mentions "Christus"—The evidence of Suetonius.

"Then he took unto him the twelve and said unto them, Behold we go up to Jerusalem, and all things that are written by the prophets concerning the Son of man shall be accomplished" (Luke 18³¹).

Out of all the journeys that Jesus undertook in his lifetime, one can be traced without difficulty—his last journey through Palestine, the journey from Capernaum to Jerusalem.

He went a long way round to get there. The shortest route from Galilee to the Holy City lies directly south through the hills of Samaria. The path keeps to the hills, over the tops of Gerizim and Ebal, the site of ancient Shechem, and then on through Bethel into the heart of Judah, along the old high road which Abraham followed with his family and his flocks.

It took three days to make this journey on foot from Galilee to Jerusalem.

Jesus too would have chosen this road through Samaria (Luke

9^{51-56}). But since the anti-Jewish feeling among the Samaritans was well known it seemed doubtful to him whether they would permit his little company to pass through their territory. To make sure, he sent his disciples James and John in advance. And indeed the Samaritans refused permission.

Jesus and his disciples therefore went by way of "the borders of Judaea and beyond Jordan" (Mark 10^1—R.V.). The road goes downstream through the middle of the wide and torrid valley, where the banks alone are fringed with tropical growth, with little clumps of tamarisks and poplars, with castor oil and liquorice trees. There is solitude and stillness in the "pride of Jordan" (Zech. 11^3; Jer. 12^5). For the valley, which for nine months of the year is as sultry as the tropics, is but thinly populated.

At the ancient ford, where once the children of Israel under Joshua's leadership had passed over in safety, Jesus crossed the Jordan and arrived in Jericho (Luke 19^1). It was no longer the fortified city of old Canaan, entrenched behind its walls. On the south side of the hill lay a new up to date city, built by Herod the Great, a gem of Graeco-Roman architecture. At the foot of the citadel called Cyprus, a magnificent palace had arisen. A theatre, an amphitheatre, cut into the hillside, and a circus, all adorned with dazzling white pillars, sparkled in the sunlight. Magnificent fountains played in the luxuriant gardens with their massed banks of flowers. Outside the town stretched the balsam plantations—the most precious plants in the whole of the Mediterranean land—while deep palm groves offered coolness and shade.

Jesus spent the night in Jericho in the house of the Jewish tax-collector Zacchaeus (Luke 19^{2ff}), far away from all this magnificence. He could not have avoided Jericho, which was a centre of Greek paganism. For the road to Jerusalem led through the city.

It is 23 miles from Jericho to Jerusalem. Twenty-three miles of dusty road winding and twisting between steep and almost barren cliffs nearly 4,000 feet high. Hardly anywhere else in the world can there be a stronger contrast than this short stretch of road affords. Straight from the wonderfully luxuriant growth and the sheer unbearable heat of a tropical sun by the Jordan's banks, one is whisked into the chill air of forbidding and barren mountain peaks.

This was the road, like a prelude to the end, which Jesus

followed with his disciples a week before the Passover. This was the time when Jews from far and near flocked to celebrate the feast in the Holy City.

At the highest point on the road, which is almost at the end of the journey, the Holy City emerges from behind the top of the Mount of Olives as if some wizard had conjured it out of the hills. The view that Jerusalem presented to Jesus and the disciples can be imagined from a contemporary description:

"Anyone who has not seen Jerusalem in all its beauty has never beheld a great and lovely city in all his life: and anyone who has not seen the structure of the second Temple has never seen an impressive building in his life." This was the proud verdict of the Jewish rabbis of the time.

Research into the appearance of old Jerusalem has been summed up by Garstang in the following words: "At no point in their history can the Temple and the city have presented a more wonderful picture. The rhythm and harmony of Graeco-Roman art, which stood out so marvellously against the eastern sky, repressed the extravagant architectural tendencies of Herod, and brought order and good taste into the traditional chaos of the city."

The great walls towered 250 feet high above the valley. Behind their battlements rose the contours of mighty edifices from a constricted chequer-board of houses, streets and alleys.

Immediately opposite the Mount of Olives lay the Temple, right in the foreground, and outshining all other buildings in its magnificence. Its façade 150 feet high and of equal breadth, faced eastward and consisted entirely of light marble. Its decorations were of pure gold. Pillared colonnades hemmed in the spacious courts and vestibules. The crowning glory was however the Tabernacle in the centre, sparkling "like a snow capped mountain", to quote Josephus' words.

Directly on the north-west side of the Temple wall rose the Tower of Antonia, perched on a rocky eminence. Each of its four great corner turrets measured nearly 120 feet high. A viaduct led from the south side of the Temple area to the palace of the Hasmoneans in the upper city. At the highest point in the city stood Herod's palace by the west wall, likewise surmounted by three towers 130, 100 and 80 feet high. Herod had named them Hippicus, Phasael and Mariamne. From this point a thick wall ran through the sea of houses to the Temple area, thus dividing the heart of the city once more into two sections.

There is an indomitable air about this city with its multiplicity of fortifications, walls and towers surrounding its Temple. As the sightseer looks over Jerusalem he almost feels that he is breathing in its obstinacy, rigidity and inflexibility. It was these very attributes of obstinacy, rigidity and inflexibility which helped Israel for more than 1,000 years to stand out against every world-power. Obstinacy, rigidity and inflexibility were also responsible for the eventual destruction of Jerusalem and the ejection of Israel from the land of their fathers.

Jesus predicted the future fate of Jerusalem. "And when he was come near, he beheld the city, and wept over it" (Luke 19[41]).

> "And straightway in the morning the chief priests held a consultation with the elders and scribes and the whole council, and bound Jesus, and carried him away, and delivered him to Pilate. . . . And so Pilate willing to content the people . . . delivered Jesus, when he had scourged him, to be crucified" (Mark 15[1,15]).

The descriptions of the trial, sentence and crucifixion in the four Gospels have been checked with scientific thoroughness by many scholars and have been found to be historically reliable accounts even to the last detail. The chief witnesses for the prosecution against Jesus have been indirectly attested and the place where sentence was pronounced has been accurately ascertained by excavations. The various incidents in the course of the trial can be verified from contemporary sources and modern research.

With the arrest the incomparable tragedy began to unfold. Jesus had gathered his disciples round him in the Garden of Gethsemane on the Mount of Olives, "and immediately, while he yet spake, cometh Judas, one of the twelve, and with him a great multitude with swords and staves, from the chief priests and the scribes and the elders" (Mark 14[43]).

A taunt-song in the Talmud reminds us of the "clubs" and "staves" of the Boethusian high priests who had been in control since Herod's day:

> "A plague on the house of Boethus: a plague on their clubs! A plague on the house of Annas: a plague on their spying!"

It ends: "For they are high priests and their sons are in the Treasury, and their sons-in-law in the Government and their servants beat the people with staves."

Among the high priests who are expressly named is one well known to us: the "Annas" in the Gospels. "Then the band and the captain and officers of the Jews took Jesus, and bound him, and led him away to Annas first: for he was father-in-law to Caiaphas, which was the high priest that same year. Now Caiaphas was he, which gave counsel to the Jews, that it was expedient that one man should die for the people" (John 18[12-14]).

Joseph ben Caiaphas had been appointed high priest by the Roman procurator Valerius Gratus. He remained in office[1] under his successor Pontius Pilate also.

After his arrest Jesus was brought before the High Council—the Sanhedrin—which at that time was the highest Jewish authority and combined within itself all spiritual and temporal power. At the same time it functioned as the highest judicial court of the Jews. It met below the Temple near the bridge which gave access to the upper city.

What were the grounds on which the council condemned Jesus to death?

"The expectation of the old Jewish prophets which centred on a future Messianic king," writes Professor Martin Noth, "had developed during the long period of foreign domination into hope of a political liberator; and the greater the resentment of the Roman government of the country the more this picture of a Messianic conqueror who would destroy the hateful foreign power filled their minds. Measured by these standards Jesus of Nazareth could not be the Messiah they were waiting for. . . . But if Jesus of Nazareth was not the Messiah, 'the Christ', then he must be a fraud and an impostor. And if he was a fraud and an impostor then for the safety and peace of the religious life of Jerusalem he must be got rid of. . . . The fact that Jesus during his trial claimed to be the Messiah and therefore, on the basis of Old Testament teaching, the Son of God was sufficient ground for condemning him to death on a charge of outrageous blasphemy."

According to the existing law the sentence had to be confirmed by the Roman procurator, to whom belonged the so-called

---

[1] From A.D. 18–36.

ius gladii. Only he could authorise the death penalty. The procurator of Judaea was Pontius Pilate.[1]

Contemporaries like Josephus and Philo of Alexandria describe him as an extortioner, a tyrant, a blood sucker and a corruptible character: "He was cruel and his hard heart knew no compassion. His day in Judaea was a reign of bribery and violence, robbery, oppression, misery, executions without fair trial and infinite cruelty."[2] That Pilate hated and despised the Jews was made unmistakably plain to them again and again.

Pilate must have recognised at once that the accused man, Jesus, was the object of a hatred which had been stirred up by the Pharisees. That alone must have been sufficient reason for him to reject their demand and to acquit him. Indeed first of all and without hesitation he actually declared him to be innocent: "Then said Pilate to the chief priests and to the people, I find no fault in this man" (Luke 23[4]).

But the mob, incited and goaded by the councillors, tumultuously repeated their demand for the death penalty. Pontius Pilate gave in.

How was it that this tyrannical enemy of the Jews yielded to their request?

St. John's Gospel contains a cogent explanation: "But the Jews cried out, saying, if thou let this man go, thou art not Caesar's friend: whosoever maketh himself a king, speaketh against Caesar" (John 19[12]).

This was a dangerous political threat which clearly implied reporting Pilate to Rome for neglect of duty in acquitting a rebel. "Making himself a king" meant treason against the Roman emperor. According to the Lex Juliana the penalty for that was death. Pilate was afraid of this unambiguous threat. He had not forgotten that the Jews had carried it out once before.

As Philo tells us, Pontius Pilate had brought to Jerusalem the golden shields bearing the emperor's name and had hung them up in Herod's palace in the middle of the city. That was a serious offence against the rights of the Jewish religious community which had been guaranteed by Rome. It was a challenge. He scornfully rejected their request to have the golden shields removed from the Holy City. Thereupon the Jews appealed to

---

[1] A.D. 26–36.
[2] Philo of Alexandria A.D. 25–50.

FIG. 72.—Coins of the Roman Procurator, Pontius Pilate.

Rome and secured their rights. The Emperor Tiberius himself ordered the removal of the golden shields. Because of this and sundry other arbitrary actions, which ran counter to Roman colonial policy, Pontius Pilate's reputation in Rome was at a low ebb at the time of the trial.

> "When Pilate therefore heard that saying, he brought Jesus forth, and sat down in the judgement seat, in a place that is called the Pavement, but in the Hebrew, Gabbatha. ... Then delivered he him therefore unto them to be crucified" (John 19[13,16]).

The Pavement in Pilate's court, where this scene took place, survived even the destruction of Jerusalem in A.D. 70. Its rediscovery was the result of years of work on the part of the archaeologist Father L. H. Vincent. His success was due to the exact description given in St. John's Gospel.

The Authorised Version has translated the word "Lithostroton" by "Pavement". It means a stone pavement. The Aramaic word "Gabbatha" means "raised ground".

Just beside the north-west perimeter wall of the Temple there lay in the time of Jesus the powerful Tower of Antonia. It stood upon a rocky eminence, therefore on "raised ground". Herod I had built it and called it after a friend. The Roman occupation troops had taken it over as a garrison. In A.D. 70, at the conquest of Jerusalem, Titus had the castle of Antonia demolished. Later buildings arose upon the ruins.

On the spot where the courtyard of the Antonia had been, Vincent was able to establish the existence of a large flat pavement nearly 3,000 square yards built in the Roman style and typical of the time of Jesus.

This was where Jesus stood before Pilate while the mob howled outside. It was on this Pavement too that the scourging took place (John 19[1]). This always preceded crucifixion, as Josephus expressly mentions twice. For this horrible punishment the body was stripped naked and flogged until the flesh hung down in bloody shreds.

Then Jesus was seized by Roman soldiers to complete the sentence of crucifixion. Cicero calls it "the most cruel and most frightful means of execution", Josephus recoils from it as "the most pitiable of all forms of death". This typically Roman death penalty was unknown in the Jewish penal code.

Still inside the court buildings the soldiers vented their wanton mischief on Jesus and "clothed him with purple and platted a crown of thorns and put it about his head" (Mark 15[17]).

So far, botanists have not been able to agree on what sort of plant this was. The only thing that is certain is that the "Christ's Crown of Thorns",[1] familiar to Europe and U.S.A. in the present day, has nothing to do with the Biblical crown of thorns. "It is a native of Madagascar and was completely unknown in Jesus' day," says the American botanist Dr. Harold Moldenke. Many other experts assume that the crown of thorns was woven from the Syrian Christ-thorn,[2] hence its name. The Syrian Christ-thorn is a bush or small tree, 10 to 15 feet high, with pliant white twigs. Its stipulae have each two strong thorns which curve backwards. According to Dr. G. E. Post, who is an expert on these matters, this plant grows in the neighbourhood of old Jerusalem, especially in the area where Golgotha is said to have been.

The way from the courthouse to Golgotha was mercifully short: "for the place ... was nigh to the city" (John 19[20]), beside the main road which entered Jerusalem from the north-west. A pilgrim from Bordeaux who visited Jerusalem in the year 333 specifically mentioned "the little hill of Golgotha[3] where the Lord was crucified".

"And they gave him to drink wine mingled with myrrh: but he received it not" (Mark 15[23]). Similar acts of mercy are frequently recorded on other occasions. We read in an old Jewish Baraita: "Anyone who is led out to execution is given a small piece of incense in a beaker of wine to numb his senses. . . . The good women of Jerusalem have a custom of dispensing this generously

---

[1] Euphorbia milii Desmoul.

[2] Sisyphus spina Christi.

[3] Monticulus Golgotha.

and bringing it to the victims.'' Moldenke, who has done much research into Biblical flora, has this to say: "Wine mixed with myrrh was given to Jesus just before the Crucifixion to lessen the pain, just as in the days before anaesthetics, intoxicating drinks were poured into the unfortunate patients on the eve of big operations." Jesus however declined the drink and endured with all his senses the torture of being nailed to the cross.

"And it was the third hour and they crucified him" (Mark 15^{25}).

According to our division of time the "third hour" in the Ancient East is 9 a.m. "And at the ninth hour", in our reckoning three o'clock in the afternoon, the tragedy came to an end. "And Jesus cried with a loud voice, and gave up the ghost" (Mark 15^{34,37}).

What was the cause of Jesus' death? Some years ago Dr. Hermann Mödder of Cologne carried out scientific tests in an attempt to answer the question from a medical point of view. In the case of a person suspended by his two hands the blood sinks very quickly into the lower half of the body. After six to twelve minutes blood pressure has dropped by 50% and the pulse rate has doubled. Too little blood reaches the heart, and fainting ensues. This leads to a speedy orthostatic collapse through insufficient blood circulating to the brain and the heart. Death by crucifixion is therefore due to heart failure.[1]

It is a well authenticated fact that victims of crucifixion did not usually die for two days or even longer. On the vertical beam there was often a small support attached called a "sedile" (seat) or a "cornu" (horn). If the victim hanging there eased his misery from time to time by supporting himself on this, the blood returned to the upper half of his body and the faintness passed. When the torture of the crucified man was finally to be brought to an end, the "crurifragium" was proceeded with: his legs were broken below the knee with blows from a club. That meant that he could no longer ease his weight on the footrests and heart failure quickly followed.

Jesus was spared the "crurifragium". "Then came the soldiers, and brake the legs of the first, and of the other which was

[1] Coronary insufficiency.

crucified with him. But when they came to Jesus, and saw that he was dead already, they brake not his legs'' (John 19[32-33]).

The Jews had asked Pilate for the ''crurifragium'', for it was ''the day before the sabbath'' (Mark 15[42]; Luke 23[54]) and also the day of preparation for the Passover. According to Jewish law the bodies of victims after crucifixion were not allowed to remain hanging overnight (Deut. 21[23]). And at 6 p.m. the Sabbath of Passover week began, when all kinds of normal activity were forbidden. The imminence of this important festival explains the precipitate haste of the events which preceded it, the arrest by night, the condemnation, execution and burial of Jesus all within a few hours.

It is barely 1,000 paces from the Ecce Homo arch, the site of Pilate's judgement seat, along the narrow Via Dolorosa to the Church of the Holy Sepulchre.

In 326 the Emperor Constantine erected a magnificent sepulchral tower over the tomb of Jesus, which had just then been rediscovered. Richly decorated pillars supported a roof of gilded beams, as can be seen from old books on pilgrimages and early Christian art. Today the Church of the Holy Sepulchre is a chaotic jumble of dim chapels. Every branch of the Christian Church has established for itself a little place of worship in this holiest of all the sites of Christendom.

In the Chapel of the Holy Sepulchre a well worn flight of steps leads down to a grotto where a 6 foot long tomb is hewn out of the rock. Is this the burial place of Jesus?

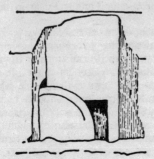

FIG. 73.—It was in a Palestinian tomb of this sort, with a millstone rolled across the entrance, that Christ was buried.

Over 1,000 graves have been found in Palestine dating from this period, but all of them were in cemeteries or family vaults. This tomb is however by itself. According to the Gospel tradition Jesus was the first to be laid in a great sepulchre: "And when Joseph had taken the body, he wrapped it in a clean linen cloth, and laid it in his own new tomb, which he had hewn out in the rock: and he rolled a great stone to the door of the sepulchre, and departed" (Matt. 27[59-60]).

One question has always been pressing for an answer since early times: How is it possible that apart from the books of the New Testament no contemporary records exist which deal with the events of those days? "World history at the time took no notice of him [Jesus of Nazareth]," writes Professor Martin Noth in his important *History of Israel*. "For one short moment his appearance stirred men's minds in Jerusalem: then it became an episode in past history and people had to concern themselves with what seemed more important things. And yet this was a final decisive crisis in the history of Israel. It was only when the numbers of his followers made them a force to be reckoned with in terms of world history that his name began to be mentioned at all."

Josephus in his *Antiquities of the Jews*, which he wrote in the last part of the 1st century A.D., in referring to the early Christian community in Jerusalem, speaks of "Jesus who was called Messiah".[1] Tacitus the Roman historian mentions Jesus specifically in his *Annals*,[2] while explaining the meaning of the word "Christians": "Christ, from whom they derive their name, was condemned to death by the procurator Pontius Pilate in the reign of the Emperor Tiberius."

The most important comment comes however from the Roman Suetonius:[3] he is describing a messianic movement during the reign of Claudius, who was Roman emperor from A.D. 41 to 54. Suetonius says of him in his account of the life of the Emperor Claudius: "He drove the Jews out of Rome who were rioting because of Chrestus." The writer Orosius mentions that this expulsion took place in the ninth year of Claudius' reign, i.e., A.D. 49. That means that a Christian community is attested in Rome not more than fifteen to twenty years after the Crucifixion.

---

[1] Antiquities XX, 9, para. 200.
[2] Annals, XV, 44—written A.D. 115–117.
[3] A.D. 65–135.

There is, in the Acts of the Apostles, an amazing corroboration of this Roman evidence. When Paul came from Athens to Corinth he found there "a certain Jew named Aquila, born in Pontus, lately come from Italy, with his wife Priscilla: because that Claudius had commanded all Jews to depart from Rome" (Acts 18²).

It cannot be denied, however, that the rare non-Biblical reports on Jesus are very problematical. Although there is a phonetic connection between Greek long "e" and "i", which is known as "itacism", so that *chrestos* meaning "capable", "skilful", "valuable", "good", could easily be confused with *christos*, which means "the anointed one" and is the Greek translation of the Hebrew word *Messias*, it is not at all certain whether the disturbances in Rome which were provoked by the question of the Messiah and which Suetonius mentions in his account of the life of the Emperor Claudius, really had anything to do with Jesus. The above quoted passage in Josephus must be considered a forgery. In its positive and approving tone it does not fit in either with Josephus' basic anti-Messianic attitude or with the surrounding text which gives an account of the uprisings of Jewish nationalists which in the opinion of Joseph were abominable and to be condemned. Moreover, the internal structure of this passage is not typical of Josephus' way of writing. It is more like the preaching style of the Evangelist Luke. The statement made by Tacitus does not yield much either. It nevertheless confirms that there were Christians who derived from Christ their name "Christians"—Christ who had been crucified at the time of the Emperor Tiberius (A.D. 14–37) under the procurator Pontius Pilate. It is an open question whether Tacitus himself thought this true. The only safe deduction we can make is that during the reign of the Emperor Nero (A.D. 54–68), whose persecution of the Christians provides the opportunity for Tacitus to make his statement about them, a Christian community was in existence in Rome and that in certain respects their traditions coincided with points in the New Testament.

The year of Jesus' death, moreover, is no less debated than the date of his birth, concerning which we were able to say with any certainty only that it must have occurred somewhere and at some time between 7 B.C. and A.D. 7. The time span between the limits set by modern specialists for the year of Jesus' death is not so great, however, as that for his birth. Today the possibilities have been narrowed down to A.D. 29, 30, 32 and 33. If we wish to be very cautious, then we have at our disposal the ten years of the period that Pontius Pilate held his office (A.D. 26–36). Caiaphas, the High Priest, held office from A.D. 18–37.

Even the day of the trial and execution of Jesus is uncertain for if we work out the dates indicated by the Evangelists Matthew, Mark and Luke and compare them with those given by John, they show a difference of a day. There is even less uniformity concerning the hour of Jesus' death.

Moreover, the Evangelists linked the crucifixion of Jesus with so many passages from the Old Testament that it would almost be possible to have doubts about Jesus' crucifixion. Can all these terrible things have been imagined merely for the sake of cross references in the Bible? And it must not be forgotten that Jesus was by no means the first god to be crucified! He had been preceded by fertility gods who suffered and were put to death. In Berlin, for example, there is a small amulet with a crucified person, the Seven Sisters and the moon which bears the inscription ORPHEUS BAKKIKOS. It has a surprisingly Christian appearance. The same can be said of a representation of the hanging Marsyas in the Capitoline Museum in Rome.

On the other hand, we know that a crucifixion took place and we also know who ordered the crucifixion and who suffered this dreadful form of death. The Dead Sea Scrolls mention as outrageous a mass crucifixion ordered by Alexander Iannaios (103–76 B.C.). The Romans showed a preference for this manner of execution. It was inflicted on persons belonging to defeated peoples who had committed crimes against the Roman State as well as on slaves. But the question arises as to the actual cause of death of the crucified person as well as to the length of time he remained alive on the cross.

There was also disagreement concerning certain details of the way in which the cruel punishment was carried out. A macabre discovery on a hill named *Givat Hamivtar* on the eastern edge of Jerusalem helped solve the problem. Two Israeli specialists, the archaeologist Vassilios Tzaferis and the pathologist Nicu Haas, have published a report on it, while the American journalist and author Jerry M. Landay has written an account of it for the general public in his book on Biblical archaeology *Silent cities, sacred stones*.

It was in the summer of 1968. In the course of construction work a bulldozer cut into graves dating from the time between the accession of Herod the Great (37 B.C.) and the destruction of

Herod's temple (A.D. 70). These graves lay on the hill of *Givat Hamivtar* so that the people buried in them must more or less have been contemporaries of Jesus. The name of one of the dead was *Johanan Ben Ha'galgol*. It was noticed with feelings of horror that his feet were separated from the smashed skeleton and were lying one on top of the other and joined together by a rusty nail which had been driven through both feet. Fragments of wood, the remains of a wooden slab, were attached to it. Behind Johanan's feet, the nail was bent obviously by having been driven into harder material. Johanan's forearms also showed signs of having had nails driven through them. In the course of Johanan's death struggles, his skin had suffered abrasions on the nails.

This discovery undeniably called for detailed investigation. Vassilios Tzaferis and Nicu Haas wondered whether any conclusions could be drawn from Johanan's injuries concerning the shape of the crucifix and the way in which the victim had been nailed to it. In fact, the nails had not been driven through the palms of the hands in the way usually depicted, but through the forearms near the wrist. Presumably this was the usual practice for this manner of execution, for the palms of the hands when pierced by nails would have torn under the weight of a body writhing in the agonised throes of death. This fact had already been established, moreover, in the gruesome experiments of Dr. Barbet of Paris in connection with the "Turin Shroud" which will be discussed in the next chapter. The crucified person, whose imprint the shroud shows, contrary to all the artistic conventions of the usual manner of depicting a crucifixion, had not had the nails driven through his palms. There was one way, however, in which the case of Johanan Ben Ha'galgol obviously differed from the normal Roman method of execution. The question has been raised whether the *crurifragium,* the smashing of the shinbones with a blunt instrument, was an additional torture or perhaps in the end an act of mercy, a "coup de grâce", for the victim then collapsed and died more quickly. In Johanan Ben Ha'galgol's case, however, this "act of mercy" was not deemed sufficient. Together with the nail and the wooden slab his feet had been cut off his smashed legs. . . .

Chapter 40
THE TURIN SHROUD

Books from Constantinople—Discovery in the photographic negative—Tests by forensic medical experts—A scientific proof of authenticity?

"Then took they the body of Jesus, and wound it in linen clothes with the spices, as the manner of the Jews is to bury" (John 19⁴⁰).

In the year 1204, during the course of the Fourth Crusade, the Crusaders captured Constantinople. In connection with this event the chronicler Robert de Clari reports that a Frenchman named Otto de la Roche came into the possession of a linen cloth as part of the spoils. This cloth, which measured 1.10 metres in width and 4.36 metres in length, had the peculiarity that it bore marks made by blood and sweat. On closer inspection the indistinct outlines of a human body, which must have measured about 1.80 metres in height, became apparent. Otto de la Roche took it with him back to France.

A century and a half later, the linen cloth reappeared in Besançon where it was worshipped as Christ's shroud. When a fire occurred, it was not consumed by the flames, it is true, but it did sustain slight damage. Its subsequent history can be followed in detail.

When the plague broke out in Milan, the devout Carlo Borromeo, bishop of the town, who was subsequently canonised, fulfilled his vow to make a pilgrimage to the shroud which had been brought for him from the south of France to Turin where it has since remained.

The linen cloth is said to have been in Jerusalem until the fifth or sixth century. Tradition has it that this is the linen cloth in which Joseph of Arimathea wrapped the body of Christ.

It is impossible to provide historical proof of these claims. There are, moreover, two pieces of linen in addition to that in Turin, for which the claim is also made that they came into contact with Christ's body.

The more important of these is the handkerchief of Saint Veronica. According to legend, the saint gave Christ her handkerchief as he was on the way to his crucifixion. When she received it back, it bore the imprint of his face.

The portrait of Christ in the possession of King Abgar V of Edessa, "Antiochia", was also considered authentic, but the French theologian and historian Chevalier came across proof to the contrary in the Papal archives in a document dated 1389 which states that an artist had painted such a cloth. When this became known, the Turin shroud was identified as a copy by that artist and consequently in the estimation of all those interested, it ceased to have any value as a contemporary document.

That might have been the end of the matter if interest in the legendary piece of linen had not been aroused anew in 1889. Technical progress had made possible the first photograph of the "Turin shroud". Something extraordinary was the result, for the photographic plate converted the impressions on the cloth into black and white. A face became clearly visible.

Specialists all over the world studied the sensational photograph. Art specialists, to whom it was submitted, noticed, moreover, that the negative was astonishingly natural and anatomically correct for, as with every human being, the features are not the same on both sides of the face. Artists in the early Middle Ages certainly did not pay any attention to this dissimilarity. Attempts made by painters showed that no artist was able, even when using a model, to convert a human face by the processes of the mind into a negative image and paint it.

The "Turin Shroud" could consequently not be a forgery insofar as it was the imprint of a human face. Even art specialists, who began by denying its authenticity, now admit that it cannot have been painted as a negative. Nobody can do that.

After this exciting discovery, scientists also began to take an interest in the shroud and a number of prominent specialists in various branches of science began their researches. Decades of study, experiments and investigations have brought certain conclusions. Concrete and very significant results have been obtained.

A whole mosaic of infinitely painstaking studies exists which were undertaken to answer the question:

How did the shroud originate?

Professor Vignon of Paris was the first to concern himself experimentally with the impression of a body on linen. He placed a cloth sprinkled with aloes in contact with a corpse. The experiments were not satisfactory, however, as considerable distortions seemed unavoidable. Italian forensic medical specialists, Professor Judica of Milan and Professor Romanese of Turin, were more successful. In their experiments they adhered to the Biblical account which indicates the correct method: "And there came also Nicodemus . . . and brought a mixture of myrrh and aloes, about an hundred weight. Then they took the body of Jesus, and wound it in linen clothes with the spices, as the manner of the Jews is to bury" (John 19[39-40]). A long series of experiments showed that the corpse must be powdered and the cloth moistened with aromatic oil. Impressions which do not show any distortion are obtained more particularly when the hair on the head prevents too close contact of the side of the face with the cloth. The results of the Italian tests provide the highest degree of correspondence.

The imprint on the "Turin shroud" shows swellings on the face. It is possible that they result from blows. "Then did they spit in his face, and buffeted him; and others smote him with the palm of their hands" (Matthew 26[67]). Patches of blood are clearly visible on the forehead and neck. "And the soldiers platted a crown of thorns, and put it on his head" (John 19[2]). Small swellings can also be seen on other parts of the body. They come from wounds on the hands and feet made by nails as well as from a wound on the right side of the chest: ". . . one of the soldiers with a spear pierced his side, and forthwith came there out blood and water" (John 19[34]).

Dr. Barbet of Paris has thoroughly investigated the nature of these wounds and here, too, the results were surprising. The wounds do not correspond to the customary manner of artistic depiction. The "Turin shroud" clearly shows the places where the nails were driven in. They were not driven through the palms of the hands, but through the wrists. From the physical and medical angle, the artistic depictions are wrong. And here, too, an unusual experiment led to a conclusion in the shroud's favour.

Dr. Barbet nailed a corpse to a crucifix. The wound in the palm of the hand was torn when bearing a weight of 40 kilos. A wide tendon runs through the wrist, however, and is strong enough to support the weight of the human body.

Some medical men believed they were able to detect two kinds of blood in the traces left by the wounds. They distinguished between blood which must have flowed while the victim was still alive—such traces are found on the head, the hands and the feet—and blood after death from the wound in the side of the chest and also on the feet.

From what period does the linen of the famous shroud date? Because of the manner of weaving, specialists have repeatedly situated the shroud in the decades around the beginning of our era, although a precise determination of the time has not yet been attempted. It would be possible to undertake this, however, by using highly sensitive Geiger counters. The C14 method developed by Professor W. F. Libby of the Chicago Institute of Nuclear Physics would allow the date to be determined within a range of a few years. We should then know at least when the flax was grown from which the linen was made (cf. also pp. 420–21).

These are the results which scientific investigation could achieve, but the question as to who the dead man was who lay in the shroud and when he lay there would still not have been answered.

In the Days of the Apostles

Chapter 41
IN THE STEPS OF ST. PAUL

The tentmaker from Tarsus—Triumphal arch in Antioch—Galatia, a Roman province—Wood digs in Ephesus—The temple of Artemis—The ruins of the gateway of Philippi—In ancient Corinth—A meat-market with a cooling system—"The Hebrew Synagogue"—A prisoner on the way to Rome.

"And ye shall be witness unto me, both in Jerusalem, and in all Judaea, and in Samaria, and unto the uttermost part of the earth" (Acts 1[8]).

"I am a man which am a Jew of Tarsus, a city in Cilicia, a citizen of no mean city." Thus Paul, who was by trade a tentmaker (Acts 18[3]), describes himself in Acts 21[39]. Tersoos, a little town of 20,000 inhabitants lying at the foot of the Taurus mountains in the south of Turkey, has preserved none of its former glory. Paul had every reason to laud his native city to the skies. An inscription calls Tarsus "the great and wondrous metropolis of Cilicia", and the Greek geographer Strabo[1] mentions that Tarsus had a university to match those of Athens and Alexandria. The famous teacher of the emperor Augustus, Athenodorus the philosopher, was one of its sons. All that remains from the past is its tentmaking. As in Paul's day, the material comes from flocks of goats who grow magnificent thick coats among the Taurus mountains where the snow lies right up to the month of May.

Long journeys by sea and land, such as Paul undertook, were in those days nothing out of the ordinary. Roman roads were in their way the finest that even Western Europe knew until the railways began to be built in the 19th century. An inscription on

[1] 63 B.C.–A.D. 20.

the tombstone of a Phrygian merchant in the heart of modern Turkey proudly proclaims that in his lifetime he made seventy-two journeys to Rome alone. The busy, well maintained Imperial roads were equipped with halts for changing chariots and horses. Inns and hostelries offered rest and refreshment to travellers. A special police force was responsible for the protection of the roads against the attacks of brigands.

The marvellous network of roads throughout the vast empire—a masterpiece of Roman skill and organisation—together with the Greek language which Paul could make use of on all his journeys contributed as much to the speedy spread of Christianity as the widely dispersed Jewish communities. "Jerusalem is not only the capital of Judaea," wrote King Herod Agrippa I[1] to the emperor Caligula, "but also of most countries in the world through the colonies which it established in neighbouring lands when it had the opportunity."

Even last century scholars had begun to search for the cities in Asia Minor whose names have become so familiar to the Christian world through the Acts of the Apostles and the Epistles of St. Paul. Where were the places whose inhabitants received the famous Epistle to the Galatians?

In 1833, Francis V. J. Arundell, British chaplain in Smyrna, discovered the ancient "Antioch in Pisidia" (Acts 13[14]) near the Turkish town of Yalovach. North of the Taurus a great arched aqueduct sweeps down from the majestic scenery of the Sultandagh mountains into the valley. In the early twenties of this century scholars of the University of Michigan stood entranced before the remains of monuments of unique beauty. In the centre of the old city the archaeologists uncovered a broad flight of steps at the top of which stood three triumphal arches. Marvellous reliefs depicted the victories of the emperor Augustus on land, while a frieze with Poseidon, Tritons and dolphins commemorated the naval victory of Augustus at Actium. In the Roman quarters they found the gaming tables where the soldiery whiled away their leisure hours. The archaeologists were looking at the Antioch, so often mentioned, where Paul founded a church on his first missionary journey (Acts 14[21]).

And they "came unto Iconium . . . unto Lystra and Derbe, . . . and unto the region that lieth round about: and there they preached the gospel" (Acts 13[51]; 14[6,7]).

[1] King Agrippa (A.D. 37–44): see Acts 12.

Konia, 60 miles south-east of Antioch and main station on the
Anatolian railway, was the Iconium of Paul's missionary activity.
In 1885 Professor J. R. Sitlington Sterrett discovered the remains
of an altar in the mountains 25 miles farther south. A thick stone
slab bore a Latin inscription to the effect that a Roman colony
had existed on this site. He was able to decipher the name
"Lustra".[1]

A day's journey farther on Sterrett also discovered the ancient
Derbe. These four cities—Antioch, Iconium, Lystra and Derbe—
belonged in Paul's day to the Roman province of Galatia, the
home of the "Galatians".

On the island of Cyprus near the ancient town of Paphos a
Roman inscription came to light. It made mention of Paulus, the
proconsul who is described as "a prudent man" in the Book of
Acts (13[7]), likewise the riot at Ephesus, as the New Testament
depicts it, has become a living reality, thanks to the tireless
efforts of the archaeologists.

"For a certain man named Demetrius, a silversmith, which
made silver shrines for Diana, brought no small gain unto the
craftsmen: whom he called together with the workmen of like
occupation, and said: Sirs, ye know that by this craft we have
our wealth." He then went on to incite them: "not alone at
Ephesus, but almost throughout all Asia, this Paul hath persuaded and turned away much people", and graphically described
how they would all be reduced to starvation as a result. "Great is
Diana of the Ephesians!" was the answering cry. "And the
whole city was filled with confusion: and having caught.... Paul's
companions in travel, they rushed with one accord into the
theatre" (Acts 19[24-29]).

This story fired an English architect J. T. Wood with a desire
to investigate the Temple of Artemis,[2] which was widely renowned in the ancient world. The British Museum put funds at
his disposal for this enterprise, and in the beginning of May 1863
Wood landed on the coast opposite the island of Samos. If he
had not been so incredibly persistent and obsessed with his
purpose he might well never have achieved it. For six long years
he dug down doggedly through layer after layer of what was left
of the masonry of the old city—and found nothing. Eventually
while digging in the old amphitheatre, the site of the riot, he
found a signpost which put him on the right road.

[1] i.e., Lystra.
[2] Artemis, the Greek goddess of hunting, was called Diana by the Romans.

An inscription listed several gold and silver images of Artemis from two to six pounds in weight which were to be offered as a gift to the goddess and placed in the temple. The vanity of that Roman donor showed Wood the way to the fulfilment of his dream without further ado. For in order to ensure that the greatest possible number of people would admire his gifts he had described in detail the exact route along which they were to be borne in solemn procession the goddess' birthday, from the temple to the ceremony in the amphitheatre and back again.

They were to be carried in through the Magnesian Gate. . . . Wood searched for the gate and found it, followed the prescribed route and found himself a mile north-east of the city, at the finishing point of the procession which was also the end of his own indefatigable quest.

Under nearly 25 feet of soil and rubble he came upon a magnificent pavement, the bases of massive pillars, and great stone cylinders adorned with sculptures: the Temple of Artemis.

Dinocrates, the famous Alexandrian architect, had designed the shrine; Alexander the Great had been responsible for completing it in such splendour that in olden times the temple was admired as one of the Seven Wonders of the World.

The foundations measured 390 feet long by 260 feet broad, sheets of white marble covered the roof, and a hundred columns 65 feet high led the way into the interior of the temple, which was extravagantly decorated with sculptures, paintings and gold ornamentation.

Thirty-five years later one of Wood's countrymen, David G. Hogarth, found under the shattered altar a large collection of statues of the goddess made of bronze, gold, ivory and silver. They had been made by those craftsmen and workers who scented in Paul's preaching of the Gospel at Ephesus a threat to their livelihood and therefore responded to Demetrius with cries of: "Great is Diana of the Ephesians."

"Immediately we endeavoured to go into Macedonia, assuredly gathering that the Lord had called us for to preach the gospel unto them. Therefore loosing from Troas. . . ." (Acts 16[10,11]).

Where once the proud stronghold of Priam's Troy held sway, St. Paul boarded a sailing ship for his first journey to Europe.

Near the fishing village of Kavalla[1] he set foot on European soil and set out on the ancient Via Egnatia which climbed up into the wild mountains of Macedonia to Philippi.

Can anyone hear the name of this city without thinking of the ominous words: "Thou shalt see me at Philippi"? For it was here in 42 B.C. that the legions of Antony and young Octavian won a brilliant victory over Brutus and Cassius, who had assassinated Caesar in an attempt to save the republic of Rome from dictatorship. But who reflects that it was outside the walls of Philippi that St. Paul won for Christianity its first congregation on European soil?

French archaeologists on the strength of the concrete evidence in the Book of Acts excavated the Roman colony. They found the old forum, the temples and public buildings, the pillared arcades, the paved streets and squares with their rain-gutters still intact. At the western exit of the city a great colonial archway spanned the Via Egnatia which soon afterwards crossed the swift narrow river Gangites. "And on the sabbath day we went forth without the gate by a river side where we supposed there was a place of prayer" (Acts 16[13]—R.V.). On the banks of the Gangites Paul's first convert was Lydia, the seller of purple.

By way of Thessalonica[2] and Athens, where he preached only for a short time, St. Paul turned his steps towards Corinth.

In 1893 dredgers cut a narrow channel through the isthmus which joined the Peloponnese with the mainland and thus realised a plan which was already in the minds of notable figures in the ancient world, Alexander the Great and Julius Caesar. In A.D. 63 Nero had indeed begun to put the plan into effect. After a song in praise of Neptune in which he accompanied himself on the harp, he dug the first sod with a golden spade. Six thousand Jews had been commandeered from Palestine to cut the canal, which was however very quickly filled in again when the suspicion was voiced that a breach in the land might wash away the Peloponnese.

Three years after the first ship passed through the new canal the American School of Classical Studies began to search for the renowned and important trading and packing centre of Corinth, where the wares of the ancient Orient met those of Europe. Here too the archaeologists followed the footsteps of St. Paul to the places which if they could only speak could tell so much about his activities.

---

[1] One of the many towns called *Neapolis* (new town) in Classical Antiquity.
[2] Now Salonika.

The road from Lechaeum, the west harbour, led into the heart of the old city of Corinth. Through the great marble arch of the Propylaeum it debouched into the market place, the agora. In those days the business quarter lay to the west of Lechaeum street, and colonnades led past its shops and up to the steps of the Temple of Apollo. What aroused genuine admiration among the hygienically-minded Americans was the ingenious system of water mains which they found immediately under the houses which fronted the broad and handsomely paved market place. It obviously provided the shops with a constant supply of fresh mountain water to keep fresh such foodstuffs as were liable to perish quickly. An inscription at this place dating from the last years of the reign of Augustus actually mentioned a "meat-market". The Christians in Corinth were allowed to make their purchases in these shops without scruple. "Whatsoever is sold in the shambles, that eat", is Paul's advice to the church in 1 Cor. 10^{25}.

At the marble steps of the Propylaeum the excavators found a heavy stone lintel on which they were able to decipher the words "Hebrew Synagogue", clearly cut out in Greek letters. The house in which Paul proclaimed the new doctrine must have stood beyond the colonnade in the region of Lechaeum street. For "he reasoned in the synagogue every sabbath, and persuaded the Jews and the Greeks" (Acts 18^4). Among the ruins of the numerous dwelling houses in the same quarter of the city must certainly be those of the house of the Justus with whom Paul lodged, "whose house joined hard to the synagogue" (Acts 18^7).

Finally the archaeologists found in the market place a raised platform, on which a Latin inscription indicated that it had been the rostra, the judgement-seat. "And when Gallio was the deputy of Achaia, the Jews made insurrection with one accord against Paul, and brought him to the judgement-seat, saying, This fellow persuadeth men to worship God contrary to the law." Gallio however declined to intervene "and drave them from the judgement seat" (Acts 18^{12-16}).

The detailed reproduction of the trial scene made it possible to establish the exact time that Paul spent in Corinth. Lucius Junius Annaeus Novatus Gallio—which was the governor's full name—was the worthy offspring of a highly respected family. His brother, Lucius Annaeus Seneca, the great Roman philosopher and tutor of Nero, dedicated two books to him.[1] And the poet Statius called him the "beloved Gallio".

[1] *De Ira* and *De Vita Beata*.

SPREAD OF CHRISTIANITY
IN THE ROMAN EMPIRE
■ 45 A.D.
▥ 325 A.D. (Emperor Constantine)

FIG. 74.

In old Delphi a letter of the emperor Claudius came to light from which it appeared that Gallio must have been in Corinth from A.D. 51–52. The letter contains the words: "As Lucius Junius Gallio, my friend the proconsul of Achaia,[1] wrote..." and is dated at the beginning of the year 52. According to a decree of Claudius newly appointed officials had to leave Rome for their provinces on June 1. Gallio must therefore have arrived in Achaia about July 1, A.D. 51. Paul "continued there a year and six months, teaching the word of God among them" (Acts 18[11]) until the Jews became incensed and dragged him before the governor. Thus it is highly probable that the apostle went to Corinth at the beginning of A.D. 50.

Two years after the crucifixion of Christ the fanatical persecutor of the Christians, Saul of Tarsus, was converted to Christianity (Acts 6[3ff]). Almost exactly thirty years later the great missionary and evangelist embarked upon his last journey, this time as a prisoner. In Judaea Festus had been procurator since A.D. 61. He sent Paul to Rome to face a serious charge in the custody of the centurion Julius (Acts 27[1]). There Paul was allowed "to dwell by himself with a soldier that kept him" (Acts 28[16]).

"And Paul dwelt two whole years in his own hired house, and

[1] The Peloponnese was in Roman times the province of Achaia.

received all that came in unto him, preaching the kingdom of God, and teaching those things which concern the Lord Jesus Christ with all confidence, no man forbidding him." With these words St. Luke concludes his narrative in the Book of Acts.

In the persecution of the Christians which took place under Nero, Paul died a martyr's death. As a Roman citizen he did not die on a cross like Peter but was beheaded.

Chapter 42
THE DESTRUCTION OF JERUSALEM

Rebellion—The Jewish War—Fighting in Galilee—General Titus—80,000 Romans advance—Order to attack—Parade outside the gates—500 crucifixions daily—Jerusalem sealed off—The spectre of famine—Castle of Antonia taken—The Temple in flames—The city is razed—Triumph in Rome.

"And as some spake of the temple, how it was adorned with goodly stones and gifts, he said, As for these things which ye behold, the days will come, in the which there shall not be left one stone upon another, that shall not be thrown down. . . . And when ye shall see Jerusalem compassed with armies, then know that the desolation thereof is nigh. . . . For there shall be great distress upon the land and wrath upon this people. And they shall fall by the edge of the sword, and shall be led away captive into all nations: and Jerusalem shall be trodden down by the Gentiles. . . ." (Luke 21[5,6,20,23,24]).

Countless royal palaces and castles, cities, mansions and temples, buildings whose foundations were laid in the first, second or even third millennium before Christ, have been wrested from the past. Archaeology has used its spades and the sharp wits of its experts to free them from the dust in which they have been buried at a cost of untold effort. But the city and Temple of Jerusalem, whose importance for posterity cannot be rated too highly, have eluded the endeavours of the archaeologists: they have been blotted out for ever from this earth. For barely within a generation after the crucifixion of Jesus they suffered in "the days of vengeance'' (Luke 21^{22}) the fate that Jesus prophesied for them.

Old Israel, whose history no longer included the words and works of Jesus, the religious community of Jerusalem which condemned and crucified Jesus, was extinguished in an inferno which is almost unparalleled in history—the "Jewish War" of A.D. 66–70.

Louder and louder grew the protests against the hated Romans. In the party of the "Zealots" fanatics and rebels banded themselves together, demanding incessantly the removal of the foreign power. Every one of them carried a dagger concealed under his cloak. Their deeds of violence disturbed the country. Autocratic encroachment by the Roman procurator heightened the tension. More and more supporters flocked to the side of the radicals.

This mounting anger broke into open revolt in May 66, when the procurator, Florus, demanded 17 talents from the Temple treasury. The Roman garrison was overrun. Jerusalem fell into the hands of the rebels. The prohibition of the daily sacrifices to the emperor meant an open declaration of war against the Roman world empire. Tiny Jerusalem threw down the gauntlet at Rome's feet and challenged the great Imperium Romanum.

This was the signal for the whole country. Rebellion flared up everywhere. Florus was no longer in command of the situation. The governor of the province of Syria, C. Cestius Gallus, marched to the rescue with one legion and a large number of auxiliary troops, but was forced to retire with heavy losses. The rebels controlled the country.

Being certain that Rome would strike back with all its might, they hastened to fortify the cities. They repaired the old defence walls and appointed military commandants. Joseph, later known as Josephus the historian, was appointed commander-in-chief of Galilee. On the Roman side, the Emperor Nero entrusted the command to General Titus Flavius Vespasianus, who had proved himself a brilliant soldier and distinguished himself during the conquest of Britain.

Accompanied by his son Titus, three of the best legions in the army and numerous auxiliaries, he attacked Galilee from the north.

The villages on the Lake of Galilee, where but a few years earlier Jesus had been preaching to the fishermen, saw the first of the bloody butchery. The whole of Galilee was subdued by October 67. Among the crowds of prisoners marched Josephus, the commander-in-chief. He was put in chains and conveyed to headquarters at Vespasian's orders. From then on he saw the Jewish War from inside the enemy's camp. Six thousand Jews went as slaves to build the Corinth canal.

In the following spring the suppression of the rebels in Judaea was resumed. In the midst of the fighting news came which for the time being halted the campaign—Nero had committed suicide.

Civil war broke out in Rome. Vespasian awaited developments. One after another three insignificant emperors lost their thrones and their lives. At last the legions in the east stepped in. A year after Nero's death the cry went up in Egypt, in Syria, in Palestine, throughout the whole of the Orient: "Vivat Caesar". Vespasian became master of the Roman empire. From Caesarea on the coast of Palestine, where the news reached him, he embarked without delay for Rome, leaving his son Titus to finish the last act of the Jewish War.

Shortly before the full moon in the spring of 70 Titus appeared with an enormous army outside Jerusalem. Marching columns filled the highways and byways leading to the city such as Judaea had never seen before. They were made up of the 5th, 10th, 12th and 15th Legions, accompanied by cavalry, engineers and other auxiliary troops, almost 80,000 men.

The Holy City was swarming with people: pilgrims had come from far and near to celebrate the Passover. Disputes between the extremists among the Zealots and the moderate party interrupted the devotions: the wounded and the dead remained untended.

Meantime the Romans moved into their camps in the environs of the city. A call to surrender was met with derisive laughter. Titus replied with the command to attack. The Roman artillery, "scorpiones", quick-firing siege engines and "ballistae", stone throwers, closed in. Every one of these heavy weapons could throw stones weighing a hundredweight a distance of 600 feet. On the north side the engineers were cracking open the Achilles heel of the fortress. On the south, east and west sharp precipices protected the ramparts. The north side was however unusually strongly fortified by three massive walls. Battering rams and siege engines began to crack and thunder as they attacked the foundations. Only when an incessant hail of great stones came

hurtling into the city, and when night and day the heavy thud of
the battering rams could be heard, did civil war end within the
fortress. The rival factions came to terms. Simon bar Giora,
leader of the moderates, took over the defence of the north side,
John of Gischala, leader of the Zealots, took over the defence of
the Temple area and the Tower of Antonia.

By the beginning of May the siege engines had in the space of
two weeks made a gaping hole in the most northerly wall. In five
more days the Romans were through the second wall. A determined counter-attack put the defenders once more in possession
of the wall and it took the Romans several days before they could
recapture it. With that the northern suburb was firmly in Roman
hands.

FIG. 75.—Roman siege technique during the conquest of Jerusalem.

Convinced that in view of this situation Jerusalem would
surrender, Titus called off the attack. The grandiose spectacle of
a great parade of his forces immediately under the eyes of the
beleaguered people would surely bring them to their senses.

The Romans doffed their battledress and polished their full-
dress uniform until it shone. The legionaries put on their armour,
their coats of mail and their helmets. The cavalry decked their
horses with the richest caparisons, and amid loud blasts from the
trumpets tens of thousands of warriors marched past Titus and

received their pay and ample rations in full view of the garrison. For four days from early morn till dusk the sound of the tramping feet of these unbeaten Roman columns echoed in the air.

It achieved nothing. Packed tight along the old wall, on the north side of the Temple, on every roof, the people spat hatred down at the Romans. The demonstration had been useless—the beleaguered garrison had no thought of surrender.

Titus made one last attempt to win them round. He sent their captive countryman Flavius Josephus, the Jewish commander-in-chief in Galilee, to harangue them under the fortress walls.

Josephus' voice hailed them from below: "O hard hearted men, throw away your weapons, have pity on your country that stands on the edge of the abyss. Look round and behold the beauty of all that you are ready to betray. What a city! What a Temple! What gifts from so many nations! Who would dare to let all of this be given to the flames? Is there one of you who can wish for all this to be no more? What more precious treasure could have been given to man to preserve—You obdurate creatures, more unfeeling than these very stones!"

In heartrending words, Josephus reminded them of the great deeds of the past, of their forefathers, of their history, of the mission of Israel—his exhortations and pleas fell on deaf ears.

The battle began anew from the second wall and surged against the castle of Antonia. The front was pushed forward through the streets of the suburbs to the Temple area and the upper part of the city. The engineers built ramps and auxiliaries dragged trees for this purpose from far and near. The Romans proceeded with all their tried methods of siege warfare. Their preparations were constantly being sorely hampered by the determined efforts of the defenders to upset them. Apart from wild sorties, no sooner were their wooden ramparts in position than they went up in flames. When darkness set in, the Roman camp was surrounded by swarms of figures who had crept out of their hiding places or through subterranean passages or over the walls.

Titus ordered reprisals to be made against these half starved ghostly figures and against deserters. Anyone caught outside—deserters, raiders or foragers—was to be crucified. Mercenaries nailed 500 of them every day to crosses just outside the city. Gradually a whole forest of crosses sprang up on the hillsides till the lack of wood called a halt to the frightful practice.

Tree after tree was sacrificed for crosses, siege ramps, scaling ladders and camp fires. The Romans had come into a flourishing countryside. Now the vineyards had disappeared as had the market gardens, the wealth of fig-trees and olive-trees; even the Mount of Olives no longer provided shade. An unbearable stench hung over the bare and desolate countryside. The corpses of those who had died of starvation and of those who had died in battle, thrown over the ramparts by the beleaguered garrison, were piled beneath the walls by the thousand. Who had the strength to bury them in the traditional way?

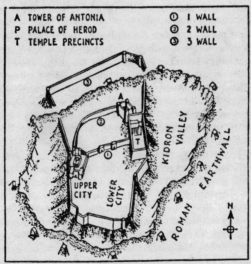

FIG. 76.—Jerusalem during the siege by Titus, A.D. 70.

"No stranger who had seen Judaea of old, and the lovely suburbs of its capital, and now saw this devastation," mourned Josephus, "could have restrained his tears and lamentations at the hideous change. For the war had turned all that beauty into a wilderness. And no man who knew these places of old and suddenly saw them again could possibly have recognised them."

To seal off the city hermetically Titus ordered the erection of a "circumvallatio". Working night and day they constructed a massive high wall of earthwork in a wide circle round Jerusalem, strengthened by thirteen fortified strong points and guarded by a close chain of pickets. If so far it had been possible to smuggle supplies and provisions into the city by night by way of secret paths through tunnels or ditches, the "circumvallatio" stopped even this last meagre reinforcement.

The spectre of famine haunted the city, which was filled to overflowing with pilgrims, and death mowed them down in a dread harvest. The craving for food, no matter of what sort, drove men beyond all bounds and killed all normal feeling.

"The terrible famine that increased in frightfulness daily annihilated whole families of the people. The terraces were full of women and children who had collapsed from hunger, the alleys were piled high with the bodies of the aged. Children and young people, swollen with lack of food, wandered around like ghosts until they fell. They were so far spent that they could no longer bury anyone, and if they did they fell dead upon the very corpses they were burying. The misery was unspeakable. For as soon as even the shadow of anything eatable appeared anywhere, a fight began over it, and the best of friends fought each other and tore from each other the most miserable trifles. No one would believe that the dying had no provisions stored away. Robbers threw themselves upon those who were drawing their last breath and ransacked their clothing. These robbers ran about reeling and staggering like mad dogs and hammered on the doors of houses like drunk men. In their despair they often plunged into the same house two or three times in the one day. Their hunger was so unbearable that they were forced to chew anything and everything. They laid hands on things that even the meanest of animals would not touch, far less eat. They had long since eaten their belts and shoes and even their leather jerkins were torn to shreds and chewed. Many of them fed on old hay and there were some who collected stalks of corn and sold a small quantity of it for four Attic drachmas.—But why should I describe the shame and indignity that famine brought upon men, making them eat such unnatural things?" asks Josephus in his history of the Wars of the Jews.

"Because I tell of things unknown to history, whether Greek or barbarian. It is frightful to speak of it and unbelievable to hear of it. I should gladly have passed over this disaster in silence, so that I might not get the reputation of recording something which must appear to posterity wholly degrading. But there were too many eye-witnesses in my time. Apart from that my country would have little cause to be grateful to me were I to be silent about the misery which it endured at this time.''

Josephus, whose own family suffered with the defenders, was not afraid to describe an inhuman occurrence which proves that the raging famine had begun to cloud the brains of the blockaded citizens.

Zealots were foraging through the lanes of the city in quest of food. From one house came the smell of roast meat. The men plunged into the house at once and were confronted by Maria, daughter of the noble line of Beth-Ezob in Transjordan, an extremely wealthy family. She had come to Jerusalem on pilgrimage for the Passover. The Zealots threatened her with death unless she handed over the roast meat to them. With a wild look she gave them what they asked for. Aghast, they found themselves looking at a half consumed infant—Maria's own child.

Soon not only the whole city learned of this, but the news also seeped out through the walls to the Roman camp. Titus swore that he would bury this dreadful deed under the ruins of the whole city.

Many fled from death by starvation under cover of darkness and ran into the arms of an equally cruel fate. The story had got around among the Romans' auxiliaries that fugitives from within the walls always carried gold and jewels, which they had swallowed in the hope of preserving them from being seized by strangers. If any of these unsuspecting people were caught they were felled to the ground and their bodies slit open in the endless quest for plunder. In one night 2,000 alone lost their lives in this way. Titus was furious. Without mercy he got his cavalry to decimate an auxiliary unit. An order of the day made the crime punishable by death. But it was of little avail, the slaughter continued secretly.

Meantime day and night the battering rams were hammering on the suburbs of Jerusalem. New ramps were laid down. Titus was in a hurry. He wanted to end this frightful nightmare as quickly as possible.

At the beginning of July his soldiers stormed the Tower of Antonia. The castle, on whose "Pavement" Jesus of Nazareth had been sentenced to death, was razed to its foundations. Its walls abutted on the north wall of the Temple.

It was now the turn of the Temple, that powerful and extremely well fortified complex of galleries, balustrades and forecourts. The commander-in-chief discussed the situation with his officers. Many of them wanted to treat the Temple like a fortress. Titus opposed them. He wanted if possible to spare this famous sanctuary which was known throughout the empire. For the last time his heralds demanded that the rebels should surrender. Once more the answer was a refusal. Titus then finally embarked upon the attack against the sacred precincts.

An incessant hail of heavy stones and a rain of arrows showered down upon its courts. The Jews fought like men possessed and did not yield an inch. They relied on Yahweh hastening to their aid at the last moment and protecting his shrine. More than once legionaries on scaling ladders reached the perimeter wall. Every time they were thrown back. Rams and siege engines were powerless against these walls. It was impossible to shatter the vast stone blocks of which Herod had built the Temple. In order to force an entry Titus set fire to the wooden Temple gates.

Hardly were they consumed when he gave instructions to put out the flames and make a passage for the legionaries to attack. Titus' order of the day read "Spare the sanctuary". But during the night the fire had reached the inner court and the Romans had their hands full to put it out. The beleaguered rebels profited by this favourable opportunity to make a violent attack. With remorseless slaughter the legionaries drove the Jews back, and pursued them through the courts. In wild tumult the battle raged round the sanctuary. Carried away by excitement, "one of the soldiers, without waiting for orders and without any sense of the horror of his deed, or rather being driven by some evil spirit, seized a blazing torch and, hoisted on the shoulders of one of his comrades, flung it through the Golden Window that opened into the rooms which lay beside the Holy of Holies."

These rooms were panelled with old wood and contained, as well as highly inflammable materials for the sacrifices, jars of holy oil. The flaming torch found instantaneous and ample fodder. Titus saw the flames springing up and tried to check the spread of the fire.

"Caesar[1] then commanded that the fire should be put out, calling in a loud voice to the soldiers who were in the thick of the fighting and giving them a signal with his right hand. But

[1] Titus became Emperor in 79.

they did not hear what he said for all his shouting. . . . And since Caesar was unable to restrain the hot rage of the soldiery, and since the flames were spreading further and further, he entered the Holy Place in the Temple together with his commander and viewed it and all its contents. . . . But since the flames had not yet reached the inner rooms, and were still devouring the rooms that surrounded the Tabernacle, Titus, assuming, as was indeed the case, that the Tabernacle itself could still be saved, hurried away and made every effort to get the soldiers to put out the fire, giving orders to Liberalius, the centurion, and to one of his own body guard, to beat the soldiers with staves if they refused and by every means to restrain them. But however great their enthusiasm for Caesar and their dread of what he had forbidden them to do, their hatred of the Jews and their eagerness to fight them was equally great.

"In addition the hope of booty spurred many of them on. They had the impression that all these rooms within were full of gold, and they saw that all around them was made of pure gold. . . . Thus the Holy Place was burnt down without Caesar's approbation."

In August A.D. 70 Roman legionaries erected their banners in the sacred precincts and sacrificed before them. Although half of Jerusalem was in the hands of the enemy, although ominous black columns of smoke rose from the burning Temple, the Zealots would not surrender.

John of Gischala escaped with quite a large band from the Temple area into the upper part of the city on the western hill. Others fled into the strong towers of Herod's palace. Once again Titus had to deploy his engineers, artillery, siege engines and all his brilliant technical skill. In September these walls too were forced, and the last bastions conquered. Resistance was finally at an end.

Murdering and plundering, the victors took possession of the city that had so fiercely and bitterly resisted them and cost them so much blood and time. "Caesar ordered the whole city and the Temple to be razed to the ground. He left standing only the towers of Phasael, Hippicus, and Mariamne and part of the city wall on the west side. This was to provide quarters for the garrison that was to remain behind."

The legion that occupied the garrison in this dreadful place for sixty long years bore the symbol "Leg XF", which meant "Tenth Fretensian Legion". Their home station was on the

"Fretum Siciliense", the straits of Messina. They left behind them in and around Jerusalem thousands upon thousands of indications of their presence. Gardeners and peasants still find occasionally small tiles with the legion's number and its emblems of a galley and a boar.

The loss of life among the Jews was unimaginably high. During the siege, according to Tacitus, there were 600,000 people in the city. Josephus gives the number of prisoners as 97,000, not counting those crucified or ripped open, and adds that within a period of three months 115,800 corpses were taken out of one of the city gates alone by the Jews.

In the year 71 Titus paraded his great victory over Jerusalem in a gigantic triumphal procession through Rome. Among 700 Jewish prisoners John of Gischala and Simon bar Giora were marched past in chains. Amid great rejoicing two other costly trophies of pure gold were borne in procession, the seven branched candlestick and the table of the shewbread from the Temple at Jerusalem. They found a new home in the Temple of Peace in Rome. Both these accessories of Jewish ritual can still be seen on the great arch of Titus which was erected to commemorate his successful campaign.

On top of these desolate and cheerless ruins, on which neither Jews nor Christians were allowed to set foot on pain of death, the emperor Hadrian[1] built a new Roman colony: Aelia Capitolina. The sight of a foreign settlement on this sacred Jewish soil provoked yet another open rebellion. Julius Severus was summoned to Judaea from his governorship in Britain and smashed the last desperate attempt of the Jews to regain their freedom. But it took him three years to do so. The emperor Hadrian then erected a race-course, two baths, and a large theatre. A statue of Jupiter was enthroned above the ruins of the Jewish Temple as if in derision, and on the site which Christian tradition believed to be that of the Holy Sepulchre, strangers climbed the terraced steps to do homage at a shrine of the pagan goddess Venus.

The greatest part of the population of the Promised Land, which was not massacred in the bloody Jewish War of 66–70 and in the Bar-Kokhba rebellion of 132–135, was sold into slavery: "And they shall fall by the edge of the sword and shall be led away captive into all nations."

Archaeologists have found no material evidence of Israel's

[1] A.D. 117–138.

existence in Palestine after the year 70, not even a tombstone with a Jewish inscription. The synagogues were destroyed, even the house of God in quiet Capernaum was reduced to ruins. The inexorable hand of destiny had drawn a line through Israel's part in the concert of nations.

But by then the teaching of Jesus was well started on its irresistible and victorious journey, uniting and giving new life to the nations.

THE DEAD SEA SCROLLS

A lost lamb—The Dead Sea Scrolls—Harding and de Vaux in Wadi Qumran—Archbishop Samuel goes to Chicago—Nuclear physicists assist with the dating—Testing linen in the "Atomic Clock"—A book of Isaiah 2,000 years old—A prophetic roll in Jesus' day—A mysterious flood of documents—In the valley of the pirate-diggers—A text that corresponds after 2,000 years.

"The grass withereth, the flower fadeth: but the word of our God shall stand for ever" (Is. 40[8]).

Mohammed Dib, a Bedouin shepherd of the tribe of Ta 'Amireh, shared the experience of young Saul, who set out to find his father's asses which were lost and acquired a kingdom (1 Sam. 9, 10).

One fine day in the spring of 1947 Mohammed was combing the rocky ravines on the north shore of the Dead Sea in quest of a lost lamb, when he unwittingly came upon a veritable royal treasure in the shape of Biblical material.

He had been clambering to no purpose for several hours up and down the clefts and gullies of the ridge, which had many a time served as a hideout for hermits and sectaries, to say nothing of bandits, when he spied a dark crevice above his head in the rock-face of Wadi Qumran. Could his lost lamb have taken refuge there? A well aimed stone whistled through the air. But instead of the sharp crack which he expected in reply, a dull rumbling noise came from the cave instead. Mohammed Dib fled in terror and fetched two of his fellow tribesmen to the scene. They approached the cave with great caution and eventually squeezed their way through its narrow entrance. To their amazement they saw in the dim light of the little vault some clay jars. Treasure was their first thought and the three shepherds pounced on the jars and smashed them. But to their disappointment they contained neither jewels, nor gold, nor coins: nothing appeared but battered looking written scrolls of ancient leather and papyrus, wrapped in linen. In their annoyance they threw their finds carelessly aside, trampling on many of them, until it suddenly dawned on them that there might be money in them. At all events they took a few of the best looking scrolls to see if perhaps they had some cash value. With that the ancient documents set out on a remarkable journey.

They were smuggled into Bethlehem and came via the black market into the hands of antique dealers. Jewish and Arab collectors bought some of the scrolls, and a bundle of four came into the possession of the Orthodox archbishop of Jerusalem, Yeshue Samuel, for a handful of coins. The archbishop had no idea how precious was the treasure he had acquired, until experts from the American School of Oriental Research paid a visit to St. Mark's Monastery, where the documents were stored. A cursory examination convinced the archaeologists that they were dealing with Biblical documents of an uncommonly early date. A 23-foot-long scroll with the complete text of the Book of Isaiah in Hebrew was among them. A short published report by the Americans on their find aroused incredulous astonishment among experts all over the world. The immediate question however as to the exact age of the leather and the papyrus could best be solved by examining the place where they were discovered.

With endless trouble and patience the origin of the documents was therefore traced back through the dealers and the black market in Bethlehem to the Arabs of the Ta 'Amireh tribe and so eventually to the cave in Wadi Qumran. But access to the cave was prohibited. For following on the establishment of the new state of Israel the Arab-Jewish war had broken out in 1948 and the whole of Palestine was a hotbed of unrest.

The persistence of a Belgian United Nations observer in Jerusalem finally helped to overcome all difficulties. Captain Philippe Lippens had studied papyrology at the ancient University of Louvain. At the end of 1948 he established contact with Gerald Lankester Harding, the British director of the Department of Antiquities in Amman, the capital of Jordan. Their united efforts succeeded in interesting officers of the Arab Legion in the cave where the discovery was made. Thirty miles in a jeep from

Amman to Wadi Qumran presented no problems. After several fruitless quests among the numerous caves they eventually found the right one. The entrance to the cave was guarded by sentries until in February 1949 G. L. Harding and Father Roland de Vaux, Dominican director of the French Ecole Biblique et Archéologique at Jerusalem, arrived at the spot in person.

Their hopes were however disappointed. They found neither complete scrolls nor undamaged jars. Everything pointed to the fact that in the meantime others had rummaged through the mysterious cave on their own. With infinite patience and labour the two scholars examined the floor of the cave, literally with their finger-nails, in search of even the tiniest remains of manuscripts or of clay jars. What they collected in the way of fragments permitted them nevertheless to draw some important conclusions. The potsherds were uniformly Graeco-Roman, dating from 30 B.C. to A.D. 70. Six hundred tiny scraps of leather and papyrus made it possible to recognise Hebrew transcriptions from Genesis, Deuteronomy and the Book of Judges. Pieces of linen fabric which had served to wrap up the scrolls completed the meagre spoils.

In response to an American invitation Archbishop Yeshue Samuel took his precious scrolls to the United States in the summer of 1949 and submitted them for examination to the Oriental Institute in Chicago. A violent dispute broke out among the experts on the question of the age and authenticity of the documents. To settle the matter, one of them proposed a course which was still unfamiliar to archaeologists, namely to invite the assistance of a nuclear physicist. This was all the easier since the Oriental Institute is next door to the University of Chicago, where nuclear physicists had begun to determine the age of organic substances with the aid of Geiger-counters.

Professor Willard F. Libby of the Chicago Institute of Nuclear Physics had already carried out his first astonishingly accurate calculations of age by the use of the so-called "atomic calendar" which he had evolved.

The idea behind this method is as follows: As a result of the bombardment of cosmic rays, which are constantly penetrating our atmosphere from outer space, nitrogen is transformed into the radioactive isotope of carbon C-14. Every living organism—men, animals, plants—absorbs this C-14 with its food and the air it breathes every day until it dies. In the course of 5,600 years this carbon loses half of its original radioactivity. In the case of any dead organic substance a highly sensitive Geiger-counter can establish how much radiation has been lost from its content of C-14. This makes it possible to calculate how many years ago it was since it absorbed carbon for the last time.

Professor Libby was asked to conduct an investigation. He took pieces of the linen, in which the Isaiah scroll had been wrapped, burned them to ashes, put them into a battery of Geiger-tubes, and came to an astonishing conclusion. The linen had been made from flax which had been harvested in the time of Christ. The documents which had been wrapped in it must therefore have been older still. After exhaustive and minute examination the papyrologists came to the same conclusion. The text of Isaiah from the cave of Qumran had actually been copied about 100 B.C., as Professor Albright once more had been first to recognise.

This discovery means more than simply a scientific sensation. To estimate the importance of the Dead Sea Scrolls it is necessary to remember that the oldest text of the Bible which we possess in the Hebrew language—the so-called Massoretic Text (Massora = tradition), which is the work of rabbinical scribes—dates from no earlier than the 9th–10th century A.D. The chief sources for our version of the scriptures are the Septuagint, the Greek translation, and the Vulgate, the Latin translation of St. Jerome (4th century A.D.). Our knowledge of the text of the Bible rested for a long time on nothing but these two translations and the very late Hebrew manuscript. But with the discovery of the Dead Sea Scroll of Isaiah we have a Hebrew text of the Bible which is 1,000 years older. And the remarkable and wonderful fact is that that ancient scroll of Isaiah, just like the book of the prophet in any printed Bible, whether in Hebrew, Greek, Latin, German or any other language, has sixty-six chapters and agrees with our present day text.

Seventeen sheets of leather, sewn together into a length of almost 23 feet—this must have been what the roll of the prophet looked like as it was handed to Jesus in the synagogue at Nazareth so that he might read from it to the congregation. "And there was delivered unto him the book of the prophet Esaias" (Luke 4[16,17]). "Every movement of Jesus' hands is brought closer to us," writes Professor André Parrot, "for we can still see on the reverse side of the leather the marks of the readers' fingers."

That first chance find made by a Bedouin in 1947 at Qumran was to lead to a whole series of most astonishing and highly significant discoveries. Soon after, for the first time a systematic investigation of the Judaean hills was undertaken with a view to finding more documents and further historical evidence. Expeditions were mounted both in Israel and Jordan. Hundreds upon hundreds of lonely gullies and hitherto unexplored caves in the Dead Sea area were searched. Many a time it was a race between the experts and unofficial explorers, because it had very quickly become clear to the natives that there was big money in these unlikely scraps of parchment and papyrus with any hint of writing on them. The result was that within ten years a whole host of documents and written records, including many Old Testament writings, came to light, providing a vast amount of new knowledge about Biblical and post-Biblical times.

In Khirbet Qumran, near the cave where the first discoveries were made, scholars came upon the ruins of a settlement and a cemetery of the Jewish sect of Essenes, of whose existence we had only previously known from the accounts given by ancient writers—Philo, Josephus, and Pliny. The Essenes—first mentioned in the time of Jonathan, brother of Judas Maccabaeus (160–143 B.C.)—were members of an ascetic order who lived strictly in accordance with the law. They formed communities which were completely self-supporting and refused to do military service. The particular group at Qumran survived up to the Roman invasion in A.D. 68. Presumably it was members of this group who were responsible for many of the copies of the books of the Old Testament which have been rescued from caves in the adjacent hills, since a proper scriptorium was discovered among the ruins of the settlement. This Jewish monastic order, as their records now disclose, recognised as their head a "Teacher of Righteousness" who had revealed to them a secret rule of life. Some scholars were at first inclined to say that Qumran had strongly influenced John the Baptist, Jesus, and the early Church. This view, which caused a stir at the time, has on closer investigation proved to be unfounded.

Almost at the same time as the Dead Sea Scrolls were discovered, a collection of manuscripts was found not far from Luxor in Egypt which was to prove highly significant for our understanding of early Christianity. Fellaheen had discovered at Nag Hammadi, near the ancient Chenoboskion, a clay jar containing thirteen leather-bound volumes with about 1,000 leaves. These papyrus manuscripts written in Coptic, dating from the 3rd and 4th centuries A.D., and including a collection of the Sayings of

Jesus ascribed to the Apostle Thomas, "the Gospel according to Thomas", shed light on an early Christian Gnostic sect of which, apart from the writings of the early Christian Fathers, we hitherto knew little or nothing. The Fathers attacked the Gnostics as heretics since they tried to combine Egyptian, Babylonian, Greek, Persian, and Jewish mysticism with Christian doctrine. The Nag Hammadi manuscripts, apart altogether from what further research discloses as to the authenticity of the teaching of Jesus which they contain, give us some idea of the formidable opposition and competition which the early Christian teachers had to face.

Following on the finds at the Dead Sea which aroused worldwide interest, came the discovery in 1952 of two inscribed copper scrolls in a cave to the north of the ruined monastery of Qumran. When eventually in the winter of 1955–56, after careful chemical experiments, experts in the Manchester College of Technology succeeded in opening them, the contents about which everyone had been agog turned out to be a curious inventory of hidden treasure. While the experts are still far from clear as to the real significance of this list, a geographical reference in the text confirmed the reliability of a piece of topographical information contained in the Fourth Gospel. According to John 5[2] "there is at Jerusalem by the sheep market a pool, which is called in the Hebrew tongue Bethesda, having five porches..." The accuracy of this description was questioned until quite recently, when Bethesda was cleared of the rubble of centuries and brought once more to the light of day: a vast double pool covering over 5,000 square yards to the north of the Temple area. It had in fact five colonnades. Four of these surrounded the whole place, but the fifth porch, in which the sick folk lay waiting to be healed, stood on a ridge of rock which divided the two pools. The text of the copper scroll makes it quite clear that the lay-out at Bethesda consisted of two pools, since one of the hiding places is given as the smaller of the two reservoirs.

In the ancient Jewish fortress of Masada on the Dead Sea, Israeli scholars in 1956 came upon armouries and storehouses of Herod the Great. A fragment of papyrus was discovered inscribed with Hebrew characters and written in black ink. According to Dr. Aharoni, the fort and Herod's palace which crowned it were destroyed by the Romans in A.D. 73 after the end of the Jewish War.

Other expeditions have made interesting discoveries which shed an odd ray of light here and there on the Jewish rebellion under Simon Bar-Kokhba, which took place after the Biblical period. Hitherto, all that was known of this great revolt of the Jews against the emperor Hadrian and their struggle against the legions of Julius Severus consisted of comments in later Jewish writings, in the works of the Greek historian Dio Cassius, and the Christian Fathers Eusebius and Jerome.

In 1951 Professor Lankester Harding and Father de Vaux had retrieved original letters of the leader of the revolt dating from A.D. 130—including several copies of a document proclaiming the liberation and issued by Bar-Kokhba—from caves to the south of Qumran in Wadi Murabba'at, one of the most desolate spots in Palestine. Then in 1960 a group of archaeologists under the direction of Professor Yigael Yadin of Jerusalem University found army orders from the leader to his subordinates in caves in the Hever Ravine. The original letters deal with arrests, confiscation of crops and removal of population from Tekoa, the birthplace of the prophet Amos. A second expedition led by Professor Yadin in 1961 found in the same place a bundle of documents— papyri in Hebrew, Greek, and Aramaic. It is thought that these are minutes dating from the year A.D. 134 from the archives of the commandant of the stronghold at En-Gedi by the Dead Sea who had been installed there by Bar-Kokhba. Together with coins of the "Son of a Star"—which was Bar-Kokhba's title—and pieces of crockery, a gruesome discovery awaited the archaeologists: skeletons of rebels indicated the desperate last act of this historical tragedy. Women and men who had taken refuge there had obviously died of starvation in their hide-out.

With all these discoveries since the first finds in 1947, quite apart from the recovery of numerous Biblical manuscripts, the period immediately after Biblical times has for the first time been illuminated in a way which no one a few years ago would have dared to hope.

So far the total number of manuscripts discovered at the Dead Sea amounts to over 400, including 100 Biblical manuscripts. Apart from the Book of Esther every book of the Old Testament is represented. The best known is the complete scroll of the Book of Isaiah. The scrolls and fragments which come from Qumran date from 200 B.C. to A.D. 68; those from Wadi Murabba'at go up to A.D. 132–135.

These unexpected discoveries in the words of Professor Lankester

Harding are "perhaps the most sensational archaeological event of our time. It will take a whole generation of Biblical scholars to assess the value of these manuscripts."

In the summer of 1947 a sheer coincidence led to the discovery of the oldest manuscripts of the Bible so far known. Among a collection of writings on leather and papyrus which Bedouin shepherds came across in a cave in Wadi Qumran on the north side of the Dead Sea was a 23-foot leather scroll containing the complete text of the Book of Isaiah in Hebrew. Expert examination of the document revealed beyond doubt that the Isaiah text dated from 100 B.C. It is an original prophetic scroll of the type that Jesus held in his hands when he read the lesson in Nazareth on the sabbath (Luke 4[16ff]). This copy of Isaiah, over 2,000 years old, is a unique proof of the reliability of the holy scriptures that have been handed down to us, for the text agrees exactly with what we have in our present day Bible.

The oldest and most complete text of the Old and New Testaments were, until recently, the famous Codex Vaticanus and Codex Sinaiticus dating from the 4th century A.D., supplemented in 1931 by the Chester Beatty papyri dating from the 2nd and 3rd centuries A.D. Besides these, there were some fragments of the Old Testament from pre-Christian times (Fuad and Rylands Fragments). But all of these documents are in Greek, that is to say translations as far as the Old Testament is concerned. The oldest and fullest MS. in Hebrew was the Codex Petropolitanus, dating from A.D. 916. By the discovery of the leather scroll of Isaiah at the Dead Sea the Hebrew text has been carried back to almost exactly 1,000 years before. In 1935 a part of St. John's Gospel in Greek—the famous Bodmer papyrus—dating from the time of Trajan (98–117) was discovered. These old MSS. are the most convincing answer to all doubts as to the reliability of the text that we have in our Bibles today.

Much has been written about Qumran in the meantime. The Dead Sea Scrolls have been the subject of publications of a strictly specialised nature, but Qumran has also figured in literature intended for the general public. The time has certainly come to ask whether Qumran has actually proved to be the sensational find it seemed to be. The answer cannot be definitely either positive or negative. Once more we shall be obliged to record that the reply to this question is: partly "yes" and partly "no". The Dead Sea Scrolls have failed to provide the spectacular discoveries concerning the lives and activities of John the Baptist

and Jesus the Nazarene, for which people had secretly hoped.
Instead the "voice from the desert" of Qumran has made us
aware of how little we really know about the historical John the
Baptist and the historical Jesus. What a part of the scrolls does
confirm, however, is the striking agreement between the Old
Testament texts on which they are based and the Masoretic version of the Hebrew Old Testament of a full thousand years
later. This fact is of the greatest importance in the textual
history of the Old Testament.

The contents of the Qumran texts with their innumerable
anticipations of Christian concepts, teachings, demands, rules
and regulations were and still are grist to the mill of the sceptics
and to those who doubt the originality of Jesus and his Church.
After the Qumran discoveries, they are not willing to grant
Christianity anything from the Beatitudes of the Sermon on the
Mount to the white baptismal robe, from the Last Supper to the
community organisation. Among the people belonging to the
Qumran sect, the Essenes, there was a "community council"
consisting of 12 men and 3 priests. The number twelve corresponds not merely to the 12 tribes of Israel but also to the 12
apostles of Jesus. The Qumran people had "elders" and the
word "priest" comes ultimately from the term loaned from the
Greek for an elder of the Christian community, "presbyter".[1]
Even the office of bishop was not unknown to the people of
Qumran. The word "bishop" has its origins in the Greek word
"episkopos" which literally means "overseer". The dignity of
"overseer", which in Aramaic is "mebagger", was not unknown to the Qumran sectarians.

In short, from the 12 apostles and the whole "community
organisation" to the value concepts and beliefs as well as to the
consciousness of guilt, the idea of redemption and the expectation of eternity, all these Christian fundamentals were already
known to the Essenes.

Occasionally the correspondences verge on the grotesque.
Thus we find in Paul the curious passage: "For this cause ought
the woman to have power on her head because of the angels" (1
Corinthians 11[10]). As a last resort we can understand this to mean
that women should wear a veil as a sign that they were in the
power of the man. But what has this to do with the "angels"?
The Qumran rule provides the explanation. The Essenes believed

[1] The German text has been slightly adapted to bring it into line with facts of English
rather than German.

that at the sacral community meal there were "holy angels" who could be offended by the presence of certain persons or groups of persons. As far as women were concerned, the early Christians acted in the same way, even if they did not go so far as the Essenes and exclude women completely from their sacral community meal. They merely imposed on them certain restrictions such as the wearing of a veil. In the case of the sick, the lame, the blind, the deaf and the maimed, the Essene ordinance went beyond what they could accept. "Go out quickly into the streets and lanes of the city, and bring in hither the poor, and the maimed, and the halt and the blind" (Luke 14[21]). Some scholars consider these words to be a clear protest and a refusal to accept the regulation of the community of Qumran.

Here we reach the differences between Qumran and Christianity. Again we find in Luke something like a disagreement. He records the parable of the unjust steward and has Jesus say: ". . . for the children of this world are in their generation wiser than the children of light" (Luke 16[8]). The Essenes were "children of light". The members of the early Christian communities are here called upon not to imitate the Essenes who isolated themselves and withdrew into the desert and so lost contact with the world. Whilst the people of Qumran concealed themselves from the rest of the world, the Christian messengers went out into "the streets and lanes" and what they preached was meant not only for the chosen, but also for "the poor, and the maimed, and the halt, and the blind". The message was not "justice", but "judge not, that ye be not judged" (Matthew 7[1]) and also ". . . love one another, As I have loved you" (John 15[12]). This was a new message which was unknown to the "voice from the desert" of Qumran. In whatever way Christianity subsequently developed and whatever cause for criticism it has offered, even its sharpest critics cannot deny that it is *kindliness* which made it different from Qumran with its strict ordinances.

REBUILDING WITH THE HELP
OF THE BIBLE

Economic planning with the help of the Old Testament—The wells of the patriarchs provide for the settlers—"Honey out of the rock"—Stone walls to collect dew—Digging again in Solomon's mines—Pioneering on the Biblical pattern.

No one would dispute that the Old Testament is filled with that imponderable moral and spiritual power which outlasts time and loses nothing with its passing. But that its power should extend to the sober and prosaic business of remoulding the economy of a country is a sensational development.

Since 1948, the Book of Books, now more than 3,000 years old, has been playing the role of a trusted adviser in the rebuilding of the modern state of Israel. In the growth of both agriculture and industry the exact historical information given in the Bible has proved to be of the highest importance.

The territory of the new state covers about 8,000 square miles. In 1948 it was only in the Plain of Jezreel and the productive lowlands by the Lake of Galilee that there seemed to be even a remote reflection of the Biblical description of the Promised Land, flowing with milk and honey. Large areas in Galilee and almost the whole of the Judaean highlands presented an entirely different picture from Biblical times. Centuries of mismanagement had even destroyed the grass roots. Careless cultivation of olive and fig groves on the hillsides had dried them up. Increasing barrenness and considerable erosion were the sequel.

The inexperienced settlers, to whom the country was a completely unknown quantity, found the Old Testament of priceless assistance. It helped them to make many a decision in questions of cultivation, afforestation or industrial development. It is nothing unusual even for experts to consult in on doubtful problems.

"Fortunately," says Dr. Walter Clay Lowdermilk, an expert on agricultural economics, "the Bible tells us what plants can grow in particular places. We know from the book of Judges that the Philistines grew corn, for Samson tied foxes tails together, 'and put a firebrand in the midst between two tails' and 'let them go into the standing corn of the Philistines'. In the same manner he set fire to their olive groves and as he was on his way to visit his lady love he passed vineyards (Judges 15⁵; 14⁵). All these plants are now doing well there."

Every attempt to settle in the Negev must have seemed hopeless. South of the mountains of Judah between Hebron and Egypt lay nothing but desert, interspersed with wadis and barren of any vegetation. Meteorological measurements showed an average annual rainfall of less than 6 inches. It was a discouraging prospect.

Nothing can grow with a rainfall as small as that. But had the stories of the days of the patriarchs nothing of value to contribute? "And Abraham journeyed from thence toward the south country, and dwelled between Kadesh, and Shur and sojourned in Gerar" (Gen. 20¹). The father of the patriarchs was a shepherd, he kept close company with his large flock, and it needed pasture and water.

A reconnaissance party spent weeks with geologists scouring the desolate sand-dunes and rocky hills of the "south country".[1] They actually found what they were looking for. And the Israelis did exactly what Isaac had done. "And Isaac departed thence, and pitched his tent in the valley of Gerar, and dwelt there. And Isaac digged again the wells of water which they had digged in the days of Abraham his father" (Gen. 26¹⁷,¹⁸). Choked with sand, the ancient wells are still there and still as before at the foot of them runs clear pure water, "springing water", as Isaac's servants called it. They meant by that drinking water, for otherwise the underground water in the Negev—as was proved by testing the soil—is brackish and unpalatable. Once again tents stood on the same spots by the water-holes. The well beside which Abraham's rejected bondwoman Hagar rested with her son Ishmael (Gen. 21¹⁴⁻¹⁹) now supplies water for sixty families of

[1]Negev.

settlers. Rumanian Jews have settled on a nearby hillside only a mile or two from the Beersheba of the Bible.

In the same area there is another remarkable feature. The settlers have planted seedlings, slender young trees which are coming along famously. "The first tree which Abraham planted in the soil of Beersheba was a tamarisk," declared Dr. Joseph Weitz, the Israeli forestry expert. "Following his example we have planted 2,000,000 of them in this area. Abraham did absolutely the right thing. For the tamarisk is one of the few trees, as we have proved, that will flourish at all in the south where the annual rainfall is under 6 inches." Here again the Bible pointed the way: "And Abraham planted a tamarisk tree in Beersheba" (Gen. 21[33]—R.V.).

Afforestation is an essential prerequisite in making a countryside which is short of water into a fertile land. Since the beginning of the return of the Jews to Palestine the settlers have been planting forests. In choosing the types of trees they could rely on the observations of their forefathers just as much as in the choice of suitable areas. A few years ago, when the question arose as to whether the bare mountain slopes in the northern part of the country could be afforested, the Book of Joshua gave them the answer. "And Joshua spake unto the house of Joseph, even to Ephraim and to Manasseh saying: 'Thou art a great people and hast great power: thou shalt not have one lot only: but the mountains shall be thine for it is a wood and thou shalt cut it down'" (Josh. 17[17-18]).

Both these tribes, it was known, settled north of Jerusalem from the mountain ridge of Bethel past Biblical Shechem at the foot of Mt. Gerizim right to the Plain of Jezreel. "Since trees are known to grow better in places where there have been trees before," argued Professor Zohary of the Hebrew University, "we are relying on the Book of Books."

Much discussion has centred round an extremely obscure reference which until a few years ago was understood by nobody: "He made him (Israel)...that he might eat the increase of the fields: and he made him to suck honey out of the rock, and oil out of the flinty rock" (Deut. 32[13]). The riddle was solved when in the Negev they came across thousands of little circular stone walls. There was no water in the neighbourhood, neither springs nor any pools of underground water worth speaking of. When the sand was shovelled out of them they found the remains of the roots of ancient olive trees and vines. The stone walls had served their ancestors as valuable collectors of dew.

Their construction indicated an astonishing practical knowledge of the process of condensation. The stones in the circles were loosely stacked to ensure that the wind could blow through them. In this way the moisture from the air was deposited inside. This moisture was enough to feed an olive or a vine. Inside each wall there was always one tree only. The sweet juice of the grapes was often extolled in ancient times as "honey". The olive-tree produces oil. Honey and oil were sucked "out of the rock ... out of the flinty rock". Present day Israelis set great store by these serviceable little dew-collectors in the redevelopment of their agriculture.

In the second half of 1953 for the first time in Israel 3,000 tons of copper were mined. Where the houses of Solomon's workmen and slaves stood 3,000 years ago, new miners' houses stand today. Copper mining still pays. Dr. Ben Tor, the geologist, had the ancient copper mines tested in 1949 as to their mineral resources and their possibilities as an economic proposition. Experts estimated that there was enough ore to provide 100,000 tons of copper. According to their calculations the ramifications of the mines could produce at least another 200,000 tons. Since then, "Ezion Geber, which is beside Eloth on the shores of the Red Sea" (1 Kings 9[26]), has been a hive of activity. Jeeps and trucks scurry around, churning up clouds of yellow dust, and gangs of sunburnt men ply pick and shovel. "Wherever the ore is particularly rich," maintains a mining engineer, "we come upon the slag and furnaces of Solomon's miners. It often seems as if they had just left the place."

In the company's main office there is a text hanging on the wall. It reads: "For the Lord thy God bringeth thee into a good land ... a land whose stones are iron, and out of whose hills thou mayest dig brass" (Deut. 8[7,9]).

Iron is however not yet being mined. But the outcrops have already been recorded. Not far from Beersheba, exactly where the iron-smelting Philistines lived, Dr. Ben Tor noticed steep hillsides with reddish-black veins, the sign of iron ore deposits. Investigation showed that they amounted to 15,000,000 tons on a rough estimate. Most of this is ore of inferior quality but in the course of the survey excellent ores were discovered with between 60%–65% of pure iron.

Another very well known Biblical passage kept running in the mind of Xiel Federmann, a shrewd business man. It was the sentence in which the destruction of Sodom and Gomorrah is described, "... and lo, the smoke of the country went up as the smoke of a furnace" (Gen. 19²⁸). He could get no peace. Did these conflagrations not indicate subterranean gas? And where there is underground gas there are also deposits of oil, as has long been recognised. A company was formed and the experts who were sent to the Dead Sea confirmed completely Federmann's guess. On November 3, 1953, the first Israeli oil-well was drilled.

More than fifty farming communities have sprung up again between the sites of the Biblical settlements of Dan and Beersheba. Almost every one of them possesses a small modern pumping station above a spring or a well dating from ancient times. Gradually many parts of the country are coming to resemble once more the cheerful picture of Old Testament times.

It is a hard task that the state of Israel has set itself. But its people are fully convinced that they and their descendants will overcome all difficulties—not least thanks to the Bible—and that the prophecy of Ezekiel to the children of Israel will be fulfilled.

"And the desolate land shall be tilled, whereas it lay desolate in the sight of all that passed by. And they shall say, this land that was desolate is become like the garden of Eden" (Ezek. 36³⁴⁻³⁵).

POSTSCRIPT TO THE REVISED EDITION
Joachim Rehork

Is the "accuracy" of the Bible important?—Inaccuracies—Problematical patriarchs—The Bible: the most diligently researched work in world literature—Endless questions—Contact with the past—Is the Bible right after all?—Ancient Israel between the fronts—Reading between the lines—The Bible as a record of events.

More than twenty years have passed since the first appearance of this book. We have now come to the end of an attempt to incorporate new knowledge into it without disturbing the substance of the original text by tendentious criticism arising from the fresh discoveries. If we now ask ourselves again: "Well, is the Bible right after all?", some readers will reply with a definite "yes", while others will answer with a no less definite "no". Between these two answers there is room for a wide variety of opinion.

There is no lack of scholars—among them historians, theologians, philologists and archaeologists—who after conscientious examination of the Biblical tradition have come to the conclusion that fundamentally it is of secondary importance whether the facts reported in the Bible are correct or not. According to them, the Bible is primarily "prophecy". It is a religious message, made known with the means available at the time of its origin, or rather the different times of its origin, for the Bible is the extraordinarily complex product of numerous "growth strata" which in the course of centuries produced the "Bible" in its present form while leaving clear indications of the stages of its growth. It is more important in their view to shed light on the *origin,* the growth process of the collection of writings known as the "Bible" and to understand how the various elements of the Biblical tradition fit into the whole in order to obtain an idea, with the help of such knowledge, of what the authors of the individual books of the Bible wanted to tell their readers. In any case, the emphasis lay on getting the message across and not on the accuracy of historical details.

For the majority of Bible readers, on the other hand, as well as for a large number of Biblical scholars, a great deal still depends on the question whether statements in the Bible can be proved. The Dominican father, Roland de Vaux, for example, one of the most prominent figures in the history of Biblical antiquity, regarded the capacity to survive of the Jewish and Christian faiths as dependent upon the agreement between "religious" and "objective" history. He stated his opinion thus: ". . . if Israel's historical faith does not have its roots in history, then it is wrong and the same is true of our faith." The no less distinguished American Biblical archaeologist George Ernest Wright expressed the opinion that in Biblical belief everything depends on whether the main events actually took place. That is exactly the spirit in which the present work had its origin twenty years ago.

These two scholars, de Vaux and Wright, however, encountered active opposition in specialist circles. Not from less deeply religious colleagues, but from specialists who took their religion no less seriously than de Vaux and Wright, but who at the same time felt the desire to base their religious convictions on a more solid foundation than the confirmation of historical statements in the Bible. This is no cause for surprise since the Bible certainly does not make things easy for the researcher. It is full of problematical statements with the consequence that representatives of the most diverse disciplines, "schools" and opinions have racked their brains again and again over contradictions, repetitions and inconsistencies in the Biblical text—inconsistencies of which the following are a few examples.

In the Bible there are *two* accounts of the Creation (Genesis $1^{1-2,3}$ and Genesis 2^{4ff}).

In the first of these two accounts of the Creation, God created man *last;* in the second, however, God created him *first,* that is to say, before all other creatures.

In one case God created mankind from the beginning as "male

and female''; then, however, only the man came into being from "the dust of the ground", while woman was formed subsequently from a rib of the man.

The second account of the Creation contains details not mentioned in the first.

The two accounts of the Creation also differ from one another in their literary form. The first is hymnal, of the nature of a litany, whilst the second is a simple narrative.

So far reference has been made only to repetitions. The name of Moses' father-in-law has been transmitted in *three* different forms, once as Jethro (Exodus 3^1; 4^{18}; 18^{1-12}), once as Reuel (Exodus 2^{18}) and finally as Hobab (Judges 4^{11}). Other passages in the Bible also make us wonder what their meaning is, for example:

What sort of darkness "over the land of Egypt" was it from which the Egyptians suffered whilst the Israelites in bondage in Egypt did not (Exodus 10^{22f})?

How could Moses describe his own death (Deuteronomy 34)? Or to put the question in another way: can the first five books of the Bible really have been written by Moses when they tell us of his death?

These are only a few examples of inconsistencies in the Bible. These and similar incongruities have raised questions, however, which have led scholars to examine the Bible time and time again and to offer fresh interpretations. For generations the Bible has been the object of critical investigation and it can claim to be not only one of the most widely distributed and best selling books, but also the work of world literature which has been subjected to the most objective and thorough scholarly research. It has long been known that it contains elements belonging to the most varied literary genres, from the edifying treatise to the thriller, from the sermon to the legal text, from the liturgical hymn to the love song, from historiography to the novel, not to mention legends, anecdotes and folk-tales. A complete "national literature" is to be found in this collection known as the "Bible". In consequence, we also know that from the outset historians and archaeologists attach more historical weight to some books of the Bible than to others which have rather to be considered as "literary". In short, we know that the Bible is certainly not homogeneous and to a certain extent we are aware of the "joins".

It was indeed a matter of centuries before the various books of the Bible were brought together and codified, that is to say, given a final written form. Perhaps what we know as the song of Miriam (Exodus 15²¹) is really a genuine example which has come down to us from the Late Bronze period (13th century B.C.), whilst the second Epistle of Saint Peter, which is probably the nearest to us in date of the Biblical works, may not have been composed until the second quarter of the second century A.D. The majority of the Biblical works were probably brought together to form the "Bible" between the sixth century B.C. and the first century A.D., although in indicating these dates a few centuries must be added at the beginning of the period for a number of books of the Bible and some source material as well as a few decades at the end for some of the books of the New Testament.

Yet however much we know about the Bible today, we still do not know nearly enough. There is no end to the problems. On the contrary, every new discovery raises new questions. And there is no lack of fresh discoveries, certainly not of those in the area of archaeology. A veritable boom in archaeology has occurred precisely in the principal region where the events of the Bible took place, in ancient and present day Israel. The results of archaeological work there achieve a publicity which it is unlikely they will ever receive here. This is no cause for surprise, since for the Israelis of today archaeology is "a handshake with the past". Archaeological finds are called "greetings from our forefathers". Archaeology is part of the search for the collective identity which is here being documented, a search for what binds together the immigrants to Israel from all over the world, whether they be religious orthodox or liberal. Each one of the "greetings from the forefathers", however, each one of the direct "handshakes with the past", is also more or less a contribution to Bible research and each of the discoveries helps not only to solve problems but also indicates fresh problems. The situation in Bible scholarship is no different from that in other branches of knowledge. This is also the reason why a book such as this was in need of revision after the passage of two decades.

The discovery of the tablets at Nuzi (Yorgan Tepe) can here be cited again as an example. It provided striking enlightenment concerning the legal customs of the patriarchs, whilst at the same time opening to question the generally accepted date for the beginning of the period of the patriarchs.

In view of such a host of questions and correspondences, can we really say that the Bible "is right"? Of course, there are quite different levels of "being right". There is the level of *belief*, of religious conviction and of subjective feeling that something is right. Such belief is not at all in question here and must remain a matter of belief. The Bible cannot be proved as a document of faith, nor for the believer can it be convincingly disproved, for belief begins where knowledge and proof have their limit. In any case, proofs such as we are seeking can only be produced for or against the Bible as a historical source.

Here we have to condemn a bad habit current these days. Recently the rather derogatory term "less than a history book" has become customary in referring to the Bible. Quite respectable writers today have adopted this bad habit. In so doing they forget that the Bible is intended to be a representation of history. This is true of at least a large number of its texts. It would be foolish to criticise these texts because their authors did not yet adhere to the standards which we are now accustomed to apply to the writing of history and which in their turn are not destined to be eternal. Let us not forget that the Bible speaks to us from the historical past! But the historical past is powerful. It has to do with the state of man, his moods, the trends of the period which affect him, the influences exerted by his environment, the spirit of the times, the fads to which he is exposed. It is only in the light, or the twilight, of all these things that we experience our environment and all these things determine what can enter our sphere of experience and thus become available to us as knowledge.

In other words, if we do not wish to subject it to force, we must not squeeze the Bible into the Procrustean bed of our demands for "historical truth" and "scientific objectivity", which are themselves sufficiently problematical. It is, or rather, it was an historical work, but not such as we understand the term. It is the account of a people and its god, whose powers his worshippers came to know in the course of history. The Bible does not attempt to be a neutral, objective account of the events it relates. It is far too committed for that, much too rooted in its own times, in the times of which it speaks the language. This, too, must not be forgotten—the Bible uses descriptive methods which are by no means always those we employ. Biblical language is naturally abstract, yet is much more rich in images than ours. What we reduce to a short, conceptual formulation, the Bible converts into a story and its descriptions are often puzzles whose ambiguity is quite often intentional.

The sacrifice of Isaac by Abraham commanded by God but not carried out just at the last moment (Genesis 22^{1-13}) may serve as an example. It can be interpreted in three ways.

In the first place it may be the vestige of a primitive initiation rite, a kind of "blood baptism". Only he who wholly and unconditionally submits himself to his god becomes a full member of the community.

Secondly, the passage is a renunciation, in more or less allegorical form, of the custom of human sacrifice and more particularly of the sacrifice of boys which was widespread in the Ancient East.

Thirdly, it is a test of faith for Abraham. The author of this chapter in the Bible himself suggests this when he writes at the beginning of his account: "God did tempt Abraham."

As our time and patience have grown short, we usually feel extremely ill at ease when faced with the task of decoding these "linguistic allegorical puzzles".

In order to transport ourselves back into the thoughts of the Bible authors, we have simultaneously to turn back the wheel of history to that point in time which marks the beginning of the codification, the definitive text of the hitherto oral or written separate traditions of Ancient Israel, and thus of the growth of the complex structure known as the "Bible".

Is the Bible always right? We shall certainly be able to answer in the affirmative for those passages which have been confirmed by non-Biblical parallel sources or by archaeological discoveries. The Bible can claim another form of "rightness", however, insofar as it brings nearer to us its times and the people of its times with their ways of thought and behaviour so that we learn how better to understand their sermons, parables, allegories, visions, symbols, and allusions. Perhaps we shall some day be in a position to affirm, even of passages which are still unclear and puzzling to us today, that the Bible is right after all, as seen through the eyes of the people of its times!

CHRONOLOGICAL TABLE OF BIBLE DEVELOPMENT

(From: Claus Westermann: Abriss der Bibelkunde, p. 266f.)

Epoch	Date	Parts of the Bible
Occupation of the land	13th century B.C.	Song of Miriam (Exodus 15[21]).
Period of the judges	c. 12th/11th century B.C.	Book of the Covenant (Exodus 20[22] to 23[33]).
David	c. 1000 B.C.	Beginning of the composition of the Psalms. Story of the Ark of the Covenant. (1 Samuel 4–6; 2 Samuel 6)
Period of the kings (Solomon and later the two kingdoms)	10th century to 722/721 B.C.	Origin of the written source by the Elohists and Jahvists.[1]
Hezekiah of Judah	727 (721) to 698 (693) B.C.	The so-called "Proto-Isaiah" (= Isaiah 1–39), Micah.
The so-called "Deuteronomistic Reform"[2] (621 B.C.)	King Josiah of Judah (639/638 to 609 B.C.)	Deuteronomy (5th Book of Moses), Habakkuk, Nahum, Zephaniah.
First exile	597 B.C.	Jeremiah (original scroll). A small part of the Book of Ezekiel.
"Babylonian exile"	586 to 539/8 B.C.	Lamentations, the so-called "Deutero-Isaiah" (= Isaiah 40–55), the so-called "Deuteronomical historical work"[3] (Joshua, Judges, Samuel, Kings), the so-called "priestly writings".
Restoration until the consecration of the "Second Temple"	539/8 to 515 B.C.	The so-called "Trito-Isaiah" (= Isaiah 56–66), Haggai, Zechariah 1–8.

Epoch	Date	Parts of the Bible
Persian period	539/8 B.C. until Alexander the Great (King 336 to 323 B.C.)	460 Malachi, around 450 probably Ezra and Nehemiah (Nehemiah was governor under Artaxerxes I [465–424 B.C.]). Between 400 and 200 B.C.: Jonah, perhaps in the 4th century B.C.: Job, 4th or 3rd century B.C.: Joel and the so-called "chroniclers' history work".
Hellenism	From Alexander the Great until Rome's annexation of Egypt (30 B.C.)	Around 332: Zechariah 9–14. 3rd century: Proverbs and Song of Solomon. Around 250: Ecclesiastes. Beginning of the Septuagint (between 285 and 246 B.C.).
Maccabees	167/166 B.C. until the intervention of Pompey (63 B.C.) or until Herod the Great (37–4 B.C.)	Between 170 and 160 B.C.: Book of Esther, Book of Daniel. (Perhaps between 166 and 160 B.C.: first canon of the Bible [under Judas Maccabaeus]?) Qumran texts.
Roman period	From A.D. 6 (A.D. 66: rebellion; A.D. 70: destruction of Herod's temple; A.D. 73: fall of Masada.	Middle of the first century A.D.: New Testament Epistles. About A.D. 70: Gospel of St. Mark. Between 75 and about A.D. 95: Matthew and Luke. Probably after 90: John's apocalypse. End of the 1st century: Acts of the Apostles and Gospel of St. John. Also the establishment of the Hebrew Bible canon at Jabneh (Jamnia). Further New Testament Epistles. Middle of the 2nd century A.D.: Second Epistle of St. Peter.

[1] The written sources of the first five books of the Bible, known as the "Pentateuch", which are attributed to Moses. The source we owe to the Jahvists employs the name "Jahveh" for "God", whilst that due to the Elohists employs the name "Elohim". The work by the Jahvists originated in Southern Judaea probably during the 10th–9th century B.C., that of the Elohists probably in the 8th century B.C. in northern Israel. The two works were later merged with one another to begin with and subsequently together with the "Second Book of the Law" (*Deuteronomy* [7th century B.C.]) and the "priestly writings" (6th century [period of exile] or not until the 5th century B.C.) to form what are known as the "five books of Moses".

[2] The "Deuteronomistic Reform" is referred to in this way because this reform carried out by King Josiah of Judah (639/8–609 B.C.) in 621 B.C. attempts to put into practice the norms of the "Second Book of the Law" (*Deuteronomy* [the so-called fifth book of Moses]) which had only recently been codified (622 B.C.); efforts were made to lend importance to it by giving it the style of an address to the people by Moses at the end of the wanderings in the wilderness.

[3] The Biblical books Joshua, Judges, Samuel and Kings are called the "Deuteronomistic History" because, having originated probably in the 6th century B.C., they are composed entirely in the spirit of the "Second Book of the Law" (*Deuteronomy* [the so-called fifth book of Moses]), which was codified in the 7th century (622 B.C.), and of the "Deuteronomistic Reform" of King Josiah (621 B.C.). It has a connection with "Deuteronomy" only by reason of *content*, however, but not of chronology, for it originated, as stated, not before the 6th century B.C. and possibly later.

BIBLIOGRAPHY

Abel, F.-M.: Géographie de la Palestine I (1933), II (1938), Histoire de la Palestine depuis la conquête d'Alexandre jusqu'à l'invasion Arabe I/II (1952).

Adams, J. M. K.: Ancient Records and the Bible (1946).

Albright, W. F.: Archaeology and the Religion of Israel (1953), Recent Discoveries in Bible Lands (1936), Exploring Sinai with the University of California (1948), Archaeology of Palestine (1954), From the Stone Age to Christianity (1949).

Alt, A.: Die Herkunft der Hyksos in neuer Sicht (1954), Kleine Schriften zur Geschichte des Volkes Israel I/II (1953).

Andrae, W.: Das wiedererstandene Assur (1938).

Augstein, R.: Jesus Menschensohn (1972).

Avigad, N.: Bullae and seals from a post-exilic Judean archive (1976).

Bailey, A. E.: Daily life in Bible Times (1943).

Barrois, A. G.: Manuel d'archéologie biblique I/II (1939/53).

Bauer, H.: Die alphabetischen Keilschrifttexte von Ras-Shamra (1936).

Begrich, J.: Die Chronologie der Könige von Israel und Juda (1929).

Ben-Chorin, Sch.: Bruder Jesus. Der Nazarener in jüdischer Sicht (1970).

Benzinger, I.: Hebräische Archäologie (1927).

Biblisches Nachschlagewerk, Stuttgarter (1955).

Bittel, K.: Die Ruinen von Bogazköy (1937).

Bittel, K., und R. Naumann: Bogazköy (1938).

Bodenheimer, Fr. S. u. O. Theodor: Ergebnisse der Sinai-Expedition 1927 (1929).

Boschke, F. L.: Die Schöpfung ist noch nicht zu Ende (Econ, 1962).

Bossert, H. Th.: Altanatolien (1942).

Breasted, J. H.: The Dawn of Conscience (1933), Ancient Records of Egypt I–V (1906/07), History of Egypt, 2nd Ed. 1954.

Budge, W. E. A.: The Babylonian Story of the Deluge and the Epic of Gilgamesh (1920), revised by C. J. Gadd (1929).

Burrows, M.: What mean these Stones? (1941).

Caiger, S. L.: Bible and Spade (1936).

Canyon, Fr.: Bible and Archaeology (1955).

Carleton, P.: Buried Empires (1939).

Chase, M. E.: The Bible and the Common Reader (1946).

Clay, A. T.: Business Documents of Murashu Sons (1898).

Clemen, C.: Die phönikische Religion nach Philo von Byblos (1939).

Clermont-Ganneau, C. S.: La Stèle de Mésa (1887).

Collart, Philippes ville de Macédoine.

Contenau, G.: La civilisation phénicienne (1949), La vie quotidienne à Babylone et en Assyrie (1953), Les civilisations anciennes du Proche Orient (1945), Manuel d'Archéologie orientale I–IV (1927/47).

Cornfeld, G., ed.: Pictorial Biblical encyclopedia; a visual guide to the Old and New Testaments. Edited by Gaalyahu Cornfeld assisted by Biblical scholars, historians and archaeologists (1964).

Craveri, M.: Das Leben des Jesus von Nazareth (1970).

Crowfoot, J. W., Kathleen M. Kenyon, E. L. Sukenik: The Buildings at Samaria (1942).

Cuneiform Texts: British Museum (Ed.).

Dalman, G.: Heilige Stätten und Wege (1935), Licht vom Osten (1923), Arbeit und Sitte in Palästina I–VII (1928/42).

Dalmas, G.: Die talmud. Texte über Jesu (1900).

Davis, J. D.: Dictionary of the Bible (1953).

Davis, J. D. and H. S. Gehman: The Westminster Dictionary of the Bible (1944).

Delitzsch, Fr.: Babel und Bibel (1903).

Deschner, K.: Jesusbílder in theologischer Sicht (1966).

Dobschütz, E. v.: Die Bibel im Leben der Völker (1954).

Dougherty, R. P.: Nabondus and Belshazzar (1929).

Duncan, G.: Digging up Biblical History I/II (1931).

Dussaud, R.: Les Découvertes de Ras Shamra et l'Ancien Testament (1941).

Ebeling, E. u. B. Meissner: Reallexikon der Assyriologie I/II (1932/38).

Eberhard, E. G.: Bible-Thesaurus (1953).

Eissfeldt, O.: Philister und Phönizier, Der Alte Orient (1930), Baal Zephon, Zeus Kasios und der Durchzug der Israeliten durchs Meer (1932), Handbuch zum Alten Testament (1935).

Ellermeier, F.: Prophetie in Mari und Israel (1968).

Elliger, K.: Ein Zeugnis der judischen Gemeinde im Alexanderjahr 332 v. Chr., in: ZAW 62 = Neue Folge 21 (1949/50), 63ff. Kleine Propheten (1975).

Ephesus, Forschungen in Veröffentl. V. Österr. Archäol. Inst. (1937).

Eusebius, Historica ecclesiastica, ed. by E. Schwartz (1914), The Life of Constantine.

Finegan, J.: Light from the Ancient Past (1954).

Frayzel, S.: A History of the Jews (1952).

Fritz, V.: Israel in der Wüste (1970).

Gadd, E.: The Fall of Nineveh (1923).

Galling, K.: Biblisches Reallexikon (1937), Textbuch zur Geschichte Israels (1950).

Gardiner, A. H. and E. Peet: The Inscriptions of Sinai (1952).

Garis-Davies, N. de: The Tomb of Rekh-mi-re at Thebes (1943).

Garlake, P. S.: Great Zimbabwe (1973).

Garstang, J. B. E.: The Story of Jericho (1940).

Gerke, S.: Die Christ. Sarkophage d. vorkonstantin. Zeit (1940).

Gese, H. u.a.: Die Religion Altsyriens (1970).

Glueck, N.: The Other Side of the Jordan (1940), The River Jordan (1946).

Goldschmidt, L.: Der Babylonische Talmud (1935).

Gordon, C. H.: The Living Past (1941), Ugaritic Literature (1949).

Götze, A.: Hethiter, Churitter u. Assyrer (1936).

Gressmann, H.: Die älteste Gesichtsschreibung und Prophetie Israels (1921), Altorientalische Texte und Bilder zum Alten Testament (1927).

Gunkel, H., W. Stark u.a.: Die Schriften des Alten Testaments in Auswahl I–VII (1921/25).

Guthe, H.: Bibelatlas (1926), Palästina, Monographien zur Erdkunde 21 (1927).

Haag, H.: Bibellexikon (1968).

Haas, N.: Skeletal Remains from Givat ha-Mivtar (1970).

Harper: Bible Dictionary (1952).

Heidel, A.: The Gilgamesh-Epic and the Old Testament (1953).

Hengel, M.: Mors turpissima crucis. Die Kreuzigung in der antiken Welt und die »Torheit« des »Wortes vom Kreuz« (1976).

Herodotus: History. Herrmann, S.: Israels Aufenthalt in Ägypten (1970).

Hogarth, D. G.: Excavations in Ephesus (1908).

Honor, L. L.: Sennacherib's Invasion of Palestine (1926).

International Standard Bible Encyclopaedia (1952).

Jannsen, E.: Juda in der Exilheit (1956).

Jansen, H. L.: Die Politik Antiochus IV (1943).

Jirku, A.: Die ägypt. Listen palästinens. u. syr. Ortsnamen (1937).

Josephus, Flavius: Antiquities, Wars of the Jews.

Junge, P. J.: Dareios I., König der Perser (1944).

Kaiser, O.: Altes Testament. Vorexilische Literatur (1973), Einleitung in das Alte Testament (1975), Der Prophet Jesaja (1977), Israel und Agypten (1963), Zwischen den Fronten (1972).

Kapelrud, A. S.: The Ras Shamra Discoveries and the Old Testament (1965).

Kaufmann, C. M.: Handbuch der christl. Archäologie I–III (1922).

Kenyon, Sir F.: Bible and Archaeology (1940).

Kenyon, K. M.: Jerusalem; excavating 3000 years of history. (New Aspects of Antiquity) Thames, London (1967), Archaeology in the Holy Land

(1970), Royal Cities of the Old Testament (1971), Digging up Jerusalem (1974).

Klausner, J.: Jesus von Nazareth (1950), Von Jesus zu Paulus (1950).

Knopf, Lietzmann, Weinel: Einführung in das Neue Testament (1949).

Knudtzon, J. A.: Die El-Amarna-Tafeln I/II (1908/15).

Koeppel, P.R.: Palästina (1930).

Kohl und Watzinger: Antike Synagogen in Galiläa (1916).

Koldewey, R.: Das wiedererstehende Babylon (1925).

Kraeling, E. G.: Gerasa. City of the Decapolis (1938).

Kugler-Schaumberger: Sternkunde und Sterndienst in Babel (1935).

Laible, H.: Jesus Christus im Talmud (1900).

Landay, J. M.: Silent Cities, sacred stones—archaeological discovery in the land of the Bible (1971).

Layard, A.: Discoveries in the Ruins of Nineveh and Babylon (1853).

Lefebvre, G.: Romans et contes égyptiens de l'époque pharaonique (1949).

Lentzen, H. J.: Die Entwicklung der Ziggurat (1942).

Lepsius, C. R.: Königsbuch der alten Ägypter (1858), Denkmäler aus Ägypten und Äthiopien (1849/56).

Lietzmann, H.: Petrus und Paulus in Rom (1927).

Loud, G.: Megiddo Ivories (1939), Megiddo II (1948).

Macalister, R. A. S.: Gezer I–III (1912), The Excavations of Gezer (1912), A Century of Excavations in Palestine (1925).

McCown, C. C.: Tell en-Hasbeh. Berkeley, Calif., The Palestine Institute of Pacific School of Religion and the American Schools of Oriental Research (1947).

Mari: Archives royales de, ed. Musée du Louvre I–V.

Meyer, Ed.: Der Papyrusfund von Elephantine (1912), Geschichte des Altertums I–III (1925/37).

Miller, M. S. and J. L.: Encyclopedia of Bible Life (1944).

Moldenke, H. N. and A. L.: Plants of the Bible (1952).

Montet, P.: Les nouvelles fouilles de Tanis (1929/32, 1933), Avaris, Pi-Ramsès, Tanis (Syria XVII 1936), Tanis (1942).

Moret, A.: The Nile and Egyptian Civilisation (1927).

Morton, H. V.: In the Steps of the Master (1953), Through Lands of the Bible (1954).

Moscati, S.: Geschichte und Kultur der semitischen Völker (1953).

Mowinckel, S.: Studien zum Buche Ezra-Nehemia I (1964).

Negev, A.: Archäologisches Lexikon zur Bibel (1972).

Newberry, P. E.: Beni Hasan I (1893).

Noth, M.: Die Welt des Alten Testaments (1953), Geschichte Israels (1954).

Origen: Contra Celsum I, 32.

Orlinski, H. M.: Ancient Israel (1954).

Otto, E.: Ägypten (1953).

Otto, W.: Handbuch der Altertumswissenschaft (1928).

Parrot, A.: Mari une ville perdue (1936), Archéologie mésopotamienne, Les Etapes I (1946), Studia Mariana (1950), Déluge et arche de Noé (1952), Découverte des mondes ensevelis (1952).

Petrie, Fl.: Researches in Sinai (1906).

Pfeiffer, R. H.: History of New Testament Times (1949), Introduction to the Old Testament (1948).

Pingré, M.: Cométographie I (1783).

Pius XII Pope: Die Gottesbeweise im Lichte der modernen Naturwissenschaft (Universitas, Okt. 1952).

Plutarch: Life of Alexander.

Post, G. E.: Flora of Syria, Palestine and Sinai (1933).

Pottier, E.: Musée du Louvre, Catalogue des Antiquités Assyriennes No. 165.

Pritchard, J. B.: Ancient Near Eastern Texts relating to the Old Testament (1950), The Ancient Near East in pictures relating to the Old Testament (1954), Solomon and Sheba (1974).

Ramsay, W. M.: The Cities of St. Paul (1900).

Redford, D. B.: A Study of the Biblical Story of Joseph (1970).

Rehork, J.: Archäologie und biblisches Leben (1972).

Reisner, Th., H. and W. O. E. Oesterley: Excavations at Samaria I–II (1924).

Ricciotti, G.: Storia d'Israele I–II (1949).

Riemschneider, M.: Die Welt der Hethiter (1954).

Rothenberg, B.: Timna—das Tal der biblischen Kupferminen (1973).

Rowe, A.: The Topography and the History of Beth-Shan (1930), The Four Canaanite Temples of Beth-Shan I (1940).

Rowley, H. H.: The Re-discovery of the Old Testament (1945), The Old Testament and Modern Study (1952), From Joseph to Joshua (1948).

Schaeffer, C. F. A.: The Cuneiform Texts of Ras Shamra-Ugarit (1939), Ugaritica I–II (1939/49).

Scharff, A.: Handbuch der Archäologie I (1939).

Scharff, A.: Moortgat, A.: Ägypten und Vorderasien im Altertum (1950).

Schmidt, E. F.: The Treasury of Persepolis and other Discoveries in the Homeland of the Achaemenians (1939).

Schmidt, W. H.: Königtum Gottes in Ugarit und Israel (1966).

Schnabel, P.: Berossos u. d. babylon.-hellenist. Literatur (1923).

Schott, A.: Das Gilgamesch-Epos (1934).

Sellin, E.: Wie wurde Sichem israelitische Stadt? (1923), Geschichte des israel.-jüd. Volkes (I–II. 1924/32).

Sethe, K.: Die Achtungstexte feindl. Fürsten, Völker u. Dinge auf altägypt. Tongefässscherben d. Mittl. Reiches (APAW 1926, Nr. 5), Zur Geschichte der Einbalsamierung b. d. alten Ägyptern (1934).

Simons, J.: Opgravingen in Palestina (1935).

Soden, W. v.: Leistung und Grenze sumerischer u. babylon. Wissenschaft, Welt als Geschichte II (1936), Das altbabylon. Briefarchiv v. Mari, Die Welt des Orients (1948).

Speiser, E. A.: Introduction to Hurrian (1941).
Starkey, J. L.: Excavations at Tell ed-Duweir 1933/34 (1934).
Starr, R. F. S.: Nuzi, Report on the Excavations at Yorgan Tepe near Kirkuk, Iraq, I–II (1937/39), Nuzi I (1939).
Steindorf, G., K. C. Seele: When Egypt Ruled the East (1942).
Strabo: Geography.
Sukenik, E. L.: Ancient Synagogues in Palestine and Greece (1934), The Third Wall of Jerusalem (1930) (with L. A. Mayer).
Svenskt Bibliskt Uppslagsverk (ed. I. Engnell and A. Fridrichsen, 1948).

Thompson, Th. L.: The Historicity of the Patriarchal Narratives. The Quest for the Historical Abraham (1974).
Torczyner, H.: Lakish I, The Lakish Letters (1938).
Tzaferis, V.: Jewish Tombs at and near Givat ha-Mivtar (1970).

Unger, E.: Babylon, die heilige Stadt (1931).
Ungnad, A.: Reallexikon der Assyriologie (1938), Die neue Grundlage f.d. alt-oriental. Chronologie (1940).

Vaux, R. de: Histoire ancienne d'Israël (1971).
Vincent, L. H.: Canaan d'après l'exploration récente (1914), Jéricho et sa chronologie (1935), L'Archéologie et la Bible (1945).

Watzinger, C.: Denkmäler Palästinas I–II (1933/35).
Weimar, P. und Zenger, E.: Exodus, Geschichten und Geschichte der Befreiung Israels (1975).
Weissbach, F. H.: Die Keilschriften der Archämeniden (1911).
Wolff, H. W.: Eine Handbreit Erde (1955).
Wood, J. T.: Modern Discoveries on the Site of Ancient Ephesus (1890).
Woolley, C. L.: Abraham, Recent Discoveries and Hebrew Origins (1936), Ur Excavations. V, The Ziggurat and its Surroundings (1939), Ur of the Chaldees (1954).
Wreszinski, Atlas zur ägyptischen Kulturgeschichte I–III (1923/40).
Wright, G. E.: Biblical Archaeology (1962).
Wright, S. E. and Fl. V. Filson: The Westminster Historical Atlas to the Bible (1953).
Würthwein, E.: Die Königsbücher (1976).

Yadin, Yigael: Masada. Der letzte Kampf . . . (1967), Hazor (1976).

Journals: Annual of American Schools of Oriental Research (AASOR), Der Alte Orient (AO), American Journal of Archaeology (AJA), Biblical Archaeologist (BA), Bulletin of the American Schools of Oriental Research (BASOR), Beiträge zur Wissenschaft vom Alten u. Neuen

Testament (BWANT), Illustrated London News, Israel Exploration Journal, Journal of the Society of Oriental Research (JSOR), Picture Post, London, Zeitschrift des Deutschen Palästinavereins (ZDPV), Revue Biblique (RB), Syria, Zeitschrift für alttestament, Wissen (ZAW).

INDEX

ABOUT THE AUTHOR

DR. WERNER KELLER was born in Germany in 1909 and was early recognized as one of the foremost journalists in the scientific field. His greatest interests have always been archaeology and the story of mankind, and in pursuit of these he has traveled extensively in Italy, the Balkans, and the Middle East. He decided to write *The Bible as History* in 1950, after studying the sensational French reports on the findings of the ancient Phoenician port of Ugarit and of the home of the patriarchs in the Kingdom of Mari on the Euphrates.

SPECIAL
MONEY SAVING
OFFER

Now you can have an up-to-date listing of Bantam's hundreds of titles plus take advantage of our unique and exciting bonus book offer. A special offer which gives you the opportunity to purchase a Bantam book for only 50¢. Here's how!

By ordering any five books at the regular price per order, you can also choose any other single book in the catalog (up to a $4.95 value) for just 50¢. Some restrictions do apply, but for further details why not send for Bantam's illustrated Shop-At-Home Catalog today!

Just send us your name and address plus 50¢ to defray the postage and handling costs.